DATE DUE

THE CENTENNIAL EDITION

OF THE WORKS OF

SIDNEY LANIER

GENERAL EDITOR

CHARLES R. ANDERSON

MARBLE BUST OF LANIER BY GUTZON BORGLUM, 1929

Modeled from the 1857 ambrotype

Washington Memorial Library, Macon, Georgia

CENTENNIAL EDITION

VOLUME I

SIDNEY LANIER

POEMS

AND

POEM OUTLINES

EDITED BY

CHARLES R. ANDERSON

BALTIMORE

THE JOHNS HOPKINS PRESS

GENERAL PREFACE

THE CENTENNIAL Edition of the works and letters of Sidney Lanier was planned as a celebration of the one hundredth anniversary of his birth, 1842-1942, but its completion was delayed by the exigencies of the war. Undertaken with the full coöperation of the family and friends of Lanier, it has been achieved by the joint labors of the editorial staff and is now published with the aid of a substantial gift from an anonymous friend.[1]

Three large collections of manuscripts and other Lanieriana belonging to the late Mr. Charles Day Lanier and Mr. Henry Wysham Lanier, sons of the poet, and to Mrs. John Tilley, daughter of the poet's brother Clifford Anderson Lanier, have been deposited at the Johns Hopkins University (the first as a gift, the others on loan) and are now for the first time fully available for the uses of scholarship. Acting as a loadstone they have drawn to the Lanier Room several smaller collections, and these have been supplemented by other manuscripts in the hands of private owners and institutions scattered over the country. All together they consist of the following: more than fifteen hundred letters by Lanier, a thousand to him, and a large number concerning him; the manuscripts of three of his major prose works, nearly half of his shorter pieces, and over a thousand miscellaneous pages not included in this edition; the manuscripts of the majority of his poems, frequently with variant versions; a small college notebook and a large literary work-book of nearly seven hundred ledger pages; over two hundred volumes from his personal library, many with annotations; a great many first editions and reprintings of his works; innumerable articles and reviews clipped from periodicals; a large collection of original musical compositions, concert programs, manuscript reminiscences, miscellaneous documents, photographs, and memorabilia of all sorts—the bulk of which are in the three collections named above.[2] By the rare generosity

[1] Grateful acknowledgment is also due to the American Philosophical Society for a grant that made it possible for the general editor to devote his entire time to the project during most of 1942.
[2] Acknowledgment to all owners of MSS is made below. The holdings are

of the owners all have been made accessible to the editorial staff without restriction and with only the most nominal exercise of the privilege of censorship.

This unusually large mass of source materials forms the basis of the Centennial Edition, furnishing it with authoritative texts and instructive variants, supplying explanatory matter for notes and introductions, and thus making it something more than a mere reprinting of Lanier's works. Even without this new matter, a complete collection of his writings has long been a desideratum, for existing editions are wholly inadequate. To begin with, his poetry, prose, and letters have never been issued in a uniform set, and none of them have been edited by scholars. All of his volumes, with the exception of the poems (and two of the juveniles), have long been out of print, and many are unknown except to the special student. Only one rather small volume of his letters has been brought before the public. Of his prose, only three volumes were published during his lifetime, two of which have become collector's items. Four more were issued posthumously; but two of them—collections of his lectures—suffered from garbled texts, and the other two—comprising a score of his " essays "—were incomplete since they omitted more than half of his ventures in the field. Of his poems, only ten were published in final book form during his lifetime; ninety more were added to a " collected " edition after his death, not always taken from the most authentic source; another score were uncollected and twice that number unpublished. Hence the available texts for over half his works have not been authoritative, the very existence of many of them has not been widely known, and a small but interesting body of previously unknown poetry and prose plus a very large number of letters have remained until now in manuscript.[3]

specifically described in the introductions and notes to the several volumes and in the bibliography and calendar, vols. VI and X.

[3] The official sales records of Lanier's books published by Hurd and Houghton, J. B. Lippincott, and Chas. Scribner's Sons have been destroyed, but the following information can be supplied from other sources. *Tiger-Lilies* seems to have sold out an edition of 962 copies, but it was never reprinted (V, ix). *Florida* ran to two editions and two reprintings, but the number of copies is not known (VI, xviii-xx). *Poems* (1877) apparently sold only about 500 copies (Lippincott wrote Lanier on May 14, 1881, that 425 copies still remained on hand, out of an edition of presumably not more than 1000). Records obtained from Scribner's in 1904 show the following number of copies of their volumes

The aim of the present edition has been to bring together in definitive form the body of Lanier's writings so they can be judged as a whole. With the poems, because of their relatively small bulk, completeness seemed a feasible goal, even to the inclusion of fragments, outlines for unfinished poems, and variant readings. With the prose, however, the exercise of some editorial discretion seemed called for. In the first place, there are a large number of fragments, plans for rejected projects, and miscellaneous notes that defy intelligent classification and so are largely unusable. In the second place, several hundred pages of college " themes," debates, and speeches have survived of too slight intrinsic value to deserve inclusion, and nearly a thousand pages of early drafts for later completed works that differ sufficiently to constitute independent compositions but are not significant enough to warrant publication. Finally, Lanier's original musical compositions—ten completed and sixty-odd fragments—seemed less suited to an edition of his writings than for special treatment by some future historian of American music.[4] Of previously published prose, Lanier's four juveniles have been omitted—his redactions of Malory, Froissart, Percy, and *The Mabinogion*—though his own contributions in these volumes, the prefaces, have been included among his essays. Further, a few short compositions that had found their way into print have been excluded from the present edition: the post-humously printed " What I Know About Flowers," written to be delivered by a boy orator at a Sunday School picnic; " King Arthur and His Knights of the Round Table," a popular version

sold up until that time (letter from George S. Wills to Edwin Mims, Sept. 9, 1904, MS Johns Hopkins University): *Poems,* 16,500; *Select Poems,* 2,750; *The Science of English Verse,* 3,700; *The English Novel,* 4,000; *Music and Poetry,* 1,590; *Retrospects and Prospects,* 1,500; *Bob: the Story of Our Mocking-Bird,* 5,400; *The Boy's Froissart,* 13,750; *King Arthur,* 20,700; *Mabinogion,* 6,500; *Percy,* 4,050. I have not been able to discover from Doubleday Doran how many copies of *Shakspere and His Forerunners* have sold.

[4] All of these omitted materials are listed in the bibliography (VI, 388-390) and are described at some length in the several introductions, where they are sifted for whatever matter they contain. The manuscripts are in the Lanier Room, Johns Hopkins University, where they are available to the curious and to the critical who may not share the editorial conscience that rejected them. (Five translations from early English poetry are credited to Lanier, III, xvi, by mistake; a re-examination of the MSS, after that volume went to press, revealed that they are in the handwriting of W. H. Browne—probably prepared as guides for metrical versions by Lanier that were not completed.)

of his preface to *The Boy's King Arthur* that was printed as a sales-promoter for that volume; and "John Barbour's *Bruce*," an interlinear modernization of the fourteenth-century Scottish poem.[5] With the letters the editorial policy adopted was frankly selective: to print all letters necessary to a complete story of Lanier's life; those omitted, less than a third, either duplicated the ones selected or were trivial in content. To have included all this matter would have added several volumes of small worth without throwing any further light on the reader's understanding of Lanier. In spite of these various omissions it can be said, in all but the most literal sense, that the Centennial Edition constitutes a complete collection of the writings of Sidney Lanier.

The plan of the edition developed into ten volumes of reasonably uniform size. Since Lanier's reputation depends largely on his poems, these were allotted to the first volume. The five major prose works logically formed the staple of five separate volumes, but they varied in length from 70,000 to 140,000 words. In addition there were a large number of short pieces (eighteen from the posthumous *Music and Poetry* and *Retrospects and Prospects*, twenty-eight previously unpublished or uncollected) which had no compelling unity as experiments in a special literary genre sufficient to call for a separate volume. The problem was solved by dividing them into general categories suitable for inclusion with the major prose works—essays on music, on the South, and so on, using these terms in their broadest sense. The order assigned to these volumes was partly chronological and partly sequential. Lanier's theory of prosody (*The Science of English Verse*) naturally followed the poems, and was in turn followed by the Peabody and Hopkins lectures out of which it had grown (*Shakspere and His Forerunners*), and this by the later lectures (*The English Novel*). The early prose, a war novel (*Tiger-Lilies*) and a travel book (*Florida*), were placed last since they fell outside this sequence. The letters were grouped in four volumes representing distinct periods in Lanier's career: his literary apprenticeship, the fallow years practicing law in Macon and travelling for his health, the first

---

[5] The last two are available in *The Lanier Book*, New York, 1914, pp. 23-35, and *Music and Poetry*, New York, 1898, pp. 212-248. The MS of the first is in the Lanier Room.

period in Baltimore devoted to music and poetry, and the last years divided between creative writing and lecturing. The sixth volume of works concludes with a bibliography consisting of two parts: I, first editions of all of Lanier's volumes, chronological lists of the first printings of his poems and short prose, and brief descriptions of all items remaining in manuscript; II, selected lists of biographical and critical studies of Lanier and reviews of his books. The last volume of letters concludes with a calendar, listing all known letters by and to Lanier and a selection of letters concerning him, with indication of the owners and location of the manuscripts. The edition opens with a general preface and closes with a general index.[6]

The purpose of the Centennial Edition being chiefly expository, the editorial apparatus has been designed as a framework of such facts as were necessary to set forth with clarity exactly what Lanier wrote and what he intended it to signify. A reasonable uniformity of matter treated and manner of treatment has been imposed upon the several volumes by the general editor, but considerable latitude seemed desirable in the special studies that constitute the introductions, and slightly different techniques were inevitable for the three categories of poems, prose, and letters. For the six volumes of works, the editorial notes have been limited largely to textual and bibliographical problems. In volume I—placed at the end for aesthetic considerations—they consist of one inclusive note for each poem, giving the facts of composition and publication, authority for the text adopted, annotation and commentary, and in a separate section formal collation of variants for a group of selected poems. In volumes II-VI the notes are placed at the bottom of the page, marked by asterisks and set in brackets to distinguish them from Lanier's own notes. They point out significant vari-

[6] The index has been prepared by Miss Eugenia Wallace of the Publisher's Emergency Bureau. The frontispieces of vols. I-VI reproduce the principal memorials of Lanier, and preceding the texts are facsimiles of original title-pages of all books published during his lifetime (except the juveniles). Scattered through the letters, vols. VII-X, are photographs of his principal correspondents, samples of his manuscripts and miscellaneous illustrations, and all known portraits of Lanier. (One exception is the group picture in Starke, facing p. 108, but the vignette head in the illustration facing p. 379, vol. VII, was apparently taken from it. One further photograph has been omitted because it cannot be positively identified—by F. A. Gerrish, Montgomery, c. 1866-1868, Charles D. Lanier Collection.)

ants and *lacunae* in the texts, correct typographical errors, and identify literary quotations; additional footnotes to the titles of the shorter prose give the facts of composition and publication. A considerably larger number of notes in another category has been added for the letters, explanatory matter to identify contemporary persons, places, and events, to clarify allusions, and to fill gaps in the narrative.[7]

The introductions vary considerably because of the different problems involved in the several volumes. For the prose, they contain a history of the genesis, composition, publication, and reception of the major work; an account of the authoritative text, the variants, and the manuscripts; and an explanation of any editorial procedure peculiar to each volume. Further, they relate the specific work to the body of Lanier's writing and to the facts in his life, especially by cross-reference to the new matter in the letters; and they include special studies such as the historical significance of his theory of prosody, his standing as an amateur scholar, his relations to the South, and the influence of illness and hack-work on him as an artist. In the introductions to the poems and letters are added general surveys of his poetic career and of the cultural life of Baltimore in which he participated. Finally, though the aim is primarily exposition, general critical estimates have been attempted.

The authoritative texts for the poetry and prose have been established by a rule of thumb as that text which last passed under Lanier's eyes and met with his approval—save in a very few cases where a contemporary copy or a posthumous print had to suffice—whether found in book, periodical, or manuscript. This text has been followed *verbatim*, except that typographical errors have been corrected, silently unless some doubt called for an explanatory note. It has not been followed *literatim*, since there could be no purpose in preserving for posterity the mechanical idiosyncrasies of various printers or careless slips of the pen in unrevised manuscripts. Thus the use of italics, quotation marks, capitals, spelling, and punctuation has been

---

[7] For poems, prose, and letters the first printing, all known reprints during Lanier's lifetime, and the first collection are given. The identification of literary allusions and quotations is limited to author and title, the sole purpose being to show the nature and scope of Lanier's reading. No effort has been made to supply the standard titles of the numerous musical compositions referred to.

regularized, following Lanier's system when he had one and standard modern usage otherwise, but with a minimum of change and with explanation for anything that went beyond mere correction in mechanics. A different policy has been followed for the letters. The aim here has been an absolutely literal text, reproduced from the original manuscripts (which have survived in all but a very few instances). For poems, prose, and letters all texts are given entire.[8]

In a large coöperative enterprise of this sort so many obligations are incurred that a prefatory listing can only approximate completeness. First of all, grateful acknowledgment is hereby made to the members of the editorial staff, not only for their splendid work but for their courtesy in yielding to the general plan on several points of procedure: to Paull F. Baum, Clarence Gohdes, Philip Graham, Garland Greever and Cecil Abernethy, Kemp Malone, Aubrey Starke—also to the first-named for expert advice concerning format and to the last for aid in the end work on volumes I and X.

Special thanks are due to Mrs. Walter D. Lamar, whose enthusiasm for Lanier was instrumental in launching this project; to Duke University, which first undertook the edition, for graciously relinquishing it when circumstances suggested a change of sponsorship; to President Isaiah Bowman and the administration of Johns Hopkins, for making available the facilities of the university and its press; to the Librarian Emeritus, John C. French, and his successor, Homer Halvorson, for unfailing coöperation; to Miss Frieda Thies, who catalogued the collections in the Lanier Room, for innumerable services including

---

[8] Fragments and *lacunae* are indicated by x x x; Lanier's own omissions are indicated by . . . , as are a few long quotations in the lectures and occasional texts of his poems in the letters which have been omitted editorially with explanation in the notes.

Examples of silent corrections in the mechanics of the text (vols. I-VI) will make clear the editorial policy. Typographical errors such as " throug " have been corrected without comment; Lanier's general use of italics for titles of short poems has been standardized; quotations of more than three lines have been uniformly set in smaller type, and missing halves of quotation marks have been supplied; capitalization of abstract words has been made consistent within a given poem or prose piece; English spellings such as " honour " (e. g., from the *Southern Magazine*) have been Americanized, and since Lanier adopted the form " Shakspere " after 1876 the few different spellings have been regularized; excessive pointing (e. g., after chapter titles) has been removed, and missing marks of punctuation have been supplied. For any change that could be argued as remotely affecting the meaning, full explanation has been made in the notes.

checking the text of the letters against the original manuscripts and aiding with the preparation of the bibliography.

For research assistance and aid of many sorts, obligation is acknowledged to the following persons: W. F. Albright, D. C. Allen, R. L. Anderson, Jr., William Charvat, H. W. L. Dana, E. M. Everett, Ernst Feise, Miss Sarah Freeman, C. J. Furness, Ferris Greenslet, R. D. Havens, Mrs. Frank Jones, Mrs. Lubov Keefer, H. C. Lancaster, Emile Malakis, Mrs. J. J. McKay, Mrs. Collin Messenger, Edwin Mims, Miss Alice Northrup, E. H. O'Neill, D. A. Randall, D. M. Robinson, Hyder Rollins, Mrs. J. L. Smith, Miss Ottilie Sutro, Mentor Williams; and to the library staffs of the following institutions: Alabama Department of Archives and History, American Antiquarian Society, Boston Public Library, Buffalo Public Library, Carnegie Library (Atlanta), Chester County (Pennsylvania) Historical Society, University of Chicago, Columbia University, Cornell University, Duke University, Enoch Pratt Free Library, University of Georgia, Georgia Historical Society, Georgia State Library, Harvard University, Howard Memorial Library, Johns Hopkins University, Kansas State Historical Society, Library of Congress, University of Maryland, Maryland Historical Society, New Jersey State Library, New York Historical Society, New York Public Library, New York State Library, University of North Carolina, Ordinary's Office (Augusta, Ga.), Peabody Institute (Baltimore), University of Southern California, Syracuse Public Library, Toledo Public Library, U. S. Department of Agriculture, U. S. War Department, Vanderbilt University, University of Virginia, Virginia State Library, Washington Memorial Library (Macon, Ga.), Western Reserve Historical Society. (Other acknowledgments are made in the notes.)

To the following private owners of manuscripts for permission to transcribe and publish: G. S. Alleman, R. L. Anderson, Mrs. W. R. Benjamin, Gordon Blair, Mrs. B. B. Comer, Miss Nannie E. Dorsey, H. S. Gulliver, J. D. Hankins (for the family of Virginia Hankins), Mrs. C. N. Hawkins, Mrs. S. J. Hinsdale, Mrs. Charles D. Lanier, Henry W. Lanier (through A. G. Lanier, H. W. Lanier, Jr., and Mrs. R. B. Livermore), Robert S. Lanier, Jr., Mrs. Sidney Lanier, Jr., H. M. Lovett, J. S. Mayfield, Edwin Mims, Miss Alice Northrup (for the family of M. H. Northrup), Miss Elizabeth Price, A. H. Starke, Philip Straus, Mrs. John Tilley, Miss Eleanor Turnbull; and to the following institutions:

Aldrich Memorial Museum, British Museum, Brown University, University of California (Los Angeles), Columbia University, Cornell University, Craigie House, Duke University, Emory University, Enoch Pratt Free Library, Harvard University, Houghton Mifflin Co., Huntington Library and Art Gallery, Johns Hopkins University, Library of Congress, Mont de Sales Academy, National Archives, Peabody Institute, Pennsylvania Historical Society, Charles Scribner's Sons, University of Texas, Washington Memorial Library and Wesleyan College (Macon), Yale University. For permission to use the large collections of Lanieriana assembled by J. C. French, J. S. Mayfield, and the late J. S. Short. (Acknowledgments for the illustrations are made in the accompanying legends.)

To the following owners of copyright for permission to quote and reprint: Charles Scribner's Sons, publishers of *Bob: the Story of Our Mocking-Bird, The Boy's Froissart, King Arthur, Mabinogion,* and *Percy, The English Novel, The Lanier Book, Letters of Sidney Lanier, Music and Poetry, Poems of Sidney Lanier, Poem Outlines, Retrospects and Prospects, The Science of English Verse, Select Poems of Sidney Lanier, Selections from Sidney Lanier;* Doubleday Doran Co., publishers of *Shakspere and His Forerunners;* the J. W. Burke Co., publishers of G. H. Clarke's *Some Early Letters and Reminiscences of Sidney Lanier;* Mrs. Horace Traubel, for Lanier's letter in *With Walt Whitman in Camden;* University of Texas Press, publishers of *Letters. Sidney Lanier to Col. John G. James;* Whittet & Shepperson, publishers of Gordon Blair's *Father Tabb;* Houghton Mifflin Co., publishers of Edwin Mims's *Sidney Lanier;* University of North Carolina Press, publishers of Aubrey Starke's *Sidney Lanier.*[9]

The generous coöperation of all has lightened the work of the general editor, who wishes to express, in conclusion, a personal debt to Eugenia Blount Anderson for sane human counsel in restraint of the excesses of scholarship.

C. R. A.[10]

Johns Hopkins University
November, 1945

[9] The last two volumes, cornerstones on which all study of Lanier must be based, are cited throughout the present edition as " Mims " and " Starke."
[10] The Introductions, which are the work of the several editors, are initialed only for those volumes in which two names appear on the title-page.

CONTENTS

xv

INTRODUCTION [1]

THE LIFE and song of Sidney Lanier are so intimately related, and the frustrations that beset his ambition for achievement as an artist so poignant, that the tendency has been to lose the poems in the poet. In the last analysis, of course, all poetry must be understood and evaluated on its own merits, quite independently of its relation to biography or milieu. But since one function of the editor, as distinguished from the critic, is to set the author's works in an adequate frame of facts, a survey of Lanier's poetic career will provide a proper approach to the poems themselves.[2] Again, though the final test is performance, when that falls short of promise an inquiry into the ups and downs of the struggle for expression should throw light on what was actually done as well as on what was left undone.

Many a lyric poet dying at Lanier's age or earlier has left behind a fuller measure of his worth, but few have been faced with so many obstacles in a life of less than forty years. Plunged into four years of war on the threshold of maturity, he emerged from it at the age of twenty-three crippled with a fatal disease and conditioned by the economic blight that paralyzed the South during ten years of Reconstruction. These harried his progress at every stage, rising to a climax in the last five desperate years; and they increased that isolation from the contemporary world of letters which he felt to be such a handicap. But though this is the best known part, it is by no means the whole story of his frustration. More disastrous, perhaps, was the proclivity to scatter his talents and energies in several fields, augmented by the untoward circumstances of his life but also stemming from originally divided aims. As early as his college days he was unable to decide between music and poetry as his natural bent, and the choice was further complicated by the yearning for an academic career. The failure to choose, resulting from outward pressure and from lack of inward

---

[1] All letters referred to in this Introduction are printed or listed in the present edition, vols. VII-X. Information contained in the notes at the end of this volume and details from other volumes that can be readily located from the general index (vol. X) are utilized in the following pages without specific citation of sources.

[2] Detailed analyses of the majority of Lanier's poems can be found in the critical biographies of Edwin Mims and Aubrey Starke (especially the latter) and in the various books and articles listed in the Bibliography (vol. VI). Only his most important poems are dealt with at length in the present Introduction, the main intention of which is expository rather than critical.

discipline, accounts in great measure for his failure to achieve more largely as poet, musician, or scholar.

During the twenty years of his career, first one and then another of these aspirations dominated his life; and the creation of poetry, though the most continuous single aim, was sometimes subordinated and on occasions thrust altogether into the background. The majority of his poems were written in two periods, of three and five years respectively, between stretches largely devoted to other fields; and even in times of his greatest productivity he was disabled by illness, harassed by economic necessity, and distracted by his activities as a professional musician and amateur scholar.[3]

These were the hostile forces that prevented the full expression of his message to mankind—the gospel of love and beauty that was to redeem a world sick with materialism. That Lanier was aware of this thwarting is evidenced in the three projected volumes of his last years, unfinished "outlines" for as many more poems as he had written in a lifetime, and especially in the note of pathos sounded in the final jotting.[4] The wonder of it is that he accomplished as much as he did; the tragedy, not that he died young, but that after many delays he died at the beginning of his period of greatest development, in originality and in sureness of technique. The loss to poetry is implicit in the progress of these last years and the unfinished plans that he left.

Lanier's poetic career began late. Referring in 1876 to "Corn," "The Symphony," and "Psalm of the West," all written during the past two years, he said: "These are my first poems, excepting short songs which have appeared in Scribner's and Lippincott's."[5] In the deepest sense this was true, for it was not until he was thirty-two years old that he gave himself with full seriousness to the composition of poetry, and only half-a-dozen pieces of importance date from before this time. In a literal sense it was far from true, for he had written as many poems before "Corn" as he was to write thereafter. But the work of these last crowded years is that on which his reputation largely rests, and the several abortive starts of the earlier period will be given only summary treatment here.

[3] A list showing the number of Lanier's poems composed in each year makes this clear: 1858-1860 (16), 1861 (1), 1862 (0), 1863 (2), 1864 (3), 1865 (8), 1866 (14), 1867 (9), 1868 (15), 1869 (2), 1870 (0), 1871 (8), 1872 (0), 1873 (1), 1874 (8), 1875 (11), 1876 (10), 1877 (18), 1878 (11), 1879 (3), 1880 (15), 1881 (9). Thus in the two periods of greatest productivity, 1865-1868 and 1874-1878, he wrote 104 poems out of a total of 164; the first came to an end when he turned to law to earn a living in 1869, the second when he turned to the academic life in 1879. Another spurt came in 1880, but was stopped by the final illness.

[4] See the "Poem Outlines," pp. 251-284, below, and especially No. 189.

[5] Letter to A. H. Dooley, Aug. 15, 1876 (omitted); to Sargent, Aug. 19, 1880.

Tradition has it that Lanier wrote verses during his early years as a pupil at the Bibb County Academy, but these have not survived. The next reference is to poems written at Oglethorpe University, in his late teens, and remembered by his brother as "*Byronesque*, if not *Wertheresque*, at least tinged with gloominess." [6] These early efforts, now first brought to light, are of very slight intrinsic merit, but they deserve a place in the history of Lanier's development. Some of them, indeed, show the influence of Byron, though this is more pervasive than specific, and it was an enthusiasm that soon cooled; for he and Byron had very little in common, and the stormy romantic played no part in Lanier's literary life beyond this momentary appeal to his adolescent imagination. Coleridge is also reflected in these juvenile efforts, one poem being actually addressed to him, with strictures on his short-comings as well as a confession of indebtedness; but though Lanier's interest in him continued for many years, he never owed him more than a divided allegiance. There is no trace here of Wordsworth or Shelley whom he later admired. In fact, the only one of the great English romanticists to exert any abiding influence on Lanier was Keats. He is alluded to in one of these early poems as "My dearest friend," but the effect of his style and theory was only slowly to permeate the writings of this late American admirer.[7]

More than all the rest, Poe was the idol during these first years. The gloom and the melancholy come directly from him, and likewise the romantic treatment of love. The only surprising thing, as a matter of fact, is that his influence should have died out so soon, for more than any other American poets of the century these two were concerned with sound effects and with theories of prosody. Both were interested in the physics of music as well as of poetry, yet Lanier finally declared the *Rationale of Verse* to be "permeated by a fundamental mistake." [8]

[6] See Clifford Lanier's reminiscences in *Gulf States Historical Magazine*, II, 10 (July, 1903) and in *Chautauquan*, XXI, 406 (July, 1895).

[7] The sixteen poems in this group are printed separately in the present volume. For imitations of Byron, see the ones on pp. 232-233; of Coleridge, pp. 224-226; for the allusion to Keats, p. 228, bottom. Lanier's later interest in all these poets can be readily traced from the index. His copy of *The Poetical Works of Coleridge, Shelley, and Keats* (Philadelphia, 1847) is inscribed on the flyleaf, "Christmas, 1878"; it contains numerous annotations, principally indicating his use of them in the Peabody and Hopkins lectures, vols. III-IV. (All vols. from Lanier's library referred to in this Introduction are in the Charles D. Lanier Collection, Johns Hopkins University.) He is said to have carried a similar volume with him through the war until it was stolen during a Federal raid (Clifford Lanier, "Reminiscences," *Chautauquan*, XXI, 407-408, July, 1895).

[8] See II, 11-12; and Poe's *Works* (Harrison Edition), XVI, 8. In a letter of 1835 Poe speaks of making "some odd chromatic experiments" by way of testing the music of his own lines (*Century Magazine*, CVII, 654, Mar., 1924). See also Starke, p. 335.

Likewise, he expressed an early admiration for the philosophic-scientific *Eureka*; but in the end he complained: " The trouble with Poe was, he did not *know* enough . . . to be a great poet." [9] Though the mature Lanier owed little to Poe, fully half of the juvenile poems are palpable imitations of him, including the only one of them he thought worthy of publication.[10] Thus all of this group are imitative, and, granting that they were written between the ages of sixteen and eighteen, still they show little if any promise. In fact, they seem quite detached from the future Lanier, except for the exaggeration of defects that he was to wrestle with to the end: blurred images, a too luxuriant diction, and a tendency to compose in terms of sound rather than meaning. Nothing came of this first flirtation with the muse, for it was hardly more than that. Aside from the letter submitting his choice effort to the editor of an unidentified magazine, there is no indication in his early correspondence of a serious interest in becoming a poet.[11] Other plans were maturing in his mind during the winter of 1861, to become a musician or to study at Heidelberg in preparation for a professorship in an American university. But all this gave way before the impending conflict, and within six months he was in Virginia as a Confederate soldier.

It was nearly three years before Lanier again turned to authorship. In 1863 he was stationed at Fort Boykin on the James River with rather light duties as a scout, and by December, under the stimulus of literary discussions at nearby Bacon's Castle, he began the composition of a novel and as an offshoot wrote a poem to the " daughter of the castle," Virginia Hankins.[12] Six weeks later, with mounting enthusiasm,

[9] See letter of May 5, 1863, to Mary Day, and *Poems* (1884), pp. xxxv-xxxvi. Killis Campbell used this as the starting point for his title essay in *The Mind of Poe* (1933), but misunderstood the meaning of Lanier, who had come to think of the poet as a religious seer " in charge of all learning to convert it into wisdom " (II, 6)—a theory quite opposite from Poe's. A comparative study of the two poets should be revealing.

[10] See the poems on pp. 5, 221-222, 229-231, 234.

[11] Letter of Feb. 5, 1861; there is no evidence that it was actually published. See also the playful reference to writing poetry in the letter to his father, Feb. 12. But R. S. Lanier's reply of Feb. 21 to a lost letter by Sidney indicates that he submitted poems to his father for criticism and received kindly advice and encouragement: " You have quick poetical sympathies, a rich fund of imagery, inexhaustible conceit, & a clever knack of versification. . . . As to the verses themselves, they show more of promise in the author than present worth in themselves." For the reference in the following sentence, see note 7, Letters of 1860.

[12] " To ——— " (153) ; see letter of Dec. 7, 1863, and Jan. 4, 1864. He had previously written a humorous quatrain, and had spoken of himself somewhat jocularly as a prospective poet (letters of Sept. 15, and Apr. 21, 24, 1863; see also his father's encouragement to authorship, quoted in note 21, Letters of 1863).

he wrote to his father (Jan. 18, 1864) : " I find that my whole soul is merging itself into this business of writing, especially of writing poetry—. I'm going to try it: and am going to test, in the most rigid way I know, the awful question whether it is my vocation—." He even indulged in the pleasant anticipation of publishing a volume of poems in collaboration with his brother; but the primary absorption in his novel and the vicissitudes and hazards of military life left him little time for poetic composition.[13] During the entire war he wrote but four poems, another love lyric to his Virginia sweetheart and two translations from the German.

Lanier's four years as a soldier marked a distinct break in his life. A serious collapse in health as a result of his imprisonment, combined with the failure of economic opportunity following the South's defeat, left him little to do for the moment but mark time. In the summer of 1865 he took a position as tutor on a plantation near Macon, as much to ward off a return of illness as to earn his meager board and keep. It was here that he again took up his pen and even began to entertain ambitions to publish, not only his novel but his poems.[14] After three months of this and a relapse in health, he turned to clerking in his grandfather's hotel in Montgomery, where he remained through 1866 and most of 1867. It was not the kind of work he could look forward to permanently, but it gave him a livelihood and slowly returning strength. Besides, he found happiness in his brother's companionship and in the literary life they began to evolve during their spare time. They joined a literary society, read avidly, and talked about books with every congenial soul they could find, though in the main they had to rely on each other and the critical encouragement in their father's letters.[15] To a northern friend Lanier wrote (May 12, 1866) :

[13] See letter of Mar. 14, 1864. In the winter of 1864 he spent two months on a campaign in North Carolina. The following summer he was detailed as a signal officer on a blockade-runner out of Wilmington, N. C. ; and in November he was captured and imprisoned at Point Lookout, Md., where he remained until the end of the war. For the poems referred to in the following sentence, see pp. 5 and 154, below.

[14] See his letters to Mary Day, Sept. 1 and Oct. 15, 1865. She took some of his poems to New York for publication, but apparently failed in her efforts. See also letter of Sept. 16, 1865, to Clifford, announcing his renewal of literary activity and implying that he had begun to keep his literary work-book or Ledger by this time.

[15] The correspondence between R. S. Lanier and his sons during these years shows his hearty approval of their literary endeavors, but his practical caution in warning them against adopting authorship as a means of support. See note 41, Letters of 1865. But cf. the comment in the letter to Milton Northrup, May 12, 1866 (quoted in the following sentence) : " beyond our father, a man of considerable literary acquirements and exquisite taste, we have not been able

Our literary life, too, is a lonely and somewhat cheerless one. . . . I'm thirsty to know what is going on in the great Art-world up there: you have no idea how benighted we all are—I've only recently begun to get into the doings of literary men, through the Round Table, which I've just commenced taking.

This New York weekly proved an important stimulus to them in their isolation, for it not only urged that there was never a riper time for young men to enter the field of authorship, but adopted a magnanimous attitude towards the South and held out a hand of friendship.[16] Lanier responded promptly, and his first two poems known to have been published were printed in the July 14, 1866, issue of the *Round Table*. This was his sole vehicle for over two years, and though there is no evidence that he received any pay for the dozen poems he contributed to its pages, it was encouragement enough to the young author merely to see his compositions in print.

Most of the energies of the two brothers went into their novels, for Clifford was writing one also, but they found time to compose a good deal of poetry, both separately and in collaboration. During the first two and a half years after the war, in addition to completing and publishing *Tiger-Lilies*, Lanier wrote some thirty poems—as high an average as he ever maintained.[17] These, and the few he had written during the war, present a striking change from the verses of his college days. Many of the juvenile crudities—the extravagant diction, the vagueness of purpose, the obscurity and diffuseness—had been corrected if not entirely overcome. The greatest improvement was undoubtedly in polishing his slipshod meters and careless rhymes into smooth and sometimes felicitous verse. Indeed, the chief value of the work of these years was in the practice Lanier gave himself in mastering the technique of his craft. He seldom used the same stanza-forms or rhyme-schemes and experimented in many directions, with occasional hints of a tendency towards that metrical irregularity he was to advocate at the end of his career in *The Science of English Verse* and to justify in

to find a single individual who sympathized in such pursuits enough to warrant showing him our little productions." A year later the Preface to *Tiger-Lilies* calls his book "a faint cry, sent from a region where there are few artists to happier lands that own many" (V, 5).

[16] See, for example, the editorials in the *Round Table* for May 12, July 7, 14, 28, 1866. For the titles of Lanier's poems published there in 1866-1868, see the bibliography, VI, 381. The first two were printed anonymously.

[17] See pp. 5-13, 153-168, for the thirty-three poems written by Lanier in 1863-1867, and pp. 213-214 for three in collaboration with his brother. There was continual talk of publishing a volume together. (See, for example, letters of May 12, 1866, and Mar. 21, 1867, but this never materialized. See also letter of June 15, 1867, for plans for a joint literary life.)

" The Marshes of Glynn " and " Sunrise." [18] That Lanier was consciously trying to improve his art in the larger aspects of style, also, is evidenced in his confessions of his own defects. As early as Jan. 18, 1864, he had written to his father:

I have frequently noticed in myself a tendency to the diffuse style—; a disposition to push my metaphors too far, employing a multitude of words to heighten the *pat*-ness of the image, and so making of it rather a *conceit* than a metaphor, a fault copiously illustrated in the poetry of Cowley, Waller, Donne.

After several years of practice, he was still modest enough to accept the criticism of the publishers to whom he submitted *Tiger-Lilies* that he needed " very severe training," and admitted that his prose was redundant and his " tendency to a profusion of metaphors deep-rooted "; but encouraged by his progress he declared rashly: " There is no single poem of mine which is not as simple in diction, in word-arrangement, and in thought, as any ballad of Burns." [19] This approaches the truth in two or three of the best, and in several written the following year; it is also true that Lanier achieved a comparative simplicity in these years that he was not to recapture except in the finest work of his maturity. But there still remained in 1865-1867 much to be corrected in his poetic style: a tendency to strained personifications, verbosity, affectation of archaisms, a sentimental vocabulary (especially in the conventional flowers of poetry—the rose, the violet, and the lily), and the old habit of choosing words for their musical sounds rather than their meaning.

For convenient summary most of the poems of these years, none of which were ambitious in scope or theme, can be divided into a few categories. First, there are the light lyrics addressed to cousins, friends, and young ladies with whom he fancied himself in love; one of them, "A Song of Eternity in Time" (12), he thought well enough of to republish many years later in a slightly revised form. Next in number, and overlapping these, are the occasional pieces, prompted by birthdays, marriages, and deaths; of one, " To Captain James DeWitt Hankins " (10), he declared, " It's the best thing I've written: approaching more nearly my ideal of simplicity." [20] Lanier's own choices may be allowed to stand as the best representatives of these two groups. In addition, there are the translations and other metrical

[18] See the analysis of the poems through 1869 in Starke, pp. 124-125.
[19] Letters of June 15 (to Clifford Lanier) and Sept. 12(?), 1867.
[20] Letter to R. S. Lanier, Nov. 5, 1866. (In this Introduction numbers in parenthesis following the titles of poems refer to the pages where they are printed in the present volume.)

experiments, and a few generalized interpretations of nature. Almost all of them are marked by the over-seriousness, and the immaturity, of a somewhat prolonged youth; and through them run the themes of love and friendship, treated sentimentally, and the repeated efforts to work out a few favorite metaphors—night, day, the sea, and the stars. But none of these have more than the most tenuous connection with Lanier's life, inner or outer. None of his war experiences were put to poetic use, which is disappointing in view of the saving realism injected into *Tiger-Lilies* by the occasional battle scenes.[21] " The Dying Words of Jackson " (156) is partly a literary exercise, and though it touches actuality in the central stanzas, the purpose is to eulogize Stonewall's character rather than his military genius. " The Tournament " (6) is in one sense an allegory of the conflict between North and South, unhappily incorporated for this purpose in " Psalm of the West " ten years later, but it owes quite as much to his reading and to his relations with Mary Day. Lanier's reticence about the war may be explained by an incidental allusion in another poem, in which he forgives, in order that he may forget, the " drunken, rude barbarity " of these four years.[22] In this he was merely representative of the rest of his generation, for excepting Whitman's *Drum Taps* little important poetry came from either side.

The truth of the matter is that, barring this one significant reservoir from which he could not bring himself to draw, the young Lanier had very little to say, so that his early poems reflect not his life but his reading. The ardent humanist places as high a value upon poetry drawn from the experience of the life of literature as upon that drawn from the author's own experience of actual life. But without going to the opposite extreme of demanding that an artist divorce himself from the cultural heritage of the past, one can find little nourishment in poetry that is merely bookish and imitative. However, since Lanier's reading explains in part not only his present limitations but also, as he was able to transmute it, his future achievements, a brief inquiry into the influences that dominated these years seems called for. Though there are lingering traces of the English romanticists and of Poe,[23] new gods had replaced those of his college days. In camp and field in Virginia he had been reading Carlyle and through him the early German romantic writers, especially Richter and Novalis; from them he

---

[21] See V, xxvii-xxx.

[22] Quoted from " To J. L." (8). Beyond these there are only the four metaphors drawn from war scenes, Poem Outlines Nos. 4, 5, 12, 13 (pp. 238-239).

[23] Cf. the attempt at the onomatopœic effect of " The Bells " in " Spring Greeting " (5) and the general resemblance in " The Wedding " (158). For the others see Starke, who also points out the influence of Shakespeare for decorative and oratorical effects.

developed his first theories of the nature and function of the poet. At the same time, and with equal enthusiasm, he discovered Philip James Bailey and the two Brownings, especially Elizabeth Barrett, committing to memory *Festus* and *Aurora Leigh*; the influence on Lanier of the metaphysical speculations of the former and the idealism and lyricism of the latter would repay study, but are beyond the limits of this Introduction.[24]

Among many new favorites, however, Tennyson by all odds held first place. The earliest reference to him is in 1862, but it is clear that already a kindred spirit had been found; and for the next ten years he is the most quoted of all authors in Lanier's letters, his journal, and his published prose.[25] At first it was Tennyson's elegiac mood and his emphasis on love and friendship that appealed to the southern poet's sentimental nature, an influence that was not always healthy. *In Memoriam*, naturally enough, was the principal source from which he drew, and two quotations from it will suffice to show the nature of its appeal. Into his Ledger (p. 37) Lanier copied in the spring of 1866 that stanza which recommends

> Short swallow-flights of song that dip
> Their wings in tears, and skim away.

And the following year he chose for the motto of his novel the one concluding

> To lull with song an aching heart,
> And give to earthly Love his dues.

The manner and purpose of Lanier's early poetry could hardly be more fittingly epitomized.[26] Elsewhere he praised Tennyson for his

---

[24] Cf. Carlyle's doctrine of the poet as seer and preacher, which was to influence Lanier's theory throughout life, and the statement of one of his prime tenets in Novalis's *Fragments*: " The true Poet is all-knowing; he is an actual world in miniature." More specifically, the symbolism of head and heart and resurrection in " The Tournament " may derive from Novalis. The influence of Richter is more diffuse, and that of all three more apparent in *Tiger-Lilies* than in the poems (see V, xviii-xxiv). His interest in Heine seems to have been confined for the most part to the translations. For the Brownings see Starke; and for general references to reading during the war see Lanier's letters to Augusta Lamar, May, 1862(?), to Mary Day during Apr., 1863, and the following: May 5, Sept. 15, 1863; Mar. 14, July 28, Aug. 1, 1864. All of these authors figure prominently in *Tiger-Lilies*.

[25] See, for example, letters of Jan. 18 and May, 1862(?); Apr. 6, 21, 1863; Apr. 9, July 28, Aug. 1, 1864; Sept. 16, 1865; Ledger, pp. 37, 38, 39, 43, 46; vol. V, 39, 54, 77, 82, 84, 239, 263, 268, 321; VI, 243 and 389—listing four of Tennyson's poems set to music by Lanier.

[26] For example, " To Captain James DeWitt Hankins " is modelled on Tennyson's poem, even in form, and Lanier himself refers to it as an " In

technical skill, his "light airy metaphors," his "etherealization" of
nature, and also for being a "singing philosopher" strong by virtue of
his "steady spiritual enthusiasm." [27] The Laureate's wrestling with the
problems of religion and science, however, did not find an echo in
Lanier's poetry until many years later. In these early years the influence
was chiefly one of mood and vocabulary, and the example of a varied
experimenter in metrics and verbal music.

As 1867 drew to a close, Lanier was beginning to feel himself
something of an author. With his novel in press and half-a-dozen
poems in print, he wrote scornfully of a new magazine, *Southern Society*
of Baltimore, which had asked him to contribute, calling it "jejune"
and saying, "I shall certainly send nothing to such a set of asses." [28]
Still not ready to risk authorship as a means of support, he had at
least taken a step in that direction by giving up his hotel clerkship to
become principal of the Academy at Prattville, Alabama, a position
which he hoped would afford more leisure for writing. In December
he married Mary Day, whom he had loved through a troubled court-
ship of four years. Ahead lay the promise of domestic happiness,
security, and peace. Meantime *Tiger-Lilies* had been published, and,
as reports of good sales and favorable reviews came in for both this
and Clifford's *Thorn-Fruit*, Lanier had a small first taste of the heady
wine of success. "What could we not do . . . if we could study, if
we could take time to polish, having some experience?" he wrote to
his brother at the beginning of the new year. "Can we not work
together, at the work which we love, and for which Nature, in the
opinion of all these critics without exception, has fitted us?" Three
days later he was stricken with his first hemorrhage from the lungs
and the fear of tuberculosis that had haunted him for several years
was confirmed.[29] But this was only the beginning of his troubles.

Shortly before his marriage he had written to his New York
friend Northrup (Dec. 16, 1867): "I think y'r people can have no
idea of the slow terrors with which this winter has invested our life

Memoriam" (letter to Virginia Hankins, Nov. 5, 1866). The stanza of the
"Lady of Shalott" is used in "Spring Greeting," and Tennyson's medievalism
(as well as Froissart's) is probably echoed in "The Tournament." Many other
resemblances, specific and general, are so apparent as to need no further citation.

[27] The quotations are from "Retrospects and Prospects," an essay written in
1867 (V, 285-287, 292, 296-297). Lanier's copy of Tennyson's *Poems*, which
he apparently carried through the war with him, has not survived (but see below,
n. 142). A copy of his *Queen Mary*, apparently purchased in 1879 according to
a statement from Turnbull & Bros. (Charles D. Lanier Collection), is preserved
in his Library, Johns Hopkins University.

[28] Letters of Oct. 10 and Dec. 16 (to Northrup), 1867.

[29] Letters to Clifford Lanier, Jan. 14, 17, 1868.

in the South." The First Reconstruction Act, dividing the southern states into military districts and setting up carpet-bag governments, had been passed the previous spring. At first Lanier was able to describe the ominous prospects in a bantering vein.[30] Then came two poems in the summer of 1867, one of hope and one of despair, that reveal his growing awareness of what was in store. "To Our Hills" (166) is an indignant complaint against the "coward hand" of the North that could smite an honorable enemy in defeat. "Barnacles" (11) is a challenge to the cumbering past growing out of his earnest need to keep alive in a world that seemed dying all around him. Writing to a friend after its appearance in the *Round Table* in the late autumn, he said: "It is incomplete: a companion piece must go with it."[31] This, he makes clear, was to have been his profession of faith in the future. In the winter of 1868, however, as the economic and social effects of the paralyzing legislation began to be felt, the prospects for the South's future were grim. On Jan. 21 he wrote of the possibility of having to leave Prattville because of danger from the Negroes who were becoming unruly under their new freedom. A series of poems dealing with the evils of Reconstruction followed almost immediately.[32]

Two of these Lanier withheld from publication, and even left them in an unrevised state, probably because the immediacy of their response to recent events—"such . . . crime and hatred and bitterness as even the four terrible years of war had entirely failed to bring about"—made them more declamatory than poetic.[33] Sometimes his indignation transcended mere name-calling, and in the gloom of "The Raven Days" (15) and the anguished remonstrance of "Laughter in the Senate" (14) he achieved a certain lyricism. Better than any of these are the two which inaugurated and closed the series: "Tyranny" (13) in which his bitterness had burned down to irony, calling on the blight

---

[30] See "The Sherman Bill" (V, 209 and xxxviii-xxxix) and his letter of Mar. 14, 1867.

[31] Letter to Virginia Hankins, Jan. 14, 1868—written on the same date that he announced his literary plans to his brother, three days before his attack of illness.

[32] The political and economic history of the Reconstruction years is too well known to need rehearsing here (see Paul H. Buck, *The Road to Reunion, 1865-1900*, Boston, 1937). For R. S. Lanier's suggestion that his sons turn to political themes in their writing, see notes 22, 23, Letters of 1868.

[33] "Steel in Soft Hands" and "Burn the Stubble" (169-170) are here first published; the MSS are rough pencil drafts only. Two-thirds of the original version of "The Raven Days" was suppressed apparently for the same reason (see p. 228, below), as well as parts of *Tiger-Lilies* (see V, xxxv-xxxvi); and "To Our Hills," similarly, was not published until after Lanier's death. ("Strange Jokes," 167, from the previous summer also belongs with this group). The quotation in this sentence is from an essay, "Retrospects and Prospects," written in 1867 (V, 303).

to finish its work; and " The Ship of Earth " (15), in which he voiced the utter despair of his leaderless region. Welling up from deeply felt emotions, these vigorous protests stand out in marked contrast to the imitative poems that had come from his reading. It is as if the threatened destruction of his native South opened his eyes for the first time to the southern scene and way of life he had so long taken for granted, and the vision gave reality to what he wrote. He may have drawn no poems from the war itself, but the evils of Reconstruction gave him something to say, and he was almost the only poet in whom it found a voice—not first-rate poetry, but eloquence such as the best of the Abolition poems achieved in ante-bellum days.

As the paralysis spread, however, Lanier too became lethargized; the poems ceased and a novel which was to record this economic catastrophe was abandoned.[34] Everything was against him. " He has not been as strong or cheerful since his sickness of two months ago," his wife wrote as spring and a relapse came on.[35] Attendance at his school fell off, and by May he was forced to close the Prattville Academy and move back to Georgia until some plan for the future could be worked out. With illness, debt, no employment, and a child expected, his fortunes reached bottom. And not the least part of his depression came from the conclusion, daily growing more inevitable, that he must give up his hopes of authorship probably forever and turn to some more certain means of livelihood, such as practising law in his father's office. The irony of all this could hardly be more pointed. For the very adverse circumstances that made this change necessary had produced his most interesting poems; and it was just at this time that he made his first acquaintance with an established poet, Paul Hayne, who had read one of these recent lyrics and sent him a warm letter of encouragement.[36] Exactly when the decision was made is not known, but it was reflected poignantly in " Life and Song " (16), written during the summer of 1868. This was not only his best poem to date but his first real success, being printed and reprinted in periodicals in New York, Baltimore, and Atlanta. It has been a favorite with anthologists and often quoted as a symbol of the union between his life and his art, combining as it does the sincerity of the Reconstruction pieces and the melodious quality of the earlier Tennysonian imitations. As much of the finest lyric poetry comes from anguish as from ecstasy; but it was a bitter pill that almost the only one of his early poems deserving to rank with his best should have been born of the desperation that made him abandon

[34] See the fragmentary " John Lockwood's Mill " and the other post-war prose (V, 231 and 200-208).
[35] Letter of Apr. 2, 1868, to Mrs. Cosby Smith.
[36] Letter of Sept. 7, 1868, and note 47.

authorship altogether.[37]   By the end of 1868 he had begun the study of law.

The next five years constitute a pathetic gap in Lanier's career as a poet. His difficulty in adjusting himself to the necessity is witnessed in his letters. Writing of his prospects in the legal world to a friend (Mar. 15, 1869), he added, "I have not however ceased my devotion to letters, wh. I love better than all things in my heart of hearts." And several months later, even after passing the bar examinations, his admonition to his brother (Nov. 19) that they must be "*lawyers, nothing but lawyers, good* lawyers, and *successful* lawyers" betrays the pain of decision beneath its bravado. The struggle between desire and need is likewise reflected in two of the very few serious poems he completed during this period. "June Dreams, In January" (29), apparently begun in 1868 and completed in 1873, is as revealing a piece of autobiography as Lanier ever wrote. Though the story is not to be taken literally, it is an accurate enough picture of his economic handicap and his abiding devotion to poetry, which could not supply his bread. Such moods of protest alternated with others of resignation. "Nirvâna" (19) is his quest for spiritual peace, written after a long illness just as he began the active practice of law in the late autumn of 1869. Both show a luxurious sensuousness that is new in his poetry, partly in reaction from the practical routine of his new profession, partly in response to new influences from his reading. There is less of Tennyson here than of Swinburne and Pre-Raphaelitism, with touches of an eclectic Orientalism.[38] More important than their literary background, however, is their originality, growing out of their relation to the poet's deeper emotional life, in which they compare favorably with "Life and Song."

[37] The early title "Work and Song" suggests even more forcibly its connection with this decision. Lanier again showed his good judgment in choosing this, along with the best of the Reconstruction poems ("Tyranny" and "The Ship of Earth"), to be included in a group of "Street-Cries" for a projected volume near the end of his life. All of the other early poems (except "A Song of Eternity in Time") were allowed to remain neglected in obscure magazines or in MS.

[38] As early as Oct. 14, 1866, he had written his father, "Mr. Swinburne has suddenly shot up into the foremost place among modern poets;" and one poem written at this time, "Will 'All Be Right in a Hundred Years'" (159), is an imitation of the French lyrics Swinburne was translating. A friend of Lanier's later called "June Dreams" Swinburnish and "too voluptuous," but Hayne approved of it as Oriental (Hayne's letter of Mar. 27, 1873; cf. especially the rejected lines, pp. 291-293, below). The most significant influence of Swinburne came many years later, however, in matters of rhythm and rhyme rather than in unconventional vocabulary and theme. A study of the sources of "Nirvâna" may be found in Arthur Christy, "The Orientalism of Sidney Lanier," *Aryan Path*, V, 638-641 (Oct., 1934); but part of the Oriental influence, at least, came at second hand through Novalis.

Though "Nirvâna" opened up to Lanier a new magazine and brought him the friendship of its editors, instead of launching a new period of literary productivity, it brought him contentment to "lie fallow." [39] In 1870 he wrote no poetry at all, and during the following year he merely amused himself with the composition of a group of verses in dialect, which he did not take seriously enough even to mention in his letters.[40] But his contemporaries found them entertaining, as indicated by reprints in newspapers all over the country, especially of the most popular one, which even attracted the pen of a comic illustrator in the mid-west (see p. 337). They appeared at a time when the "Pike County" ballads of Bret Harte and John Hay had started something of a vogue, but the importance of these two as pioneers has been greatly exaggerated and it seems reasonably certain that Lanier hit upon this literary type quite independently.[41] Humorous dialect writing, we know now, is as old in America as journalism itself. He was undoubtedly acquainted with the Georgia exponents of this genre from boyhood as he was most certainly acquainted at first hand with the Cracker's character and speech; and he had already tried his hand at it in prose as early as 1867.[42] Moreover, the distinguishing feature of Lanier's dialect poems is not their humor but their moral earnestness, and it is this which sets them apart from the better known work of Harte and Hay, which depends for its effectiveness upon romantic exaggeration and surprise. Though he chose a light form, his theme was serious. The poems draw strength from their concern

[39] Letters of Feb. 22, Mar. 4, Apr. 13, 1870. The *New Eclectic* was edited by Lawrence Turnbull and William Hand Browne, who gave him encouragement through these lean years and became valuable friends after his removal to Baltimore. But Lanier's chief contributions to their magazine (and its successor, the *Southern*) were prose.

[40] The only reference to the dialect poems is the brief allusion in his letter of Mar. 11 (?) 1871. No evidence has been found to substantiate the dates of 1869-1870 assigned by Lanier's wife to "Thar's More in the Man" (22), "Jones's Private Argument" (24) and "9 from 8" (194). On the contrary, the original publication date of the first two has now been established as 1871. More conclusive is the allusion in "Them Ku Klux" (191), now first published, which places its composition after Dec. 21, 1870; and from the less skilful handling of both dialect and theme this seems to have been the first of the series.

[41] His first reference to an acquaintance with Harte's poetry is in a letter of Nov. 3, 1874, where he points out that it is not at all like his own just published "Civil Rights" (40), a fifth poem in Cracker dialect voicing his protest against the final piece of Reconstruction legislation. Recent studies of this genre are curiously silent about Lanier (see Walter Blair, *Native American Humor*, New York, 1937, and *Horse Sense in American Humor*, Chicago, 1942).

[42] See V, xxx-xxxii. He was later to meet and describe the western Pike (letter of Nov. 22, 1872) and the Florida Cracker (VI, 13-14, 21-22). The last of his Cracker dialect poems, "A Puzzled Ghost in Florida" (99), depends entirely upon comic effects, and is decidedly inferior to the earlier ones.

with the economic problems of the region he knew and loved, and so form a link with the earlier Reconstruction pieces. Even more than their portrayal of folk character, it is this grappling with realities in the world around him, a trait all too rare in his poetry, that gives them their importance for the modern reader. Yet, though he was soon to win his first prominence with a more exalted treatment of the same theme in " Corn," he seems to have considered his experiments in dialect beneath the dignity of the poet's high calling.

After this little flurry of writing, Lanier attempted no new poems in 1872 or 1873.[43] Indeed, during most of the Macon period the struggle was less between poetry and law than it was between law and health. The exertions of practice, especially in court, drained his small reserves of strength, and half of each year was spent in New York for medical treatment or in health resorts to escape the climate which he felt was so fatal to him. He was not only too busy for authorship, but much of the time too ill even to read his favorite authors. Gradually it became apparent that this was a losing game; and when he went to Texas for the winter of 1872-1873, after a particularly long and severe attack, he took stock of his prospects. The bravery of his decision lies in the fact that it was based not upon the recovery of his health but, on the contrary, upon his realization of how few years he had left to live. So it was that he determined to leave the only work which promised security and launch himself in the precarious profession of an artist. For five years he had kept alive the smouldering fires of authorship by working spasmodically on a long narrative poem, " The Jacquerie," which he planned as his *magnum opus,* and by occasional correspondence with the few literary friends he had. Now, he wrote to his wife from Texas, " Ineffable poems—of music and words— torment me." For the flute meant almost as much to him as the pen, and it was more certain as a means of earning a living. This practical feature of his plan, to support himself by playing in an orchestra while he wrote his books, probably accounts for the exaggeration in his letter to Hayne: " Whatever turn I have for Art, is purely musical; poetry being, with me, a mere tangent into which I shoot sometimes." [44]

[43] In the last half of 1871 he had written three occasional pieces (see pp. 196-199) and in " The Homestead " (25) made a first effort to put the theme of diversified farming into serious poetry, but it is conventional and uninspired. In 1873 his only poetic activity was to revise and probably expand " June Dreams." (For the prose of this period, four public addresses and two essays of earlier date refurbished for publication, see V, 247-321.)

[44] The two quotations are from letters of Feb. 25 and May 26, 1873. For the conflict of these two interests at this crucial period of decision see also letters of Feb. 8, 24, 28, May 24, 27, July 21, Sept. 24, and Nov. 29, 1873, and note 40. (His career as a musician is discussed in the Introduction to vol. VII.)

However this may be, most of his energies during the next year were devoted to music, as first flute in the Peabody Orchestra of Baltimore.

Lanier's real career as a poet did not begin until the summer of 1874. He was thirty-two years old but still almost completely unknown. Though he had written half the poems he was ever to write, few were significant and not more than a score had been published—all privately printed or in periodicals with a small or local circulation. Occasionally a poem had taken his reputation momentarily beyond the boundaries of his native Georgia, but not a single one had appeared in a leading national magazine. The reading public had not discovered him,[45] and what is more serious, he had not found himself. " I seem so poor, so insignificant," he wrote to his wife at the time of making his decision (Jan. 10, 1873) : " I have not yet dealt so much as a good sword-stroke in life." He had had from Paul Hayne encouragement and advice, but none of the stimulating and disciplinary criticism he so sorely needed.

Such were his handicaps, but he was not a raw beginner. For fifteen years of practice, however desultory, had taught him the rudiments of his craft, and in the past few years by drawing upon his own emotional and imaginative resources he had learned to lean less heavily on his models. Further, he had found new ones who offered a healthy corrective to the early sentimental influence of Tennyson. In Texas Lanier had discovered Chaucer, and his letters are filled with quotations showing his delight in this new world. In an essay he was writing at this period he declared that " all modern poets would do well to drink much of Chaucer and little of Morris," thus renouncing the author of *The Earthly Paradise* he had admired so extravagantly a few years before.[46] Shakespeare, whom he had known all along, he was now reading with a new enthusiasm as reflected in the dictum, " Let us not forget that Shakespeare is first poet and Chaucer second poet." During his first winter in Baltimore, when asked to name his favorite poets, these two headed the list.[47] Tennyson was not even mentioned; and just how far he had moved away from his old master is revealed in his curiously erratic comment to Hayne: " Tennyson (let me not blaspheme

[45] The selections and biographical sketch in J. W. Davidson's *Living Writers of the South* (New York, 1869), pp. 321-324—with p. 323 a misprint of a critique on another writer—probably reached only a limited audience, chiefly in the South.

[46] The quotation is from " Paul H. Hayne's Poetry " (V, 323; that in the following sentence, from p. 325). For Morris see letter of July 7, 1869.

[47] See " Lanier's Mental Photograph " (X, 376). The others named are Lucretius and Robert Browning, whose more robust influence was a valuable complement to that of his wife, still listed however as his favorite poetess. (For Lanier's admiration of *The Ring and the Book*, see his letter of Apr. 13, 1870.)

against the Gods!) is not a musical tho' in other respects (particularly in that of phrase making) a very wonderful writer." [48] Though this apostasy was only temporary, it indicates an important trend at the time of his new beginning in poetry. To Virginia Hankins whose reading he had guided in an earlier period, he summed up his new allegiance succinctly. " No, Tennyson and William Morris are not the masters," he wrote (Aug. 15, 1875): " Chaucer and Shakespeare— these are the masters." The sturdy vocabulary of the one and the deep humanity of the other are reflected in " Corn " and the poems that followed, less as direct imitation than as an assimilated influence.

Lanier rarely composed spontaneous lyrics, nor were his studied revisions always happy. His best poems invariably came when he drew from deeply felt experiences to body forth themes over which he had long brooded. The genesis of " Corn " (34) goes back to the Reconstruction poems of 1868 (especially " Tyranny "), which had first turned his attention to the economic plight of the post-war South, and to the dialect verses of three years later, in which he had proposed diversified crops as his solution to the collapse of the old agricultural system. Returning to Georgia in 1874 after his first winter in Baltimore, his vision sharpened by the contrasting progress of that city, he was " struck with alarm, in seeing the numbers of deserted old homesteads and gullied hills in the older counties." The earlier poems came back to him, but this time he desired to carry these same " prosaic matters up to a loftier plane." [49] When he had chosen for the symbol of this tragedy the illiterate small farmer, his treatment had been comic; if he should now choose the old-school planter, it would be sentimental. Wisely, instead, he turned his eyes to the land itself. Spending the summer at Sunnyside, just north of Macon, he was surrounded by farms whose prosperity had come from planting corn instead of the single traditional money-crop, cotton. Here then was the new life that could spring from the old soil, and here was the theme of the poem that had been germinating so long in Lanier. Having determined the previous spring (letter of Mar. 15) to revolt against the " trim smugness and clean-shaven propriety" of conventional poetic form, he chose as his model the dignity of the Cowleyan ode and began experimenting in the

---

[48] Letter of May 26, 1873. This judgment is contradicted by the score of quotations and comments on Tennyson's technical skill, especially in sound effects, in *The Science of English Verse* (1880). His influence in this as well as in theme and attitude persisted to the end of Lanier's life, but in modified form.

[49] Quoted from a letter to Logan Bleckley, Oct. 9, 1874, describing the origin of the poem. The lines most like the dialect poems are those on pp. 38-39, below (see also the rejected lines referring to westward migration, p. 295, ll. 130 ff.).

direction of that musical irregularity which was to distinguish his best work. From his reading of Chaucer and Shakespeare he found the language and metaphor he needed to heighten his timely drama to one of universal significance. The result was the most original poem he had written.

Encouraged by his friends and confident that he had something worthy of the leading literary magazines, Lanier submitted "Corn" to *Scribner's* and the *Atlantic Monthly*, but it was rejected by both. The hurt was so deep that he could not bring himself to describe it until long afterwards, but the soul-searching that resulted brought him such confidence in himself that he wrote to his wife: " I *know*, through the fieriest tests of life, that I am, in soul, and shall be, in life and in utterance, a great poet." [50] An ambitious scheme to publish it as a separate booklet also fell through. After an extensive revision and three months of shopping around, he finally sold his poem to *Lippincott's*. This was indeed a second best, with a level of contributors distinctly below the company Lanier was ambitious to join, but as matters turned out it was a stroke of fortune. For this Philadelphia magazine, considering itself a rival to the older ones of New York and New England, was anxious to ferret out and sponsor new talent, especially from the middle Atlantic and southern states. During the next three years it bought fifteen of his poems, at higher prices than he ever received elsewhere, gave him several good commissions for prose, and issued through its publisher a selected volume of his poems. The house of J. B. Lippincott launched Lanier on his career. And when "Corn" appeared in the issue of February, 1875, it was another Philadelphia institution that undertook to spread his reputation. Gibson Peacock, editor of the *Evening Bulletin*, took up the cudgels in his behalf, praised his poem as "a great and noble one," better than anything the New England poets had produced in years, and pronounced it, to the author's delight, "Keats at his best . . . with an American fibre in it." [51] As a result of this fanfare the poem was widely reprinted,

[50] Letter of Oct. 23, 1874; the account of his reaction to Howells's rejection is in a letter to Spencer, Apr. 1, 1875. (The letter submitting the poem to the *Atlantic*, discovered too late to be incorporated in its chronological place, is printed in an appendix, X, 341.)

[51] See Lanier's letters of Jan. and Feb., 1875, and notes 25, 28. Lanier was also particularly pleased with the comparison: "After the trash and sensationalism of the ' dialect ' poets, the Walt Whitmans and the Joaquin Millers, . . . a new and true poet has made his *début*" (quoted in a letter to his father, Jan. 26, 1875). Cf. the soberer estimate by Starke, pp. 190-194, who discusses the defects as well as the merits of " Corn " in great detail. In addition, it may be pointed out that though Lanier in his revision " simplified the opening—which was too labyrinthine " (letter of Oct. 25, 1874; cf. the variants for this part listed on p. 294, below), it is still a hindrance to the effectiveness of the poem. Only a

and the name of Sidney Lanier was now one to conjure with in American letters. Better still, he had an eager publisher and an enthusiastic sponsor.

" Corn " was not only his best and most successful poem to date; it was also his most ambitious effort, marking a new departure from the " short swallow flights of song " which he had previously confined himself to. Even more ambitious was his next important poem, " The Symphony," which as he wrote his wife (Mar. 28, 1875), " says some things I have very long wanted to say." This, indeed, has its roots deep in Lanier's past, and an understanding of its development calls for an account of the evolution and abandonment of an even longer poem which for many years he cherished as his masterpiece, but never finished. " The Jacquerie " (171) had been begun just at the time when he entered upon the study of law. It was planned as a novel in verse founded on " a very remarkable popular insurrection " in fourteenth-century France, he wrote to his brother (Nov. 4, 1868) : " But, unfortunately, I have only the very meagre account of the business given in Froissart, and am terribly crippled in my historical allusions by this fact." Lanier's copy of the *Chronicles* is heavily marked in the sections dealing with this uprising and on the flyleaves has a brief outline of the background facts that were used in the first chapter of his poem and sketched in his summary of what the whole was to contain.[52] It seems quite possible that Chapter I was all he wrote at this time, for Froissart contains no mention of the persons and events that figure in the ensuing chapters. In fact, though Lanier is known to have worked on his poem during the next four years, no specific evidence of its progress appears until he wrote to his father from Texas (Dec. 6, 1872) that he had discovered a book by Michelet with which he " managed to advance very largely [his] conception of the Jacquerie." An examination of Jules Michelet's *Histoire de France* makes clear

faulty sense of proportion—one of his besetting sins—could have devoted one-fifth of a poem on corn to a description of the surrounding woods. It was good enough in itself to have been formed into a separate poem.

[52] Jean Froissart, *Chronicles of England, France, Spain, etc.*, translated by Thomas Johnes (New York, 1849), marked in the handwriting of Mary Day Lanier as the copy that her husband " pored over in his early childhood." On pp. 108-112 is the historical background used in Chap. I and following this, a very brief account of the principal events in the " Jacquerie " culminating in their defeat at the battle of Meaux and the hanging of the peasant leader. The notes at the back contain in addition to what he used in Chap. I only the following: a sketch of Marcel, provost of the Paris merchants, an account of a second " free company " of brigands (in addition to that of Arnold de Cervoles), and a few scattered jottings such as " Song names—*virelay, rondeau*." For Lanier's plan of the whole see the description of MS *JT*ᵃ, p. 374, below. His use of historical detail, so far as it can be checked, is accurate except for a few spellings of proper names and the date 1359 instead of 1358.

what this means. For he differs radically from Froissart in taking sides not with the nobility but with the peasants, and he dates the beginning of modern French history from their insurrection.[53] Although he likewise gives none of the details used in Chapters II-V, his attitude is nearer than the older historian's to Lanier's so far as this is revealed in the surviving fragment and in the expressed intention to treat the Jacquerie uprising as " the first time that the big hungers of *the People* appear in our modern civilization." [54] All available evidence seems to indicate that the plot of " The Jacquerie " is largely original, however, for none of the authorities that he was so anxious to consult in the Peabody Library contained any material appropriate to the main body of his story beyond what he had found in Froissart and Michelet.[55]

Lanier had gone a long way in the matter of creative invention since *Tiger-Lilies*, and with such a promising start it seems necessary to inquire why he abandoned his long cherished narrative poem just after coming to Baltimore. The last significant reference to it is in a letter of November 15, 1874. Here, though he seems in sympathy with the insurrection in which " Trade arose & overthrew Chivalry," the second half of his comment was directed against the deadening spirit of commercialism in modern civilization: " Thus in the reversals of time, it

---

[53] For example: " The sufferings of the peasant had exceeded endurance: all had rained blows upon him, as on a brute that had fallen down under its load. The brute, maddened, recovered its legs and bit, . . . forced the castles and cut the throats of the barons . . . [who] had never dreamed of such a height of daring. . . . Jacques Bonhomme will pay off his lord centuries of arrears. His vengeance was that of the despairing, of the damned. God seemed to have sickened him of this world." (Quotations from the New York edition of 1865, pp. 445, 447.)

[54] Letter to Bleckley, Nov. 15, 1874.

[55] See letter of Dec. 23, 1873, and note 145. Of the works there cited Buchon's voluminous collection of Chronicles (47 vols.) contains nothing but Froissart for this period, and nothing is added to his account by the following: C. Leber, *Collection des meilleurs dissertations, notices et traités particuliers relatifs à l'histoire de France* (Paris, 1838), XX, 248-255; and C. B. Petitot, *Collection complète des memoires relatifs à l'histoire de France* (Paris, 1824), IV, 136-137. Since Lanier also mentioned the " Chronicle of the Continuator of Guillaume de Nangis " (letter of Dec. 6, 1872), this has also been examined but without avail (see Jean d'Achéry, ed., *Spicilegium sive collectio veterum aliquot scriptorum qui in Galliae bibliothecis delituerant*, Paris, 1723, III, 119-122). The scholarly study of Siméon Luce, *Histoire de La Jacquerie* (Paris, 1894), giving a detailed account of the entire insurrection, has so little in common with Lanier's narrative as to make it reasonably certain that Chaps. II-V, though true to history in a general way, were largely invented. Luce does state that the troubles first broke out in the neighborhood of Clermont, and he relates the episode of how Raoul de Clermont et de Nesle was killed and his houses burned by the peasants, two of whom (" Henniquet père et fils ") were hamstrung and otherwise mutilated by the lord's brother in revenge—but this is all that in any way parallels Lanier's story (see pp. 69-70, 160).

is *now* the *gentleman* who must arise & overthrow Trade." He favored the oppressed peasants of medieval France, but not the materialistic merchants of his own America. For years these two themes had appeared in his poetry, prose, and letters. His earliest poem protesting against trade for oppressing the masses is a newly discovered one, advocating, romantically, that Niagara be harnessed to a factory wheel so that its grandeur might be brought to the poor as well as the rich.[56] But this was written in 1867 when he was living in the model factory village of Prattville. Several years later when he saw what industrialism was doing to West Virginia, he wrote of the "blaring furnaces and flaming chimneys and pitchy smoke-clouds" in an anguished letter to his wife (Apr. 16, 1874):

O how I do abhor these trade-matters, as they are carried on here. God, to see the great stalwart men, in these acres of rolling-mills, sweating, burning, laboring, with only enough time betwixt tasks to eat in and sleep in,—far too little time to wash in! Why should this be so? The men who own these mills do not so: they have plenty.

This has often been cited as the germ of Lanier's "Symphony" (46), but it is a mistake to think of that poem as a protest only against industrialism. The misery caused by the mercantile prosperity of places like Baltimore affected him the same way, as revealed, for example, in a letter to his brother (Dec. 16, 1873):

Scarcely a day, indeed, when I do not see, in going about the streets of these great cities, the forlorn faces of the starving, of the rag-people, of the criminals, of the all-wanting, anything-grasping folk who are rogues by birth and by necessity and who suffer, suffer, throughout life. What can one do *quoad* these people, whom one cannot possibly relieve? One can only shut one's heart with a great gulping sigh . . . ; otherwise one is paralyzed by one's sympathy, and hindered from work.

Lanier had written to Hayne, Apr. 17, 1872, praising his poetry for being uncommercial and unworldly, adding significantly: "It was Trade that hatched the Jacquerie in the 14th Century . . . and now sits in the throne." But a year or so later, when writing an essay on his *Legends and Lyrics*, though he mentioned approvingly that they contained no polemical discussion—"no 'progress,' no 'Comtism'"—he

[56] See p. 168, and the prose jotting of about the same date cited in the note, pp. 372-373. See also the incidental indictments of trade running through the prose of 1867-1870 (V, 231-272, 280-305), and the rejected passages in "Nirvâna" and "June Dreams" (p. 290, ll. 56† and pp. 292-293, ll. 36†, 55†). See also his somewhat confused solution of the problems of industrialism, again by means of music, in a poem written many years later "To Richard Wagner" (102—and the rejected stanzas on pp. 315-316).

took the older poet to task for following William Morris into " dreams of the past " rather than writing of the " manners of his living time." [57] This shift of emphasis coincides with Lanier's own turning from the past to the present in the winter of 1874-1875. And it seems to offer the best explanation of why just at this time he abandoned his medieval narrative; for though its theme was modern ("the big hungers of *the People*"), the machinery and setting obscured the emphasis that he now wanted to place on the current aspect of the problem. So, in a sense " The Symphony " (46) was a revision of " The Jacquerie "; and when he wrote to Peacock (Mar. 24, 1875) that a new poem in which he discussed "various deep social questions of the times" had taken hold of him " like a real James River Ague," this must not be thought of as a spontaneous growth of the two months that had passed since the publication of " Corn." [58] Like all his best work it was long maturing. Nor was there anything incongruous to Lanier in evolving a modern poem out of a medieval one, for his interest in the past was not that of an antiquarian but always of one anxious to relate the old to the new. For example, the second entry in his Ledger, probably written in 1865, declares: " The days of chivalry are not gone, they are only spiritualized. . . . In these times, the knight of the 19th century fights, not with trenchant sword, but with trenchant soul." And out of the times of the Jacquerie a knight rides into " The Symphony," blowing defiance to the philosophy of profit and loss and invoking the spirit of the quixotic Sir Philip Sidney as a model for the modern gentleman.   As in the earlier so in the later poem the evil effects of trade were to be overcome not by economic reforms but by chivalry, in the most idealistic Christian interpretation of that code of unselfish service.[59]

For " The Symphony " is less a plea for a fairer distribution of the world's goods on socialistic principles than it is for a broader and deeper love of humanity, less an outcry of the poor against the hardness of their lot than a voice to express their longing for a larger life, in nature and in art. Yet, though twentieth-century champions of the proletariat find little to admire in Lanier's solution, it was the first

---

[57] V, 322-326. The essay was probably completed in the summer of 1873 though not published until Jan., 1875.

[58] Starke, p. 202, calls attention briefly to this connection between the two poems. Lanier's active work on " The Jacquerie " seems to have ended with the composition of the intercalary song, " Special Pleading," in Feb., 1875, though there are occasional references in later letters that suggest he still contemplated finishing the long narrative.

[59] So until the end of his life, in his lectures to adults and his books for boys, Lanier continued to interpret the ideals of the past to his own generation (see III and IV, *passim*).

important American poem protesting against economic tyranny and the enslavement of the spirit by commercialism, and his contemporaries found it satisfying.[60] Next to love, and making an equation with it, music was to him the religion of the new age, to redeem it from trade, and " The Symphony " was his first major effort to relate the two arts between which his life was divided. Much of the imagery of the poem is drawn from his enthusiastic experiences as an orchestral player during the past two seasons, though there is no attempt to parallel the structural design of a symphonic composition. Instead, this is a sort of counter-part to program music, as if the impressions made on him by a sym-phony had been translated into words which would in turn recreate for the reader the original music. So Lanier himself explained it, quoting from a sonnet by Shakespeare to back up his own declaration of purpose: " In my ' Symphony ' Love's fine wit—the love of one's fellow-men—attempts (not to hear with eyes, but precisely the reverse) to see with ears." [61] And the experiment has the fascination and the hazards of all efforts to interpret one art in terms of another. He also considered this another step in his conscious program of freeing himself from poetic conventions, declaring at the time of its publication (letter of June 15, 1875): " I have dared *almost* to write quite at my ease in the matters of rhythm, rhyme, and substance, in this poem." But these are matters of technique and theory; more important to the poet and his audience was the message which the music brought. Nearly a decade earlier the heroine of *Tiger-Lilies* had been made to say: " Music means harmony, harmony means love, and love means—God! " [62] This like-

[60] For example, Granville Hicks (in *The Great Tradition,* New York, 1933, p. 28), though granting that Lanier was " outspokenly critical of commercialism," regrets that " all he could propose was to substitute love of art for love of money." (For objections by recent critics on other scores, see the entries in the bibliography, vol. VI, under Ransom, Tate, and Warren.) " The Symphony " is, indeed, less akin to the reformist poetry of the Victorians and of today than it is to Ruskin in *Unto this Last,* a book admired by Lanier and most of his American contemporaries. Similar protests against materialism may be found in the prose of Emerson and Thoreau, and in many novels after 1865, but the first poems written in America comparable to Lanier's came a quarter of a century later. (No study has been made of the poetry of social protest such as W. F. Taylor and L. A. Rose have recently published on the economic novel.)

[61] Letter to Spencer, Feb. 12, 1876 (written just after he had completed the Cantata, another experiment in the same direction). See H. C. Thorpe, " Sidney Lanier: A Poet for Musicians," *Musical Quarterly,* XI, 377 (July, 1925), for a defense of this feature of the poem. The personification of musical instruments, frequently objected to by critics as fanciful, was a lifelong habit with Lanier (see the essay written in 1867, V, 291 ff., and the extended similarities in " The Orchestra of Today," II, 296-303, written in 1876).

[62] V, 31. It is significant that the villain of the novel, who crashes into this world made utopian by music and love, is described as a soul " warped by Trade."

wise is the theme of " The Symphony," his first deeply religious poem, and the core of Lanier's philosophy throughout life. It was also his first truly national poem—a vein he was to work in the following year.

All of these qualities appealed to the idealists of the late nineteenth century, but by and large it was the timeliness of his two long poems— their applicability to current problems—that brought Lanier so quickly out of his obscurity. As " Corn " had been declared the finest American poem ever written on an agricultural topic, so now commentators were amazed that anyone could make real poetry out of the money question. And those who praised the originality of " The Symphony " linked it with the earlier poem, giving a cumulative lift to his reputation. Peacock again was the prime mover in all this. After the first poem he introduced Lanier to the celebrated actress Charlotte Cushman, who became his devoted friend and admirer, and invited him to Philadelphia for a visit where he met the literati of that city. After the second, he called the attention of Bayard Taylor to both poems. Taylor, the most prominent of the younger generation of writers, hailed the new author as a " rightfully annointed poet, in whom are the elements of a great success." [63] Before the summer was out they met, and in him Lanier found the best critic and literary friend he was ever to have. And through these new acquaintances was opened up to him the " great Art-world " of New York and to a lesser degree of Boston, so that he no longer felt isolated from that companionship he had yearned for all these years.[64] Peacock was also instrumental in bringing about the first serious magazine discussion of his poetry, a warm and appreciative review in the Golden Age for June by an established critic, George Calvert, who found in " Corn " and " The Symphony " " a deep basis upon which may be built up a great reputation." [65] Perhaps an even better measure of his progress in the popular mind is a casual aside in the New York World, June 7, 1875, describing him as " that new and happy singer, SIDNEY LANIER, [who] rapidly mounts the wave of recognition like a strong swimmer as he is." In the ears of one who, less than a year before, had begun his career completely unknown, this must have sounded pleasantly like fame.

Unfortunately he was not able at first to take full advantage of this

---

[63] His comments from a letter of June 3, 1875, to Peacock are quoted at length in note 99, Letters of 1875. See also note 95 and letters of Jan. 26, Mar. 7, and June 16, 1875. On Aug. 17, before their first meeting, he wrote Lanier of " how much joy the evidence of a new, true poet always gives me— such a poet as I believe you to be."

[64] See the often quoted letter to Taylor, Aug. 7, 1875.

[65] See note 108, Letters of 1875; for other notices, including an unfavorable one in the Nation, see note 107.

success, for at this juncture one of his old enemies, the need of money, put a lull on his creative writing. Ironically it was this same success that brought him, of all things, a commission to write a travel book. The prospect of being able to establish a home for his family in Baltimore made him willing to devote the six months from April to November to putting this pot-boiler through the press, and as a result of this, other paying prose was offered him.[66] Meanwhile he did manage to write a few songs, to spend some delightful evenings at the Century Club with Taylor, Stoddard, and Stedman, and at least to have the pleasure of meeting Longfellow and Lowell.[67] Of all these Taylor alone became a close friend, but by the end of 1875 it was apparent just how valuable it could be to have even one friend among the leading authors of the day. For it was through his suggestion that Lanier was invited to write the Cantata for the opening ceremonies of the Centennial Exposition.[68]

Writing to his wife of the year that lay ahead (Jan. 1, 1876) Lanier said: " I wonder if the new king will be so good a friend to my fame as was the dead one." His hopes were amply fulfilled; for " The Centennial Meditation of Columbia " (60) and the " Psalm of the West " (62), which he had been previously commissioned to write for the July issue of *Lippincott's*, brought him into national prominence. But since they are less important as poems than as documents in the development of his career, they are treated here chiefly in the latter connection.[69] The composition of these two poems, written to order, occupied most of Lanier's time and creative energy during the first half of 1876. Taylor laid down for him, quite sensibly, the principles

---

[66] See VI, vii, xx.

[67] See, for example, the letter of Oct. 4, 1875, and notes 193, 194, Letters of 1875. Lanier also met Bryant and exchanged a letter or so with Aldrich and Holmes. But he had no relations with Whittier, Whitman (who failed to respond to his invitation to correspondence), Mark Twain, Howells, James, Harte, Miller, or any of the lesser figures—except the Baltimore group, discussed in the Introduction to vol. VII. Melville had abandoned authorship, Emily Dickinson was too secluded, Emerson too old; and the rest of the early group were dead by 1865. In the final analysis Lanier had only two literary friends: Hayne, whom he never met, and Taylor with whom he found a certain intimacy during the three years that followed, though they were together less than a score of times.

[68] Since Whittier had been selected to write the Hymn for the same occasion, the Centennial Commission wanted for the Cantata " a poet *not* of New England." Stedman, who was first considered, had gone to Panama; Taylor, who had already accepted the invitation to write the Fourth of July Ode, suggested a southern poet, naming Lanier specifically (see Starke, p. 235).

[69] The full story of both poems is told in the letters, Jan.-June, 1876 (and summarized in the notes, pp. 345-349, below)—especially the controversy over the Cantata, which is quite out of proportion to its intrinsic worth.

which should govern occasional poetry: "One dare not be imaginative or *particularly* original," he wrote; "make the lines simple and strong, keep down the play of fancy . . . and aim at expressing the *general* feeling of the nation rather than individual ideas." [70] Lanier replied that he had "tried hard to think—in a kind of average and miscellaneousness" in order not to be too original, and that his purpose was to write a text that was "entirely large, simple, and melodious." But when against his judgment it was published without benefit of the music, the critics did not find it so. Although Peacock and Taylor as well as the southern press came to its defense, and some few wrote prose summaries to prove that it really was intelligible, the great majority of the newspapers over the country showered it with abuse, chiefly on the grounds of its obscurity. The attacks ranged all the way from humorous comparisons of it to the "Jabberwocky" (in its combination of "uproarious nonsense with pretentious gravity") to serious denunciations such as "Walt Whitman with the jim-jams" and "a communication from the spirit of Nat Lee, rendered through a Bedlamite medium." [71]

Indeed, as an occasional poem to be recited or even privately read— and as such all of the newspaper critics treated it—Lanier's Cantata is not successful; for it is too filled with his own ideas to evoke the stock response which should be the aim of the occasional poet, and many of its lines are too involved to be immediately clear in meaning. Though he wrote a surprisingly large number of poems for special occasions, this was not his forte. But for a proper evaluation of his Cantata, his intentions on this particular occasion must be understood. Statements in his letters must be supplemented by the elaboration of his principles and purposes which he published in the New York *Tribune*, from which the first criticism had emanated.[72] Then it becomes apparent that the "large and artless simplicity" refers not to the words themselves but to the musical conception, that his aim was to write not a poem to be read but a song to be sung through the "voices" of a hundred and fifty instruments as well as a chorus of eight hundred singers. Only general conceptions are capable of being rendered by orchestral music, he declared, and the "subordinate related ideas" must be sketched in "gigantic figures" contrasted with each other

---

[70] Letters of Dec. 28, 1875, and Jan. 7, 1876. For the quotations in the following sentence, see Lanier's letters of Jan. 13, 15, 1876.

[71] The quotations are from the New York *Times,* May 12, 1876; an unidentified clipping in the Lanier Collection, Duke University Library; and the *Nation,* XXII, 247 (Apr. 13, 1876). A score or more of contemporary notices are preserved in the Lanier Room, Johns Hopkins University, many of which are quoted in the notes to the letters.

[72] This defense is reprinted in the present edition, II, 266-273.

in " broad outlines of tone-color." The individual words, he insisted, did not necessarily have to be " perfectly clear, smooth, and natural " ; performed in the open air for an audience of fifteen thousand, whole lines would lose their identity and survive only in these " broad bands of color." Knowing this he composed in terms of sound rather than idea, in " movements " rather than in words or even lines; and he wrote his text not with the reader but the musical composer in mind. Sufficient vindication perhaps lies in the fact that Dudley Buck was " immensely pleased " with the text and was soon begging for more poems to set to music; that Theodore Thomas was " delighted with the musical conception " and invited him to join his orchestra; that the actual performance was an acknowledged success.[73] The experiment was one of many that Lanier made in the relations between poetry and music, and as such the final evaluation lies outside the scope of this Introduction.[74] For present purposes its chief importance is what it brought him—if not fame, at least notoriety; for when a poet becomes the subject of parodies (see p. 346, below), he is not likely to be forgotten soon.

To his wife Lanier wrote: " I think the [Cantata] business has been of great value to all my artistic purpose, just at this stage of it." And to his father: " Meantime, there can be no doubt that my personal interests are on the whole advanced by the commotion; for I am presented with an audience familiar at least with my name very much sooner than I could otherwise have been." [75] His diagnosis was confirmed when the " Psalm of the West " appeared as the featured number of the centennial issue of *Lippincott's*, in July; it had an assured reading public and seems to have been on the whole well received.[76]

[73] See letters of Jan. 13 (to Taylor), Jan. 25 (to Peacock), May 12, 1876, and note 91.

[74] Materials for such a study may be found in his poems that were set to music by Buck and others, and those of his own and Tennyson's that he himself set; in his musical conception of " The Symphony " and " The Jacquerie " (as a music-drama) ; and in his discussion of the relations of the two arts in *The Science of English Verse*. That he was satisfied with his experiment in the Cantata is evidenced by his statement (May 23, 1876): " It is really the first English poem written in such a way that the whole body of it could be genuinely set to music." But his attitude towards it as a poem is perhaps clarified by remembering that he never afterwards reprinted it in his published or projected volumes; and his wife, who best knew his desires in such matters, put it in an appendix to the collected *Poems* (1884).

[75] Letters of May 27 and May 18, 1876.

[76] The favorable comments will be found in the reviews of his *Poems* (1877) discussed below. The only unfavorable notice I have found was in the *Nation*, XXIII, 11 (July 6, 1876), which said in part: " Whoever struggles through the Swinburnian prelude, . . . here and there, amid a mass of conceits, he will find a stanza which does not require to be defended against critics ignorant of

And well it may have been, for although an occasional poem it was the best thing of that sort he ever wrote. He had put much of himself into it—too much, in fact. Lanier certainly knew the limitations placed on an artist when writing for an occasion or on commission, yet he was never able to withhold; the fault, though springing from admirable motives, is just another part of the tragic story of scattered energies. The day he completed the "Psalm of the West" he wrote to Taylor in all sincerity (Apr. 4, 1876) : "I now only know how divine has been the agony of the last three weeks during which I have been rapt away to heights where all my own purposes as to a revisal of artistic forms lay clear before me." This deep emotional involvement in an assignment that most poets would have executed perfunctorily, even though competently, is partly explained by his concern at this time with artistic theories. For, like the other long poems of the period, this was conceived as a symphonic poem that should "carry or create its own musical accompaniment," and he actually began the composition of a musical setting for it.[77] Further, he was experimenting again in the direction of freer poetic form, the chief evidences of which are his interest in the dactyls of the "Swinburnian prelude" and the variety of meters employed in the different movements in accordance with a newly evolving theory of architectural structure.[78] But no small part of his excitement came from the renewed sense of nationality that was stirred in him by the composition of these two poems. The worst aspects of Reconstruction were over, and like many other forward-looking southerners he felt the need of living in the present. Two years of living in Baltimore, that "middle ground" where "Southern courtesy and Northern vigor meet," [79] had helped to heal the scars of the past. If the Cantata was a song of reconciliation, the "Psalm" was a hymn of Lanier's devotion to his country, nowhere better revealed than in the early title for it, "To the United States of America"—a title savoring of the full bodied patriotism of Whitman. As a result he wrote

the relations between genuine poetry and the number of pieces in the modern orchestra. In this category we place the better part of the Columbus soliloquy. On the other hand, the fraternal reconciliation of North and South can never be so hollow a thing as to make either party to the civil war regard as anything but puerile Mr. Lanier's . . . 'The Tournament.' " But the *Nation,* Lanier's most persistent critic, was not typical.

[77] See Starke, p. 248. No trace has been found of the "Choral Symphony," the music he planned for it, except in his letter of Feb. 12, 1881.

[78] See letters of Mar. 11, 18, 20, 1876, and note 66. The former look forward to the distinctive rhythms of "The Marshes of Glynn"; the latter may owe something to his old master Tennyson, in *Maud.*

[79] Quoted from D. C. Gilman, "Baltimore," *St. Nicholas,* XX, 729 (Aug., 1893).

a rhapsodic epitome of American history and, in spite of its obvious defects, a forceful national poem.[80]

The creative activity of these first years in Baltimore did not spend itself entirely in the composition of these long poems. In addition he wrote some twenty-five poems between 1874 and 1876, all but a few of which found their way into the magazines, Scribner's as well as Lippincott's, so that Lanier's name was constantly before the public. In the midst of his work on the " Psalm of the West," dedicating himself to what he now knew was his " Great Passion," he wrote to his friend Bleckley (Mar. 20, 1876) : "As for me, life has resolved simply into a time during which I want to get upon paper as many as possible of the poems with which my heart is stuffed like a schoolboy's pocket." And there was variety as well as quantity in the product of these years.

Two of these poems, written in collaboration with Clifford Lanier, were experiments in the portrayal of Negro character and dialect. From the available evidence it would seem that the original conceptions and first drafts are attributable to his brother, the polishing of meter and dialect and considerable artistic revisions in " shape but not in matter " the work of Lanier himself.[81] " The Power of Prayer " (215) dramatizes an episode revealing the Negro's superstitions about the Devil; "Uncle Jim's Baptist Revival-Hymn " (217) is a sort of comic spiritual. Both are quite true in the picturesque manner of the local color writers who followed a few years later, such as Joel Chandler Harris, whose " Uncle Remus " stories he was to praise as " fiction . . . founded upon fact," " as nearly perfect as any dialect can well be." [82] Though the modern attitude favors the use of idiom and speech tune rather than dialectal misspelling—feeling a false exaggeration in the phonetic representation of illiterate speech which implies that educated speech corresponds to standard spelling—Lanier was more meticulous and accurate than most of his contemporaries in recording the actual language of the Negro, as well as of the Cracker. And if he had continued in this vein, his later theories about the tunes and colors of speech (as revealed in The Science of English Verse) might have

---

[80] See Dorothy L. Werner, The Idea of Union in American Verse, 1776-1876 (Philadelphia, 1932). Though the imagery is often strained and obscure the principal criticism must be directed at the lack of proportion, only one-fifth of his poem being saved for the century of American history since the Revolution. Although Lanier's war experiences were still too close for realistic handling, his use of the " Tournament " to represent this conflict was a sentimental evasion; similarly the omission of the founding of Virginia and the other southern colonies betrays a too self-conscious anxiety not to be sectional. The high point of the poem is indisputably the Columbus sonnets, as both his contemporaries and posterity agree.

[81] The evidence is summarized on pp. 327-328, 384-385, below.

[82] In " The New South," written in 1880 (see V, 348).

resulted in some valuable pioneering.[83] As it is, he and his brother share with Irwin Russell the honor of being the first to discover the literary value of the Negro, and their poems, which were widely copied, prepared the way for a new vogue.[84] As secure a niche as Lanier's dialect poems have, they belong more to his past than to his future plans.

By far the largest number of short poems written during these years were the lyrics, best of all being those celebrating his love for Mary Day Lanier. During his first winter in Baltimore after an evening of Schubert's songs, he wrote out for her his definition of what " all lyric poetry must be, *i. e.*, each poem expressing but a single idea, . . . and in the simplest, noblest, most beautiful, and most musical words." And ten days later " My Two Springs " (33) was inclosed in a letter to his wife (Mar. 15, 1874), the first poem he felt to be worthy of his adoration, though admitting that his desire to print it had made him conform to conventions more than he had wished. In spite of a simplicity and directness of expression that he had achieved only once before (in " Life and Song ") and its undeniable sincerity as a statement of his great love, it is too reminiscent of his early imitations of Tennyson in sentiment as well as melody. This, of course, is more objectionable to the modern reader than it would have been to Lanier's contemporaries, who were undoubtedly as pleased with it as his wife was.[85] But " My Two Springs," though it has continued a popular favorite, falls short of being a fine lyric for quite other reasons. The failure is in Lanier's definition. He makes no mention of that unerring sense for the inevitable word which produces the magic of the best lyric poetry. Here whole stanzas could be omitted or added without material alteration, and no spell of enchantment takes the reader out of himself.

Next Lanier turned to the sonnet, addressing a sequence of ten of them to his wife between the autumn of 1874 and 1875.[86] Though

[83] Lanier's inconsistent spelling of dialect has been retained, since it was deliberate (see letter of Nov. 23, 1879; also Aug. 7, 1874, and May 27, 1875).

[84] The discovery of a previously unknown prose sketch in Negro dialect, written by Lanier in 1865 (V, xxxviii, 200-203), seems to place his work ahead of Russell's. He contemplated one further collaboration with his brother (letter of June 29, 1876) and, in the last year of his life, an anthology of Negro dialect poems (Clifford Lanier to Scribner's, Oct. 31, 1881—MS Charles Scribner's Sons), but neither project materialized. He seems to have felt that these, as well as the earlier Cracker poems, somehow needed apology from a serious poet, as evidenced by his appealing to the example of Chaucer, Burns, and Tennyson in justification (see letters of Aug. 22, 1874, June 15 and 17, 1875).

[85] See letter of Mar. 15, 1874, and note 44; cf. C. Brooks and R. P. Warren, *Understanding Poetry* (New York, 1938), pp. 442-445.

[86] " In Absence " (42), " Acknowledgment " (56), " Laus Mariæ " (44) and " Whate'er has been " (200)—the first two being groups of four each. For the

they show progressive improvement, they are studied and frankly imitative of Shakespeare. They were good discipline in the craft of poetry and paved the way for the Columbus sequence in " Psalm of the West " and two years later " The Harlequin of Dreams " (112), the best sonnet he ever wrote. Desiring more flexibility of form, he then tried his hand at an experiment in his " own peculiar style " allowing himself " to treat both words, similes and metres with such freedom as I desire." [87] The result, " Special Pleading " (45), is somewhat hard to fit with this description until one remembers that his interests at this time were focused upon the relation between music and poetry. But his concern with sound effects was such that his involved imagery and idea failed to come clear. During the next year some half-dozen of these experimental songs were written, all intended apparently to be set to music. Four of them, at any rate, were sent to Dudley Buck in June, 1876, in response to a request from his collaborator on the Cantata, but they were returned as unsuitable for musical settings, with the implication that they were too unconventional.[88] One suspects, rather, that it was their lack of spontaneity which troubled him. The artificiality of one of them is revealed by its survival in manuscript in four entirely different forms, which seem more like copy-book exercises than lyrical utterances; of another, by its use to bolster up a rather elaborate discussion about architectonic structure in poetry.[89] Taylor had warned him that an application of the laws of music to poetry would produce a " too conscious air of design." It was Lanier's practice rather than his theory, however, that was at fault. For it was as a conscious artist, applying the principles of musical construction to poetry, that he wrote his first fine lyric in the autumn of 1876. Buck found the " Evening Song " (88), for which he composed the music at one sitting, " simply lovely and as new as lovely," [90] and he is only one

relation of these poems to each other see note on p. 341. For the Shakespearian influence, mentioned in the following sentence, see letter of Nov. 8, 1874.

[87] See letter of Feb. 11, 1875, which makes it clear that this song for " The Jacquerie " was addressed to his wife.

[88] See note 117, Letters of 1876; identification of the four poems is made in the note to " Rose-Morals," p. 345, below. In this same group besides " Special Pleading," should be included the best of them all, " A Song of the Future " (59).

[89] See the variant versions of " A Song of Love," pp. 300-301, below. For the analysis of " Rose-Morals " see Lanier's letters to Taylor, Mar. 11, 20, 1876; Taylor's reply of Mar. 17 is quoted in the following sentence.

[90] Letter of Nov. 7, 1876; see also note 12, Letters of 1877. Buck was an ideal composer for Lanier, with a religious quality in his longer pieces and sentimental in the shorter. He also set to music poems by Drake and Lognfellow and was inspired to some longer compositions by the Spanish writings by Irving (J. T. Howard, *Our American Music,* New York, 1939, pp. 349-352).

of many composers who have expressed their delight in it. Here at last was his true love song to Mary Day Lanier—spontaneous but controlled, sincere as a personal expression yet with a touch of magic for the reader who knows nothing of the facts behind it.

This is an appropriate time for a summing up in Lanier's career, for the end of 1876 marks a turning point. In November the firm of J. B. Lippincott issued a volume containing the ten poems that had appeared in their magazine during the past two years.[91] For the first time critics and reading public had the opportunity to survey his work in collected form. The volume seems to have had a small-to-normal sale; beyond this there is no available evidence of the general reader's reaction;[92] but for a first book of poems, it had a fairly wide and generally favorable reception from the periodical press.[93] Since there was a remarkable unanimity among the reviewers, a summary of their opinions offers a reasonably accurate estimate of Lanier's reputation among his contemporaries at this time. Almost without exception they granted him a " rich poetic nature," and though the *Nation* whittled this down to " a thin vein of real poetic sentiment," *Harper's* called it " genuine poetic genius " and the *Evening Mail* declared him " the most promising of our rising poets." However, all qualified this praise by pointing out the over-richness and obscurity resulting from a want of discipline. The most favorable found these defects not serious since they were born of even greater virtues and needed only time and hard work to eliminate. For example, Eggleston in the *Post* said that his lavishness

[91] The publication date was Nov. 12, 1876 (see letter same date). The volume contained: " Corn," " The Symphony," " Psalm of the West," " In Absence," " Acknowledgment," " Betrayal," " Special Pleading," " To Charlotte Cushman," " Rose-Morals," " To—, with a Rose," and a new " Dedication " to Charlotte Cushman. Three other poems written during 1874-1876 will be discussed below; the rest were occasional pieces.

[92] The few comments that have come down, from friends and relatives, are naturally eulogistic. The most interesting of these is from his father, who wrote of the new volume to Clifford Lanier (Jan. 8, 1877): " Sid is bound to be famous if he can only have a few years more. . . . I read his poems with more delight as I get his meaning more clearly." The records of J. B. Lippincott & Co. for this period were destroyed by fire, but a letter to Lanier over four years after publication (May 14, 1881) states that 425 copies remain on hand, out of an original edition of probably not more than 1000; and their offer to sell these " at the actual cost to us " suggests that the volume was printed at the publisher's expense. It was never reprinted.

[93] Ten reviews have been located: seven of these are listed in the bibliography (VI, 411); the others were *Evolution*, I, 182-183 (June, 1877), and two undated clippings in the Lanier Room from the *Evening Mail* and the *Commercial.* (All are from New York except the last named, which is from Pittsburgh. The first three are quoted from at length in notes 158 and 162, Letters of 1876, and note 15, Letters of 1877. Other periodicals searched without success are: *Atlantic, Lippincott's, Scribner's,* and the newspapers of Macon and Baltimore.)

and compression "overwhelms the reader and confuses him," but that condensation was the chief merit of his poems and their peculiar luxuriance in imagery and poetic suggestion, which already showed "the beginnings of order and symmetry," were "a source of very great power for the future." At the other extreme the *Nation* found little hope for this poet who revealed no symptom of relaxing his "convulsive and startling mode of utterance" in which "the entire absence of simplicity spoils everything." More soberly Taylor pointed out the real problem in his long *Tribune* article, suggesting that the author's "redundancy and apparent *abandon* to the starts and bolts of ... Fancy," in singular contrast to the maturity of his ideas, was the result of over-richness of material uncontrolled by proper training:

But just such technical splendors of poetry require the firmest hand, the finest ear, the most delicate sense of Art. It is still too soon to decide whether Mr. Lanier's true course is to train or carefully prune this luxuriance.

The benefit Lanier derived from this advice is demonstrated in his major poems of the next few years. Yet the resemblance of this criticism to that which had pointed out the defects in his poetry and prose of ten years before is striking. The battle was only partly won.

The minor pieces being mostly passed over in silence or discounted as inferior, the praise was divided between "Corn" and "The Symphony." [94] Admiration for the noble aspirations embodied in the latter was balanced by objections to the attempted fusion of music with poetry, though, as the *Times* declared, "almost everybody can admire the portions that allude to nature." And it was on this score that "Corn" proved the favorite of the critics, even the recalcitrant *Nation* finding in it "a genuine feeling for nature." Almost with one accord they pointed to the sub-tropical luxuriance of the deep South as the chief source of Lanier's strength, both in theme and style, and he was soon to prove them right in their diagnosis. He may have been somewhat disappointed that so little mention was made of what he felt was new in his poetry; one said that his versification belonged to the "new school," another that he had read too much of Swinburne,

[94] The only review to comment at length on the "Psalm of the West" was that in the *Graphic*, which quite absurdly misinterpreted Lanier's love of country as a repudiation of the spurious caste system and the "real rottenness of the former South" (see quotations in note 15, Letters of 1877). The review in *Evolution* by Edgar Fawcett, whose poetry was frequently compared to Lanier's by contemporary critics, was violently unfavorable: "Mr. Lanier . . . disfigures his best passages by shameless neologisms, atrocious distortions of syntax, intentional obscurities, oddities of phrase that almost suggest insanity, and a general contempt for the sacredness of art that his incidental excellencies make all the more lamentable and shocking."

and only Taylor called attention to his daring originality in "poetic aim, form, and choice of theme." But he must have been pleased that many took this occasion to survey his rapid rise to a "national reputation" and to speak with confidence of his "uncommonly rich promise of excellence yet to come."

Anticipating his critics, Lanier had written to Taylor (Nov. 13, 1876) just as his *Poems* came from the press that he already felt himself entering a new period of development:

I can't tell you with what ravishing freedom and calmness I find myself writing, in these days, nor how serene and sunny the poetic region seems to lie, in front, like broad upland fields and slopes. . . . I hope to have out another volume soon, of work which will show a much quieter technique than this one.

He failed to add that he was confined to his bed with an illness now entering its fifth month and daily growing more serious. The way in which his recurring attacks coincide with his periods of greatest progress seems like some malignant fate trying to rob him of his few pitiful moments of success, until it becomes clear that excitement and overwork were almost invariably the immediate causes.[95] And in the present collapse of his health another familiar old enemy had played a part—economic need and worry. Anxious to realize his dream of establishing a permanent home, he had brought his family north in June, 1876, depending upon the commissions promised him for writing a biography of the late Charlotte Cushman. The failure of this scheme, through no fault of his own,[96] left him with no means of support and worried with the debt of an advance payment already spent. Worn with the activity of the past winter and spring, his strength failed and he fell ill. Stranded penniless at a farm in West Chester, with lingering resentment of the abuse meted out to his Cantata, depression of spirit followed as he brooded over the plight of the artist. One of his most promising poems, "Clover" (84), reflects the mood of this despairing summer, but is marred by it. Beginning with a description of the broad upland fields of Pennsylvania, with a sensuous texture assimilated from his reading of Shakespeare and Keats, it gives promise of that

[95] Note, for example, the two weeks illness that followed the triumph of "Corn" and his meeting with Peacock and the literary group in Philadelphia, Mar., 1875; the same after his meeting with Taylor and the members of the Century Club and the resulting poetic activity of Sept., 1875; the severe illness at the end of 1875 brought on by the over-work on the pot-boiler, *Florida*; and the attack in Mar., 1876, between work on the Cantata and the "Psalm"—which he was completing under stress to get funds so he could go to Georgia for a rest.

[96] See letters of Feb. 27, July 19, 24, 1876, and note 121.

quieter technique he felt as the beginning of his new period; but the allegory in the latter part, which attempts to define the role of the poet in a materialistic and hostile world, is strained and distorted— the hurt was too recent.[97] In the autumn came another disappointment in the failure of his hope for a chair of Music and Poetry at the newly established Johns Hopkins University. As illness and worry reacted on each other his situation became desperate. At last, just as the heartening reviews of his first volume of poems began to come in, his physician ordered him to a warmer climate for the winter as his only chance for life. With a gift from an anonymous friend he set out with his wife for Florida, but before leaving he wrote Taylor (Dec. 6) that no " conceivable combination of circumstances could induce me to die before I've written and published my fine additional volumes of poems."

Lanier's resiliency was as remarkable as his courage, and within less than a month of his arrival in Tampa he wrote of his improvement, declaring (Jan. 11, 1877) : " I ' bubble song' continually during these heavenly days, and it is as hard to keep me from the pen as a toper from his tipple." Thus began the most prolific period of his entire career. The first two poems he wrote form a pair, " The Stirrup-Cup " (90) announcing with quiet bravery his resignation to death if that is inevitable, " Tampa Robins " (92) voicing his intention to sing blithely while life remained. These were the beginning of a spray of songs which he sent out to the magazines, finding with the aid of friends a number of new vehicles in *Appleton's, Harper's, Leslie's,* and the *Galaxy.* In this manner his name was kept before the public, his purse modestly replenished, and his spirit revived. Though none of the dozen poems that came out of his three months in Florida [98]

---

[97] Another poem written this summer and touching the same theme, " The Waving of the Corn " (83), likewise suffered from the immediacy of the personal protest out of which it grew; but it was improved by omitting the final stanza with its obtrusive moral (see p. 307, ll. 30†) upon the advice of Taylor, who said that it clashed with the tranquil pastoral tone of the rest of the poem (letter of Oct. 6, 1876, and note 140). A similar revision would have helped the conclusion of " Clover," which Lanier was two years in placing with a magazine. See letter of May 18, 1876 (to his father) for a specific linking of the Cantata controversy with the brutal treatment by contemporaries of almost exactly the same list of the great that are named in " Clover." This poem is discussed further in connection with a group of poems dealing with the function of the artist in society (see pp. lxxvii ff.). Lanier's sensitiveness to criticism is further witnessed by a surviving envelope of slips, probably written about this time, containing notes apparently for an essay and entitled " Contemporary Criticism," the theme of which is to show how posterity reverses the judgments of the " dapper art critics of the newspapers " (Charles D. Lanier Collection, Johns Hopkins University).

[98] All of the poems on pp. 90-101, below (except " The Dove "), were written

are of first importance, they are indicative of considerable poetic vitality in their variety and in their hint of a new trend. Several are short comic scribblings that reveal the cheerful invalid on the balcony of his hotel making versified puns for his wife's amusement; another is the last of his humorous dialect verses; yet another is his hymn of gratitude to his principal literary friend and helper, Bayard Taylor. More interesting by far are those which grew out of a combination of two new influences, one from within, one from without.

As Lanier struggled back to life, the sunshine and luxuriance of this sub-tropical land began to vitalize his poetry as well. Here are orange groves and robins, "bosky avenues" and mocking birds, bees rioting in the "huge nectary" of jessamine vines that wreathe the live-oaks, green paroquets, palm trees, and pelicans poised above the shallows. Here also are wide expanses of sky and sea on the sunny beaches, followed significantly by a yearning from the "drear sand-levels" back to the more familiar landscape of his native Georgia. Nature had figured in Lanier's writings from the beginning, but at first it was a purely literary treatment, with ever-recurring images drawn from the conventional lily and rose, morning star and ocean wave. Admiring as he did the "etherealization of nature" in Tennyson, his own nature-metaphors (defined as the transference of human thoughts and feelings to natural phenomena) all too often had resulted in the pathetic fallacy.[99] True, in "Corn" and the poems that followed he had begun to look at the scene around him, with a resulting realism in his translations from nature; but accurate as many of his observations are, Lanier's talent was not that of the realist. In Florida, as the world of eye and ear thronged upon his outward senses, it was informed with a new spirit that came from his discovery of a kindred author whom he had somehow missed all these years. It was Emerson who stung him fertile, to borrow a phrase from "The Bee" (91), a poem whose setting comes from just such a personal experience of nature as those which abound in the essays and poems of his new teacher. From these he first became aware of the vast spiritual background of the sensuous world and of the essential kinship of each and all, which produced the religious tranquility of "A Florida Sunday" (94), the best fruit of these months of convalescence.[100] "Emerson, whom I have been reading all winter," he wrote to Taylor, "gives me immeasurable delight because he does not propound to me disagreeable systems and hideous creeds but simply walks along high and bright

or planned there. "On a Palmetto" (208) is certainly drawn from the experiences of this winter, though it was dated "1880" by Lanier's wife.

[99] See especially the essay "Nature-Metaphors," written in 1868 (V, 306-321).

[100] Starke, p. 275, points out also the influence of Keats on the imagery of this poem.

ways where one loves to go with him." [101] And in discovering Emerson, he found himself as a poet. His true vein lay, not in social protest nor in celebrating the national spirit nor even, except subordinately, in the marriage of music to words—it lay in his religious interpretation of nature. This was the best thing that happened to him in Florida, though it was another year before he realized it in a memorable poem and one worthy of his great discovery.

Very little is known, unfortunately, of the composition of "The Marshes of Glynn" (119). The only external evidence is the statement in a letter to his father, July 13, 1878, that he has just sent it off "hot from the mint." It was his contribution to an anonymous anthology in response to a request of the past spring.[102] Beyond quoting the judgment of his friend R. M. Johnston that it was "the greatest poem written in a hundred years," Lanier says nothing here or in later letters about this important poem except for passing comments on the form in which it was cast. Though it seems clear that it was written specifically for *A Masque of Poets,* and probably during the few weeks preceding the known date of its completion in mid July, 1878, it would be ingenuous to think of "The Marshes of Glynn" as a perfunctory piece composed on order or an experiment to illustrate a prosodical theory. It is, instead, the inevitable product of the slow

[101] Letter of May 25, 1877. This is clearly Lanier's first serious reading of Emerson. There are only two earlier references to him, both in 1867, and neither indicates more than casual acquaintance (see V, 32, and note 30, Letters of 1867). He is also referred to as "our wise Emerson" in an essay that may have been written as early as 1876 (see II, 288). Beyond these there are scarcely more than a dozen further references to Emerson, all dating from the last three years of Lanier's life, but they show a deep sense of kinship even in the two which mark a point of difference. The poems quoted, always with warm approval, are significant: "Each and All" (II, 338, IV, 86, 234), "Brahma" (II, 136, III, 313), "Initial, Demonic, and Celestial Love" (IV, 236), and "Beauty" (IV, 238). The prose volume most frequently referred to is *Representative Men,* which may well be the one he was reading in Florida. Lanier's copy of this has not come down, but the outline for a poem that he wrote on a flyleaf ("I fled in tears from the men's ungodly quarrel about God," No. 125, p. 268, below) is a reminder of the essential religious quality that permeates all of Emerson's writing. In 1879 Lanier bought three more of his volumes (statement from Turnbull Bros., Apr. 11, 1879, Charles D. Lanier Collection): *Poems* (1869), *Society and Solitude,* and *May-Day and Other Pieces.* The last named only has been preserved; the two poems marked therein are not significant.

[102] Letter from G. P. Lathrop, Apr. 20, 1878, quoted in note 66, Letters of 1878. The reference in the following sentence is to Lanier's letters of Oct. 20 and Dec. 21, 1878. One reason for the paucity of Lanier's comments on this poem is that there are few letters in this period addressed to the correspondents with whom he usually discussed his poems: his wife was with him, Taylor had gone to Europe, and no letters to Hayne have been discovered between 1875 and 1880.

convergence of several forces which rank as the most important in his entire career as a poet. In a general way it is implicit in all that he wrote and was; and from scattered bits of evidence in his poetry, prose and letters, its evolution can now be traced over a period of at least three years.

Lanier had been intimately acquainted with the coastal regions of Georgia for more than a decade.[103] The description of the landscape around Brunswick in a letter of April 18, 1875, probably represents what he had long felt. In it he speaks of this as the idyllic land for a battered soul, with its " unbroken forest of oaks, of all manner of clambering and twining things and of pines," its " divine atmosphere . . . unspeakably bland, bringing strange secrets rather of leaves than of flowers." This was written at the beginning of a three-months' tour of the deep South collecting materials for *Florida*. And when his guide book was published, it contained, in addition to practical aids for the traveler, romantic descriptions of the moss-hung oaks and " manifold vine-growths," of the trees as religious symbols which offered a refuge for the tired man from " the fever of the unrest of trade." Lanier's developing interest in southern scenery is revealed in several of the long poems of the next two years, but nowhere so clearly as in the manuscript draft of " Psalm of the West." There, in describing the mosses and oaks and palms of this region, as the new world dawned upon the first explorers, he makes as many as six revisions to the line before he is satisfied.[104] The next winter in Tampa as he walked along the Gulf, fresh from his reading of Emerson, he named over in quiet ecstasy all sights and sounds that made up his " Florida Sunday " only to say that he held them merged in his own being: cross-threads of bird songs weaving like " shuttles of music " among the trees of a natural temple, " Pale in-shore greens and distant blue delights " of a coastline swerving like " The grace of God made manifest in curves "— a God whom he now addressed as the "All-One." Again he jotted down in his notebook his contemplations after a forest stroll when, in semi-mystical mood, he had begun to " glide out of the idea that this multiform beauty is familiar, that it is a clump of trees and vines and flowers." Tentatively he suggested that it was " Silence, which . . . has caught form," " Music, in a siesta," " Mystery, grown communicative," " Trade, done into a flower," a " revelation of the enormous Besides and Overplus " that business men and pleasure-seekers suspect as lying beyond their routines. Unable to decide the real meaning and value of this tranquility, his fumblings remained in prose.[105] As he

[103] See letter of July 17?, 1868, and note 45.
[104] See the textual variants of ll. 145 ff., p. 304, below.
[105] See the full entry from the Ledger quoted on p. 358 below. It is not

passed through Brunswick on his return trip he wrote to Taylor (Apr. 26, 1877) of his excursions on horseback "through the green overgrown woodpaths . . . now in full leaf and overflowing song":

The whole air seems full of fecundity: as I ride, I'm like one of those insects that are fertilized on the wing,—every leaf that I brush against breeds a poem. God help the world, when this now-hatching brood of my Ephemeræ shall take flight and darken the air.

Emerson had sensitized him to the spiritual values in nature, but at present he lacked that serenity needed to produce the poem that was stirring within him, and the gestation period was long.[106]

Lanier's concern about his own unorthodoxy may furnish an explanation as to why he was so late in discovering that he was primarily a religious poet. Undoubtedly it was under the influence of his mother's piety and deep devotion to the church that he had been received into the Presbyterian communion during his first year in college, yet even this early he was asking questions about sectarian differences.[107] There are occasional references to church attendance in his letters of the next ten years, apparently in the Episcopalian congregation of which his wife was an ardent member as well as at services in his family denomination, but they are usually concerned with playing the organ.[108] During the years following the war evidences of his tendency towards unorthodoxy begin to appear, as in the Ledger entry quarrelling with a sermon he had just heard for "throwing obstacles in the way of honest inquirers" and in the metaphysical essays where his concern was chiefly with working himself free from the dilemmas of theology to the more satisfying doctrine that religion, poetry, and music are the same.[109] And for the last fifteen years of his life, as his attack on

---

dated, but from its position on pp. 602-603 and from the handwriting it apparently belongs to 1877.

[106] See letters of May 25 and Aug. 26, 1877.

[107] The records of the First Presbyterian Church, Macon, Ga., show that he became a member on Apr. 4, 1858. A letter from his parents of May 20, 1858 (printed in the present edition), answering some questions from a lost letter by Lanier, reveals their own somewhat differing attitudes.

[108] See the interview with the Rev. E. F. Rees, rector of Christ Church, who married Mary Day to Lanier and who says that he was "his pastor in Macon for many years," adding: "His religion was not one of doctrines. It was one of broad, impulsive human faith and sympathy" (quoted in "The World's Charity," Atlanta Constitution, Feb. 23, 1890). See also, for example, Lanier's letter of Nov. 3, 1866.

[109] Ledger, p. 44, probably written in the spring of 1866. For the essays, based on his study of Sir William Hamilton and Victor Cousin, see V, xlix, note 95; and cf. the notation on the flyleaf of his copy of Cousin's Elements of Psychology: "Poetry at its highest flight meets and merges into philosophy," by which, as the rest of the note explains, he means religion (copy in the

creeds grew to a major issue, he only went once in a while to hear
the music in the big city churches and perhaps, on rare occasions, to
please his wife.[110] It was quite possibly the contrasting orthodoxy of
family and friends that made Lanier think of himself for so many
years as merely a member of the unorganized Party of Humanity, and
confined the religious element in his poetry to preachments of the
social ethics of Christianity as in " The Symphony." The experiences of his winter in Florida touched the deeper springs of his
transcendental longings, and it is in the marsh hymns that flowed from
this that we first see the high priest of nature at his devotions. Yet
Lanier felt himself to be poet and musician as well as seer, and
Emerson's halting rhythms could not give form to his vision. One
more influence was necessary before he could fashion to his harp the
rhapsodic chords of " The Marshes of Glynn."

In the winter of 1878 Lanier discovered for the first time the poetry
of Walt Whitman. Writing to Taylor, from whose library he had
borrowed the volume, he declared:

LEAVES OF GRASS was a real refreshment to me—like rude salt spray
in your face—in spite of its enormous fundamental error that a thing
is good because it is natural, and in spite of the world-wide difference
between my own conceptions of art and its author's.[111]

Three months later, when his scant budget allowed him to purchase
this coveted volume, he wrote an enthusiastic letter to the Good Gray
Poet, repeating his reservations but revealing candidly the excitement
of his discovery:

Although I entirely disagree with you in all points connected with
artistic form [and taste] . . . my dissent in these particulars becomes
a very insignificant consideration in the presence of that unbounded
delight which I take in the bigness and bravery of all your ways and

Charles D. Lanier Collection, Johns Hopkins University, inscribed " Sidney
Lanier—1865 ").

[110] See Mary Day Lanier's letter to Lawrence Turnbull, Feb. 2, 1881: " [Lanier
is] not in exact accord with any of the established forms of worship . . . still,
he finds himself able sometimes to join in our church worship by using what
seem to him larger interpretations of the same general truths. . . . I think
orthodox people are very peaceful and enviable but *we* have no prospect of
bringing up an orthodox family!" Cf. the similar estimate by the Rev. William
Kirkus, who preached Lanier's funeral sermon (*American Literary Churchman*,
I, 34, Nov. 1, 1881).

[111] Letter of Feb. 3, 1878; he goes on to declare that it was " worth at least
a million " of the other two volumes of poetry he had borrowed, by Lowell and
Swinburne. The earlier references to Whitman (Oct. 23, 1874, Jan. 26 and
Dec. 19, 1875) indicate disapproval, but without actual acquaintance with
his poetry.

thoughts. It is not known to me where I can find another modern song at once so large and so naive . . . , propounded in such strong and beautiful rhythms.[112]

Indeed, in spite of obvious differences between them, they had much in common, especially in their interest in new and freer forms.[113] Perhaps the greatest likeness is betwen Whitman's practice and Lanier's theory. Though *The Science of English Verse* makes no direct reference to *Leaves of Grass*, poetic experiments of this sort—as well as the free rhythms and run-on lines of Shakespeare's later plays—undoubtedly prompted such radical suggestions as:

I am strongly inclined to believe that English poetry might a great gainer if we would at once frankly recognize . . . rhythmic but unmetric verse as a strictly-rhythmized prose, and print it as such without the deceptive line-division. . . . A development of English rhythm lies, I feel sure, in this direction.

For Lanier points out specifically in this connection poetry with a predominance of dactyls, in combination with the spondee and iambus, and this was the typic scheme he marked out not only for *The Battle of Maldon* but, in another connection, for "Song of Myself." [114] Though he never accepted Whitman's "theory of formlessness," he maintained that the sponsor of the new school did not actually practice this in his own poems, declaring, in his most unfavorable criticism:

It seems like a curious sarcasm of time that even the form of Whitman's poetry is not the poetry of the future but tends constantly into the

[112] May 5, 1878; the letter states explicitly: "I had never read this book before." Lanier's copy of the 1876 edition, with numerous passages lined in the margin, is preserved in the Charles D. Lanier Collection. Whitman's only reply to this invitation to friendship was a postal card, dated May 27 [1878] saying that the volume had been sent.

[113] This was commented on by at least one contemporary: " [Lanier's] taste made him an open critic of the robust poet of democracy; but it is manifest that the two . . . were moving in the same direction; that is, for an escape from conventional trammels to something free, from hackneyed time-beats to an assimilation of nature's larger rhythm " (E. C. Stedman, *The Nature and Elements of Poetry*, Boston, 1892, p. 196).

[114] See II, 184-185, 114-119; for Whitman's opinion of Lanier, see note 180. For the quotation in the following sentence, see IV, 54-55. The thesis in these Johns Hopkins lectures of 1881 (the spiritualization of personality through civilization) and Whitman's extreme views in a recent magazine article (" The Poetry of the Future "), which was the point of departure for Lanier's attack on his muscular democracy of bearded roughs chanting their formless and savage songs, undoubtedly accounts in some measure for the emphasis on their differences rather than their likenesses in this extended critique (see IV, 43-55). A. H. Starke has collected all the available evidence in an effort to present a more balanced picture of their relations (" Lanier's Appreciation of Whitman," *American Scholar*, II, 398-408, Oct., 1933).

rhythm of . . . the earliest [English poetry]. The only difference which Whitman makes is in rejecting the alliteration, in changing the line-division, so as to admit longer lines, and the allowance of much liberty in interrupting this general rhythm for a moment.

Then, after citing Landor's dictum that the dactyl is the "bindweed of English prose," he quotes side by side from the oldest and the newest English poetry:

> Brimmanna boda abeod eft ongean

> Walt Whitman am I, a cosmos of mighty Manhattan the son

—to which he might have added the opening line of his own hymn:

> Glooms of the live-oaks, beautiful-braided and woven.

Without pressing a parallel in the niceties of metrical scansion for these lines written from three such different prosodical theories, one can point to their similarity in general effect: the swinging chant of the Old English, the "strong and beautiful rhythms" Lanier had admired in *Leaves of Grass*, and the range and sweep of his own "Marshes of Glynn." [115]

In connection with his studies in the "Science of Poetry" and his reading of Old English poems for a course of lectures delivered in the spring of 1878, Lanier wrote "an experiment . . . with logaoedic dactyls" called "The Revenge of Hamish" (112), a remarkably good poem considering the circumstances of its composition. [116] "Another freer treatment of the same rhythm by me," he wrote modestly of "The Marshes of Glynn," "reads well if a man understands the long roll of dactyls in which it is written." He had had his practice in the earlier poem, and by the time he came to the composition of the second he had elaborated his theories into a manual on "The Physics of Poetry," with a long section on the "tendency of English rhythmical feeling towards the running [or logaoedic] dactyl" as opposed to the ponderous classical dactyl. [117] Lanier was also a musician interested in

---

[115] Another resemblance to Whitman comes from the parallelism and the long flowing sentences—for example, the first 36 lines. But the most Whitmanesque of all Lanier's experiments are his "poem outlines" (pp. 237 ff., below), though it is difficult to tell which, if any, of them he considered finished in the matter of form.

[116] The plot was taken bodily from a current novel by William Black (see note), and the form was clearly an exercise to illustrate a theory of prosody presumably discussed in the Bird Lectures (see III, vii-viii). For the reference to it as an experiment see his letter of Oct. 20, 1878. The quotation in the following sentence is a composite from this letter and one of Dec. 21, 1878.

[117] MS in the Henry W. Lanier Collection, Part I, pp. 88-92. The same matter is treated in *The Science of English Verse* (II, 176-179). See letters of July 13, Aug. 16, 1878 (to R. S. Lanier).

the "colors" of verse as well as its rhythms, and the same treatise
lays emphasis not only on rhyme and alliteration but on consonant-
sequence and vowel-distribution, qualities he had admired in the works
of Swinburne and Tennyson.[118] And out of all this came the orchestral
effects that he needed to give shape to his vision of spiritual values
he had found in the trees and marshes of the southern coast, best
described by a modern critic as:

not one melody artfully varied, but a bewildering succession of winding
and darting melodies . . . a full, rich, complex background of sound,
of crescendo and decrescendo restlessly alternating, of a rapid tempo
bespeaking eagerness and wonder, relieved perhaps too rarely by a
brief tranquil interlude; and everywhere words are poured out lavishly
like so many notes, not so much expressing a meaning as illustrating it.[119]

In spite of the many influences that went into the making of "The
Marshes of Glynn," it was essentially original, the poem of Lanier's
aesthetic and spiritual maturity.

   This important poem did not get the publication it deserved, for it
appeared not only anonymously but in a volume which he himself
described as "an intolerable collection of mediocrity." It is easy to
understand why Lanier willingly contributed to *A Masque of Poets,*
which he was told would be "representative of the best poets in this
country"; but it is unfortunate that he should have sent in his best
poem to a "no-name" anthology made up of second-rate verse—even
the few contributions that came from prominent poets.[120] It went into
three editions, however, and was widely though not favorably reviewed.
Lanier's poem indeed "won most of the honors of the book," as he
wrote to his father (Feb. 1, 1879), but only a few guessed him as the
author, others attributing it to Edgar Fawcett, Jean Ingelow, and
Tennyson. He must have derived some satisfaction from the praise
in the *Atlantic* (presumably from the pen of Howells, who had consistently rejected his offerings), which singled it out as the pick of

---

[118] Part III, pp. 40-50; cf. II, 228 ff. There is surprisingly little dissyllabic
or internal rhyme in "The Marshes of Glynn," but considerable attention is
paid to the other matters of color, as he had suggested in the lectures. It is
also interesting to note that in spite of an appearance of irregularity the pre-
vailing pattern in pentameter lines rhymed in couplets. (See the articles by
Snoddy in the bibliography, VI, 405.)
[119] Norman Foerster, *Nature in American Literature* (New York, 1923), pp.
235-236. It was this very musicalness in Lanier's poetry, incidentally, that
Whitman objected to (Horace Traubel, *With Walt Whitman in Camden,* New
York, 1906, III, 207-209).
[120] See note 66, Letters of 1878, and letter of Dec. 21, 1878. A full account
of the volume, its contributors, and its contemporary reception may be found in
A. H. Starke, "An Omnibus of Poets," *Colophon,* IV, Part 16 (Mar., 1934).
Lanier apparently received no compensation for his poem.

the volume, calling it " a fine Swinburnian study . . . in which the poet
has bettered, in some passages, his master's instructions."[121] The only
other interesting comment was in the London *Spectator*, which pointed
to it as one of the few poems showing signs of power, but gave the
author a piece of sound advice: "let his substantive be strong, his
adjectives few and quiet, and he will gain in effectiveness." Finally,
Longfellow selected it for reprinting in his *Poems of Places*. Neither
" The Marshes of Glynn " nor any of the hymns that followed, however,
served to advance his reputation during his lifetime, though they were
of the first importance in maturing him as an artist and are the foundation on which his fame must rest.

Lanier had found his true church, and having sounded his prelude
he planned a whole book of hymns that would chant his new gospel.
But the last three years of his life were subject to many interruptions—
from work, sickness, and the crossing of his purposes by new ideas that
he did not have time to assimilate—and it is only in his recessional
that all of his powers of rhapsody again found adequate expression.
" Sunrise " (144), his last important poem, is the only real companion
piece to " The Marshes of Glynn," and much that has been said of the
one applies to the other. Lanier's final illness, which continued through
more than a year with mounting intensity, had begun in the last half
of 1880. By December he was prostrated with a temperature of 104°,
yet it was while he lay all but extinguished by the fire of this fever
that he penciled the faint script of his splendid " Sunrise." The relation
of this poem to his life has been aptly phrased by his biographer:

> The restlessness and the burning of his fever pervade the lines; it is
> into the dream-troubled sleep of illness, no restful, natural sleep, that
> the clean nature odors of marsh and forest and sea come . . . to trouble
> Lanier and to waken him. But the sleep is . . . the sleep of life, and
> awakening is to the freedom of all-releasing death.[122]

Though this first draft has not survived the second and third have, and
the manuscripts furnish an instructive picture of Lanier as a craftsman.
Almost without exception the revisions are in the direction of a richer
and more varied music, and one feels certain that the orchestral effects

[121] *Atlantic*, XLIII, 410 (Mar., 1879) ; but see note 14, Letters of 1876, for
Lanier's changed attitude towards Swinburne, and for his relations with the
Atlantic see A. H. Starke, " William Dean Howells and Sidney Lanier," *American Literature*, III, 79-82 (Mar., 1931). The quotation in the following sentence
is from the *Spectator*, LII, 247-248 (Feb. 22, 1879). The Boston *Literary World*
called it " in some respects the strongest poem in the book; " most of the
other reviews, such as *Appleton's, Harper's*, and the *Nation*, failed to discuss
it or many of the other poems individually.

[122] Starke, p. 408. All known facts of its composition are collected in the note,
p. 366, below.

of all his hymns were the result of careful and repeated polishings.[123] In spite of its beauty of phrase and rhythm it does not come up to the technical achievement of "The Marshes of Glynn," though happier circumstances might have resulted in further improvement in the matter of execution. But, even more than the earlier poem, "Sunrise" is a summing up of Lanier as both man and poet. Here his courage in facing death has become triumphant acceptance, the social gospel of "The Symphony" has been transmuted into a chant for a better world sung with the conviction of poetic vision rather than the querulousness of the reformer, the adoration of nature has been exalted into unqualified worship of the sun as the divine source of life—but also as the symbol of immortality. For "Sunrise" is pagan only in its symbolism, and even that may have come from his reading of Swedenborg.[124] The manuscripts now available make clear for the first time the poem's underlying Christianity, though it was a far cry from the current orthodoxy. The line that describes the dawn, preceding the actual rising of the sun, read in its first form: "Sweet Baptist, prepar'st thou the way of the light?"[125] And his meaning is confirmed beyond any doubt by a surviving poem outline, in which he says, "about this Matter it was not intended we should be sure, else Christ would rise with the sun every day;" but he adds quickly: "And doth He not rise with the sun, Yea, dear, art thou not it?" Lanier created his own symbol for God, an original and a daring one for that day, and he realized it grandly in "Sunrise."

That this major poem is not mentioned in any of his letters can only be accounted for by the stress and strain of the few remaining months. That it was never even submitted to a publisher is explained by his intention of using it to lead off his projected book of "Hymns of the Marshes." Lanier completed only one other long poem for this volume, "The Cloud," but this is a troubled poem and a labored one, belonging with the group that grew out of his scientific reading rather than here. However, though there were no further hymns there were shorter songs of the marshes, five of which he wrote out and a dozen more he left in outline form. The finished songs are all interesting, either in themselves or because of their lyricism; the unfinished ones are mere brush strokes and musical notations to record fleeting impressions on eye and ear.[126] Some of them probably date from the

[123] See the variants given on pp. 323-325, below. No MS of "The Marshes of Glynn" has been found.
[124] His copy of *Concerning Heaven and its Wonders, and Concerning Hell* (New York, 1863) is preserved in the Charles D. Lanier Collection.
[125] Line 123, p. 324, below. The quotation in the following sentence is from No. 141, p. 272, below.
[126] Poem Outlines Nos. 154-164, pp. 276-277, seem like the germs of such

" Ephemerae " he began jotting down at the time of his return from
Florida, when he lacked the serenity needed for composition. " I'm
taken with a poem pretty nearly every day," he wrote (May 26, 1877),
" and have to content myself with making a note of its train of thought
on the back of whatever letter is in my coat pocket." Others date
from a later period. Much of the work of these last years is so fragmentary as to furnish only a hint of direction, but the fortunate
survival of at least a dozen prose drafts of ideas that were actually
worked out into poems indicates just how meaningful to the poet were
jottings that show small promise to the reader. And Lanier's plans
for three projected volumes can be sketched in from the evidence of
these surviving outlines and the few poems he actually completed in
each of these categories.[127] From scattered references it may be conjectured that he planned to include in one of these volumes all of his
Hymns of the Marshes, the Fields, and the Mountains. The most
suggestive of these, though there is not a single completed poem for
proof, are the last named. For, in spite of the poetic rapture he found
in the marshes, it was not flat lands but mountains which drew the
deepest responses from Lanier; and if there was one thing he loved
in nature above all others, it was trees. Of all the outlines that have
come down, those written during the final illness in western North
Carolina, summer of 1881, are most unmistakably the germs of poems.[128]
The springs and rivers, the laurel thickets filled with birds, and most
of all the balsams that crowned these mountains had messages for him
of the sources of life and the meaning of death; but he learned the
meaning before he had time to complete, " in obedience to the dream,"
his songs against death.

The religious tone of these reveals their connection with another
unfinished volume, " Credo and Other Poems," several actually bearing
the alternate title.[129] Though few of the outlines in this group approach
true lyricism, the impact of scientific thought on Lanier was deeply
significant, and if he had lived to resolve this discordant note the result
might have been stronger if less harmonious music than the concord
of his more confident songs. The half-dozen completed poems in this

transcripts from nature as " Between Dawn and Sunrise " and " A Sunrise
Song " (143). The best of the completed songs are " Marsh Song—At Sunset "
(142), with its magical adjectives, and "A Ballad of Trees and the Master,"
the finest lyric he ever wrote. (The latter and " To the Sun " are discussed
below.) Three of them were originally incorporated as intercalary songs in
" Sunrise " (see note, pp. 366-367).

[127] See the headnote to the section of Poem Outlines, p. 236, below. For the
following sentence, see p. 276 n.

[128] See Nos. 177-189, pp. 280-284, below.

[129] Poem Outlines Nos. 109-153, pp. 262-275 (cf. the notes on pp. 262 and
276).

group are but a token of what might have followed. Like other intelligent Victorians he was swept into the controversy between science and religion, excited by the widening of the boundaries of the mind but disturbed by the doubts that were unsettling old beliefs. One result, that is now for the first time clear, was that it hastened the development of his unorthodoxy. The progress of his disillusionment can be traced in the outlines which reproach the church for its temporizing institutionalism and its members for their indifference or hypocrisy. Declaring that the true church was in each man's heart, he threw overboard the whole body of theological dogma. His attack on creeds, indeed, found voice in at least one finished poem, "Remonstrance" (122),[130] the most outspoken protest against convention that he ever submitted for print. This denunciation of the age for its intolerance, written in the summer of 1878, reveals a very different attitude from "Acknowledgment" (56), written three years before, which had denounced the age for its skepticism—heart in the temple but head out, with eyes blinking at "o'er-bright science." *Lippincott's* which had accepted the one rejected the other, specifically because it was an attack on orthodoxy, which may explain why more of the poems planned for the "Credo" volume were never completed.[131]

In his private notes he was far more outspoken than in his published poems, and the reason for this is evidenced in such a jotting as the one in which he weighs the inevitable misunderstanding that would follow "if for example you declare you believe in one God—and that Christ is not God but the sweetest man who ever lived." Such conclusions were not reached without a struggle, as witness his anguished cry, "O Science, wilt thou take away my Christ," his concern that Christ

[130] The relationship between Lanier's outlines and his finished poems can be traced in five of the poems here assigned to the "Credo" volume: "Remonstrance," "How Love Looked for Hell," "The Crystal," "The Cloud," and "Opposition" (see pp. 317, 321, 360, 361, 364, below).

[131] *Lippincott's* likewise rejected "The Cloud" two years later—in fact, published none of Lanier's poems from 1878 on. This date marks his shift to two other magazines, the *Independent* and *Scribner's*, in which most of his remaining poems appeared, both during his lifetime and posthumously. The editor of the former became Lanier's first biographer; the house of the latter, his official publisher. *Century*, the continuator of *Scribner's*, accepted both "Remonstrance" and "The Cloud" with praise and substantial payments to his widow. Of the other magazines which had been opened up to Lanier in 1877 two of them, *Appleton's* and *Leslie's*, he probably dropped because they were second-rate. The *Galaxy*, which had accepted three of his poems, was a good magazine, but its merger with the *Atlantic* in 1878 closed this door to him. No explanation has been discovered as to why he contributed only one poem to *Harper's*. But his independence in the matter of publication during his last years is demonstrated by his turning down the invitation of *Evolution*, a New York weekly that solicited his contributions in a letter of Feb. 15, 1879.

should not be taken away from the normally religious men and women who need him, and the question broken off in the middle " but if he was only man x x x." [132] If science made him revise his old notions of deity, he was guided to his new attitude by Emerson, whose position, that Christ was not so much God becoming man as man becoming God, is restated in one of the outlines. But his adoration of the person of Jesus, as revealed in another, is not Emersonian: " The Church is too hot, and Nothing is too cold. I find my proper Temperature in Art. Art offers me a method of adoring the sweet master Jesus Christ, the beautiful souled One." Lanier's final solution was his own. He simply passed over the question of the divinity of Christ for other aspects that concerned him more. And as in " The Symphony " he had expounded the social gospel of the New Testament, so five years later in " The Crystal " (136) it is Jesus as the great ethical teacher who is praised as the paragon of men. The one godlike attribute assigned to him in the printed version, " King," reads in the manuscript signifi-cantly " Friend "— this much to convention.

One more influence was brought to bear on his thinking about Christ before he produced the poem that had lain in his heart so long. In Lanier's copy of Sir John Seeley's *Ecce Homo, A Survey of the Life and Work of Jesus* (Boston, 1866), opposite the sentence: " He who was to reconcile God and man needed to be first at peace with himself " (p. 13), there is a marginal query: " As a matter of fact, was the state of Jesus's mind one of inward tranquility? " The healing effect of nature had been an accepted belief with Lanier from the beginning. After his reading of Emerson this came to take on a more transcen-dental tone, as revealed in the Peabody lectures delivered in the winter of 1878 (III, 39): " Day by day," he declared in an autobiographical aside, "we find that the mystic influence of Nature on our human personality grows more intense and individual." And the illustration that followed was an enraptured account of the ministry of trees on the troubled spirit of man. Two years later all this found expression in " A Ballad of Trees and the Master " (144). It was composed, we are told by his wife, in " fifteen or twenty minutes . . . , without erasure or correction "; [133] it was the product we now know, of as many years—

---

[132] The Poem Outlines treating the matters discussed in this paragraph are Nos. 109-125, 136-139, pp. 262-268, 271.

[133] See note 124, Letters of 1880. Describing the composition of this poem, she wrote: " It was different from any thing I happened to note, beside this, for Mr. Lanier's wont was to polish his verse with much interlining, until the artist's keen sense of the right color in words found rest " (letter to Mrs. Charlotte Ware, Sept. 13, 1910). For Lanier's comments on spontaneity in composition see his letter of Mar. 3, 1878. In connection with his lyrics it is also interesting to note his definition of the " song " as a composite of music and poetry, in

and there could be no better formula for the composition of lyric poetry. The most spontaneous lyrical utterance of Lanier's career, " A Ballad of Trees and the Master" is in a sense an epitome of his religion and art. Here is the conscious architecture of the musician-poet, its melody the product of a haunting refrain, of strong substantives, of adjectives few and quiet. Here is the most significant episode of human history interpreted in a way that is equally satisfying to orthodox and unorthodox. If Lanier had lived longer the conflict between religion and science might have produced other examples of this new and simpler music.

In problems of a purely theological cast Lanier had little difficulty in reaching conclusions satisfactory to himself. None of the new thought seems to have shaken his belief in personal immortality, which indeed he rarely mentions except in poetic imagery, such as that where as a bird facing death he says, " I will fly to another tree." [134] Nor did it drive him towards agnosticism, for he remained a convinced theist, but he was satisfied with vaguer formulations of the " God whom I but dream I dream." Thus positive science simply broke down rather painlessly the dogmatic definitions of his early religious creed. But some of its broader philosophic implications were not accepted into his practical thinking without a real struggle. Although he declared himself satisfied that there was no revelation of God except in " trees, music, and a running stream," he confessed that it was easier to find him in the " rosy hues " than in the " inexorable *quid pro quo* of Nature and the hateful measure of Evil." [135] Like others brought up in the romantic school of nature worship, the theory of the survival of the fittest was shocking to Lanier:

It is, some how, a terrible reflection to me. . . . My grasses against my oaks! My ferns stabbing at the serene-shining mountain-beeches, my violets snatching the last drop of moisture from a parching and dying daisy. Good God! who is there, after this, that can prate of the " Evidences from design " and declare that one can trace any (so-called) goodness in the Creator from the operations of nature. No, in the ordinary sense of the term, God is *not* " good." The suffering that goes on by His command, under His Eye, and preventable by His Hand, is unspeakable. . . . Nevertheless I believe that God is God, and that Faith can see Him as infinitely loveable.

His conclusion was a *non sequitur* and he knew it. Later he resolved

which the words are used " not as vehicles of ideas but as vehicles of tones " (see the " Physics of Poetry," Part II, MS, Henry W. Lanier Collection).

[134] Poem Outline No. 186, p. 283. That quoted in the following sentence is No. 131, p. 269.

[135] Nos. 126, 127, 129, pp. 268-269. The quotation in the following sentence is from his Ledger, pp. 600-601.

his dismay over this struggle for existence less evasively by interpreting it within his theory of "oppositions," quoting Darwin to show that nature is the mother of death as well as of life; and this was the theme of one of his most promising mountain hymns, jotted down in outline form during the summer of 1881.[136]

Of all theories of contemporary science it was evolution, naturally enough, that disturbed Lanier most. Confusing biological evolution with various ideas of moral and social progress, like many other Victorians he feared the acceptance of it meant adopting a philosophy of materialistic determinism.[137] Though he had wrestled with this problem over a period of years, he never really clarified his attitude towards it.[138] It is this confusion, rather than the halting rhythms, that mars the one completed poem that wrung itself out of his agonizing over

[136] No. 180, p. 282. Darwin was used to substantiate the apparently contradictory treatments of nature in *Hamlet* and *A Midsummer Night's Dream* in a lecture delivered at Johns Hopkins, Dec., 1879 (III, 397).

[137] Two doctoral dissertations on the general subject have been recently completed but are unavailable to the present writer: F. W. Conner, "Cosmic Optimism: The Influence of Darwinian Evolution on American Poets" (Pennsylvania, 1944); and J. M. Turner, "The Response of Major American Writers to Darwinism" (Harvard, 1945). A volume based on a seminar on the same theme at Princeton, edited by Stow Persons, has been announced as in preparation. Richard Hofstadter's *Social Darwinism in American Thought, 1860-1915* (Philadelphia, 1944) gives only incidental treatment of the reaction of literary men, with no mention of Lanier. (For Lanier's worst example of confusion in the matter, see IV, 248.)

[138] The earliest references are in two Ledger entries that from their handwriting seem to date from the early 1870's: "The theological mind looks for God . . .: the philosophical mind works out a theory of evolution-from-One" (p. 328); and "Grant the development or evolution theory: the question must occur why did the atom develope to just that particular sort of being called a man?" (p. 597). A miscellaneous MS page in a later hand begins: "Crude enough seems to me the well loved notion of Science that all phenomena are only the outcome of a tendency which God first impressed upon the primordial germ, and that God then left Things to develop according to law. Did God indeed do this, and then retire? O God, hast thou left us? Whither has thou gone?" (MS, Charles D. Lanier Collection). On the back flyleaves of his copy of Pietro Blaserna's *The Theory of Sound in its Relation to Music* (New York, 1876) he wrote out two and a half pages of examples to prove the general uniformity of natural forces only to conclude: "But the uniformity seems to disappear when we come to consider those peculiar forces usually called spiritual forces."

Lanier's first teacher in science at Oglethorpe University, James Woodrow, had been ardent in his attempts to reconcile natural and revealed religion (see Philip Graham's article in *Sewanee Review*, XL, 307-315, July, 1932, and the expansion in "Lanier and Science," *American Literature*, IV, 288-292, Nov., 1932). Later Lanier had made the acquaintance of a similar advocate in a kinsman of his favorite aunt, Joseph LeConte, whose *Religion and Science* he apparently read (see June 13, 1877, to R. S. Lanier). His chief reading in science, however, seems to have come in the last four years of his life, as will be shown below.

the conflict between religion and science. Its later title, "The Cloud" (139), was adopted when he decided to make it one of his marsh hymns; but the earlier title, "Individuality," better states its theme and its relation with the "Credo" volume. In a letter recounting the genesis of "The Cloud," Lanier declared that though evolution was "a noble and beautiful and true theory" for whatever can be proved to have been evolved, not a single case of species differentiation had been so proved.[139] Hence the "enormous modern generalizations" of science end precisely where the subject of his poem begins and "the doctrine of evolution when pushed beyond this point appears to me . . . to fail." For Lanier was at this time working out a moral doctrine of his own—that the sacredness of the modern personality was the most significant phenomenon of human history—and this poem, he declared, was "a passionate reaffirmation of the artist's autonomy, threatened alike from the direction of the scientific fanatic and the pantheistic devotee."

This explanation accounts for the fact that he could find no help at this crisis in his thinking from Emerson, whose emphasis on the importance, even the potential divinity, of the individual he had found so stimulating.[140] For Lanier could not follow transcendentalism to its logical conclusion as to the unity of the one and the many. Indeed, it is in connection with this same theme of personality, in the lectures of the following winter, that he voiced his one serious disagreement with Emerson, specifically rejecting "that most marvellous delusion of his—the strange wise man!—that personality is to die away into the first cause."[141] Instead he turned back for confirmation to Tennyson, who is quoted at great length and with warm approval in the same lectures. "In Memoriam" is cited to prove that this modern has not found science a destructive force but an aid to his confidence in the mission of the poet; and in his own copy of the poem he wrote in the margin: "Personality and love. Here we have a certain compensation against genius and the favoritism of nature."[142] "The Two Voices"

---

[139] Letter to J. F. Kirk, June 15, 1880. The quotations in the following sentences are from the same letter. (Kirk, editor of Lippincott's, rejected the poem, and it was not published during Lanier's lifetime.)

[140] See, for example, Poem Outlines Nos. 149-152, pp. 273-275.

[141] IV, 165-166. Cf. the reference in "The Crystal," p. 138, to "Emerson,/ Most wise, that yet, in finding Wisdom, lost/ Thy Self, sometimes." Even in "A Florida Sunday," his most Emersonian poem, it may be pointed out that the tone is more orthodox and the approach is religious rather than philosophical. Finally, though Lanier tentatively implied his acceptance of the transcendental doctrine that evil is the absence of good in "How Love Looked for Hell," he later abandoned this for his theory of opposition. (Cf. the partial resemblance to "The Cloud" in the central stanzas and rejected lines of "To Beethoven," pp. 89, 310-311, below—a poem written in Dec., 1876.)

[142] Lanier's copy of Tennyson's Poems has not survived, but the marginal

is given as an example of how his poetry is stronger and richer "by as much as he has been trained and beaten and disciplined with the stern questions which scientific speculation has put." And a new poem, "De Profundis," is praised for its noble treatment of "the poetic idea of that personality which I have just tried to express from the point of view of science, of the evolutionist." If Lanier had lived, he might have composed such "sombre and terrible" music instead of "The Cloud," with its unblended form and meaning. For interpreters like Asa Gray were clarifying the air; and in John Fiske, a popular defender of both religion and evolution, he had already found some comfort in the explanation that human genius can be accounted for by the scientific principle of spontaneous variation.[143] There was not time enough for assimilation, however, and his response to Darwinism never achieved adequate expression in his poetry.

Though he balked at some of the philosophic implications of science, Lanier was more successful in applying its findings to the theory and practice of his poetry. During the last years of his life he was reading avidly, if only as a beginner, in many fields. "I have been studying science, biology, chemistry, evolution, and all," he wrote on June 15, 1880; and he should have added geology, mineralogy, astronomy, and the others as well. For some twenty scientific books are known to have been in his small library, representing almost as many branches of study. Though many of them were elementary texts, others were important documents in the history of nineteenth-century thought: Darwin's *Origin of Species*, Spencer's *The Principles of Psychology*, and Huxley's *The Crayfish*.[144] That he read them is witnessed by his marginal

annotation was recorded by one who examined it shortly after his death (see W. M. Lind, "A Dead Poet's Library. Sidney Lanier's Literary Treasures," Baltimore *Sunday News*, July 24, 1892). The lecture reference to "In Memoriam" is taken from IV, 34-38; those in the two following sentences from IV, 38-39, and 27-29. The name of Tennyson had been notably missing from the list of favorites in "Clover" and "The Stirrup-Cup," written in 1876-1877. Even though he is praised in "The Crystal" three years later as the "largest voice since Milton," the qualification is significant: "yet some register of wit wanting."

[143] See the prose jotting quoted in the notes, p. 364, below, which is used in the lectures (IV, 6) and also seems to be the germ of "The Cloud" (or a revision of it) or of a new marsh hymn on the same theme. The most interesting books by Fiske that Lanier may have read were *The Unseen World* (1876) and *Darwinism and Other Essays* (1879). Asa Gray, the champion of the group trying to reconcile religion and science, had published *Darwiniana* (1876) and *Natural Science and Religion* (1880), two books which Lanier may well have been acquainted with, since he owned other volumes by Gray, discussed below.

[144] The last named has not come down, but it is on the list of books bought by Lanier from Cushings and Bailey, Mar. 10, 1880 (statement in the Charles

markings, in a few cases with notes that show the drift of his thoughts. Though it is of little moment how much science Lanier learned, since he is less important for what he thought than what he felt, it is instructive to see what it meant to him as a poet. In his copy of Darwin, opposite a passage on domestic pigeons (p. 21), he wrote: " Man, moving up out of the dark of time, attended by his friends— the pigeon, the dog, the horse, and the cow." Again, beside a discussion of adaptations in nature, as of the woodpecker and the mistletoe (p. 48): " Darwin's hearty use of such adjectives as ' exquisite ' and ' beautiful ' in these connections, is very suggestive of pleasant relations between Science and Poetry." Even in the more technical volumes he found matter to stir his imagination. Where Gray's *Botany* (p. 182) explained that all the essentials of vegetable growth are contained in the air, Lanier wrote: " Every tree then must have existed in the atmosphere first. We breathe potential forests." In Foster's *Physiology* his sensitive pencil responded with several outlines for poems, such as " The cloud,/ White corpuscle, floating in the plasm of air " and " Death masticating the bodies of men,/ For some large digestion." And on a miscellaneous slip of paper the epigram: " Rooted in the soil of Science,/ Fruited in the air of Art." [145]

There is reason to believe that science would in time have created the friction needed to bring the spark of a new life to his poetry. Already it had begun to influence the imagery of some of the later completed poems. Instead of the bird's song coming from some more romantic source, it follows the satisfaction of eating " a dull insect "; the world rejecting a poet's message is likened to a contrary flower setting its " stamen's spear-point " against the pollen-bearing bee; intellect and emotion become psychological symbols, and " dream-taught wisdom " a harlequin to " mock the daily round "; instead of the sun rising " the sea-rim sinks," and the sun itself is praised, in a newly discovered song, as the chemist of storms.[146] Though fancy still tends

D. Lanier Collection), and the references in his letters of June 1 and 15, 1880, show that he read it, and imply that it was the starting point for " The Cloud."

[145] Lanier's copy of Darwin was purchased on Apr. 11, 1879 (Turnbull Bros. statement, Charles D. Lanier Collection) and Gray's *Introduction to Structural and Systematic Botany* (1878) probably about the same time. His copy of Sir Michael Foster's *A Textbook of Physiology* has not come down, but the outlines quoted are preserved on a memorandum along with the MS slip quoted in the last sentence (Lanier Room, Johns Hopkins University).

[146] See " The Mocking Bird," " The Bee," " How Love Looked for Hell," " The Harlequin of Dreams," " Sunrise," and " To the Sun " (143)—all written between 1877 and 1880. Two of them seem to reflect his reading of Spencer's *Psychology* (see letter of July 21, 1873). Lanier's interest in chemistry may have been augmented by his friendship with Prof. Ira Remsen of Johns Hopkins, whose attitude towards religion and science conformed with

to supplant imagination, Lanier seems aware of the direction in which his improvements should tend, as evidenced in his late pronouncement:

just as science has pruned our faith (to make it more fruitful)—so it has pruned our poetic form and technic, cutting away much unproductive wood and efflorescence and creating richer yields. . . . I do not mean that you are to versify Biology, but . . . at this stage of the world you need not dream of winning the attention of sober people with your poetry unless that poetry, and your soul behind it, are informed and saturated at least with the largest final conceptions of current science.[147]

He was beginning to see with some clarity the function of science in its relation to art, and though he made only tentative applications in his practice he realized it significantly in his theory. His most elaborate formulation, in *The Science of English Verse*, was based upon the latest researches in the physics of sound, especially those of Helmholtz. Now it can be shown that his second important contribution to literary criticism, the principle of opposition, was derived from that compendium of nineteenth-century scientific generalizations, Herbert Spencer's *First Principles*.[148]

In his earliest as well as his latest treatises on the technique of poetry Lanier was echoing Spencer when he called to witness modern scientific theory (that matter is merely motion in various modes) as breaking down the conventional distinction between substance and form, in order to substantiate his emphasis on the need for studying the latter

his own (see VII, xlix-l, and the sketch in *Dictionary of American Biography*). A similar improvement in craftsmanship can be found in the sharper eye to nature that guides such revisions as those in " Owl Against Robin " (131), written in the summer of 1879. In the first draft the flight of the owl is bookish, in the second it is drawn from observation: " To flit from the woods to the dreams of men . . . Down the hill and over the vale " becomes " To wheel from the wood to the window [sill] . . . Aslant with the hill and a-curve with the vale" (cf. pp. 132 and 319, ll. 56 and 60).

[147] Quoted from the Johns Hopkins lectures, winter of 1881 (IV, 34, 43).

[148] See Collin Wilsey (Messenger), " Certain Influences of Contemporary Science Upon the Critical Theory and Practice of Sidney Lanier," Master's Thesis, University of Southern California, 1942. I am indebted to the author for permission to use here some of the specific information first called to my attention in this excellent study. Her thorough account of the scientific background of Lanier's treatise on prosody lies beyond the limitations of this Introduction, as does her detailed analysis of his literary criticism in the Peabody and Hopkins lectures (which she finds unique because " The most complete formulation of contemporary science [Spencer's *First Principles*] furnished the actual concept around which each of these works is organized "). But in addition to her new light on Lanier's theory of opposition, attention should be called to the suggestion that his theory of personality in " The Cloud " is closer akin to Agassiz's theory of recapitulation than to Spencer's interpretation of evolution.

as the "science" of English verse.[149] Similarly he was laying down good Spencerian doctrine when he defined evolution as "a process from the uniform and indefinite to the multiform and definite," as an argument for freer forms rather than formlessness in literature, and when he summed up man's various relations to the material world (defined as "motion in many forms") as follows:

Science is the knowledge of these forms, . . . Art is the creation of beautiful forms, . . . Religion is the faith in the infinite Form-giver. . . . Life is the control of all these forms to the satisfaction of our human needs.[150]

The most important discovery for his poetry that came out of Spencer, however, was the theory that all the motions of nature resulted from an antagonism of forces. In a lecture at the Peabody Institute in November, 1878, Lanier allowed himself an aside on this new concept that stirred his imagination: " From the string stretched in one direction, plucked in another, to the world in space executing its rhythmic revolution . . . , OPPOSITION has revealed itself as underlying rhythm." And when he expanded this the following summer into the most poetic chapter in *The Science of English Verse*—" Rhythm in Nature," which is almost a summary of Chapter X of *First Principles*—he at least suggested his source:

Mr. Herbert Spencer has formulated the proposition that where opposing forces act, rhythm appears, and has traced the rhythmic motions of nature to the antagonistic forces there found. . . .
Perhaps this view may be made, without strain, to bind together even facts so remote from each other as the physical and the moral . . . the fret, the sting, the thwart, the irreconcilable me as against all other me's, the awful struggle for existence . . . may also result in rhythm.[151]

[149] " The Physics of Poetry," Pt. I, pp. 107-108, written in the summer of 1878, names Spencer as the source; but the treatment in the Johns Hopkins lectures of 1879 (No. VII, p. 45) only names him as the first to announce that those motions are rhythmical (both MSS are in the Henry W. Lanier Collection). Cf. the expansion of this in *The Science of English Verse* (1880), II, 193. Specific parallels between Spencer and Lanier for the matters in this paragraph are given in the study cited in note 148.

[150] See IV, 27, 61. Cf. Lanier's favorite dictum (p. 32) to prove that technic is not the enemy of spontaneity since the " raptus " must be controlled: " He who will not answer to the rudder must answer to the rocks."

[151] The first quotation is from the surviving fragment of Lecture II, Peabody Course (MS, Henry W. Lanier Collection) ; the second from II, 194-195, of the present edition. (The theory of opposition is notably absent from Lanier's first statement of his theory in " The Physics of Poetry," written in the summer of 1878. But it appears in the Hopkins lectures of 1879—No. VII, p. 47— with the application to morals: " as opposition is the foundation of physical music so trouble is the foundation of spiritual music." Lanier's theory also owes

Though Lanier did strain when he tried to develop this idea into a philosophy capable of explaining all the phenomena of life and literature, it was one of his most important contributions to critical theory. Better still, it produced one of his most interesting poems, " Opposition " (130), his reconciliation of science, art and morals—if not religion— drawn bodily from his treatise on prosody and the lectures of his last years.[152]

a debt, which he acknowledges, to Poe's *Eureka,* but that too was drawn ,from the formulations of contemporary science (see *Selections from Poe,* New York, 1934, ed. Alterton and Craig, Introduction).

[152] A fragmentary essay left in MS by Lanier seems to have grown out of this theory of opposition (MS, Charles D. Lanier Collection). He begins by saying: " I conceive that a great step towards true religion is gained by the clear recognition of the substantial identity of the following contradictions." He then lists in parallel columns such opposites as individuality and the infinite, diversity and unity, the economic and the beautiful, reason and love, nature and art. After stating that though reason cannot find God in nature, love can find him in art, he proceeds:

" The difference between Nature and Art is in brief: that there are in Nature economic purposes which are inconsistent with any possible ideals of the Beautiful. This is the fundamental error of the school of Walt Whitman and his predecessors. When Whitman declares that he thinks the smell of his arm-pits more than prayer, he attempts to force upon the aesthetic sense of man an element which is not nutritious to that organ of him (the aesthetic), not meant to be nutritious to it, and which is rejected by the aesthetic sense with as purely a reflex action as the repugnant physiological phenomenon which he cites is rejected by the sense of smell. As against this view the Argument from the Absurd may be employed with unanswerable effect. For if it be true, that whatever occurs in the order of nature is for that sole reason beautiful and worshipful, then it necessarily follows that the Venus of Milo would have been equally as beautiful as she is now, if she had had bow-legs, squint eyes, and a mole with seven red hairs on her chin: For unless these were miracles (which the Natural School flout with contempt) then they were results purely of the laws of nature governing physical descent: they were therefore exactly in the order of nature, i. e. beautiful.

" That fierce and unappeasable Curiosity after Unity which exhibits itself in the prodigious generalizations of the modern philosophers is, strictly speaking, the Love of God. From this sentiment no man, so far as my information goes, has been able to escape. The confidence with which the physicist accepts a phenomenon as universal, in spite of the fact that no phenomenon has ever been, or can possibly be, *proved* universal by experimental verification (which all physicists now hold to be the only conclusive proof) only presents to my mind a new evidence of the underlying conviction which is bred by this Love in every mind of that One-ness to which all things are referable, however dimly. This confidence shows itself strikingly in the extension of the discovered properties of earthly matter, to the substance of other stars. . . .

" This doctrine, of Love, of Religion, of Art, is the Heat of the world, Science is the Light of the world. At present I am to be found studying the blue end of the spectrum, where the heat is greatest. Men—noble and admirable in all respects—such as Mill, Spencer, Tyndall, Helmholtz, and many

" Opposition " also forms the connecting link between " Credo " and the third volume of poems that Lanier left unfinished, the " Songs of Aldhelm," a collection dealing with the theory and function of poetry which he began in the autumn of 1878.[153] In his study of Old English literature he had discovered Aldhelm and had idealized him into the type *poeta,* representing not only poetic authority but leadership among men. The figure of the Saxon bishop, " standing on the bridge, . . . singing ballads and sweet gospels to the traders as they passed by," became a symbol of what he also might be to his generation, " burning at once with music, with poetry, and with love of his kind." [154] Of the outlines for poems in this volume, two set the scene with the poet at the edge of town importuning the merchants to hear him; and there follows a series of serenades to " my Fellow Man, My Love," with the mission to preach to a materialistic world clearly announced: " I am hungry for . . . this business man of stocks and dry-goods." [155] That Lanier intended to include in his " Songs of Aldhelm " other poems he had already written on the same theme is proved by the fortunate survival of printer's copy for yet another volume, hastily prepared for publication the following spring. Of the twenty-odd pieces here gathered together under the title of " Clover, and Other Poems," all but a very few fit with the plan outlined above.[156] One group, headed

more, are simply at the red end of the spectrum. Their conclusions are to be accepted in most instances as strictly true: but they are at the same time to be carefully discriminated as conclusions from only one end, and as by no means covering the whole matter."

[153] Letter to Taylor, Oct. 20, 1878: " in a pigeon-hole in my desk half jotted down."

[154] See II, 206; III, 309.

[155] See pp. 251-261, below, especially Nos. 68, 69, 73, 75-77. (Cf. Lanier's letter of Feb. 3, 1860.)

[156] The copy that has come down (Henry W. Lanier Collection) consists of a title page, subjects for illustrations, and pp. 1-84 of the text (with a few pages missing)—made up of pasted and revised prints and MS pages. The poems included were written, with three exceptions, between 1876 and 1879. Those which seem related to the Aldhelm volume are: " Clover," " Song of the Chattahoochee," " The Mocking Bird," " Tampa Robins," " The Stirrup-Cup," " To Beethoven," " The Bee," " To Our Mocking Bird," and " Street-Cries " (I " Remonstrance," II " The Ship of Earth," III " How Love Looked for Hell," IV " Tyranny," V " Life and Song," VI " To Richard Wagner," VII " A Song of Love "). Four others were apparently space-fillers (" The Revenge of Hamish," " To Bayard Taylor," " To Nannette Falk-Auerbach," " The Hard Times in Elfland "), and two more seem to have been included in the package by mistake (" To My Class " and " On Violet's Wafers "). Pp. 11, 13-15, 18-19, 32-36, 43-45, 49 are missing, but the table of illustrations indicates that four of these poems were " From the Flats," " The Harlequin of Dreams," " The Waving of the Corn," and " The Marshes of Glynn." Further, Lanier's letter of May 16, 1879, indicates his intention to

by a poem called " Street-Cries " which echoes the scene at the bridge, seems like songs that could have been placed in the mouth of Aldhelm: pleas for a leader in time of crisis and for the need of making one's life a poem, remonstrance against intolerance and tyranny among men, praise to Beethoven for dissolving the world's despair in chords of harmony and to Wagner for revivifying ancient virtues in an industrial age. Even more interesting are those poems that state Lanier's own poetic creed, three of which deserve mention. The title-poem " Clover " (84), after an invocatin to beauty which does not go to market, declares that the artist likewise works for love and not for gain, his market being the heart of man. It preaches the lesson of purpose in the poet's life, however dimly understood, and, as a " solemn protest against the doctrine of ' Art for Art's Sake,' " it sets the key for the volume.[157] Lanier's poetic idealism is likewise revealed in " The Bee " (91), where he answers the question " What profit e'er a poet brings? " by saying that his service is not merely to suck the sweet from life, but to bring to the " world-flower " the rich wisdom of experience that clings to him. The connection of the " Song of the Chattahoochee " (103) with his theory of the artist's function is somewhat obscured by the onomatopœia, a skilfull handling of musical effects that nevertheless lulls the meaning to sleep, and by the disconcerting imagery, the downward pull of gravity as a symbol for the swift response to the call of duty. The application to poetry is made clearer in his similar description of another river, the Nerbadá, which " leaps out eagerly toward the low lands he is to fertilize, like a young poet anxious to begin his work of grace in the world." [158]

Lanier's consecration to the priesthood of his high calling, his gospel of love preached through music and poetry, his fusion of art and morality in a broader religion, run like a theme song through all that

include " The Symphony " and " Psalm of the West " if he could buy the copyright. His letter of May 22, 1879, submitting the volume for publication, states that it consisted of only 84 pp. It was rejected by Scribner, who was unwilling to make a cash payment for it, and possibly by other publishers (see notes 30, 35, Letters of 1879). There is no mention of the title " Songs of Aldhelm " in Lanier's letters after this period (the outlines intended for this volume seem to have been merged in " Credo," see note, p. 262). It is not included in his last reference to his unfinished volumes, letter of Feb. 12, 1881, which names " Hymns of the Marshes," " Credo and Other Poems," and " Clover and Other Poems."

[157] The quotation is from a lost letter by Lanier submitting the poem to Scribner's (see note 135, Letters of 1876). Cf. the line in " A Florida Sunday," " The great bird Purpose bears me 'twixt her wings."

[158] VI, 277. Lanier, however, thought the " Song of the Chattahoochee " one of his best poems (letter of Nov. 30, 1877), and it has proved to be his most popular.

he wrote.[159] These noble aspirations, of course, were common to all the idealists of the nineteenth-century from the romantic poets to Tennyson and Emerson, but the lights they lived by flicker only dimly through the darker years that have followed. In these matters Lanier belongs with the generation preceding him, whose poetry he found more congenial than that of his own. One group of outlines for the "Songs of Aldhelm," indeed, sounds like the nucleus for another "Crystal," pointing out the defects of contemporary poets: the triviality of the "culture" school of Aldrich, the surface glitter of Swinburne, the romantic escapism of Morris, and the "sausage-grinding" naturalism of Whitman.[160] Nor was he content, on the other hand, with the orthodoxy represented by Longfellow. Lanier was convinced that he was an unconventional poet, and the references in his letters to his "newness" are many, and sometimes confusing. At the time of his first success, for example, he declared that the originality of his poetry was not in its words or forms but "in its ideas, which have not been heretofore advanced." [161] As a matter of fact, he was somewhat in advance of his day, at least in America, in writing poems on social and economic problems and in drawing subjects from the discoveries of science, so that he does show originality in matter and idea as compared with Taylor, Stedman and the other transitional poets who clung to the traditions of the past.

It was in quite a different direction, however—that of technique, in his theory and to a lesser extent in his practice—that Lanier showed his closest kinship with the poetry of the future. That his poems with the greatest number of irregularities are the long ones of his last years, which he rightly thought of as his most important, is proof of the deliberateness of his experimentation towards freer and more varied forms. Yet they are not aiming towards formlessness, for analysis shows that they are surprisingly regular on the whole. Rather, they achieve the impression of freedom by carefully chosen and consciously controlled devices, sparingly employed but of considerable variety:

[159] Cf. the statement of his creed in an address delivered in 1869 (V, 260-262) with that in his letter of Aug. 28, 1880, to Browne. Three jottings (MSS, Charles D. Lanier Collection) sum up his position: "Art is the representation, in terms of Sense, of the Beautiful in conduct"; "I wish the time to arrive when Conscience disappears in the love of the Beautiful"; "I wish to reduce religion to terms of all the arts."

[160] Nos. 102-108, pp. 259-261. For Lanier's attacks on Bohemianism in art see especially V, 5-6; VI, 337, 348-349.

[161] Letter of Aug. 15, 1875, to Virginia Hankins, just after the publication of "Corn" and "The Symphony." See also Aug. 28, 1880, to Browne, accounting for the ridicule and misunderstanding that had greeted some of his works as the result of "a certain essential non-conformity which seems to beat in the blood of all reformers and preachers like myself."

occasional extremes of line-length, the frequent use of run-on lines, skilfull foot-substitutions, and the reproduction in words of all the sound effects known to the ear of the professional musician.[162] Others had made such experiments before him, of course; Lanier's contribution lies in the elaborateness with which he tried to combine music and poetry, and this is the explanation of why his poems are both liked and disliked. More to the taste of the modern reader than the orchestral rhapsodies of the marsh hymns, perhaps, would have been that simpler music of which there are hints in the subdued lament of " A Ballad of Trees and the Master" and the rougher rhythms suggestive of conflict in " Opposition "—where science has pruned away the " unproductive wood and efflorescence." For his practice had not caught up with his theory.

It is a misconception to treat *The Science of English Verse* as a set of rules peculiarly applicable to Lanier's poetry, for the author makes clear that his purpose was to analyze the " physical principles of classification for all possible phenomena of verse " from Beowulf to Tennyson in order to put criticism of the poetic art on " a scientific basis." [163] Yet this historical interpretation of how poetry has been written was the work of a radical, and there are hints here and there of new directions that are tempting to follow out. In the neglected

---

[162] The line-length in " Sunrise " varies from 1 to 21 syllables. About one-third of the lines in " The Marshes of Glynn " are run-on. In some lines of the marsh hymns every foot is different (" The wīde | sēa marsh|es of Glynn " and " Ăffable | līve-oăks | leăning | lŏw ỹ "). An example of how consciously he employed rhythmical variation may be pointed out in " Sunrise," where the lines preceding the rising of the sun are not only irregular but interspersed with numerous rests to increase the suspense before the climax, " Good morrow, lord Sun," which is immediately followed by lines that are flowing and regular. (The reverse is true of " The Mocking Bird," in which the first eight lines describing the bird in the tree are in strict iambics followed by numerous substitutions in the last six lines to suggest the action where he swoops to the grass below.) In all there is considerable variety in the employment of rhyme—double, identical, and internal—and abundant use of alliteration to break the metrical monotony (with a distinct effect of conflict in such a poem as " Opposition "). Here and in the shorter lyrics there is skilfull use of repetition and slightly varied refrains to give balance, as in the harp accompaniment suggested by " A Ballad of Trees and the Master "; careful attention to vowel distribution and consonant sequence, as in the flowing " Song of the Chattahoochee " (where one-third of the consonants are liquids and sibilants); and effective onomatopœia as in the choppy wave rhythms of " Marsh Song—At Sunset." Yet, in his best, none of these devices are used excessively. (See the exhaustive analysis by Pearl Brown, " A Study of Sidney Lanier's Verse Technique," Master's Thesis, Chicago, 1921, and the study by Ruth Willcockson, " Rhythmical Principles and Practices of Sidney Lanier," Master's Thesis, Chicago, 1928.)

[163] See II, 5-12; letter to Stedman, May 14, 1880; and IV, 30 (an explanation of Stedman's misunderstanding of the book).

INTRODUCTION lxxxi

matter of speech tunes he found "a fascinating field for a possible extension of our poetic achievement" towards a more "complete expression of all the complex needs or hopes or despairs of modern life," anticipating the development of Robert Frost's theory of "the sound of sense." [164] He felt as strongly as Vachel Lindsay that poetry depends for its full effect upon being read aloud, and sanctioned the latters's practice of giving directions to the reader in his own marginal notations for the Centennial Cantata. Finally, in a number of suggestions, scattered through his treatise on prosody, the twentieth-century imagists could have found justification for many of their experiments. Lanier advised the poet who did not find rhyme useful to avoid it altogether, directing his attention to other and more subtle devices for securing "tone-color"; in pointing out the disappearing boundaries between prose and verse, he made a step towards "polyphonic prose"; and in denying the primary importance of accent and advocating a freer development of "rhythmic but unmetric verse" without the conventional line division, he laid part of the groundwork for *vers libre* [165] Indeed, it is possible that Lanier tried his own hand in these directions, for a few at least of the poem outlines seem like finished experiments in free verse, suggestive of the work of Amy Lowell and Carl Sandburg.[166]

However interesting, all this must remain in the realm of conjecture. For Lanier's poetic activity during the last years of his life was subjected to constant interruptions from his familiar enemies, and most of his plans were left incomplete. During the two years following "The Marshes of Glynn" he wrote only a dozen poems, all but a few of which were unimportant pieces written for special occasions.[167] His

[164] II, 211. See R. S. Newdick, "Robert Frost and the Sound of Sense," *American Literature*, IX, 289-300 (Nov. 1937). Frost read *The Science of English Verse* but deliberately rejected it (see Lawrance Thompson, *Fire and Ice: The Art and Thought of Robert Frost*, New York, pp. 40, 96).

[165] II, 47-48, 73, 184, 217 ff. Amy Lowell's copy of *The Science of English Verse* is preserved in the Houghton Library, Harvard, but there are no markings in it nor any indication of what she thought of it. A search of American magazines during the free-verse controversy, 1915-1920, should reveal whether or not Lanier exerted any actual influence on imagistic theory.

[166] See especially Nos. 57, 159, and 178 (pp. 248, 277, 281, below). Such as these may be what Lanier had in mind when he gave as one reason for writing *The Science of English Verse* (which is concerned with form, not idea): "I had some poems which I hope soon to print but which I could not hope to get understood generally, without educating their audience" (letter of May 14, 1880).

[167] "Opposition," "The Crystal," and "The Cloud" have already been discussed. The only other interesting one was "Owl Against Robin." Curiously enough this and the other two best minor poems of the last years ("The Hard

success as a poet had opened up to him the field of lecturing, and the supplementary one of textbook making. The summer of 1878 he spent writing " The Physics of Poetry," a first draft of his treatise on prosody; the following winter was occupied with his " Shakspere Course " at the Peabody Institute and with the preparation of two juvenile pot-boilers that grew out of his reading in medieval literature. All this led, as he had hoped it would, to his appointment as lecturer in English at Johns Hopkins. Hoping to turn this into a permanent " chair " he spent the summer of 1879 completing his *Science of English Verse*; and the next winter he worked himself to the bone seeing this through the press, preparing several abortive textbooks, and conducting the scholarly studies necessary for his lectures and class courses at the university. Here the question naturally arises as to why Lanier should have allowed himself to be turned aside from poetry just when he was reaching artistic maturity. One answer is that he could not resist the temptation to fulfill his lifelong yearning for an academic career. Another, that in this direction alone could he find relief from the economic necessity—or " poverty," as he called it—that still pressed him hard.[168]

Times in Elfland " and " The Revenge of Hamish ") were products of his illness, his economic distress, and his academic studies—three forces that interfered with his poetic activity. During 1879 he wrote only three poems and published only one, the lowest ebb since his years as a lawyer in Macon. Yet even during this period of inactivity his reputation continued to grow, as indicated by the invitations to contribute to anthologies: *A Masque of Poets* (1878), Longfellow's *Poems of Places* (1879), James's *Southern Students' Handbook* (1879), *The Art Autograph* (1880), Sargent's *Cyclopaedia of British and American Poetry* (1881), and Stedman's volumes (which did not appear until after Lanier's death). See also letter of April 21, 1878, and note 44.

[168] The term " poverty " so often applied to Lanier's financial condition is less accurate than that of economic harassment. During the years before he moved to Baltimore he seems to have earned a modest but competent living as clerk, teacher, and lawyer, though what little money he made from his writing was more than balanced by his losses. (There is no evidence that he was paid for any of the 24 poems published prior to " Corn "; and the only known fees for his short prose are $63 for " San Antonio," $22 for " Nature-Metaphors," a promised $33 for " The Three Waterfalls," and a " trifling " compensation for the " Letters from Texas." Against this must be set off the deficit of more than $250 incurred in the publication of *Tiger-Lilies*—see V, ix). The real struggle came during the last eight years, 1873-1881. Yet it would seem from scattered bits of evidence that his average expenditures during this period amounted to at least $1800 a year—equivalent in spending value to more than $5000 today—which was certainly enough to provide a reasonably comfortable living even for a family that grew from three to six in number (see, for example, letters of Oct. 12, 1875; July 23, 1877; and note 57, 1879). But Lanier's improvidence in money matters, the heavy expenses of constant medical treatment, and his wife's confessed lack of competence at housekeeping (see note 68, Letters of 1872, and X, 366-367) made heavy inroads on their small budget.

In spite of his enthusiasm as an amateur scholar, however, he knew that this was not his " true work " and hoped always to relegate it to a subordinate place. After his first year at Hopkins he wrote to one of his publishers: " With inexpressible delight I have got a singing-pen in my hand again, after eight months of bookmaking and lecture making and teach[ing] "; and to a friend: " To be an artist, and preach the gospel of poetry: that is the breath of my life." [169] But it was too late to mend: the intense work of these two years had broken down

The really distressing feature of his economic condition was that only a part of what he spent was earned income, and even that came in sporadically. For the rest he was dependent on his father and brother, whose generosity only increased his reluctance to call on them, with the result of continual desperate crises when rent, board, and doctors' bills came due. Ingenuously he wrote to Taylor, Mar. 4, 1878: " I find I cannot at all maintain our supplies of daily bread by poetry alone." Indeed, this was the smallest source of his income. The known fees he received for 14 poems amounted to only $675, and since $450 of this was for three long and somewhat special poems, the average pay was $20 a poem. (" Corn " $50, " The Symphony " $100, " In Absence " $35, " A Song of the Future " $10, " Psalm of the West " $300, " The Waving of the Corn " $15, " Evening Song " $10, " To Beethoven " $25, " The Stirrup-Cup " $20, " The Dove " $20, " Clover " $25, " The Revenge of Hamish " $30, " The Crystal " $20, " A Ballad of Trees and the Master " $15.) Of the remain-ing 33 poems published during the Baltimore period, at least 8 can be con-jectured to have paid him nothing, so that a safe estimate for his total income for poetry would be $1200. His prose was much more remunerative. *Florida* netted him somewhere between $750 and $1000, above expenses (see VI, xii, xvi) ; the four Boy's Books another $1400 (see Charles Scribner's Sons to Mary Day Lanier, May 31, 1899) ; and six shorter pieces of prose brought in an additional $654 (" Sketches of India " $300, " The Story of a Proverb " I $24, II $25, " The Orchestra of Today " $80, " The New South $200, " Lanier Genealogy " I $25). What further pay he may have received for short prose pieces was hardly more than enough to balance the deficit of $430.27 incurred in publishing *The Science of English Verse* (see note 2, Letters of 1881). To these may be added his salary in the Peabody Orchestra, which did not average more than $300 for the six years of his active connection; $100 which he was paid for the Bird Lectures (letter of Mar. 10, 1878; the Peabody Lectures the following year did not pay expenses—see letter of Jan. 5, 1879) ; a probable $1200 from his teaching in private schools, 1878-1880 (letter of Sept. 25, 1879) ; and $2000 from his Johns Hopkins salary, 1879-1881. Yet the grand total of all his desperate efforts to earn money amounted to only about $1000 a year, a little more than half of his actual expenditures, and much of this came only towards the end. This accounting explains much of the financial turmoil with which the letters are filled—the frantic borrowings from friends, efforts to sell his wedding silver and his flutes, mortification over his repeated calls on his family, and worrying over his inability to repay advances for writing projects that did not materialize. It also explains why he eagerly accepted the economic relief offered by lecturing and book-making in the last years, even though it very nearly put an end to his composition of poetry.

[169] Letter of June 15, 1880, note 45; and May 30, 1880. For the following sentence see letter of Aug. 10, 1880.

his health and brought on the persistent fever that prostrated him in the summer of 1880. To the end his letters are filled wtih protests against the cruel necessity of lecturing and writing for bread and with recurrent expressions of faith that he will regain his strength and live to compose many another poem.[170] In the midst of illness and the exhaustion of preparing more books and lectures came the final onset of creative energy that produced "Sunrise" and a handful of songs of the marshes. For the rest there are only scraps and fragments and uncompleted plans. The printer's copy of "Clover and Other Poems," abandoned when the forlorn hope to sell it for cash failed, and the scribbled outlines for enough poems to fill three more volumes survive as pathetic testimonials to a shattered career.

Lanier died with more than half of his poems still unpublished, including some of his very best, and with only one small volume gathered from his fugitive magazine printings to present him to his public.[171] It is from the reviews of the posthumous collection, *Poems* (1884), therefore, that the estimate of his poetry by his contemporaries must be derived. Some twenty of them have been found, of sufficient variety and distribution to furnish a cross-section of his reputation at this time.[172] The notices were on the whole full and quite favorable,

[170] See letters of July 31, Aug. 10, Oct. 30, Nov. 19, Dec. 6, 13, 1880; and Feb. 12, Mar. 7, 1881.

[171] Only 71 of his poems had been printed during his lifetime, and at least a third of these were in obscure periodicals. For the ten in the Lippincott *Poems* (1877) see note 91, above. The posthumous *Poems* (1884, *et seq.*) included all of his best. (See p. lxxviii, below.) A note that appeared in *Scribner's* XXII, 786 (Sept., 1881), just before his death, indicates the esteem in which he was held even before his work was known in collected form: "Sidney Lanier is a rare genius. No finer nature than his has America produced. His work is not popular, nor is it likely to become so, for his mind is of an unusual cast and his work is of an exceptional character. . . . The world of American letters will unite with us in the hope that the delicacy of his health will not interfere with the full unfolding and expression of his power." But this probably appeared too late for Lanier's eyes, since he died on September 7.

[172] Four are from New England (that in the *Literary News* being a reprint from the Boston *Advertiser*), four from New York, three from Philadelphia, scattered ones from Chicago, Louisville, Minneapolis, and Canada, and four from England (the last named coming somewhat later, after publication of the English edition of Lanier's *Poems*.) Newspapers, weeklies, monthlies, and quarterlies represent varying levels of critical ability; only three were by critics predisposed to be favorable to Lanier. Seventeen of these are listed in the bibliography, VI, 411. The others, all from London, are as follows: *Academy*, LVIII, 147-148 (Feb. 11, 1900), by Richard Le Gallienne; *Quarto* (1896), pp. 15-27, by W. G. Horder; and *Times*, reprinted in an unidentified clipping dated Aug. 18, 1906 (Charles D. Lanier Collection). I have also searched without success *Harper's* and *Century* (successor to *Scribner's*), the two other principal American magazines of the period.

with the keynote struck by the appreciative "Memorial" written by William Hayes Ward. The heroic struggle of Lanier's life, his high moral purpose, and the nobility of his character won the sympathy of almost every reviewer, so that some, such as the Boston *Advertiser,* were even led to declare that his life was greater than his poems, since he had not time to achieve mastery over his material. This was usually emphasized by those whose criticism was least favorable. The *Atlantic Monthly* found in the poems little more than the promise of one who, under more propitious circumstances, "would have given some noble melodies." The *New Englander* and the *Literary World,* though granting him lofty ideals and the true poetic temperament, found that his work was "fragmentary, hindered, almost rudimentary," and though his theories were original the poems themselves were labored, obscure, and lacking in spontaneity. Even *Lippincott's,* his first sponsor, though lamenting that he had just begun to "unfold his own beautiful dreams," said with some asperity: "To the last he was still haunted and waylaid by ecstatic fancies . . . The penetrative vision of the greatest poets he had not attained to." [173] But in general it was the New England magazines who stinted their praise and refused to rank Lanier with "the first princes of American song," naming over with pride their native sons.

Among the favorable reviews there was considerable unaminity in the opinion that the virtues of Lanier's poetry came from its fusion with music, and considerable speculation that his theories as expressed in *The Science of English Verse* had exerted a "radical" and "profoundly beneficial" influence on his practice.[174] As a consequence, much was made of his technical skill, in which he was pronounced second only to Tennyson, Swinburne trailing behind them both because his "flow of rhythmic words" though similar was artificial. And the praise was largely concentrated on those poems most notable for their musical quality. Of the shorter lyrics "Song of the Chattahoochee" shared equally with the far superior "Ballad of the Trees and the Master," and of the longer ones "The Symphony" with the more genuinely imaginative "Corn." With very few exceptions, however, the hymns of the marshes were declared to be his finest, usually with emphasis on their relationship to the author's musical theory of poetry.

---

[173] The most unfavorable review, in the Chicago *Times,* which declared that Lanier was "one of those misguided people who mistake the capacity to feel poetry for the capacity to express it in words," is too poor a piece of criticism for serious consideration.

[174] *St. John Globe*; see also *Evening Bulletin, Dial, Independent, Methodist Quarterly Review,* and *Saturday Union.* The most eulogistic treatment of Lanier's poems on this basis was in the Minneapolis *Tribune,* but the praise is too indiscriminate to be of any value.

For example, Richard Le Gallienne declared that it was in "The Marshes of Glynn" and "Sunrise" alone that Lanier had succeeded in his high poetic ambition:

In the other poems you see . . . the impassioned observation of nature, the Donne-like "metaphysical" fancy, the religious and somewhat mystic elevation of feeling expressed often in terms of a deep imaginative understanding of modern scientific conceptions; in fact, you find all save the important quality of that ecstasy which in the "Hymns" fuses all into one splendid flame . . .

This ecstasy was the same trance-like state produced in him by music, the critic said, and this "apparently 'loose,' Atlantic-roller metre" was the result of conscious experiments to prove his prosodical theory.[175] If the palm was awarded to any one poem, it was to "Sunrise." Perhaps the greatest triumph was that Lanier's most persistent critic, the *Nation,* was at last won over by this volume, which it found to be of "absorbing interest" and with real proof of promise in that "his latest poems are his best," "Sunrise" being unequalled in its way in all of American literature:

It is especially worth study by the young followers of Whitman, because it seems to be constructed on Whitman's methods; yet what a difference! In affluence, in breadth of handling it goes far beyond Whitman; while, instead of bald and formless iteration, it is everywhere suffused with music as with light; every stanza chants itself, instead of presenting a prosaic huddle of long lines.[176]

More even than by the praise, Lanier would have felt his long struggle rewarded by the widespread acclaim of originality. The *Dial* found in him "a new and rare poetic force . . . of unsuspected power"; the *St. John Globe* "a marvellous wealth of new rhythmical effects, sometimes odd, but for the most part of startling loveliness." The *Independent* declared that this individuality, "so marked that it may

---

[175] London *Academy.* The other British reviewers were not inclined to put the marsh hymns first, but singled out for praise "My Two Springs," "The Revenge of Hamish," "The Harlequin of Dreams," and other poems largely overlooked by the Americans. In spite of scattering comments, however, most of the discussion was confined to about a dozen poems; in addition to those named above the favorites were "A Song of the Future," "Evening Song," "The Stirrup-Cup," and "Tampa Robins"—only one critic naming "Opposition" as among the best.

[176] Of course this might have been a different reviewer from the one who had attacked almost everything Lanier wrote from "Corn" through *The Science of English Verse* (see especially II, xxvii ff.). But the reiteration on this occasion that his "intellectual" theories of prosody were his chief error and responsible for his lack of simplicity suggests that it was the same critic, converted by the later poems.

be at first mistaken for mannerism," was responsible for the slow growth of his reputation; and the *Critic* and the London *Quarto* agreed that his "exceptional originality" made his work as a whole "so entirely unlike the poems of the day, that one has no standard to judge them by." In spite of this, many attempted a final estimate by making comparisons. Among the critics at home one said he was the best southern poet since Poe, another that he was second only to Poe and Emerson on the American Parnassus, a third that he belonged among the first three or four poets of the century on both sides of the Atlantic.[177] Curiously enough the highest rank was assigned to Lanier by the English reviewers. Surveying the post-bellum poets, the London *Times* found him the most considerable of them all, and went further to say: "He remains the most fearless and passionate, the widest in range, the greatest master of melody of any of the American poets." [178] The *Spectator* was even more enthusiastic, contrasting his "vigorous imagination and depth of passion" with the "refinement and fancy" that had chiefly distinguished American poetry in the past and declaring that, though he was cut down in his prime,

As it is, . . . there is more of genius in this volume than in all Poe's poems, or all Longfellow's, or all Lowell's (the humorous poems excepted) . . . Lanier [is] an original poet,—more original, we think, than the United States has ever yet produced, more original than any poet whom England has produced during the last thirty years at least.[179]

To this may be added, in conclusion, the prophecy made in the American *Nation* at about the same time:

To some minds he appears obscure; to some he seems like a poet of another age discoursing on modern themes; to others—and this number is growing—he seems a poet of the future, the herald of better things to come from the pens of those who are inspired by the ideas that

[177] *Critic, St. John Globe, Evening Bulletin,* respectively. The *Saturday Union,* saying that we no longer need to look solely to New England for our authors, pronounced Lanier "the most spiritual of American poets," deserving to be placed in "the first ranks"; and that, though he took "startling liberties" with language, he had succeeded in inventing his own, like other "masters of style."

[178] The *Times* (as well as the *Spectator*) found him a pleasant relief from the "Massachusetts chill and fastidiousness," and with a smaller proportion of fudge to genius than in Poe. Joaquin Miller lacked his technical mastery, Harte and Taylor suffered from "artistic timidity," and Whitman from braggadocio and too much imitation of Emerson. Lanier had "lived for poetry" as no other American poet had done.

[179] This was in 1890. The *Quarto,* six years later, confirmed this judgment. The reference in the following sentence is to the *Nation,* XLVII, 118 (Feb. 9, 1888).

animated him . . . It is nearly seven years since he died, and his fame appears to be constantly increasing.

These are, of course, only the personal opinions of a score of critics, but they seem a representative measure of the blame and praise meted out to Lanier's poetry by his contemporaries.[180] Though the tides of taste have changed somewhat in the half-century that has followed, the present edition, it is hoped, will facilitate the critic in arriving at a more balanced final estimate.

The Text

Lanier's canon, as now established, includes 164 poems. Of these, 100 were collected in *Poems* (1884 *et seq.*) edited by his wife, 20 were previously uncollected, and 44 unpublished.[181] In the present

[180] The comments of contemporary poets on Lanier are interesting but fragmentary and of uncertain value. Tennyson is reported to have said that he was "worth more than a hundred Longfellows," and Swinburne that he was "one of the only two real poets yet produced in America"—the other being Poe (unidentified clipping, reprinting a notice from the Louisville *Courier-Journal*, in the Clifford A. Lanier Collection, Johns Hopkins University; see also note 14, Letters of 1876). On the American side, Longfellow praised "The Marshes of Glynn" and Holmes *The Science of English Verse*; Lowell made the rather strange judgment that he had "a rare gift for the happy word," and Whitman gave voice to several contradictory opinions, the most favorable of which was: "He had genius—a delicate, clairvoyant genius: but his over-tuning of the ear, this extreme deference paid to oral nicety, reduced the majesty, the solid worth, of his rhythms" (see notes 7 and 74, Letters of 1879, 1880; Lowell's letter to Gilman in *The Forty-sixth Birthday of Sidney Lanier*, Baltimore, 1888; and Horace Traubel, *With Walt Whitman in Camden*, New York, 1906, III, 207-209). Of all his fellow poets only two made any detailed comments on Lanier. Bayard Taylor's last extended criticism, his review of the 1877 volume (see p. liii, above), though friendly and appreciative, treated him as only a promising younger poet; E. C. Stedman damned him with two pages of faint praise in a chapter devoted to minor figures in his *Poets of America*, Boston, 1885, pp. 449-451—a book which devoted a full chapter to Taylor.

[181] Following Lanier's practice in publication, the two parts of "The Tournament" and the several "Songs for 'The Jacquerie'" have been treated separately, the two parts of "Rose-Morals" as one; further, the German version of "To Nannette Falk-Auerbach" has been relegated to the notes. All finished verses in standard form have been treated as poems, including three transferred from the printed volume of *Poem Outlines* (specified in the notes); all fragments and possible experiments in *vers libre* have been placed with the "poem outlines" (pp. 235 ff.), including "Control" which was formerly printed in *Poems*. The only volume published during Lanier's lifetime, by Lippincott in 1877, contained but 10 poems. The 1884 edition contained 91 poems; seven more were added in 1891 ("A Sunrise Song," "On a Palmetto," "Struggle," "Control," "To Captain James DeWitt Hankins," "Between Dawn and Sunrise," and "Thou and I"); two more in 1916 ("To Our Hills" and "Laughter in the Senate").

edition his poems are divided into four groups, and in each they are arranged chronologically according to date of composition in order to show his development as a poet. The first, and main, group includes those poems that were selected by Lanier himself for publication. All of them appeared in print during his lifetime, with the exception of a few which he tried in vain to get published or which he intended to include in one of the projected volumes left at his death (as indicated in the notes). The second group consists of those poems which for one reason or another Lanier had not planned to publish; they were printed posthumously or survive only in unrevised manuscripts. The third is a small group of poems written in collaboration with his brother Clifford. Last comes a group of juvenile poems, separated from the preceding because of their inferior worth. Though the chronological arrangement places a few relatively unimportant poems at the beginning of the volume, the division into groups transfers the majority of his early and lesser efforts to the end.[182]

This volume, first issued on Nov. 25, 1884, has been reprinted more than twenty-five times. All of these reprintings have not been collated line by line; but those poems whose texts were in any way unusual have been checked and the correction of errors by Mary Day Lanier pointed out in the notes. The English editions of Lanier's *Poems*—by Gay & Bird, 1892, and by A. F. Bird, 1906—are presumably reprints of the American editions. The latter was printed in New York, apparently from the Scribner plates (copy in the Lanier Room, Johns Hopkins University; no copy of the former has been located).

At the end of each poem in the present edition the date of composition is given in roman type, the date of first publication in italic. In the bibliography (VI, 381-385) may be found a chronological list of first printings of separate poems, those previously uncollected being marked by an asterisk (omitted by error from " A Weather-Vane," " A Song," and " Fame "); this is followed by an alphabetical list of those previously unpublished (in which " Fame " is incorrectly included).

[182] These are followed by an appendix containing a selection of surviving outlines for poems, many of which are now first published; formal collation of all known variants for a group of 42 poems; a section of notes, with full bibliographical data and annotative commentary for each poem; and an index of titles and first lines.

Four poems previously ascribed to Lanier have been excluded from the present edition. " Now bends the lily like a nun at prayer " is proved definitely by the copy in Lanier's Ledger, p. 32, to have been written by his brother Clifford; " To Lucie " has been identified as by Frances Litchfield Turnbull (see Mary Day Lanier's note in the copy of Kate P. Minor's *From Dixie*, 1893, preserved in the Lanier Room) ; " Sea-Foam " has to recommend it only a slight resemblance to Lanier's style and the fact that it appeared anonymously in the *Round Table* two months after a poem known to be by Lanier was similarly published there (these three are listed by Starke, p. 458, who prints the text of the last named on pp. 79-80). The fourth is an untitled sonnet that appeared without signature in the *Southern Literary Messenger* for May, 1862. It is reprinted by A. H. Starke, " An Uncollected Sonnet by Sidney Lanier," *American Literature*, VII, 460-463 (Jan., 1936) ; but the external evidence for Lanier's authorship is

The last revised version known to have been made by Lanier has been adopted as the basic text for each of his poems.[183] For the great majority, this text has been followed exactly. For a few poems in which the most authoritative text was a newspaper print or an unrevised manuscript, however, a small number of corrections in mechanics has been made in conformity with the editorial policy laid down in the General Preface. All corrections of misprints and regularization of punctuation, spelling, and capitalization are specified in the notes. The aim has been less to achieve over-all uniformity than a reasonable mechanical consistency within the given poem, with due care not to alter even the slightest shade of meaning. Further, to modernize the typography, a few changes have been made in the printing style, such as the elimination of rules to indicate divisions in the longer poems and of roman numerals for stanzas (except in the sonnet sequences); and a standard system of indention has been adopted, based upon rhyme-scheme, line-length, and stanzaic pattern.[184] For a very few poems, in order to make the significance more immediately clear, titles or subtitles have been supplied in brackets.

only circumstantial, and in quality it is considerably more mature than his known poems of this period.

[183] Four exceptions have been made to this rule. "Marsh Song—At Sunset," "On a Palmetto," and "Thou and I" have survived only in posthumous prints. For one poem, "The Marshes of Glynn," the version in *Poems* (1884) has been preferred to those printed during his lifetime, no MS being known, for reasons detailed in the notes (see p. 358). Mary Day Lanier certainly knew more about her husband's work than anyone else, and for one without training her editing was painstaking and faithful according to the standards of that day. (Her letter to Scribner, Feb. 4, 1884—MS, Charles Scribner's Sons—makes it clear that W. H. Ward's part in the volume was confined to writing the "Memorial.") Hence *Poems* (1884) can be relied on as furnishing fair texts for these few poems. For all the rest, more authoritative texts have been found; the reasons for adoption are given in each of the notes, and the differences in wording between the basic text and all others are pointed out there and in the textual variants.

[184] Lanier's final policy in all this is demonstrated in a partially corrected copy of *Poems* (1877) and in the surviving printer's copy of "Clover and Other Poems," prepared by him for publication in May, 1879, which furnishes the basic text for twenty-odd poems. (The latter is in the Henry W. Lanier Collection, the former in that of Charles D. Lanier. On the accuracy of the text of the 1877 volume see letters of Jan. 20, 1878; June 17, 1879, and Aug. 26, 1880.)

POEMS

POEMS.

BY

SIDNEY LANIER.

PHILADELPHIA
J. B. LIPPINCOTT & CO.
LONDON:
16 SOUTHAMPTON ST., COVENT GARDEN.
1877

On Reading of One Who Drowned Herself
in a Certain Lake, for Love

Thou rippleless, dim lake, enspelled
   By the basilisk eyes of stars, at night:
With thy lilies calm as sweet thoughts, upheld
   On thy bosom's waveless chrysolite;

Red under Sunsets, in Dawns silver-misted;
Pure as the troths on thy fair banks trysted:
Thou smile to the loved, thou grave to the loveless
Driven from the world so cold and moveless:—

Float the Unloved to the lilies, O Lake,
And cover the Loveless with lilies, Good Lake:
No flowers on land (in life!) had she:
Let her have flowers (in death!), in thee.

1861   *1945*

Spring Greeting

All faintly through my soul, to-day,
As from a bell that, far away,
Is tinkled by some frolic fay,
   Floateth a lovely chiming.
Thou magic-bell, to many a fell,
And many a winter-saddened dell,
Thy tongue a tale of spring doth tell,
   Too passionate-sweet for rhyming!

Chime out, thou little Song-of-Spring,
Chime in the blue skies, ravishing;
Thy Song-of-Life a joy doth bring,
   That's sweet, albeit fleeting.
Float on the spring-winds to my home,
And when thou to a rose shalt come
That hath begun to show her bloom,
   Tell her, I send her greeting!

1864   *1866*

5

The Tournament: Joust First

Being the Right Pleasant Joust betwixt Heart and Brain

Bright shone the lists, blue bent the skies,
And the knights still hurried amain
To the tournament under the ladies' eyes,
Where the Jousters were Heart and Brain.

Flourished the trumpets: entered Heart,
A youth in crimson and gold.
Flourished again: Brain stood apart,
Steel-armored, dark, and cold.

Heart's palfrey caracoled gayly round,
Heart tra-li-ra'd merrily;
But Brain sat still, with never a sound,
So cynical-calm was he.

Heart's helmet-crest bore favors three
From his ladye's white hand caught;
While Brain wore a plumeless casque; not he
Or favor gave or sought.

The herald blew; Heart shot a glance
To find his ladye's eye,
But Brain gazed straight ahead his lance
To aim more faithfully.

They charged, they struck; both fell, both bled.
Brain rose again, ungloved.
Heart, dying, smiled and faintly said,
" My love to my beloved! "

The Tournament: Joust Second

Being the Rare Joust of Love and Hate

A-many sweet eyes wept and wept,
A-many bosoms heaved again,
A-many dainty dead hopes slept
With yonder Heart-knight prone o' the plain.

Yet stars will burn through any mists,
　　And the ladies' eyes through rains of fate,
Still beamed upon the bloody lists
　　And lit the joust of Love and Hate.

O strange! or ere a trumpet blew,
　　Or ere a challenge-word was given,
A knight leapt down i' the lists; none knew
　　Whether he sprang from earth or heaven.

His cheek was soft as a lily-bud,
　　His grey eyes calmed his youth's alarm;
Nor helm nor hauberk nor even a hood
　　Had he to shield his life from harm.

No falchion from his baldric swung,
　　He wore a white rose in its place.
No dagger at his girdle hung,
　　But only an olive-branch, for grace.

And " Come, thou poor mistaken knight,"
　　Cried Love, standing unarmèd there,
" Come on, God pity thee!—I fight
　　Sans sword, sans shield; yet, Hate, beware! "

Spurred furious Hate; he foamed at mouth,
　　His breath was hot upon the air,
His breath scorched souls, as a dry drought
　　Withers green trees and burns them bare.

Straight drives he at his enemy,
　　His hairy hands grip lance in rest,
His lance it gleams full bitterly,
　　God!—gleams, true-point, on Love's bare breast!

Love's grey eyes glow with a heaven-heat,
　　Love lifts his hand in a saintly prayer;
Look! Hate hath fallen at his feet!
　　Look! Hate hath vanished in the air!

Then all the throng looked kind on all;
　　Eyes yearned, lips kissed, dumb souls were freed;
Two magic maids' hands lifted a pall
　　And the dead knight, Heart, sprang on his steed.

Then Love cried, " Break me his lance, each knight!
Ye shall fight for blood-athirst Fame no more! "
And the knights all doffed their mailèd might
And dealt out dole on dole to the poor.

Then dove-flights sanctified the plain,
And hawk and sparrow shared a nest.
And the great sea opened and swallowed Pain,
And out of this water-grave floated Rest!

1865, 1867   *1867*

To J. L.

A kind war-wave dashed thee and me together;
So we have drifted to the shores of peace,
A wintry shore, attained in wintry weather.
    Must here our loving cease?

Ah, was not ancient Love born of the ocean?
And is not *our* Love a tempest child
That rose from out the seething war's commotion
    And blessed it, as she smiled?

The buffets of this storm I have forgiven,
And all its drunken, rude barbarity,
Aye, I have begged a blessing on't from heaven
    Because it brought me thee!

My soul doth utterly refuse to render
Back to the waters of forgetfulness
This sister-love of thine, that grew more tender
    The greater my distress.

Shall, then, our wave-born love by waves be swallowed,
And foam to foam, as dust to dust, return?
Not so! I never cease to hold it hallowed,
    Nor cease for thee to yearn.

Never cease we, while on this side we wander,
To go like children singing hand in hand,
Until our Father smiles, and calls us yonder
    Into the home-like land.

1865   *1866*

Little Ella

Her bright soul burn'd in her fathomless eye,
Like a silver star in the morning sky,
And my heart all tired of life's lone night
Like a bird sang songs to morning-light.

As soft as the passion of flowers for dew,
As wild as a wave when tempests woo,
As high as a lark's flight up the blue,
As fair and pure and sweet as you,
    As you, as you, as you.

O, exquisite rare, O, past compare
Was that young star-soul shining there,
In an eye that gleam'd dark-bright like dawn,
When dews first sparkle on the lawn.

1866   *1868*

A Birthday Song. To S. G.

For ever wave, for ever float and shine
Before my yearning eyes, oh! dream of mine
Wherein I dreamed that time was like a vine,

A creeping rose, that clomb a height of dread
Out of the sea of Birth, all filled with dead,
Up to the brilliant cloud of Death o'erhead.

This vine bore many blossoms, which were years.
Their petals, red with joy, or bleached by tears,
Waved to and fro i' the winds of hopes and fears.

Here all men clung, each hanging by his spray.
Anon, one dropped; his neighbor 'gan to pray;
And so they clung and dropped and prayed, alway.

But I did mark one lately-opened bloom,
Wherefrom arose a visible perfume
That wrapped me in a cloud of dainty gloom,

And rose—an odor by a spirit haunted—
And drew me upward with a speed enchanted,
Swift floating, by wild sea or sky undaunted,

Straight through the cloud of death, where men are free.
I gained a height, and stayed and bent my knee.
Then glowed my cloud, and broke and unveiled thee.

" O flower-born and flower-souled! " I said,
" Be the year-bloom that breathed thee ever red,
Nor wither, yellow, down among the dead.

" May all that cling to sprays of time, like me,
Be sweetly wafted over sky and sea
By rose-breaths shrining maidens like to thee! "

Then while we sat upon the height afar
Came twilight, like a lover late from war,
With soft winds fluting to his evening star.

And the shy stars grew bold and scattered gold,
And chanting voices ancient secrets told,
And an acclaim of angels earthward rolled.

1866   *1867*

To Captain James DeWitt Hankins

If Birth be bitterer than Death, we know
 That Heaven is Life and Death New-birth.
Who's here that hath no secret woe?
 Who's here that dreams not the New Earth?

Dear Friend, forgive a wild lament
 Insanely following thy flight.
I would not cumber thine ascent
 Nor drag thee back into the Night;

But the great sea-winds sigh with me,
 The fair-faced stars seem wrinkle-old,
And I would that I might lie with thee
 There in the grave so cold, so cold.

Grave-walls are thick, I cannot see thee,
And the round skies are far and steep.
A-wild to quaff some cup of Lethe
Pain is proud and scorns to sleep.

My heart breaks, if it cling about thee,
And still breaks, if far from thine.
O drear, drear death,—to live without thee;
O sad life,—to keep thee mine!

Do thou go borrow some flesh-eye
And read the words I write to thee.
Then wait at the Gate, till we, too, die,
O Friend, O Brother, O Mystery!

1866   *1866?, 1886*

Barnacles

My soul is sailing through the sea,
But the Past is heavy and hindereth me.
The Past hath crusted cumbrous shells
That hold the flesh of cold sea-mells
    About my soul.
The huge waves wash, the high waves roll,
Each barnacle clingeth and worketh dole
    And hindereth me from sailing.

Old Past, let go, and drop i' the sea
Till fathomless water cover thee!
For I am living, but thou art dead;
Thou drawest back, I strive ahead
    The day to find.
Thy shells unbind! Night comes behind,
I needs must hurry with the wind
    And trim me best for sailing!

1867   *1867*

A Song of Eternity in Time

Once, at night, in the manor wood
My Love and I long silent stood,
Amazed that any heavens could
Decree to part us, bitterly repining.
My Love, in aimless love and grief,
Reached forth and drew aside a leaf
That just above us played the thief
And stole our starlight that for us was shining.

A star that had remarked her pain
Shone straightway down that leafy lane,
And wrought his image, mirror-plain,
Within a tear that on her lash hung gleaming.
" Thus Time," I cried, " is but a tear
Some one hath wept 'twixt hope and fear,
Yet in his little lucent sphere
Our star of stars, Eternity, is beaming."

1867   *1870*

In the Foam

Life swelleth in a whitening wave
    And dasheth thee and me apart.
I sweep out seaward!—be thou brave
    And reach the shore, sweetheart.

Beat back the backward-thrusting sea,
    Thy round white arm his blows may thwart.
Christ buffet the strong surge with thee
    'Till thou'rt ashore, sweetheart!

Ah! now thy face groweth dim apace,
    Seemeth of yon white foam a part.
Canst hear me through the water-bass,
    Cry, " To the shore, sweetheart? "

Now Christ thee soothe upon the shore,
   My lissome-armed sea-Britomart.
I sweep out seaward, nevermore
   To find the shore, sweetheart.

1867   *1868*

Tyranny

Spring-germs, spring-germs,
I charge you by your life, go back to death.
This glebe is sick, this wind is foul of breath.
   Stay: feed the worms.

Oh! every clod
Is faint, and falters from the war of growth
And crumbles in a dreary dust of sloth,
   Unploughed, untrod.

What need, what need,
To hide with flowers the curse upon the hills,
Or sanctify the banks of sluggish rills
   Where vapors breed?

And—if needs must—
Advance, O Summer-heats! upon the land,
And bake the bloody mould to shards and sand
   And barren dust.

Before your birth,
Burn up, O Roses! in your natal flame.
Good Violets, sweet Violets, hide shame
   Below the earth.

Ye silent Mills,
Reject the bitter kindness of the moss.
O Farms! protest if any tree emboss
   The barren hills.

Young Trade is dead,
And swart Work sullen sits in the hillside fern
And folds his arms that find no bread to earn,
   And bows his head.

Spring-germs, spring-germs,
Albeit the towns have left you place to play,
I charge you, sport not. Winter owns to-day,
   Stay: feed the worms.

1868   *1868*

Laughter in the Senate

In the South lies a lonesome, hungry Land:
He huddles his rags with a cripple's hand;
He mutters, prone on the barren sand,
   What time his heart is breaking.

He lifts his bare head from the ground;
He listens through the gloom around:
The winds have brought him a strange sound
   Of distant merrymaking.

Comes now the Peace, so long delayed?
Is it the cheerful voice of Aid?
Begins the time, his heart has prayed,
   When men may reap and sow?

Ah, God! Back to the cold earth's breast!
The sages chuckle o'er their jest;
Must they, to give a people rest,
   Their dainty wit forego?

The tyrants sit in a stately hall;
They jibe at a wretched people's fall;
The tyrants forget how fresh is the pall
   Over their dead and ours.

Look how the senators ape the clown,
And don the motley and hide the gown,
But yonder a fast-rising frown
   On the people's forehead lowers.

1868   *1868*

The Raven Days

Our hearths are gone out, and our hearts are broken,
    And but the ghosts of homes to us remain,
And ghostly eyes and hollow sighs give token
    From friend to friend of an unspoken pain.

O, Raven Days, dark Raven Days of sorrow,
    Bring to us, in your whetted ivory beaks,
Some sign out of the far land of To-morrow,
    Some strip of sea-green dawn, some orange streaks.

Ye float in dusky files, forever croaking—
    Ye chill our manhood with your dreary shade.
Pale, in the dark, not even God invoking,
    We lie in chains, too weak to be afraid.

O Raven Days, dark Raven Days of sorrow,
    Will ever any warm light come again?
Will ever the lit mountains of To-morrow
    Begin to gleam across the mournful plain?

1868   *1868*

The Ship of Earth

Thou Ship of Earth, with Death, and Birth, and Life, and
        Sex aboard,
    And fires of Desires burning hotly in the hold,
I fear thee, O! I fear thee, for I hear the tongue and sword
    At battle on the deck, and the wild mutineers are bold!

The dewdrop morn may fall from off the petal of the sky,
    But all the deck is wet with blood and stains the crystal red.
A pilot, GOD, a pilot! for the helm is left awry,
    And the best sailors in the ship lie there among the dead!

1868   *1868*

Life and Song

If life were caught by a clarionet,
    And a wild heart, throbbing in the reed,
Should thrill its joy and trill its fret
    And utter its heart in every deed,

Then would this breathing clarionet
    Type what the poet fain would be;
For none o' the singers ever yet
    Has wholly lived his minstrelsy,

Or clearly sung his true, true thought,
    Or utterly bodied forth his life,
Or out of Life and Song has wrought
    The perfect one of man and wife;

Or lived and sung, that Life and Song
    Might each express the other's all,
Careless if life or art were long
    Since both were one, to stand or fall:

So that the wonder struck the crowd,
    Who shouted it about the land:
His song was only living aloud,
    His work a singing with his hand!

1868   *1868*

Resurrection

Sometimes, in morning sunlights by the river,
    Where in the early fall long grasses wave,
Light winds from over the moorland sink and shiver
    And sigh as if just blown across a grave.

And then I pause and listen to this sighing,
    And look with strange eyes on the well-known stream,
And hear wild birth-cries uttered by the dying,
    And know men waking who appear to dream.

Then from the water-lilies there uprises
  The vast still face of all the life I know,
Changed now, and full of wonders and surprises,
  With fire in eyes that once were glazed with snow.

Smooth are the brows old Pain had erewhile wrinkled,
  And peace and strength about the calm lips dwell.
Clean of the ashes that repentance sprinkled,
  The meek head poises like a flower-bell.

All ancient scars of wanton wars have vanished;
  And what blue bruises grappling Sense had left,
And sad remains of redder stains, are banished,
  And the dim blotch of heart-committed theft.

Oh! vast still vision of transfigured features,
  Unvisited by secret crimes and dooms,
Remain, remain above yon water-creatures,
  Stand, shine above yon water-lily blooms.

For eighteen centuries ripple down the river,
  And windy times the stalks of empires wave;
Let the winds come from the moor and sigh and shiver.
  Fain, fain am I, O CHRIST, to pass the grave!

1868   *1868*

The Golden Wedding of Sterling and Sarah Lanier

A rainbow span of fifty years,
Painted upon a cloud of tears,
In blue for hopes and red for fears,
  Finds end in a golden hour to-day.
Ah, *you* to our childhood the legend told,
" At the end of the rainbow lies the gold,"
And now in our thrilling hearts we hold
  The gold that never will pass away.

Gold crushed from the quartz of a crystal life,
Gold hammered with blows of human strife,
Gold burnt in the love of man and wife,
  Till it is pure as the very flame:

Gold that the miser will not have,
Gold that is good beyond the grave,
Gold that the patient and the brave
    Amass, neglecting praise and blame.

O golden hour that caps the time
Since, heart to heart like rhyme to rhyme,
You stood and listened to the chime
    Of inner bells by spirits rung,
That tinkled many a secret sweet
Concerning how two souls should meet,
And whispered of Time's flying feet
    With a most piquant silver tongue.

O golden day,—a golden crown
For the kingly heads that bowed not down
To win a smile or 'scape a frown,
    Except the smile and frown of Heaven!
Dear heads, still dark with raven hair;
Dear hearts, still white in spite of care;
Dear eyes, still black and bright and fair
    As any eyes to mortals given!

Old parents of a restless race,
You miss full many a bonny face
That would have smiled a filial grace
    Around your Golden Wedding wine.
But God is good and God is great.
His will be done, if soon or late.
Your dead stand happy in yon Gate
    And call you blessed while they shine.

So, drop the tear and dry the eyes.
Your rainbow glitters in the skies.
Here's golden wine: young, old, arise:
    With cups as full as our souls, we say:
" Two Hearts, that wrought with smiles through tears
This rainbow span of fifty years,
Behold how true, true love appears
    True gold for your Golden Wedding day! "

1868   *1868*

Betrayal

The sun has kissed the violet sea,
And burned the violet to a rose.
O Sea, O Sea, mightst thou but be
Mere violets still? Who knows? who knows?
Well hides the violet in the wood:
The dead leaf wrinkles her a hood,
And winter's ill is violet's good;
But the bold glory of the rose,
It quickly comes and quickly goes—
Red petals whirling in white snows,
Ah me!

The sun has burnt the rose-red sea:
The rose is turned to ashes gray.
O Sea, O Sea, mightst thou but be
The violet thou hast been to-day!
The sun is brave, the sun is bright,
The sun is lord of love and light;
But after him it cometh night.
Dim anguish of the lonesome dark!—
Once a girl's body, stiff and stark,
Was laid in a tomb without a mark,
Ah me!

1868-1871?   *1875*

Nirvâna

Through seas of Dreams and seas of Phantasies,
Through seas of Solitudes and Vacancies,
And through my Self, the deepest of the seas,
I strive to thee, Nirvâna.

O, long ago the billow-flow of Sense,
Aroused by Passion's windy vehemence,
Upbore me out of depths to heights intense,
But not to thee, Nirvâna.

By waves swept on, I learned to ride the waves;
I served my masters till I made them slaves;
I baffled Death by hiding in his graves,
    His watery graves, Nirvâna.

And once I clomb a mountain's stony crown,
And stood, and smiled no smile and frowned no frown,
Nor ate, nor drank, nor slept, nor faltered down,
    Five days and nights, Nirvâna.

Sunrise and noon, and sunset and strange night,
And shadow of large clouds and faint starlight,
And lonesome Terror stalking round the height,
    I minded not, Nirvâna.

The silence ground my soul keen like a spear;
My bare thought, whetted as a sword, cut sheer
Through time and life, and flesh and death, to clear
    My way unto Nirvâna.

I slew bodies of old ethnic Hates
That stirred long race-wars betwixt states and states;
I stood and scorned these foolish dead debates,
    Calmly, calmly, Nirvâna.

I smote away the filmy base of Caste;
I thrust through antique blood, and riches vast,
And all big claims of the pretentious Past
    That hindered my Nirvâna.

Then all fair types, of form, and sound, and hue,
Up-floated round my sense and charmed anew;
I waved them back into the void blue:
    I love them not, Nirvâna.

And all outrageous ugliness of time,
Excess, and Blasphemy, and squinting Crime,
Beset me; but I kept my calm sublime:
    I hate them not, Nirvâna.

High on the topmost thrilling of the surge
I saw, afar, two hosts to battle urge:
The widows of the victors sang a dirge,
    But I wept not, Nirvâna.

I saw two lovers sitting on a star;
He kissed her lip, she kissed his battle-scar;
They quarrelled soon, and went two ways afar:
    O Life! I laughed, Nirvâna.

And never a king but had some king above,
And never a law to right the wrongs of Love,
And ever a fangèd snake beneath a dove,
    Saw I on earth, Nirvâna.

But I, with kingship over kings, am free;
I love not, hate not: right and wrong agree;
And fangs of snakes and lures of doves to me
    Are vain, are vain, Nirvâna.

So by mine inner contemplation long,
By thoughts that need no speech nor oath nor song,
My spirit soars above the motley throng
    Of days and nights, Nirvâna.

O Suns, O Rains, O Day and Night, O Chance,
O Time besprent with seven-hued circumstance,
I float above ye all, into the trance
    That draws me nigh Nirvâna.

Gods of small worlds, ye little deities
Of humble heavens under my large skies,
And governor-spirits all, I rise, I rise,
    I rise into Nirvâna.

The storms of Self below me rage and die;
On the still bosom of mine ecstasy,
A Lotus on a lake of balm, I lie
    Forever in Nirvâna.

1869   *1870*

Thar's More in the Man Than
Thar Is in the Land

I knowed a man, which he lived in Jones,
Which Jones is a county of red hills and stones,
And he lived pretty much by gittin' of loans,
And his mules was nuthin' but skin and bones,
And his hogs was flat as his corn-bread pones,
And he had 'bout a thousand acres o' land.

This man—which his name it was also Jones—
He swore that he'd leave them old red hills and stones,
Fur he couldn't make nuthin' but yallerish cotton,
And little o' *that*, and his fences was rotten,
And what little corn he had, *hit* was boughten,
And dinged ef a livin' was in the land.

And the longer he swore the madder he got,
And he riz and he walked to the stable lot,
And he hollered to Tom to come thar and hitch,
Fur to emigrate somewhar whar land was rich,
And to quit rasin' cock-burrs, thistles and sich,
And a wastin' ther time on the cussed land.

So him and Tom they hitched up the mules,
Pertestin' that folks was mighty big fools
That 'ud stay in Georgy ther lifetime out,
Jest scratchin' a livin' when all of 'em mought
Git places in Texas whar cotton would sprout
By the time you could plant it in the land.

And he driv by a house whar a man named Brown
Was a livin', not fur from the edge o' town,
And he bantered Brown fur to buy his place,
And said that bein' as money was skace,
And bein' as sheriffs was hard to face,
Two dollars an acre would git the land.

They closed at a dollar and fifty cents,
And Jones he bought him a waggin and tents,
And loaded his corn, and his wimmin, and truck,
And moved to Texas, which it tuck
His entire pile, with the best of luck,
To git thar and git him a little land.

But Brown moved out on the old Jones farm,
And he rolled up his breeches and bared his arm,
And he picked all the rocks from off'n the groun',
And he rooted it up and he plowed it down,
Then he sowed his corn and his wheat in the land.

Five years glid by, and Brown, one day
(Which he'd got so fat that he wouldn't weigh),
Was a settin' down, sorter lazily,
To the bulliest dinner you ever see,
When one o' the children jumped on his knee
And says, " Yan's Jones, which you bought his land."

And thar was Jones, standin' out at the fence,
And he hadn't no waggin, nor mules, nor tents,
Fur he had left Texas afoot and cum
To Georgy to see if he couldn't git sum
Employment, and he was a lookin' as hum-
Ble as ef he had never owned any land.

But Brown he axed him in, and he sot
Him down to his vittles smokin' hot,
And when he had filled hisself and the floor
Brown looked at him sharp and riz and swore
That, " whether men's land was rich or poor
Thar was more in the *man* than thar was in the *land*."

1869-1871?   *1871*

Jones's Private Argument

That air same Jones which lived in Jones,
   He had this p'int about him;
He'd swear, with a hundred sighs and groans,
That farmers *must* stop gittin' loans,
   And git along without 'em;

That bankers, warehousemen and sich,
   Was fattenin' on the planter,
And Tennessee was rotten-rich
A raisin' meat and corn, all which
   Draw'd money to Atlanta.

And th' only thing (says Jones) to do
   Is, *eat no meat that's boughten,*
But tare up every I O U,
And plant ALL *corn, and swear for true*
   To quit a raisin' cotton!

Thus spouted Jones (whar folks could hear,
   At court and other gatherin's),
And thus kept spoutin' many a year,
Proclaimin' loudly far and near
   Sich fiddlesticks and blatherins.

But, one all-fired sweatin' day,
   It happened I was hoein'
My lower corn field, which it lay
Along the road that runs my way,
   Whar I can see what's goin'.

And after twelve o'clock had cum
   I felt a kinder faggin'
And laid myself un'neath a plum
To let my dinner settle some,
   When 'long cum Jones's waggin.

And Jones was settin' in it, *so*;
    A readin' of a paper.
His mules was goin' powerful slow,
Fur he had tied the lines into
    The staple of the scraper.

The mules. they stopped about a rod
    From me, and went to feedin'
'Longside the road upon the sod;
But Jones (which he had took a tod)
    Not knowin' kept a readin'.

And presently says Jones: " Hit's true;
    That Clisby's head is level.
Thar's *one* thing farmers all must do
To keep therselves from goin' tew
    Bankruptcy and the devil!

" More corn! More corn! *Must* plant less ground,
    And *mustn't* eat what's boughten!
Next year they'll do it; reas'nin' 's sound!
(And cotton will fetch 'bout a dollar a pound,
    Tharfore, *I'll* plant *all* cotton! ")

1870-1871?   *1871*

The Homestead

The State spread out her arms and said:
My Children, Hate to-day is dead,
And Love and Law, together wed,
    Sit on the hills to rule you.

I will that they with equal reign
Shall keep your weal, and clear the stain
Red war hath left on my domain,
    And strengthen you and school you.

Let Law have eye on work and trade
Lest wrong be sped and right delayed,
Or weakness faint and be afraid
    My power shall not uphold it.

Let Love go floating, fair and grand,
By every homestead in the land,
And clasp her sweet white-shining hand
      About it and enfold it.

Behold, by Love full long besought,
And by the woes of battle taught,
My hand a gracious work hath wrought
      To crown all honest labor.

I will, no man shall homeless be,
I will, no weeping wife shall flee
From shadow of her own roof-tree
      Forth driven by hard neighbor.

I know the large sweet sanctities
That grow in homes, and unto these
I add the might of my decrees
      To make the home-strength stronger;

To foster and confirm the place
Where Birth hath glory, Life hath grace
And Death hath smiles upon his face
      When Life hath grace no longer.

Build me my homesteads firmly then!
Hew me, from mountain-side and glen,
Stones that outlast the sons of men
      To latest generations.

And train me vine and wind me vines
About my homes in looping lines,
For symbols and for leafy signs
      Unto the homeless nations,

That, as the vines of other lands,
Trained round a home by Georgian hands,
With bloom and bounteous fruit expands
      In more than native glory.

So hearts that pine across the sea
May wind, with larger liberty,
About this Homestead of the Free
      That Georgia builds in story.

Bower my homesteads in great trees,
Whose trunks the lusty grasses seize
Like children reaching at the knees
    Of fathers, stalwart standing:

The baby-grasses, trees in small,
Catching tree-whispers as they fall,
And lisping back a baby call
    To the great leaves commanding.

Set me my homes like diamonds large
In the great grain-fields' golden marge,
That life's chief staff may have chief charge
    Of Life's most worthy treasure.

Aye gleam, my hills and fecund plains,
With wheat-spears and tall soldier-grains,
Whose serried stateliness constrains
    The hunger-tyrant's pleasure!

What tyrant wields so trenchant brand
That he may manfully withstand
The great grain-army's calm demand,
    Up the time-road advancing?

Lean Hunger starves with plenteous fright;
Want dies, death-stricken with delight;
And Crime slinks back into his night;
    Where Plenty rides proud prancing.

Spread, too, the pied exquisite glow
Of reddening lights from flesh-like snow,
Of fruits whose tense sweet veins o'er flow,
    With mellow nectars bursting.

Spread round my homes this richer hue
Of fruits that charm the yeoman's view,
And yield their juices cool as dew
    To yeomen's tongues hot-thirsting.

From my home-yards let cheery cries
Of homely cattle upward rise,
What time the cock salutes the skies
    With heartsome, bold good-morrow.

People my meadows with great kine,
Whose large eyes from the clover shine
With calm regard, in peace benign
    That has forgotten sorrow.

When, as the sunset-shadow falls,
The cow-boy chants his silver calls
That waver down long leafy walls
    The clover-vales enclosing;

And the sleek, generous-uddered file
Winds slowly past the home-yard stile,
What time the far hills seem to smile
    In sunset lights reposing;

Ah, then the homestead roof ascends,
And with the roofing heaven blends,
And earth unto its utmost ends
    Seems for one homestead given!

Shelter, O homesteads, shelter well
Yon aged pair whose dim eyes spell
Day-long the holy words that tell
    Of death and Christ and Heaven.

For lingering Age that calmly dies
'Mid tending hands and tender eyes,
Reaches the threshold of the skies
    Ere that of earth is ended!

Aye, doth anticipate his right,
And vanisheth from mortal sight
'Midst fair earth-angels, flesh-bedight,
    With Heaven-angels blended.

So let my Love-queen on her hill
Be honored in her loving will,
That homes shall stand to guard from ill
    The living and the dying.

Then shall my homesteads light the land
With gem-rays warm on every hand,
Like red heart rubies in the sand
    Of a fair country lying!

1871?   *1871*

June Dreams, In January

" So pulse, and pulse, thou rhythmic-hearted Noon
    That liest, large-limbed, curved along the hills,
In languid palpitation, half a-swoon
    With ardors and sun-loves and subtle thrills;

" Throb, Beautiful! while th' intense hours exhale
    As kisses faint-blown from thy finger-tips
Up to the sun, that turn him passion-pale
    And then as red as any virgin's lips!

" O tender darkness, when June-day hath ceased,
    —Faint odor, of the crushed day-flower born,
—Dim, visible sigh out of the mournful East
    That cannot see her lord again till morn:

" And many leaves, broad-palmed towards the sky
    To catch the sacred raining of star-light:
And pallid petals, fain, all fain to die,
    Soul-stung by too keen passion of the night:

" And short-breath'd winds, under yon gracious moon
    Doing mild errands for mild violets,
Or carrying sighs from the red lips of June
    What aimless way the odor-current sets:

" And stars, ring'd glittering in whorls and bells,
    Or bent along the sky in looped star-sprays,
Or vine-wound, with bright grapes in panicles,
    Or bramble-tangled in a sweetest maze,

" Or lying like young lilies in a lake
    About the great white Lotus of the moon,
Or blown and drifted, as if winds should shake
    Star-blossoms down from silver stems too soon,

" Or budding thick about full open stars,
    Or clambering shyly up cloud-lattices,
Or trampled pale in the red path of Mars,
    Or trim-set in quaint gardener's-fantasies:

" And long June night-sounds crooned among the leaves,
    And whispered confidence of dark and green,
And murmurs in old moss about old eaves,
    And tinklings floating over water-sheen! "

Then he that wrote, laid down his pen and sighed;
And straightway came old Scorn and Bitterness,
Like Hunnish kings out of the barbarous land,
And camped upon the transient Italy
That he had dreamed to blossom in his soul.
" I'll date this dream," he said: " So: ' Given, these,
On this, the coldest night in all the year,
From this, the meanest garret in the world,
In this, the greatest city in the land,
To you, the richest folk this side of death,
By one, the hungriest poet under heaven,
—Writ while his candle sputtered in the gust,
And while his last, last ember died of cold,
And while the mortal ice i' the air made free
Of all his bones and bit and shrunk his heart,
And while lewd Night along the street below
Drove her sly bargain with old Lechery
Who hid in church-wall angles till the folk
Should pass and let him to his rendevous,
And while soft Luxury made show to strike
Her gloved hands together and to smile
What time her weary feet unconsciously
Trode wheels that lifted Avarice to power,
—And while, moreover,—O thou God, thou God—
His worshipful sweet wife sat still, afar,
Within the village whence she sent him forth
Into the town to make his name and fame,
Waiting, all confident and proud and calm,
Till he should make for her his name and fame,
Waiting—O Christ, how keen this cuts!—large-eyed,
With Baby Charley till her husband make
For her and him a poet's name and fame.'
—Read me," he cried, and rose, and stamped his foot
Impatiently at Heaven, " read me this,"
(Putting th' inquiry full in the face of God)
" Why can we poets dream us beauty, so,
But cannot dream us bread? Why, now, can I
Make, aye, create this fervid throbbing June
Out of the chill, chill matter of my soul,

Yet cannot make a poorest penny-loaf
Out of this same chill matter, no, not one
For Mary though she starved upon my breast?"
　　And then he fell upon his couch, and sobbed,
And, late, just when his heart leaned o'er
The very edge of breaking, fain to fall,
God sent him sleep.
　　　　　　　　There came his room-fellow,
Stout Dick, the painter, saw the written dream,
Read, scratched his curly pate, smiled, winked, fell on
The poem in big-hearted comic rage,
Quick folded, thrust in envelope, addressed
To him, the critic-god, that sitteth grim
And giant-grisly on the stone causeway
That leadeth to his magazine and fame.
　　Him, by due mail, the little Dream of June
Encountered growling, and at unawares
Stole in upon his poem-battered soul
So that he smiled,—then shook his head upon't—
Then growled, then smiled again, till at the last,
As one that deadly sinned against his will,
He writ upon the margin of the Dream
A wondrous, wondrous word that in a day
Did turn the fleeting song to very bread.
—Whereat Dick Painter leapt, the poet wept,
And Mary slept with happy drops a-gleam
Upon long lashes of her serene eyes
From twentieth reading of her poet's news
Quick-sent, " O sweet my Sweet, to dream is power,
And I can dream thee bread and dream thee wine,
And I will dream thee robes and gems, dear Love,
To clothe thy holy loveliness withal,
And I will dream thee here to live by me,
Thee and my little man thou hold'st at breast,
—Come, Name, come, Fame, and kiss my Sweetheart's
　　feet!"

1868-1873?　　　　　　　　　　　　*1884*

On Huntingdon's " Miranda "

The storm hath blown thee a lover, sweet,
And laid him kneeling at thy feet;
But—guerdon rich for favor rare!—
The wind hath all thy holy hair
To kiss and to sing through and to flare
Like torch-flames in the passionate air,
      About thee, O Miranda.

Eyes in a blaze, eyes in a daze,
Bold with love, cold with amaze,
Chaste, thrilling eyes, fast-filling eyes,
With daintiest tears of love's surprise,
Ye draw my soul unto your blue,
As warm skies draw the exhaling dew—
      Divine eyes of Miranda.

And if I were yon stolid stone
Thy tender arm doth lean upon,
Thy touch would turn me to a heart,
And I would palpitate and start—
Content, when thou wert gone, to be
A dumb rock by the lonesome sea
      Forever, O Miranda.

1874   *1874*

My Two Springs

In the heart of the Hills of Life, I know
Two springs that with unbroken flow
Forever pour their lucent streams
Into my soul's far Lake of Dreams.

Not larger than two eyes, they lie
Beneath the many-changing sky
And mirror all of life and time,
—Serene and dainty pantomime!

Shot through with lights of stars and dawns,
And shadowed sweet by ferns and fawns,
—Thus heaven and earth together vie
Their shining depths to sanctify.

Always when the large Form of Love
Is hid by storms that rage above,
I gaze in my two springs and see
Love in his very verity.

Always when Faith with stifling stress
Of grief hath died in bitterness,
I gaze in my two springs and see
A Faith that smiles immortally.

Always when Charity and Hope,
In darkness bounden, feebly grope,
I gaze in my two springs and see
A Light that sets my captives free.

Always, when Art on perverse wing
Flies where I cannot hear him sing,
I gaze in my two springs and see
A charm that brings him back to me.

When Labor faints, and Glory fails,
And coy Reward in sighs exhales,
I gaze in my two springs and see
Attainment full and heavenly.

O Love, O Wife, thine eyes are they,
—My springs from out whose shining gray
Issue the sweet celestial streams
That feed my life's bright Lake of Dreams.

Oval and large and passion-pure
And gray and wise and honor-sure;
Soft as a dying violet-breath
Yet calmly unafraid of death;

Thronged, like two dove-cotes of gray doves,
With wife's and mother's and poor folk's loves,
And home-loves and high glory-loves
And science-loves and story-loves,

And loves for all that God and man
In art and nature make or plan,
And lady-loves for spidery lace
And broideries and supple grace

And diamonds and the whole sweet round
Of littles that large life compound,
And loves for God and God's bare truth,
And loves for Magdalen and Ruth,

Dear eyes, dear eyes and rare complete—
Being heavenly-sweet and earthly-sweet,
—I marvel that God made you mine,
For when He frowns, 'tis then ye shine!

1874   1882

Corn

To-day the woods are trembling through and through
With shimmering forms, that flash before my view,
Then melt in green as dawn-stars melt in blue.
    The leaves that wave against my cheek caress
    Like women's hands; the embracing boughs express
        A subtlety of mighty tenderness;
The copse-depths into little noises start,
That sound anon like beatings of a heart,
Anon like talk 'twixt lips not far apart.
    The beech dreams balm, as a dreamer hums a song;
    Through that vague wafture, expirations strong
    Throb from young hickories breathing deep and long
With stress and urgence bold of prisoned spring
        And ecstasy of burgeoning.
    Now, since the dew-plashed road of morn is dry,
    Forth venture odors of more quality
    And heavenlier giving. Like Jove's locks awry,
        Long muscadines
Rich-wreathe the spacious foreheads of great pines,

And breathe ambrosial passion from their vines.
I pray with mosses, ferns and flowers shy
That hide like gentle nuns from human eye
To lift adoring perfumes to the sky.
I hear faint bridal-sighs of brown and green
Dying to silent hints of kisses keen
As far lights fringe into a pleasant sheen.
I start at fragmentary whispers, blown
From undertalks of leafy souls unknown,
Vague purports sweet, of inarticulate tone.

Dreaming of gods, men, nuns and brides, between
Old companies of oaks that inward lean
To join their radiant amplitudes of green
I slowly move, with ranging looks that pass
Up from the matted miracles of grass
Into yon veined complex of space
Where sky and leafage interlace
So close, the heaven of blue is seen
Inwoven with a heaven of green.

I wander to the zigzag-cornered fence
Where sassafras, intrenched in brambles dense,
Contests with stolid vehemence
The march of culture, setting limb and thorn
As pikes against the army of the corn.

There, while I pause, my fieldward-faring eyes
Take harvests, where the stately corn-ranks rise,
Of inward dignities
And large benignities and insights wise,
Graces and modest majesties.
Thus, without theft, I reap another's field;
Thus, without tilth, I house a wondrous yield,
And heap my heart with quintuple crops concealed.

Look, out of line one tall corn-captain stands
Advanced beyond the foremost of his bands,
And waves his blades upon the very edge
And hottest thicket of the battling hedge.

Thou lustrous stalk, that ne'er mayst walk nor talk,
Still shalt thou type the poet-soul sublime
That leads the vanward of his timid time
And sings up cowards with commanding rhyme—

Soul calm, like thee, yet fain, like thee, to grow
By double increment, above, below;
Soul homely, as thou art, yet rich in grace like thee,
Teaching the yeomen selfless chivalry
That moves in gentle curves of courtesy;
Soul filled like thy long veins with sweetness tense,
By every godlike sense
Transmuted from the four wild elements.
Drawn to high plans,
Thou lift'st more stature than a mortal man's,
Yet ever piercest downward in the mould
And keepest hold
Upon the reverend and steadfast earth
That gave thee birth;
Yea, standest smiling in thy future grave,
Serene and brave,
With unremitting breath
Inhaling life from death,
Thine epitaph writ fair in fruitage eloquent,
Thyself thy monument.

As poets should,
Thou hast built up thy hardihood
With universal food,
Drawn in select proportion fair
From honest mould and vagabond air;
From darkness of the dreadful night,
And joyful light;
From antique ashes, whose departed flame
In thee has finer life and longer fame;
From wounds and balms,
From storms and calms,
From potsherds and dry bones
And ruin-stones.

Into thy vigorous substance thou hast wrought
Whate'er the hand of Circumstance hath brought;
  Yea, into cool solacing green hast spun
  White radiance hot from out the sun.
So thou dost mutually leaven
Strength of earth with grace of heaven;
  So thou dost marry new and old
  Into a one of higher mould;
  So thou dost reconcile the hot and cold,
    The dark and bright,
And many a heart-perplexing opposite,
    And so,
  Akin by blood to high and low,
Fitly thou playest out thy poet's part,
Richly expending thy much-bruisèd heart
  In equal care to nourish lord in hall
    Or beast in stall:
  Thou took'st from all that thou might'st give to all.

O steadfast dweller on the selfsame spot
Where thou wast born, that still repinest not—
Type of the home-fond heart, the happy lot!—
  Deeply thy mild content rebukes the land
  Whose flimsy homes, built on the shifting sand
Of trade, for ever rise and fall
With alternation whimsical,
  Enduring scarce a day,
  Then swept away
By swift engulfments of incalculable tides
Whereon capricious Commerce rides.

Look, thou substantial spirit of content!
Across this little vale, thy continent,
  To where, beyond the mouldering mill,
  Yon old deserted Georgian hill
Bares to the sun his piteous aged crest
    And seamy breast,
  By restless-hearted children left to lie
  Untended there beneath the heedless sky,
  As barbarous folk expose their old to die.

Upon that generous-rounding side,
   With gullies scarified
Where keen Neglect his lash hath plied,
Dwelt one I knew of old, who played at toil,
And gave to coquette Cotton soul and soil.
   Scorning the slow reward of patient grain,
   He sowed his heart with hopes of swifter gain,
   Then sat him down and waited for the rain.
He sailed in borrowed ships of usury—
A foolish Jason on a treacherous sea,
Seeking the Fleece and finding misery.
   Lulled by smooth-rippling loans, in idle trance
   He lay, content that unthrift Circumstance
   Should plough for him the stony field of Chance.
Yea, gathering crops whose worth no man might tell,
He staked his life on games of Buy-and-Sell,
And turned each field into a gambler's hell.
   Aye, as each year began,
   My farmer to the neighboring city ran;
Passed with a mournful anxious face
Into the banker's inner place;
Parleyed, excused, pleaded for longer grace;
   Railed at the drought, the worm, the rust, the grass;
   Protested ne'er again 'twould come to pass;
   With many an *oh* and *if* and *but alas*
Parried or swallowed searching questions rude,
And kissed the dust to soften Dives's mood.
At last, small loans by pledges great renewed,
   He issues smiling from the fatal door,
   And buys with lavish hand his yearly store
   Till his small borrowings will yield no more.
Aye, as each year declined,
With bitter heart and ever-brooding mind
He mourned his fate unkind.
   In dust, in rain, with might and main,
   He nursed his cotton, cursed his grain,
   Fretted for news that made him fret again,
Snatched at each telegram of Future Sale,
And thrilled with Bulls' or Bears' alternate wail—

In hope or fear alike for ever pale.
  And thus from year to year, through hope and fear,
  With many a curse and many a secret tear,
  Striving in vain his cloud of debt to clear,
      At last
He woke to find his foolish dreaming past,
  And all his best-of-life the easy prey
  Of squandering scamps and quacks that lined his way
    With vile array,
From rascal statesman down to petty knave;
Himself, at best, for all his bragging brave,
A gamester's catspaw and a banker's slave.
  Then, worn and gray, and sick with deep unrest,
  He fled away into the oblivious West,
    Unmourned, unblest.

Old hill! old hill! thou gashed and hairy Lear
Whom the divine Cordelia of the year,
E'en pitying Spring, will vainly strive to cheer—
  King, that no subject man nor beast may own,
  Discrowned, undaughtered and alone—
Yet shall the great God turn thy fate,
And bring thee back into thy monarch state
    And majesty immaculate.
Lo, through hot waverings of the August morn,
  Thou givest from thy vasty sides forlorn
  Visions of golden treasuries of corn—
Ripe largesse lingering for some bolder heart
That manfully shall take thy part,
    And tend thee,
    And defend thee,
With antique sinew and with modern art.

1874   *1875*

Civil Rights

Yistiddy—which he does it every Sunday, pretty nigh—
Old Uncle Johnny Stiles, my neighbor, come a-ridin' by,
And passed the time o' day with me, and lit, and hitched his
    mar',
And come and tuk his usual cheer in my pyazer thar;
And chawed, and chawed, and chawed, but never spit and never
    stirred,
And thunk, and grunted twiced or thriced, but uttered nar' a
    word;
Twell finnilly he spit a powerful wad, and worked his lip,
And—" Jeems," said he, " d'you hear about yan row in
    Massissip?
" I've just been over to the Squire's, a'readin' of the news:
My son, this here oncivil rights is givin' me the blues.
" It *do* look like them Yankees is the curiousest set;
They *will* make treuble jest as sure as water'll make you wet!
" I jest was startin' out to learn to like 'em some agin;
And that was not an easy thing, right after what had bin!
" Right after they had killed my boy, had—eh—had killed my
    Bill—
And after Sherman's folks had broke my dam and burnt my mill;
" And stole my watch, and mules, and horses, and my cotton
    and my corn,
And left my poor old Jane and me, about as we was born!
" I say, 'twas monstrous hard, right after all these things was
    done,
To love them men. My Bill—eh—he—he—was a splendid son!
" But then I tried to see it right, allowin' all along
They saw *ther* side as we saw *our'n*, and maybe both was wrong.
" *I* didn't want no war at fust; but when it had to be
I holp old Georgy; for I nat'ally could *not* stand, and see

" No lot of mortal men a'holdin' her in base restraint;
No, Jeems, my skin *is* tolubble white, but, sir, my liver ain't!

" My blood is red—I am a man—I love old Georgy true,
And what the Guv'nor says to do, that thing I'm gwine to do.

" But now, as I was sayin', when I jest had come to see
My way was clear to like 'em, and to treat 'em brotherlee;

" When every nigger's son is schooled (I payin' of the tax,
For not a mother's son of 'em has more than's on ther backs),

" And when they crowds and stinks me off from gittin' to the
    polls,
While Congress grinds ther grain, as 'twere, 'thout takin' of no
    tolls;

" And when I stands aside and waits, and hopes that things will
    mend,
Here comes this Civil Rights and says, this fuss shan't have no
    end!

" Hit seems as ef, jest when the water's roughest, here of late,
Them Yanks had throwed us overboard from off the Ship of
    State.

" Yes, throwed us both—both black and white—into the ragin'
    sea,
With but one rotten plank to hold; while they, all safe and free,

" Stands on the decks, and rams their hands into ther pockets
    tight,
And laughs to see we both must drown, or live by makin' fight!

" For, Jeems, what in this mortal world of trouble *kin* be done?
They've made this Southern plank so rotten, it will not bear
    but one! "

Then Uncle Johnny riz, and slowly walked towards the gate,
And swung it powerful slow, like he was liftin' of a weight;

Then give a sudden grunt, and spryly h'isted on his mar';
And sot, and hilt his right hand up, high up into the a'r,

As if he was about to make his 'davy 'fore the co'te;
" Yes, Jeems," says he, " they'll make it so that both of us
    cain't float.

" Now, ef I'm drowned, I'd like to know who'll gather in my
    grain,
And feed my gals, and care for wife—my dear old faithful
    Jane? "
(And here I'll say I've knowed him now for fifty year or more,
And never heerd him swear, nor cuss a single cuss before:)
" I tell you, Jeems, I *kin* not help it—*maybe* it's a sin;
By God! ef they don't fling a rope, I'll push the nigger in! "

1874   *1874*

In Absence

I

The storm that snapped our fate's one ship in twain
    Hath blown my half o' the wreck from thine apart.
O Love! O Love! across the gray-waved main
    To thee-ward strain my eyes, my arms, my heart.
I ask my God if e'en in His sweet place,
    Where, by one waving of a wistful wing,
My soul could straightway tremble face to face
    With thee, with thee, across the stellar ring—
Yea, where thine absence I could ne'er bewail
    Longer than lasts that little blank of bliss
When lips draw back, with recent pressure pale,
    To round and redden for another kiss—
        Would not my lonesome heart still sigh for thee.
        What time the drear kiss-intervals must be?

II

So do the mottled formulas of Sense
    Glide snakewise through our dreams of Aftertime;
So errors breed in reeds and grasses dense
    That bank our singing rivulets of rhyme.
By Sense rule Space and Time; but in God's Land
    Their intervals are not, save such as lie

Betwixt successive tones in concords bland
   Whose loving distance makes the harmony.
Ah, there shall never come 'twixt me and thee
   Gross dissonances of the mile, the year;
But in the multichords of ecstasy
   Our souls shall mingle, yet be featured clear,
      And absence, wrought to intervals divine,
      Shall part, yet link, thy nature's tone and mine.

III

Look down the shining peaks of all my days
   Base-hidden in the valleys of deep night,
So shalt thou see the heights and depths of praise
   My love would render unto love's delight;
For I would make each day an Alp sublime
   Of passionate snow, white-hot yet icy-clear,
—One crystal of the true-loves of all time
   Spiring the world's prismatic atmosphere;
And I would make each night an awful vale
   Deep as thy soul, obscure as modesty,
With every star in heaven trembling pale
   O'er sweet profounds where only Love can see.
      Oh, runs not thus the lesson thou hast taught?—
      When life's all love, 'tis life: aught else, 'tis naught.

IV

Let no man say, *He at his lady's feet*
   Lays worship that to Heaven alone belongs;
Yea, swings the incense that for God is meet
   In flippant censers of light lover's songs.
Who says it, knows not God, nor love, nor thee;
   For love is large as is yon heavenly dome:
In love's great blue, each passion is full free
   To fly his favorite flight and build his home.

Did e'er a lark with skyward-pointing beak
Stab by mischance a level-flying dove?
Wife-love flies level, his dear mate to seek:
God-love darts straight into the skies above.
 Crossing, the windage of each other's wings
 But speeds them both upon their journeyings.

1874

1875

Laus Mariæ

Across the brook of Time man leaping goes
 On stepping-stones of epochs, that uprise
Fixed, memorable, 'midst broad shallow flows
 Of neutrals, kill-times, sleeps, indifferences.
So 'twixt each morn and night rise salient heaps:
 Some cross with but a zigzag, jaded pace
From meal to meal: some with convulsive leaps
 Shake the green treacherous tussocks of disgrace;
And some advance, by system and deep art,
 O'er vantages of wealth, place, learning, tact.
But thou within thyself, dear manifold Heart,
 Dost bind all epochs in one dainty Fact.
 Oh, Sweet, my pretty Sum of history,
 I leapt the breadth of Time in loving thee!

1874

1875

To Miss Charlotte Cushman (With a Copy of "Corn")

O what a perilous waste from low to high,
 Must this poor book from me to you o'er leap,—
From me, who wander in the nights that lie
 About Fame's utmost vague foundations deep,
 To you, that sit on Fame's most absolute height,
 Distinctly starred, e'en in that awful light!

1875

1878

Special Pleading

Time, hurry my Love to me:
Haste, haste! Lov'st not good company?
   Here's but a heart-break sandy waste
   'Twixt Now and Then. Why, killing haste
Were best, dear Time, for thee, for thee!

Oh, would that I might divine
Thy name beyond the zodiac sign
   Wherefrom our times-to-come descend.
   He called thee *Sometime*. Change it, friend:
Now-time sounds so much more fine!

Sweet Sometime, fly fast to me:
Poor Now-time sits in the Lonesome-tree
   And broods as gray as any dove,
   And calls, *When wilt thou come, O Love?*
And pleads across the waste to thee.

Good Moment, that giv'st him me,
Wast ever in love? Maybe, maybe
   Thou'lt be this heavenly velvet time
   When Day and Night as rhyme and rhyme
Set lip to lip dusk-modestly;

Or haply some noon afar,
—O life's top bud, mixt rose and star,
   How ever can thine utmost sweet
   Be star-consummate, rose-complete,
Till thy rich reds full opened are?

Well, be it dusk-time or noon-time,
I ask but one small boon, Time:
   Come thou in night, come thou in day,
   I care not, I care not: have thine own way,
But only, but only, come soon, Time.

1875   *1876*

Martha Washington

Down cold snow-stretches of our bitter time,
  When windy shams and the rain-mocking sleet
Of Trade have cased us in such icy rime
  That hearts are scarcely hot enough to beat,
Thy fame, O Lady of the lofty eyes,
  Doth fall along the age, like as a lane
Of Spring, in whose most generous boundaries
  Full many a frozen virtue warms again.
To-day I saw the pale much-burdened form
  Of Charity come limping o'er the line,
And straighten from the bending of the storm
  And flush with stirrings of new strength divine,
    Such influence and sweet gracious impulse came
    Out of the beams of thine immortal name!

1875   *1875*

The Symphony

" O Trade! O Trade! would thou wert dead!
The Time needs heart—'tis tired of head:
We're all for love," the violins said.
" Of what avail the rigorous tale
Of bill for coin and box for bale?
Grant thee, O Trade! thine uttermost hope:
Level red gold with blue sky-slope,
And base it deep as devils grope:
When all's done, what hast thou won
Of the only sweet that's under the sun?
Ay, canst thou buy a single sigh
Of true love's least, least ecstasy? "

Then, with a bridegroom's heart-beats trembling,
All the mightier strings assembling
Ranged them on the violins' side
As when the bridegroom leads the bride,
And, heart in voice, together cried:
" Yea, what avail the endless tale
Of gain by cunning and plus by sale?
Look up the land, look down the land—
The poor, the poor, the poor, they stand
Wedged by the pressing of Trade's hand
Against an inward-opening door
That pressure tightens evermore:
They sigh a monstrous foul-air sigh
For the outside leagues of liberty,
Where Art, sweet lark, translates the sky
Into a heavenly melody.
' Each day, all day ' (these poor folks say),
' In the same old year-long, drear-long way,
We weave in the mills and heave in the kilns,
We sieve mine-meshes under the hills,
And thieve much gold from the Devil's bank tills,
To relieve, O God, what manner of ills?—
The beasts, they hunger, and eat, and die;
And so do we, and the world's a sty;
Hush, fellow-swine: why nuzzle and cry?
Swinehood hath no remedy
Say many men, and hasten by,
Clamping the nose and blinking the eye.
But who said once, in the lordly tone,
Man shall not live by bread alone
But all that cometh from the Throne?
   Hath God said so?
   But Trade saith *No:*
And the kilns and the curt-tongued mills say *Go:*
There's plenty that can, if you can't: we know.
Move out, if you think you're underpaid.
The poor are prolific; we're not afraid;
   Trade is trade.' "

Thereat this passionate protesting
  Meekly changed, and softened till
It sank to sad requesting
  And suggesting sadder still:
" And oh, if men might some time see
How piteous-false the poor decree
That trade no more than trade must be!
Does business mean, *Die, you—live, I?*
Then ' Trade is trade ' but sings a lie:
'Tis only war grown miserly.
If business is battle, name it so:
War-crimes less will shame it so,
And widows less will blame it so.
Alas: for the poor to have some part
In yon sweet living lands of Art,
Makes problem not for head, but heart.
Vainly might Plato's brain revolve it:
Plainly the heart of a child could solve it."

And then, as when from words that seem but rude
We pass to silent pain that sits abrood
Back in our heart's great dark and solitude,
So sank the strings to gentle throbbing
Of long chords change-marked with sobbing—
Motherly sobbing, not distinctlier heard
Than half wing-openings of the sleeping bird,
Some dream of danger to her young hath stirred.

Then stirring and demurring ceased, and lo!
Every least ripple of the strings' song-flow
Died to a level with each level bow
And made a great chord tranquil-surfaced so,
As a brook beneath his curving bank doth go
To linger in the sacred dark and green
Where many boughs the still pool overlean
And many leaves make shadow with their sheen.
  But presently
A velvet flute-note fell down pleasantly
Upon the bosom of that harmony,
And sailed and sailed incessantly,

As if a petal from a wild-rose blown
Had fluttered down upon that pool of tone
And boatwise dropped o' the convex side
And floated down the glassy tide
And clarified and glorified
The solemn spaces where the shadows bide.
From the warm concave of that fluted note
Somewhat, half song, half odor, forth did float,
As if a rose might somehow be a throat:
" When Nature from her far-off glen
Flutes her soft messages to men,
The flute can say them o'er again;
Yea, Nature, singing sweet and lone,
Breathes through life's strident polyphone
The flute-voice in the world of tone.
   Sweet friends,
   Man's love ascends
To finer and diviner ends
Than man's mere thought e'er comprehends.
   For I, e'en I,
   As here I lie,
A petal on a harmony,
Demand of Science whence and why
Man's tender pain, man's inward cry,
When he doth gaze on earth and sky?
I am not overbold:
   I hold
Full powers from Nature manifold.
I speak for each no-tonguèd tree
That, spring by spring, doth nobler be,
And dumbly and most wistfully
His mighty prayerful arms outspreads
Above men's oft-unheeding heads,
And his big blessing downward sheds.
I speak for all-shaped blooms and leaves,
Lichens on stones and moss on eaves,
Grasses and grains in ranks and sheaves;
Broad-fronded ferns and keen-leaved canes,
And briery mazes bounding lanes,

And marsh-plants, thirsty-cupped for rains,
And milky stems and sugary veins;
For every long-armed woman-vine
That round a piteous tree doth twine;
For passionate odors, and divine
Pistils, and petals crystalline;
All purities of shady springs,
All shynesses of film-winged things
That fly from tree-trunks and bark-rings;
All modesties of mountain-fawns
That leap to covert from wild lawns,
And tremble if the day but dawns;
All sparklings of small beady eyes
Of birds, and sidelong glances wise
Wherewith the jay hints tragedies;
All piquancies of prickly burs,
And smoothnesses of downs and furs
Of eiders and of minevers;
All limpid honeys that do lie
At stamen-bases, nor deny
The humming-birds' fine roguery,
Bee-thighs, nor any butterfly;
All gracious curves of slender wings,
Bark-mottlings, fibre-spiralings,
Fern-wavings and leaf-flickerings;
Each dial-marked leaf and flower-bell
Wherewith in every lonesome dell
Time to himself his hours doth tell;
All tree-sounds, rustlings of pine-cones,
Wind-sighings, doves' melodious moans,
And night's unearthly under-tones;
All placid lakes and waveless deeps,
All cool reposing mountain-steeps,
Vale-calms and tranquil lotos-sleeps;—
Yea, all fair forms, and sounds, and lights,
And warmths, and mysteries, and mights,
Of Nature's utmost depths and heights,
—These doth my timid tongue present,
Their mouthpiece and leal instrument

And servant, all love-eloquent.
I heard, when '*All for love*' the violins cried:
So, Nature calls through all her system wide,
Give me thy love, O man, so long denied.
Much time is run, and man hath changed his ways,
Since Nature, in the antique fable-days,
Was hid from man's true love by proxy fays,
False fauns and rascal gods that stole her praise.
The nymphs, cold creatures of man's colder brain,
Chilled Nature's streams till man's warm heart was fain
Never to lave its love in them again.
Later, a sweet Voice *Love thy neighbor* said;
Then first the bounds of neighborhood outspread
Beyond all confines of old ethnic dread.
Vainly the Jew might wag his covenant head:
'*All men are neighbors*,' so the sweet Voice said.
So, when man's arms had circled all man's race,
The liberal compass of his warm embrace
Stretched bigger yet in the dark bounds of space;
With hands a-grope he felt smooth Nature's grace,
Drew her to breast and kissed her sweetheart face:
Yea man found neighbors in great hills and trees
And streams and clouds and suns and birds and bees,
And throbbed with neighbor-loves in loving these.
But oh, the poor! the poor! the poor!
That stand by the inward-opening door
Trade's hand doth tighten ever more,
And sigh their monstrous foul-air sigh
For the outside hills of liberty,
Where Nature spreads her wild blue sky
For Art to make into melody!
Thou Trade! thou king of the modern days!
    Change thy ways,
    Change thy ways;
Let the sweaty laborers file
    A little while,
    A little while,
Where Art and Nature sing and smile.
Trade! is thy heart all dead, all dead?

And hast thou nothing but a head?
I'm all for heart," the flute-voice said,
And into sudden silence fled,
Like as a blush that while 'tis red
Dies to a still, still white instead.

Thereto a thrilling calm succeeds,
Till presently the silence breeds
A little breeze among the reeds
That seems to blow by sea-marsh weeds:
Then from the gentle stir and fret
Sings out the melting clarionet,
Like as a lady sings while yet
Her eyes with salty tears are wet.
" O Trade! O Trade! " the Lady said,
" I too will wish thee utterly dead
If all thy heart is in thy head.
For O my God! and O my God!
What shameful ways have women trod
At beckoning of Trade's golden rod!
Alas when sighs are traders' lies,
And heart's-ease eyes and violet eyes
    Are merchandise!
O purchased lips that kiss with pain!
O cheeks coin-spotted with smirch and stain!
O trafficked hearts that break in twain!
—And yet what wonder at my sisters' crime?
So hath Trade withered up Love's sinewy prime,.
Men love not women as in olden time.
Ah, not in these cold merchantable days
Deem men their life an opal gray, where plays
The one red Sweet of gracious ladies'-praise.
Now, comes a suitor with sharp prying eye—
Says, *Here, you Lady, if you'll sell, I'll buy:*
Come, heart for heart—a trade? What! weeping? why?
Shame on such wooers' dapper mercery!
I would my lover kneeling at my feet
In humble manliness should cry, *O sweet!*
I know not if thy heart my heart will greet:

I ask not if thy love my love can meet:
Whate'er thy worshipful soft tongue shall say,
I'll kiss thine answer, be it yea or nay:
I do but know I love thee, and I pray
To be thy knight until my dying day.
Woe him that cunning trades in hearts contrives!
Base love good women to base loving drives.
If men loved larger, larger were our lives;
And wooed they nobler, won they nobler wives."

There thrust the bold straightforward horn
To battle for that lady lorn,
With heartsome voice of mellow scorn,
Like any knight in knigthood's morn.
    " Now comfort thee," said he,
      " Fair Lady.
For God shall right thy grievous wrong,
And man shall sing thee a true-love song,
Voiced in act his whole life long,
    Yea, all thy sweet life long,
      Fair Lady.
Where's he that craftily hath said,
The day of chivalry is dead?
I'll prove that lie upon his head,
    Or I will die instead,
      Fair Lady.
Is Honor gone into his grave?
Hath Faith become a caitiff knave,
And Selfhood turned into a slave
    To work in Mammon's Cave,
      Fair Lady?
Will Truth's long blade ne'er gleam again?
Hath Giant Trade in dungeons slain
All great contempts of mean-got gain
    And hates of inward stain,
      Fair Lady?
For aye shall name and fame be sold,
And place be hugged for the sake of gold,
And smirch-robed Justice feebly scold

At Crime all money-bold,
    Fair Lady?
Shall self-wrapt husbands aye forget
Kiss-pardons for the daily fret
Wherewith sweet wifely eyes are wet—
    Blind to lips kiss-wise set—
      Fair Lady?
Shall lovers higgle, heart for heart,
Till wooing grows a trading mart
Where much for little, and all for part,
    Make love a cheapening art,
      Fair Lady?
Shall woman scorch for a single sin
That her betrayer can revel in,
And she be burnt, and he but grin
    When that the flames begin,
      Fair Lady?
Shall ne'er prevail the woman's plea,
We maids would far, far whiter be
If that our eyes might sometimes see
    Men maids in purity,
      Fair Lady?
Shall Trade aye salve his conscience-aches
With jibes at Chivalry's old mistakes—
The wars that o'erhot knighthood makes
    For Christ's and ladies' sakes,
      Fair Lady?
Now by each knight that e'er hath prayed
To fight like a man and love like a maid,
Since Pembroke's life, as Pembroke's blade,
    I' the scabbard, death, was laid,
      Fair Lady,
I dare avouch my faith is bright
That God doth right and God hath might,
Nor time hath changed His hair to white,
    Nor His dear love to spite,
      Fair Lady.
I doubt no doubts: I strive, and shrive my clay,
And fight my fight in the patient modern way

For true love and for thee—ah me! and pray
  To be thy knight until my dying day,
    Fair Lady."
Made end that knightly horn, and spurred away
Into the thick of the melodious fray.

And then the hautboy played and smiled,
And sang like any large-eyed child,
Cool-hearted and all undefiled.
  " Huge Trade! " he said,
" Would thou wouldst lift me on thy head,
And run where'er my finger led!
Once said a Man—and wise was He—
Never shalt thou the heavens see,
Save as a little child thou be."
Then o'er sea-lashings of commingling tunes
The ancient wise bassoons,
  Like weird
  Gray-beard
Old harpers sitting on the high sea-dunes,
  Chanted runes:
" Bright-waved gain, gray waved loss,
The sea of all doth lash and toss,
One wave forward and one across:
But now 'twas trough, now 'tis crest,
And worst doth foam and flash to best,
  And curst to blest.

" Life Life! thou sea-fugue, writ from east to west,
  Love, Love alone can pore
  On thy dissolving score
  Of harsh half-phrasings,
    Blotted ere writ,
  And double erasings
    Of chords most fit.
Yea, Love, sole music-master blest,
May read thy weltering palimpsest.
To follow Time's dying melodies through,
And never to lose the old in the new,

And ever to solve the discords true—
Love alone can do.
And ever Love hears the poor-folks' crying,
And ever Love hears the women's sighing,
And ever sweet knighthood's death-defying,
And ever wise childhood's deep implying,
But never a trader's glozing and lying.

" And yet shall Love himself be heard,
Though long deferred, though long deferred:
O'er the modern waste a dove hath whirred:
Music is Love in search of a word."

1875   *1875*

Acknowledgment

I

O Age that half believ'st thou half believ'st,
    Half doubt'st the substance of thine own half doubt,
And, half perceiving that thou half perceiv'st,
    Stand'st at thy temple door, heart in, head out!
Lo! while thy heart's within, helping the choir,
    Without, thine eyes range up and down the time,
Blinking at o'er-bright science, smit with desire
    To see and not to see.   Hence, crime on crime.
Yea, if the Christ (called thine) now paced yon street,
    Thy halfness hot with His rebuke would swell;
Legions of scribes would rise and run and beat
    His fair intolerable Wholeness twice to hell.
        Nay (so, dear Heart, thou whisperest in my soul),
        'Tis a half time, yet Time will make it whole.

II

Now at thy soft recalling voice I rise
    Where thought is lord o'er Time's complete estate,
Like as a dove from out the gray sedge flies
    To tree-tops green where coos his heavenly mate.

From these clear coverts high and cool I see
 How every time with every time is knit,
And each to all is mortised cunningly,
 And none is sole or whole, yet all are fit.
Thus, if this Age but as a comma show
 'Twixt weightier clauses of large-worded years,
My calmer soul scorns not the mark: I know
 This crooked point Time's complex sentence clears.
  Yet more I learn while, Friend! I sit by thee:
  Who sees all time, sees all eternity.

III

If I do ask, How God can dumbness keep
 While Sin creeps grinning through His house of Time,
Stabbing His saintliest children in their sleep,
 And staining holy walls with clots of crime?—
Or, How may He whose wish but names a fact
 Refuse what miser's-scanting of supply
Would richly glut each void where man hath lacked
 Of grace or bread?—or, How may Power deny
Wholeness to th' almost-folk that hurt our hope—
 These heart-break Hamlets who so barely fail
In life or art that but a hair's more scope
 Had set them fair on heights they ne'er may scale?—
  Somehow by thee, dear Love, I win content:
  Thy Perfect stops th' Imperfect's argument.

IV

By the more height of thy sweet stature grown,
 Twice-eyed with thy gray vision set in mine,
I ken far lands to wifeless men unknown,
 I compass stars for one-sexed eyes too fine.
No text on sea-horizons cloudily writ,
 No maxim vaguely starred in fields or skies,
But this wise thou-in-me deciphers it:
 Oh, thou'rt the Height of heights, the Eye of eyes.
Not hardest Fortune's most unbounded stress
 Can blind my soul nor hurl it from on high,

Possessing thee, the self of loftiness,
And very light that Light discovers by.
Howe'er thou turn'st, wrong Earth! still Love's in sight:
For we are taller than the breadth of night.

1875   *1876*

To Charlotte Cushman

Look where a three-point star shall weave his beam
Into the slumb'rous tissue of some stream,
Till his bright self o'er his bright copy seem
Fulfillment dropping on a come-true dream;
So in this night of art thy soul doth show
Her excellent double in the steadfast flow
Of wishing love that through men's hearts doth go:
At once thou shin'st above and shin'st below.
E'en when thou strivest there within Art's sky
(Each star must o'er a strenuous orbit fly),
Full calm thine image in our love doth lie,
A Motion glassed in a Tranquillity.
So triple-rayed, thou mov'st, yet stay'st, serene—
Art's artist, Love's dear woman, Fame's good queen!

1875?   *1876*

A Song of Love

Hey, rose, just born
Twin to a thorn;
Was't so with you, O Love and Scorn?

Sweet eyes that smiled,
Now wet and wild;
O Eye and Tear—mother and child.

Well: Love and Pain
Be kinsfolk twain:
Yet would, Oh would I could love again.

1875?   *1884*

A Song of the Future

Sail fast, sail fast,
Ark of my hopes, Ark of my dreams;
Sweep lordly o'er the drownèd Past,
Fly glittering through the sun's strange beams;
Sail fast, sail fast.
Breaths of new buds from off some drying lea
With news about the Future scent the sea:
My brain is beating like the heart of Haste:
I'll loose me a bird upon this Present waste;
Go, trembling song,
And stay not long; oh, stay not long:
Thou'rt only a gray and sober dove,
But thine eye is faith and thy wing is love.

1875?   *1876*

Rose-Morals

Red

Would that my songs might be
What roses make by day and night—
Distillments of my clod of misery
Into delight.

Soul, could'st thou bare thy breast
As yon red rose, and dare the day,
All clean, and large, and calm with velvet rest?
Say yea—say yea!

Ah, dear my Rose, good-bye;
The wind is up; so; drift away.
That songs from me as leaves from thee may fly,
I strive, I pray.

White

Soul, get thee to the heart
Of yonder tuberose; hide thee there,
There breathe the meditations of thine art
Suffused with prayer.

Of spirit grave yet light,
How fervent fragrances uprise
Pure-born from these most rich and yet most white
Virginities!

Mulched with unsavory death,
Reach, Soul! yon rose's white estate:
Give off thine art as she doth issue breath,
And wait,—and wait.

1875, 1876   *1876*

The Centennial Meditation of Columbia

A Cantata

MUSICAL
ANNOTATIONS
Full chorus:
sober, measured
and yet majestic
progressions of
chords

From this hundred-terraced height,
Sight more large with nobler light
Ranges down yon towering years:
Humbler smiles and lordlier tears
    Shine and fall, shine and fall,
While old voices rise and call
Yonder where the to-and-fro
Weltering of my Long-Ago
Moves about the moveless base
Far below my resting-place.

Chorus:
the sea and the
winds mingling
their voices with
human sighs

Mayflower, Mayflower, slowly hither flying,
Trembling westward o'er yon balking sea,
Hearts within *Farewell dear England* sighing,
Winds without *But dear in vain* replying,
Gray-lipp'd waves about thee shouted, crying
    No! It shall not be!

Jamestown, out of thee—
Plymouth, thee—thee, Albany—
Winter cries, *Ye freeze: away!*
Fever cries, *Ye burn: away!*
Hunger cries, *Ye starve: away!*
Vengeance cries, *Your graves shall stay!*

Quartette:
a meagre and
despairing
minor

Then old Shapes and Masks of Things,
Framed like Faiths or clothed like Kings—
Ghosts of Goods once fleshed and fair,
Grown foul Bads in alien air—
War, and his most noisy lords,
Tongued with lithe and poisoned swords—
    Error, Terror, Rage and Crime,
    All in a windy night of time
    Cried to me from land and sea,
    No! Thou shalt not be!

Full chorus:
return of the
motive *of the*
second move-
ment, *but*
worked up
with greater
fury, to the cli-
max of the
shout at the
last line

Hark!
Huguenots whispering *yea* in the dark,
Puritans answering *yea* in the dark!
Yea, like an arrow shot true to his mark,
Darts through the tyrannous heart of Denial.
Patience and Labor and solemn-souled Trial,
    Foiled, still beginning,
    Soiled, but not sinning,
Toil through the stertorous death of the Night,
Toil when wild brother-wars new-dark the Light,
Toil, and forgive, and kiss o'er, and replight.

A rapid
and intense
whisper-chorus

Now Praise to God's oft-granted grace,
Now Praise to Man's undaunted face,
Despite the land, despite the sea,
I was: I am: and I shall be—
How long, Good Angel, O how long?
Sing me from Heaven a man's own song!

Chorus of jubi-
lation, until the
appeal of the
last two lines
introduces a
tone of doubt:
it then sinks to
pianissimo

Basso solo:
the good Angel
replies:

" Long as thine Art shall love true love,
Long as thy Science truth shall know,
Long as thine Eagle harms no Dove,
Long as thy Law by law shall grow,
Long as thy God is God above,
Thy brother every man below,
So long, dear Land of all my love,
Thy name shall shine, thy fame shall glow! "

Full chorus:
jubilation and
welcome

O Music, from this height of time my Word unfold:
In thy large signals all men's hearts Man's Heart behold:
Mid-heaven unroll thy chords as friendly flags unfurled,
And wave the world's best lover's welcome to the world.

1876   *1876*

Psalm of the West

Land of the willful gospel, thou worst and thou best;
Tall Adam of lands, new-made of the dust of the West;
Thou wroughtest alone in the Garden of God, unblest
Till He fashioned lithe Freedom to lie for thine Eve on thy
    breast—
Till out of thy heart's dear neighborhood, out of thy side,
He fashioned an intimate Sweet one and brought thee a Bride.
Cry hail! nor bewail that the wound of her coming was wide.
Lo, Freedom reached forth where the world as an apple hung
    red;
Let us taste the whole radiant round of it, gayly she said:
If we die, at the worst we shall lie as the first of the dead.
Knowledge of Good and of Ill, O Land! she hath given thee;
Perilous godhoods of choosing have rent thee and riven thee;
Will's high adoring to Ill's low exploring hath driven thee—
Freedom, thy Wife, hath uplifted thy life and clean shriven
    thee!
Her shalt thou clasp for a balm to the scars of thy breast,
Her shalt thou kiss for a calm to thy wars of unrest,
Her shalt extol in the psalm of the soul of the West.
For Weakness, in freedom, grows stronger than Strength
    with a chain;

And Error, in freedom, will come to lamenting his stain,
Till freely repenting he whiten his spirit again;
And Friendship, in freedom, will blot out the bounding of race;
And straight Law, in freedom, will curve to the rounding of
 grace;
And Fashion, in freedom, will die of the lie in her face;
 And Desire flame white on the sense as a fire on a height,
 And Sex flame white in the soul as a star in the night,
 And Marriage plight sense unto soul as the two-colored light
 Of the fire and the star shines one with a duplicate might;
And Science be known as the sense making love to the All,
And Art be known as the soul making love to the All,
And Love be known as the marriage of man with the All—
 Till Science to knowing the Highest shall lovingly turn,
 Till Art to loving the Highest shall consciously burn,
 Till Science to Art as a man to a woman shall yearn,
   —Then morn!
When Faith from the wedding of Knowing and Loving shall
 purely be born,
And the Child shall smile in the West, and the West to the
 East give morn,
And the Time in that ultimate Prime shall forget old regret-
 ting and scorn,
Yea, the stream of the light shall give off in a shimmer the
 dream of the night forlorn.

   Once on a time a soul
    Too full of his dole
In a querulous dream went crying from pole to pole—
  Went sobbing and crying
  For ever a sorrowful song of living and dying,
  How *life was the dropping and death the drying*
  Of a Tear that fell in a day when God was sighing.
And ever Time tossed him bitterly to and fro
As a shuttle inlaying a perilous warp of woe
In the woof of things from terminal snow to snow,
   Till, lo!
   Rest.
And he sank on the grass of the earth as a lark on its nest,

And he lay in the midst of the way from the east to the west.
Then the East came out from the east and the West from the
    west,
  And, behold! in the gravid deeps of the lower dark,
  While, above, the wind was fanning the dawn as a spark,
  The East and the West took form as the wings of a lark.
One wing was feathered with facts of the uttermost Past,
And one with the dreams of a prophet; and both sailed fast
And met where the sorrowful Soul on the earth was cast.
  Then a Voice said: *Thine, if thou lovest enough to use;*
  But another: *To fly and to sing is pain: refuse!*
  Then the Soul said: *Come, O my wings! I cannot but choose.*
And the Soul was a-tremble like as a new-born thing,
Till the spark of the dawn wrought a conscience in heart as in
    wing,
Saying, *Thou art the lark of the dawn; it is time to sing.*

Then that artist began in a lark's low circling to pass;
And first he sang at the height of the top of the grass
A song of the herds that are born and die in the mass.
  And next he sang a celestial-passionate round
  At the height of the lips of a woman above the ground,
  How *Love was a fair true Lady, and Death a wild hound,*
  And she called, and he licked her hand and with girdle was
    bound.
And then with a universe-love he was hot in the wings,
And the sun stretched beams to the worlds as the shinning
    strings
Of the large hid harp that sounds when an all-lover sings;
  And the sky's blue traction prevailed o'er the earth's in might,
  And the passion of flight grew mad with the glory of height,
  And the uttering of song was like to the giving of light;
And he learned that hearing and seeing wrought nothing alone,
And that music on earth much light upon Heaven had thrown,
And he melted-in silvery sunshine with silvery tone;
  And the spirals of music e'er higher and higher he wound
  Till the luminous cinctures of melody up from the ground
  Arose as the shaft of a tapering tower of sound—
  Arose for an unstricken full-finished Babel of sound.

But God was not angry, nor ever confused his tongue,
For not out of selfish nor impudent travail was wrung
The song of all men and all things that the all-lover sung.
  Then he paused at the top of his tower of song on high,
  And the voice of the God of the artist from far in the sky
Said, *Son, look down: I will cause that a Time gone by*
Shall pass, and reveal his heart to thy loving eye.

       Far spread, below,
The sea that fast hath locked in his loose flow
All secrets of Atlantis' drownèd woe
  Lay bound about with night on every hand,
  Save down the eastern brink a shining band
  Of day made out a little way from land.
Then from that shore the wind upbore a cry:
Thou Sea, thou Sea of Darkness! why, oh why
Dost waste thy West in unthrift mystery?
  But ever the idiot sea-mouths foam and fill,
  And never a wave doth good for man or ill,
  And Blank is king, and Nothing hath his will;
And like as grim-beaked pelicans level file
Across the sunset toward their nightly isle
On solemn wings that wave but seldomwhile,
  So leanly sails the day behind the day
  To where the Past's lone Rock o'erglooms the spray,
  And down its mortal fissures sinks away.

    Master, Master, break this ban:
      The wave lacks Thee.
    Oh, is it not to widen man
      Stretches the sea?
    Oh, must the sea-bird's idle van
      Alone be free?

    Into the Sea of the Dark doth creep
      Björne's pallid sail,
    As the face of a walker in his sleep,
      Set rigid and most pale,
    About the night doth peer and peep
      In a dream of an ancient tale.

Lo, here is made a hasty cry:
Land, land, upon the west!—
God save such land! Go by, go by:
Here may no mortal rest,
Where this waste hell of slate doth lie
And grind the glacier's breast.

The sail goeth limp: hey, flap and strain!
    Round eastward slanteth the mast;
As the sleep-walker waked with pain,
    White-clothed in the midnight blast,
Doth stare and quake, and stride again
    To houseward all aghast.

Yet as, *A ghost!* his household cry:
    He hath followed a ghost in flight.
Let us see the ghost—his household fly
    With lamps to search the night—
So Norsemen's sails run out and try
    The Sea of the Dark with light.

Stout Are Marson, southward whirled
    From out the tempest's hand,
Doth skip the sloping of the world
    To Huitramannaland,
Where Georgia's oaks with moss-beards curled
    Wave by the shining strand,

And sway in sighs from Florida's Spring
    Or Carolina's Palm—
What time the mocking-bird doth bring
    The woods his artist's-balm,
Singing the Song of Everything
    Consummate-sweet and calm—

Land of large merciful-hearted skies,
    Big bounties, rich increase,
Green rests for Trade's blood-shotten eyes,
    For o'er-beat brains surcease,
For Love the dear woods' sympathies,
    For Grief the wise woods' peace,

For Need rich givings of hid powers
  In hills and vales quick-won,
For Greed large exemplary flowers
  That ne'er have toiled nor spun,
For Heat fair-tempered winds and showers,
  For Cold the neighbor sun.

Land where the Spirits of June-Heat
  From out their forest-maze
Stray forth at eve with loitering feet,
  And fervent hymns upraise
In bland accord and passion sweet
  Along the Southern ways:

" O Darkness, tawny Twin whose Twin hath ceased,
  Thou Odor from the day-flower's crushing born,
Thou visible Sigh out of the mournful East,
  That cannot see her lord again till morn:
O Leaves, with hollow palms uplifted high
  To catch the stars' most sacred rain of light:
O pallid Lily-petals fain to die
  Soul-stung by subtle passion of the night:
O short-breath'd Winds beneath the gracious moon
  Running mild errands for mild violets,
Or carrying sighs from the red lips of June
  What wavering way the odor-current sets:
O Stars wreathed vinewise round yon heavenly dells,
  Or thrust from out the sky in curving sprays,
Or whorled, or looped with pendent flower-bells,
  Or bramble-tangled in a brilliant maze,
Or lying like young lilies in a lake
  About the great white Lily of the moon,
Or drifting white from where in heaven shake
  Star-portraitures of apple trees in June,
Or lapp'd as leaves of a great rose of stars,
  Or shyly clambering up cloud-lattices,
Or trampled pale in the red path of Mars,
  Or trim-set quaint in gardners'-fantasies:
O long June Night-sounds crooned among the leaves;

O whispered confidence of Dark and Green;
O murmurs in old moss about old eaves;
O tinklings floating over water-sheen."

    Then Leif, bold son of Eric the Red,
        To the South of the West doth flee—
    Past slaty Helluland is sped,
        Past Markland's woody lea,
    Till round about fair Vinland's head,
        Where Taunton helps the sea,

    The Norseman calls, the anchor falls,
        The mariners hurry a-strand:
    They wassail with fore-drunken skals
        Where prophet wild grapes stand;
    They lift the Leifsbooth's hasty walls
        They stride about the land—

    New England, thee! whose ne'er-spent wine
        As blood doth stretch each vein,
    And urge thee, sinewed like thy vine,
        Through peril and all pain
    To grasp Endeavor's towering Pine,
        And, once ahold, remain—

    Land where the strenuous-handed Wind
        With sarcasm of a friend
    Doth smite the man would lag behind
        To frontward of his end;
    Yea, where the taunting fall and grind
        Of Nature's Ill doth send

    Such mortal challenge of a clown
        Rude-thrust upon the soul,
    That men but smile where mountains frown
        Or scowling waters roll,
    And Nature's front of battle down
        Do hurl from pole to pole.

Now long the Sea of Darkness glimmers low
With sails from Northland flickering to and fro—
Thorwald, Karlsefne, and those twin heirs of woe,

Hellboge and Finnge, in treasonable bed
Slain by the ill-born child of Eric Red,
Freydisa false. Till, as much time is fled,
Once more the vacant airs with darkness fill,
Once more the wave doth never good nor ill,
And Blank is king, and Nothing works his will;
  And leanly sails the day behind the day
  To where the Past's lone Rock o'erglooms the spray,
  And down its mortal fissures sinks away,
As when the grim-beaked pelicans level file
Across the sunset to their seaward isle
On solemn wings that wave but seldomwhile.

> Master, Master, poets sing;
>   The Time calls Thee;
> Yon Sea binds hard on everything
>   Man longs to be:
> Oh, shall the sea-bird's aimless wing
>   Alone move free?

Santa Maria, well thou tremblest down the wave,
  Thy *Pinta* far abow, thy *Niña* nigh astern:
Columbus stands in the night alone, and, passing grave,
  Yearns o'er the sea as tones o'er under-silence yearn.
Heartens his heart as friend befriends his friend less brave,
  Makes burn the faiths that cool, and cools the doubts that
    burn:—

" 'Twixt this and dawn, three hours my soul will smite
  With prickly seconds, or less tolerably
  With dull-blade minutes flatwise slapping me.
Wait, Heart! Time moves.—Thou lithe young Western Night,
Just-crownèd king, slow riding to thy right,
  Would God that I might straddle mutiny
  Calm as thou sitt'st yon never-managed sea,
Balk'st with his balking, fliest with his flight,
Giv'st supple to his rearings and his falls,
  Nor dropp'st one coronal star about thy brow
    Whilst ever dayward thou art steadfast drawn!
Yea, would I rode these mad contentious brawls
  No damage taking from their If and How,
    Nor no result save galloping to my Dawn!

" My Dawn? my Dawn? How if it never break?
How if this West by other Wests is pieced,
And these by vacant Wests on Wests increased—
One Pain of Space, with hollow ache on ache
Throbbing and ceasing not for Christ's own sake?—
  Big perilous theorem, hard for king and priest:
  Pursue the West but long enough, 'tis East!
Oh, if this watery world no turning take!
Oh, if for all my logic, all my dreams,
Provings of that which is by that which seems,
  Fears, hopes, chills, heats, hastes, patiences, droughts, tears,
  Wife-grievings, slights on love, embezzled years,
    Hates, treaties, scorns, upliftings, loss and gain,—
    This earth, no sphere, be all one sickening plane!

" Or, haply, how if this contrarious West,
  That me by turns hath starved, by turns hath fed,
  Embraced, disgraced, beat back, solicited,
Have no fixed heart of Law within his breast,
Or with some different rhythm doth e'er contest
  Nature in the East? Why, 'tis but three weeks fled
  I saw my Judas needle shake his head
And flout the Pole that, east, he Lord confessed!
  God! if this West should own some other Pole,
  And with his tangled ways perplex my soul
Until the maze grow mortal, and I die
  Where distraught Nature clean hath gone astray,
  On earth some other wit than Time's at play,
Some other God than mine above the sky!

" Now speaks mine other heart with cheerier seeming:
  Ho, Admiral! o'er-defalking to thy crew
  Against thyself, thyself far overfew
To front yon multitudes of rebel scheming?
Come, ye wild twenty years of heavenly dreaming!
  Come, ye wild weeks since first this canvas drew
  Out of vexed Palos ere the dawn was blue,
O'er milky waves about the bows full-creaming!
Come set me round with many faithful spears
  Of confident remembrance—how I crushed

Cat-lived rebellions, pitfalled treasons, hushed
Scared husbands' heart-break cries on distant wives,
Made cowards blush at whining for their lives,
Watered my parching souls, and dried their tears.

" Ere we Gomera cleared, a coward cried,
Turn, turn: here be three caravels ahead,
From Portugal, to take us: we are dead!
Hold Westward, pilot, calmly I replied.
So when the last land down the horizon died,
Go back, go back! they prayed: *our hearts are lead.—*
Friends, we are bound into the West, I said.
Then passed the wreck of a mast upon our side.
See (so they wept) *God's Warning! Admiral, turn!—*
Steersman, I said, *hold straight into the West.*
Then down the night we saw the meteor burn.
So do the very Heavens in fire protest:
Good Admiral, put about! O Spain, dear Spain!—
Hold straight into the West, I said again.

" Next drive we o'er the slimy-weeded sea.
Lo! herebeneath (another coward cries)
The cursèd land of sunk Atlantis lies:
This slime will suck us down—turn while thou'rt free!—
But no! I said, *Freedom bears West for me!*
Yet when the long-time stagnant winds arise,
And day by day the keel to westward flies,
My Good my people's Ill doth come to be:
Ever the winds into the West do blow;
Never a ship, once turned, might homeward go;
Meanwhile we speed into the lonesome main.
For Christ's sake, parley, Admiral! Turn, before
We sail outside all bounds of help from pain!—
Our help is in the West, I said once more.

" So when there came a mighty cry of *Land!*
And we clomb up and saw, and shouted strong
Salve Regina! all the ropes along,
But knew at morn how that a counterfeit band
Of level clouds had aped a silver strand;

So when we heard the orchard-bird's small song,
And all the people cried, *A hellish throng*
To tempt us onward by the Devil planned,
Yea, all from hell—keen heron, fresh green weeds,
Pelican, tunny-fish, fair tapering reeds,
  Lie-telling lands that ever shine and die
  In clouds of nothing round the empty sky.
    Tired Admiral, get thee from this hell, and rest!—
    Steersman, I said, *hold straight into the West.*

" I marvel how mine eye, ranging the Night,
  From its big circling ever absently
  Returns, thou large low Star, to fix on thee.
Maria! Star? No star: a Light, a Light!
Wouldst leap ashore, Heart? Yonder burns—a Light.
  Pedro Gutierrez, wake! come up to me.
  I prithee stand and gaze about the sea:
What seest? *Admiral, like as land—a Light!*
Well! Sanchez of Segovia, come and try:
What seest? *Admiral, naught but sea and sky!*
  Well! But *I* saw It. Wait! the Pinta's gun!
  Why, look, 'tis dawn, the land is clear: 'tis done!
Two dawns do break at once from Time's full hand—
God's, East—mine, West: good friends, behold my Land! "

> Master, Master! faster fly
> Now the hurrying seasons by;
> Now the Sea of Darkness wide
> Rolls in light from side to side;
> Mark, slow drifting to the West
> Down the trough and up the crest,
> Yonder piteous heartsease petal
> Many-motioned rise and settle—
>
> Petal cast a-sea from land
> By the awkward-fingered Hand
> That, mistaking Nature's course,
> Tears the love it fain would force—
> Petal calm of heartsease flower
> Smiling sweet on tempest sour,

Smiling where by crest and trough
Heartache Winds at heartsease scoff,
Breathing mild perfumes of prayer
'Twixt the scolding sea and air.

Mayflower, piteous Heartsease Petal!
Suavely down the sea-troughs settle,
Gravely breathe perfumes of prayer
'Twixt the scolding sea and air,
Bravely up the sea-hills rise—
Sea-hills slant thee toward the skies.
Master, hold disaster off
From the crest and from the trough;
Heartsease, on the heartache sea
God, thy God, will pilot thee.

Mayflower, Ship of Faith's best Hope!
Thou art sure if all men grope;
Mayflower, Ship of Hope's best Faith!
All is true the great God saith;
Mayflower, Ship of Charity!
Love is Lord of land and sea.
Oh, with love and love's best care
Thy large godly freightage bear—
Godly Hearts that, Grails of gold,
Still the blood of Faith do hold.

Now bold Massachusetts clear
Cuts the rounding of the sphere.
Out the anchor, sail no more,
Lay us by the Future's shore—
Not the shore we sought, 'tis true,
But the time is come to do.
Leap, dear Standish, leap and wade;
Bradford, Hopkins, Tilley, wade:
Leap and wade ashore and kneel—
God be praised that steered the keel!
Home is good, and soft is rest,
Even in this jagged West:
Freedom lives, and Right shall stand;
Blood of Faith is in the land.

Then in what time the primal icy years
Scraped slowly o'er the Puritans' hopes and fears,
Like as great glaciers built of frozen tears,
   The Voice from far within the secret sky
   Said, *Blood of Faith ye have? So; let us try.*
      And presently
The anxious-masted ships that westward fare,
Cargo'd with trouble and a-list with care,
Their outraged decks hot back to England bear,
   Then come again with stowage of worse weight,
   Battle, and tyrannous Tax, and Wrong, and Hate,
   And all bad items of Death's perilous freight.

O'er Cambridge set the yeomen's mark:
Climb, patriot, through the April dark.
O lanthorn! kindle fast thy light,
Thou budding star in the April night,
For never a star more news hath told,
Or later flame in heaven shall hold.
Ay, lanthorn on the North Church tower,
When that thy church hath had her hour,
Still from the top of Reverence high
Shalt thou illume Fame's ampler sky;
For, statured large o'er town and tree,
Time's tallest Figure stands by thee,
And, dim as now thy wick may shine,
The Future lights his lamp at thine.

Now haste thee while the way is clear,
     Paul Revere!
Haste, Dawes! but haste thou not, O Sun!
     To Lexington.

Then Devens looked and saw the light:
He got him forth into the night,
And watched alone on the river-shore,
And marked the British ferrying o'er.

John Parker! rub thine eyes and yawn:
But one o'clock and yet 'tis Dawn!
Quick, rub thine eyes and draw thy hose:

The Morning comes ere darkness goes.
Have forth and call the yeomen out,
For somewhere, somewhere close about
Full soon a Thing must come to be
Thine honest eyes shall stare to see—
Full soon before thy patriot eyes
Freedom from out of a Wound shall rise.

Then haste ye, Prescott and Revere!
Bring all the men of Lincoln here;
Let Chelmsford, Littleton, Carlisle,
Let Acton, Bedford, hither file—
Oh hither file, and plainly see
Out of a wound leap Liberty.

Say, Woodman April! all in green,
Say, Robin April! hast thou seen
In all thy travel round the earth
Ever a morn of calmer birth?
But Morning's eye alone serene
Can gaze across yon village-green
To where the trooping British run
        Through Lexington.

Good men in fustian, stand ye still;
The men in red come o'er the hill.
Lay down your arms, damned Rebels! cry
The men in red full haughtily.
But never a grounding gun is heard;
The men in fustian stand unstirred;
Dead calm, save maybe a wise bluebird
Puts in his little heavenly word.
O men in red! if ye but knew
The half as much as bluebirds do,
Now in this little tender calm
Each hand would out, and every palm
With patriot palm strike brotherhood's stroke
Or ere these lines of battle broke.

O men in red! if ye but knew
The least of the all that bluebirds do,

Now in this little godly calm
Yon voice might sing the Future's Psalm—
The Psalm of Love with the brotherly eyes
Who pardons and is very wise—
Yon voice that shouts, high-hoarse with ire,
     Fire!
The red-coats fire, the homespuns fall:
The homespuns' anxious voices call,

Brother, art hurt? and *Where hit, John?*
And, *Wipe this blood,* and *Men, come on,*
And, *Neighbor, do but lift my head,*
And *Who is wounded? Who is dead?*
Seven are killed. My God! my God!
Seven lie dead on the village sod.
Two Harringtons, Parker, Hadley, Brown,
Monroe and Porter,—these are down.
Nay, look! Stout Harrington not yet dead!
He crooks his elbow, lifts his head.
He lies at the step of his own house-door;
He crawls and makes a path of gore.
The wife from the window hath seen, and rushed;
He hath reached the step, but the blood hath gushed;
He hath crawled to the step of his own house-door,
But his head hath dropped: he will crawl no more.
Clasp, Wife, and kiss, and lift the head:
Harrington lies at his doorstep dead.

But, O ye Six that round him lay
And bloodied up that April day!
As Harrington fell, ye likewise fell—
At the door of the House wherein ye dwell;
As Harrington came, ye likewise came
And died at the door of your House of Fame.

Go by, old Field of Freedom's hopes and fears;
Go by, old Field of Brothers' hate and tears:
Behold! yon home of Brothers' Love appears
     Set in the burnished silver of July,
     On Schuylkill wrought as in old broidery
     Clasped hands upon a shining baldric lie.

New Hampshire, Georgia, and the mighty ten
That lie between, have heard the huge-nibbed pen
Of Jefferson tell the rights of man to men.
They sit in the reverend Hall: *Shall we declare?*
Floats round about the anxious-quivering air
'Twixt narrow Schuylkill and broad Delaware.
Already, Land! thou *hast* declared: 'tis done.
Ran ever clearer speech than that did run
When the sweet Seven died at Lexington?
Canst legibler write than Concord's large-stroked Act,
Or when at Bunker Hill the clubbed guns cracked?
Hast ink more true than blood, or pen than fact?
Nay, as the poet mad with heavenly fires
Flings men his song white-hot, then back retires,
Cools heart, broods o'er the song again, inquires,
Why did I this, why that? and slowly draws
From Art's unconscious act Art's conscious laws;
So, Freedom, writ, declares her writing's cause.
All question vain, all chill foreboding vain.
Adams, ablaze with faith, is hot and fain;
And he, straight-fibred Soul of mighty grain,
Deep-rooted Washington, afire, serene—
Tall Bush that burns, yet keeps its substance green—
Sends daily word, of import calm yet keen,
Warm from the front of battle, till the fire
Wraps opposition in and flames yet higher,
And Doubt's thin tissues flash where Hope's aspire;
And, *Ay, declare,* and ever strenuous *Ay*
Falls from the Twelve, and Time and Nature cry
Consent with kindred burnings of July;
And delegate Dead from each past age and race,
Viewless to man, in large procession pace
Downward athwart each set and steadfast face,
Responding *Ay* in many tongues; and lo!
Manhood and Faith and Self and Love and Woe
And Art and Brotherhood and Learning go
Rearward the files of dead, and softly say
Their saintly *Ay,* and softly pass away
By airy exits of that ample day.
Now fall the chill reactionary snows

Of man's defect, and every wind that blows
Keeps back the Spring of Freedom's perfect Rose.
Now naked feet with crimson fleck the ways,
And Heaven is stained with flags that mutinies raise,
And Arnold-spotted move the creeping days.
Long do the eyes that look from Heaven see
Time smoke, as in the spring the mulberry tree,
With buds of battles opening fitfully,
Till Yorktown's winking vapors slowly fade,
And Time's full top casts down a pleasant shade
Where Freedom lies unarmed and unafraid.

Master, ever faster fly
Now the vivid seasons by;
Now the glittering Western land
Twins the day-lit Eastern Strand;
Now white Freedom's sea-bird wing
Roams the Sea of Everything;
Now the freemen to and fro
Bind the tyrant sand and snow,
Snatching Death's hot bolt ere hurled,
Flash new Life about the world,
Sun the secrets of the hills,
Shame the gods' slow-grinding mills,
Prison Yesterday in Print,
Read To-morrow's weather-hint,
Haste before the halting Time,
Try new virtue and new crime,
Mould new faiths, devise new creeds,
Run each road that frontward leads,
Driven by an Onward-ache,
Scorning souls that circles make.

Now, O Sin! O Love's lost Shame!
Burns the land with redder flame:
North in line and South in line
Yell the charge and spring the mine.
Heartstrong South would have his way,
Headstrong North hath said him nay:
O strong Heart, strong Brain, beware!
Hear a Song from out the air:

" Lists all white and blue in the skies;
  And the people hurried amain
To the Tournament under the ladies' eyes
  Where jousted Heart and Brain.

" *Blow, herald, blow!* There entered Heart,
  A youth in crimson and gold.
Blow, herald, blow! Brain stood apart,
  Steel-armored, glittering, cold.

" Heart's palfrey caracoled gayly round,
  Heart tra-li-raed merrily;
But Brain sat still, with never a sound—
  Full cynical-calm was he.

" Heart's helmet-crest bore favors three
  From his lady's white hand caught;
Brain's casque was bare as Fact—not he
  Or favor gave or sought.

" *Blow, herald, blow!* Heart shot a glance
  To catch his lady's eye;
But Brain looked straight a-front, his lance
  To aim more faithfully.

" They charged, they struck; both fell, both bled;
  Brain rose again, ungloved;
Heart fainting smiled, and softly said,
  My love to my Beloved."

  Heart and Brain! no more be twain;
  Throb and think, one flesh again!
  Lo! they weep, they turn, they run;
  Lo! they kiss: Love, thou art one!

  Now the Land, with drying tears,
  Counts him up his flocks of years,
  " See," he says, " my substance grows;
  Hundred-flocked my Herdsman goes,
  Hundred-flocked my Herdsman stands
  On the Past's broad meadow-lands.
  Come from where ye mildly graze,

Black herds, white herds, nights and days.
Drive them homeward, Herdsman Time,
From the meadows of the Prime:
I will feast my house, and rest.
Neighbor East, come over West;
Pledge me in good wine and words
While I count my hundred herds,
Sum the substance of my Past
From the first unto the last,
Chanting o'er the generous brim
Cloudy memories yet more dim,
Ghostly rhymes of Norsemen pale
Staring by old Björne's sail,
Strains more noble of that night
Worn Columbus saw his Light,
Psalms of still more heavenly tone,
How the Mayflower tossed alone,
Olden tale and later song
Of the Patriot's love and wrong,
Grandsire's ballad, nurse's hymn—
Chanting o'er the sparkling brim
Till I shall from first to last
Sum the substance of my Past."

Then called the Artist's God from in the sky:
" This Time shall show by dream and mystery
The heart of all his matter to thine eye.
Son, study stars by looking down in streams,
Interpret that which is by that which seems,
And tell thy dreams in words which are but dreams."

The Master with His lucent hand
Pinched up the atom hills and plains
O'er all the moiety of land
The ocean-bounded West contains:
The dust lay dead upon the calm
And mighty middle of His palm.

And lo! He wrought full tenderly,
And lo! He wrought with love and might,
  And lo! He wrought a thing to see
Was marvel in His people's sight:
  He wrought His image dead and small,
  A nothing fashioned like an All.

Then breathed He softly on the dead:
" Live Self!—thou part, yet none, of Me;
  Dust for humility," He said,
" And my warm breath for Charity.
  Behold my latest work, thou Earth!
  The Self of Man is taking birth."

Then, Land, tall Adam of the West,
Thou stood'st upon the springy sod,
  Thy large eye ranging self-possest,
Thy limbs the limbs of God's young god,
  Thy Passion murmuing *I will*—
  Land of the Lordship Good-and-Ill.

O manful arms, of supple size
To clasp a world or a waist as well!
  O manful eyes, to front the skies
Or look much pity down on hell!
  O manful tongue, to work and sing,
  And soothe a child and dare a king!

O wonder! Now thou sleep'st in pain,
Like as some dream thy soul did grieve:
  God wounds thee, heals thee whole again,
And calls thee trembling to thine Eve.
  Wide-armed, thou dropp'st on knightly knee:
  Dear Love, Dear Freedom, go with me!

Then all the beasts before thee passed—
Beast War, Oppression, Murder, Lust,
  False Art, False Faith, slow skulking last—
And out of Time's thick-rising dust
  Thy Lord said, " Name them, tame them, Son;
  Nor rest, nor rest, till thou hast done."

Ah, name thou false, or tame thou wrong,
At heart let no man fear for thee:
Thy Past sings ever Freedom's Song,
Thy Future's voice sounds wondrous free;
    And Freedom is more large than Crime,
    And Error is more small than Time.

Come, thou whole Self of Latter Man!
Come o'er thy realm of Good-and-Ill,
    And do, thou Self that say'st *I can*,
And love, thou Self that say'st *I will;*
    And prove and know Time's worst and best,
    Thou tall young Adam of the West!

1876   *1876*

To ——, with a Rose

I asked my heart to say
Some word whose worth my love's devoir might pay
Upon my Lady's natal day.

Then said my heart to me:
*Learn from the rhyme that now shall come to thee
What fits thy Love most lovingly.*

This gift that learning shows;
For, as a rhyme unto its rhyme-twin goes,
I send a rose unto a Rose.

1876   *1876*

Dedication

To Charlotte Cushman

As Love will carve dear names upon a tree,
Symbol of gravure on his heart to be,

So thought I thine with loving text to set
In the growth and substance of my canzonet;

But, writing it, my tears begin to fall—
This wild-rose stem for thy large name's too small!

Nay, still my trembling hands are fain, are fain
Cut the good letters though they lap again;

Perchance such folk as mark the blur and stain
Will say, *It was the beating of the rain;*

Or, haply these o'er-woundings of the stem
May loose some litle balm, to plead for them.

1876   *1876*

The Waving of the Corn

Ploughman, whose gnarly hand yet kindly wheeled
Thy plough to ring this solitary tree
    With clover, whose round plat, reserved a-field,
In cool green radius twice my length may be—
    Scanting the corn thy furrows else might yield,
To pleasure August, bees, fair thoughts, and me,
        That here come oft together—daily I,
        Stretched prone in summer's mortal ecstasy,
Do stir with thanks to thee, as stirs this morn
        With waving of the corn.

Unseen, the farmer's boy from round the hill
Whistles a snatch that seeks his soul unsought,
    And fills some time with tune, howbeit shrill;

The cricket tells straight on his simple thought—
Nay, 'tis the cricket's way of being still;
The peddler bee drones in, and gossips naught;
    Far down the wood, a one-desiring dove
    Times me the beating of the heart of love:
And these be all the sounds that mix, each morn,
        With waving of the corn.

From here to where the louder passions dwell,
Green leagues of hilly separation roll:
    Trade ends where yon far clover ridges swell.
Ye terrible Towns, ne'er claim the trembling soul
    That, craftless all to buy or hoard or sell,
From out your deadly complex quarrel stole
    To company with large amiable trees,
    Suck honey summer with unjealous bees,
And take Time's strokes as softly as this morn
        Takes waving of the corn.

1876   *1877*

Clover

Inscribed to the Memory of John Keats

Dear uplands, Chester's favorable fields,
My large unjealous Loves, many yet one—
A grave good-morrow to your Graces, all,
Fair tilth and fruitful seasons!
                            Lo, how still!
The midmorn empties you of men, save me;
Speak to your lover, meadows! None can hear.
I lie as lies yon placid Brandywine,
Holding the hills and heavens in my heart
For contemplation.
                        'Tis a perfect hour.
From founts of dawn the fluent autumn day
Has rippled as a brook right pleasantly
Half-way to noon; but now with widening turn
Makes pause, in lucent meditation locked,
And rounds into a silver pool of morn,

Bottom'd with clover-fields. My heart just hears
Eight lingering strokes of some far village-bell,
That speak the hour so inward-voiced, meseems
Time's conscience has but whispered him eight hints
Of revolution. Reigns that mild surcease
That stills the middle of each rural morn—
When nimble noises that with sunrise ran
About the farms have sunk again to rest;
When Tom no more across the horse-lot calls
To sleepy Dick, nor Dick husk-voiced upbraids
The sway-back'd roan for stamping on his foot
With sulphurous oath and kick in flank, what time
The cart-chain clinks across the slanting shaft,
And, kitchenward, the rattling bucket plumps
Souse down the well, where quivering ducks quack loud,
And Susan Cook is singing.
                                    Up the sky
The hesitating moon slow trembles on,
Faint as a new-washed soul but lately up
From out a buried body. Far about,
A hundred slopes in hundred fantasies
Most ravishingly run, so smooth of curve
That I but seem to see the fluent plain
Rise toward a rain of clover-bloom, as lakes
Pout gentle mounds of plashment up to meet
Big shower-drops. Now the little winds, as bees,
Bowing the blooms come wandering where I lie
Mixt soul and body with the clover-tufts,
Light on my spirit, give from wing and thigh
Rich pollens and divine sweet irritants
To every nerve, and freshly make report
Of inmost Nature's secret autumn-thought
Unto some soul of sense within my frame
That owns each cognizance of the outlying five,
And sees, hears, tastes, smells, touches, all in one.

Tell me, dear Clover (since my soul is thine,
Since I am fain give study all the day,
To make thy ways my ways, thy service mine,

To seek me out thy God, my God to be,
And die from out myself to live in thee)—
Now, Cousin Clover, tell me in mine ear:
Go'st thou to market with thy pink and green?
Of what avail, this color and this grace?
Wert thou but squat of stem and brindle-brown,
Still careless herds would feed. A poet, thou:
What worth, what worth, the whole of all thine art?
Three-Leaves, instruct me! I am sick of price.

Framed in the arching of two clover-stems
Where-through I gaze from off my hill, afar,
The spacious fields from me to Heaven take on
Tremors of change and new significance
To th' eye, as to the ear a simple tale
Begins to hint a parable's sense beneath.
The prospect widens, cuts all bounds of blue
Where horizontal limits bend, and spreads
Into a curious-hill'd and curious-valley'd Vast,
Endless before, behind, around; which seems
Th' incalculable Up-and-Down of Time
Made plain before mine eyes. The clover-stems
Still cover all the space; but now they bear,
For clover-blooms, fair, stately heads of men
With poets' faces heartsome, dear and pale—
Sweet visages of all the souls of time
Whose loving service to the world has been
In the artist's way expressed and bodied. Oh,
In arms' reach, here be Dante, Keats, Chopin,
Raphael, Lucretius, Omar, Angelo,
Beethoven, Chaucer, Schubert, Shakspere, Bach,
And Buddha (sweetest masters! Let me lay
These arms this once, this humble once, about
Your reverend necks—the most containing clasp,
For all in all, this world e'er saw!), and there,
Yet further on, bright throngs unnamable
Of workers worshipful, nobilities
In the Court of Gentle Service, silent men,
Dwellers in woods, brooders on helpful art,

And all the press of them, the fair, the large,
That wrought with beauty.
                Lo, what bulk is here?
Now comes the Course-of-things, shaped like an Ox,
Slow browsing, o'er my hillside, ponderously—
The huge-brawned, tame, and workful Course-of-things,
That hath his grass, if earth be round or flat,
And hath his grass, if empires plunge in pain
Or faiths flash out. This cool, unasking Ox
Comes browsing o'er my hills and vales of Time,
And thrusts me out his tongue, and curls it, sharp
And sicklewise, about my poets' heads,
And twists them in, all—Dante, Keats, Chopin,
Raphael, Lucretius, Omar, Angelo,
Beethoven, Chaucer, Schubert, Shakspere, Bach,
And Buddha, in one sheaf—and champs and chews,
With slanty-churning jaws, and swallows down;
Then slowly plants a mighty forefoot out,
And makes advance to futureward, one inch.
So: they have played their part.
                And to this end?
This, God? This, troublous-breeding Earth? This, Sun
Of hot, quick pains? To this no-end that ends,
These Masters wrought, and wept, and sweated blood,
And burned, and loved, and ached with public shame,
And found no friends to breathe their loves to, save
Woods and wet pillows? This was all? This Ox?
" Nay," quoth a sum of voices in mine ear,
" God's clover, we, and feed His Course-of-things;
The pasture is God's pasture; systems strange
Of food and fiberment He hath, whereby
The general brawn is built for plans of His
To quality precise. Kinsman, learn this:
The artist's market is the heart of man;
The artist's price, some little good of man.
Tease not thy vision with vain search for ends.
The End of Means is art that works by love.
The End of Ends . . . in God's Beginning's lost."

1876   *1878*

Evening Song

Look off, dear Love, across the sallow sands,
    And mark yon meeting of the sun and sea;
How long they kiss, in sight of all the lands!
    Ah, longer, longer, we.

Now in the sea's red vintage melts the sun,
    As Egypt's pearl dissolved in rosy wine,
And Cleopatra Night drinks all. 'Tis done!
    Love, lay thine hand in mine.

Come forth, sweet stars, and comfort Heaven's heart;
    Glimmer, ye waves, round else unlighted sands;
O Night, divorce our sun and sky apart—
    Never our lips, our hands.

1876   *1877*

To Beethoven

In o'er-strict calyx lingering,
    Lay music's bud too long unblown,
Till thou, Beethoven, breathed the spring:
    Then bloomed the perfect rose of tone.

O Psalmist of the weak, the strong,
    O Troubadour of love and strife,
Co-Litanist of right and wrong,
    Sole Hymner of the whole of life,

I know not how, I care not why,—
    Thy music sets my world at ease,
And melts my passion's mortal cry
    In satisfying symphonies.

It soothes my accusations sour
    'Gainst thoughts that fray the restless soul:
The stain of death; the pain of power;
    The lack of love 'twixt part and whole;

The yea-nay of Freewill and Fate,
    Whereof both cannot be, yet are;
The praise a poet wins too late
    Who starves from earth into a star;

The lies that serve great parties well,
    While truths but give their Christ a cross;
The loves that send warm souls to hell,
    While cold-blood neuters take no loss;

Th' indifferent smile that nature's grace
    On Jesus, Judas, pours alike;
Th' indifferent frown on nature's face
    When luminous lightnings strangely strike

The sailor praying on his knees
    And spare his mate that's cursing God;
How babes and widows starve and freeze
    Yet Nature will not stir a clod;

Why Nature blinds us in each act
    Yet makes no law in mercy bend,
No pitfall from our feet retract,
    No storm cry out *Take shelter, friend;*

Why snakes that crawl the earth should ply
    Rattles, that whoso hears may shun,
While serpent lightnings in the sky
    But rattle when the deed is done;

How truth can e'er be good for them
    That have not eyes to bear its strength,
And yet how stern our lights condemn
    Delays that lend the darkness length;

To know all things, save knowingness;
    To grasp, yet loosen, feeling's rein;
To waste no manhood on success;
    To look with pleasure upon pain;

Though teased by small mixt social claims,
    To lose no large simplicity,
And midst of clear-seen crimes and shames
    To move with manly purity;

To hold, with keen,. yet loving eyes,
  Art's realm from Cleverness apart,
To know the Clever good and wise,
  Yet haunt the lonesome heights of Art;

O Psalmist of the weak, the strong,
  O Troubadour of love and strife,
Co-Litanist of right and wrong,
  Sole Hymner of the whole of life,

I know not how, I care not why,
  Thy music brings this broil at ease,
And melts my passion's mortal cry
  In satisfying symphonies.

Yea, it forgives me all my sins,
  Fits life to love like rhyme to rhyme,
And tunes the task each day begins
  By the last trumpet-note of Time.

1876   *1877*

The Stirrup-Cup

Death, thou'rt a cordial old and rare:
Look how compounded, with what care!
Time got his wrinkles reaping thee
Sweet herbs from all antiquity.

David to thy distillage went,
Keats, and Gotama excellent,
Omar Khayyám, and Chaucer bright,
And Shakspere for a king-delight.

Then, Time, let not a drop be spilt:
Hand me the cup whene'er thou wilt;
'Tis thy rich stirrup-cup to me;
I'll drink it down right smilingly.

1877   *1877*

The Bee

What time I paced, at pleasant morn,
    A deep and dewy wood,
I heard a mellow hunting-horn
    Make dim report of Dian's lustihood
Far down a heavenly hollow.
Mine ear, though fain, had pain to follow:
    Tara! it twang'd *tara-tara!* it blew,
    Yet wavered oft, and flew
Most ficklewise about, or here, or there,
A music now from earth and now from air.
    But on a sudden, lo!
    I marked a blossom shiver to and fro
With dainty inward storm; and there within
A down-drawn trump of yellow jessamine
        A bee
Thrust up its sad-gold body lustily,
All in a honey madness hotly bound
        On blissful burglary.
        A cunning sound
In that wing-music held me: down I lay
In amber shades of many a golden spray,
Where looping low with languid arms the Vine
In wreaths of ravishment did overtwine
Her kneeling Live-Oak, thousand-fold to plight
Herself unto her own true stalwart knight.

As some dim blur of distant music nears
The long-desiring sense, and slowly clears
    To forms of time and apprehensive tune,
    So, as I lay, full soon
Interpretation throve: the bee's fanfare,
Through sequent films of discourse vague as air,
Passed to plain words, while, fanning faint perfume,
The bee o'erhung a rich unrifled bloom:
    " O Earth, fair lordly Blossom, soft a-shine

Upon the star-pranked universal vine,
    Hast nought for me?
      To thee
Come I, a poet, hereward haply blown,
From out another worldflower lately flown.
Wilt ask, *What profit e'er a poet brings?*
He beareth starry stuff about his wings
To pollen thee and sting thee fertile: nay,
If still thou narrow thy contracted way,
    —Worldflower, if thou refuse me—
    —Worldflower, if thou abuse me,
    And hoist thy stamen's spear-point high
    To wound my wing and mar mine eye—
Nathless I'll drive me to thy deepest sweet,
Yea, richlier shall that pain the pollen beat
From me to thee, for oft these pollens be
Fine dust from wars that poets wage for thee.
But, O beloved Earthbloom soft a-shine
Upon the universal Jessamine,
      Prithee, abuse me not,
      Prithee, refuse me not,
Yield, yield the heartsome honey love to me
      Hid in thy nectary!"
And as I sank into a dimmer dream
The pleading bee's song-burthen sole did seem:
  " Hast ne'er a honey-drop of love for me
      In thy huge nectary?"

1877   *1877*

Tampa Robins

The robin laughed in the orange-tree:
" Ho, windy North, a fig for thee:
While breasts are red and wings are bold
And green trees wave us globes of gold,
Time's scythe shall reap but bliss for me
—Sunlight, song, and the orange-tree.

" Burn, golden globes in leafy sky,
My orange-planets: crimson, I
Will shine and shoot among the spheres
(Blithe meteor that no mortal fears)
And thrid the heavenly orange-tree
With orbits bright of minstrelsy.

" If that I hate wild winter's spite—
The gibbet trees, the world in white,
The sky but gray wind over a grave—
Why should I ache, the season's slave?
I'll sing from the top of the orange-tree
Gramercy, winter's tyranny.

" I'll south with the sun, and keep my clime;
My wing is king of the summer-time;
My breast to the sun his torch shall hold;
And I'll call down through the green and gold
Time, take thy scythe, reap bliss for me,
Bestir thee under the orange-tree."

1877   *1877*

Under the Cedarcroft Chestnut

Firm-set in ancient sward, his manful bole
  Upbore his frontage largely toward the sky.
We could not dream but that he had a soul:
  What virtue breathed from out his bravery!

We gazed o'erhead: far down our deepening eyes
  Rained glamours from his green midsummer mass.
The worth and sum of all his centuries
  Suffused his mighty shadow on the grass—

A Presence large, a grave and steadfast Form
  Amid the leaves' light play and fantasy,
A Calmness conquered out of many a storm,
  A Manhood mastered by a chestnut-tree!

Then, while his monarch fingers downward held
   The rugged burrs wherewith his state was rife,
A voice of large authoritative Eld
   Seemed uttering prickly parables of life:

How *Life in truth was sharply set with ills;*
   A kernel cased in quarrels; yea, a sphere
Of stings, and hedgehog-round of mortal quills:
   How *most men itched to eat too soon i' the year,*

And took but wounds and worries for their pains,
   Whereas the wise withheld their patient hands,
Nor plucked green pleasures till the sun and rains
   And seasonable ripenings burst all bands

And opened wide the liberal burrs of life.
   There, O my Friend, beneath the chestnut-bough
Gazing on thee immerged in modern strife,
   I framed a prayer of fervency—that thou,

In soul and stature larger than thy kind,
   Still more to this strong Form might'st liken thee,
Till thy whole Self in every fibre find
   The tranquil lordship of thy chestnut-tree.

1877   *1878*

A Florida Sunday

From cold Norse caves or buccaneer Southern seas
   Oft come repenting tempests here to die;
Bewailing old-time wrecks and robberies,
   They shrive to priestly pines with many a sigh,
Breathe salutary balms through lank-lock'd hair
   Of sick men's heads, and soon—this world outworn—
Sink into saintly heavens of stirless air,
   Clean from confessional. One died, this morn,
And willed the world to wise Queen Tranquil: she,
   Sweet sovereign Lady of all souls that bide
In contemplation, tames the too bright skies

Like that faint agate film, far down descried,
Restraining suns in sudden thoughtful eyes
   Which flashed but now. Blest distillation rare
Of o'er-rank brightness filtered waterwise
   Through all the earths in heaven—thou always fair,
Still virgin bride of e'er-creating thought—
Dream-worker, in whose dream the Future's wrought—
Healer of hurts, free balm for bitter wrongs—
Most silent mother of all sounding songs—
Thou that dissolvest hells to make thy heaven—
Thou tempest's heir, that keep'st no tempest leaven—
But after winds' and thunders' wide mischance
Dost brood, and better thine inheritance—
Thou privacy of space, where each grave Star
As in his own still chamber sits afar
To meditate, yet, by thy walls unpent,
Shines to his fellows o'er the firmament—
Oh! as thou liv'st in all this sky and sea
That likewise lovingly do live in thee,
So melt my soul in thee, and thine in me,
Divine Tranquillity!

Gray Pelican, poised where yon broad shallows shine,
Know'st thou, that finny foison all is mine
In the bag below thy beak—yet thine, not less?
For God, of His most gracious friendliness,
Hath wrought that every soul, this loving morn,
Into all things may be new-corporate born,
And each live whole in all: I sail with thee,
Thy Pelican's self is mine; yea, silver Sea,
In this large moment all thy fishes, ripples, bights,
Pale in-shore greens and distant blue delights,
White visionary sails, long reaches fair
By moon-horn'd strands that film the far-off air,
Bright sparkle-revelations, secret majesties,
Shells, wrecks and wealths, are mine; yea, Orange-trees,
That lift your small world-systems in the light,
Rich sets of round green heavens studded bright
With globes of fruit that like still planets shine,
Mine is your green-gold universe; yea, mine,

White slender Lighthouse fainting to the eye
That wait'st on yon keen cape-point wistfully,
Like to some maiden spirit pausing pale,
New-wing'd, yet fain to sail
Above the serene Gulf to where a bridegroom soul
Calls o'er the soft horizon—mine thy dole
Of shut undaring wings and wan desire—
Mine, too, thy later hope and heavenly fire
Of kindling expectation; yea, all sights,
All sounds, that make this morn—quick flights
Of pea-green paroquets 'twixt neighbor trees,
Like missives and sweet morning inquiries
From green to green, in green—live oaks' round heads,
Busy with jays for thoughts—grays, whites and reds
Of pranked woodpeckers that ne'er gossip out,
But alway tap at doors and gad about—
Robins and mocking-birds that all day long
Athwart straight sunshine weave cross-threads of song,
Shuttles of music—clouds of mosses gray
That rain me rains of pleasant thoughts alway
From a low sky of leaves—faint yearning psalms
Of endless metre breathing through the palms
That crowd and lean and gaze from off the shore
Ever for one that cometh nevermore—
Palmettos ranked, with childish spear-points set
Against no enemy—rich cones that fret
High roofs of temples shafted tall with pines—
Green, grateful mangroves where the sand-beach shines—
Long lissom coast that in and outward swerves,
The grace of God made manifest in curves—
All riches, goods and braveries never told
Of earth, sun, air and heaven—now I hold
Your being in my being; I am ye,
And ye myself; yea, lastly, Thee,
God, whom my roads all reach, howe'er they run,
My Father, Friend, Belovèd, dear All-One,
Thee in my soul, my soul in Thee, I feel,
Self of my self. Lo, through my sense doth steal
Clear cognizance of all selves and qualities,

Of all existence that hath been or is,
Of all strange haps that men miscall of chance,
And all the works of tireless circumstance:
Each borders each, like mutual sea and shore,
Nor aught misfits his neighbor that's before,
Nor him that's after—nay, through this still air,
Out of the North come quarrels, and keen blare
Of challenge by the hot-breath'd parties blown;
Yet break they not this peace with alien tone,
Fray not my heart, nor fright me for my land,
—I hear from all-wards, allwise understand,
The great bird Purpose bears me twixt her wings,
And I am one with all the kinsmen things
That e'er my Father fathered. Oh, to me
All questions solve in this tranquillity:
E'en this dark matter, once so dim, so drear,
Now shines upon my spirit heavenly-clear:
Thou, Father, without logic, tellest me
How this divine denial true may be,
—How *All 's in each, yet every one of all
Maintains his Self complete and several.*

1877   *1877*

From the Flats

What heartache—ne'er a hill!
Inexorable, vapid, vague, and chill
The drear sand-levels drain my spirit low.
With one poor word they tell me all they know;
Whereat their stupid tongues, to tease my pain,
Do drawl it o'er again and o'er again.
They hurt my heart with griefs I cannot name:
Always the same, the same.

Nature hath no surprise,
No ambuscade of beauty 'gainst mine eyes
From brake or lurking dell or deep defile;

No humors, frolic forms—this mile, that mile;
No rich reserves or happy-valley hopes
Beyond the bends of roads, the distant slopes.
Her fancy fails, her wild is all run tame:
    Ever the same, the same.

    Oh, might I through these tears
But glimpse some hill my Georgia high uprears,
Where white the quartz and pink the pebble shine,
The hickory heavenward strives, the muscadine
Swings o'er the slope, the oak's far-falling shade
Darkens the dogwood in the bottom glade,
And down the hollow from a ferny nook
    Bright leaps a living brook!

1877   *1877*

The Mocking Bird

Superb and sole, upon a plumèd spray
    That o'er the general leafage boldly grew,
    He summ'd the woods in song; or typic drew
The watch of hungry hawks, the lone dismay
Of languid doves when long their lovers stray,
    And all birds' passion-plays that sprinkle dew
    At morn in brake or bosky avenue.
Whate'er birds did or dreamed, this bird could say.
Then down he shot, bounced airily along
The sward, twitched-in a grasshopper, made song
    Midflight, perched, primped, and to his art again.
    Sweet Science, this large riddle read me plain:
      How may the death of that dull insect be
      The life of yon trim Shakspere on the tree?

1877   *1877*

The Dove

If haply thou, O Desdemona Morn,
   Shouldst call along the curving sphere, "Remain,
Dear Night, sweet Moor; nay, leave me not in scorn!"
   With soft halloos of heavenly love and pain;—

Shouldst thou, O Spring! a-cower in coverts dark,
   'Gainst proud supplanting Summer sing thy plea,
And move the mighty woods through mailèd bark
   Till mortal heart-break throbbed in every tree;—

Or (grievous *if* that may be *yea* o'er-soon!),
   If thou, my Heart, long holden from thy Sweet,
Shouldst knock Death's door with mellow shocks of tune,
   Sad inquiry to make—*When may we meet?*

Nay, if ye three, O Morn! O Spring! O Heart!
   Should chant grave unisons of grief and love;
Ye could not mourn with more melodious art
   Than daily doth yon dim sequestered dove.

1877   *1878*

A Puzzled Ghost in Florida

Down saintly shores of milk-white sand,
   By slender cape and broadening bay,
'Twixt billowy pines—a surf asleep on land—
   And the great Gulf at play;

Past far-off palms that filmed to nought,
   And in and out the cunning Keys
That laced the land like fragile patterns wrought
   To edge old broideries:

The sail sighed on all day for joy,
   The prow each pouting wave did leave
All smile and song, with sheen and ripple coy,
   Till the dusk diver, Eve,

Brought up from out the brimming East
    The oval moon, a perfect pearl.
In that large lustre all our haste surceased,
    The sail seemed fain to furl,

The silent steersman landward turned,
    And ship and shore set breast to breast.
Beneath a palm wherethrough a planet burned
    We ate, and sank to rest.

But soon from sleep's dear death (it seemed)
    I rose, and strolled along the sea,
Down silver distances that faintly gleamed
    On to infinity,

Till suddenly I paused, for lo!
    A shape—from whence I ne'er divined—
Appeared before me, pacing to and fro,
    With head far down inclined.

A wraith, I thought, *that walks the shore*
    To solve some old perplexity.
Full heavy hung the draggled gown he wore,
    His hair flew all awry.

He waited not, as ghosts oft use,
    To be *dear-heaven'd*, and *oh'd,*
But briskly said: " Good-evenin'; what's the news?
    Consumption? After boa'd?

" Or mebbe you're intendin' of
    Investments? Orange-plantin'? Pine?
Hotel? or sanitarium? What above
    This ye'ath *can* be your line?

" Speakin' of sanitariums, now,
    Jest look 'ee here, my friend;
I know a little story—well, I swow—
    Wait till you hear the end:

" Some year or more ago, I s'pose,
    I roamed from Maine to Floridy,
And—see where them there tall Palmettos grows?
    I bought that little Key,

" Cal'latin' for to build right off
    A c'lossal sanitarium.
Big surf! Hot Gulf! Jest death upon a cough!
    I run it high, to hum!

" Well, sir, I went to work in style;
    Bought me a steamboat, loaded it
With my hotel (pyazers more'n a mile!)
    Already framed and fit,

" Insured 'em, fetched 'em safe around,
    Put up my buildin', moored my boat,
Com-plete! then went to bed and slept as sound
    As if I'd paid a note.

" Now on that very night a squall
    Cum up from some'eres—some bad place!
An' blowed, an' tore, an' rared, an' pitched, an' all—
    I had to run a race

" Right out o' bed from that hotel
    An' git to yonder risin' ground;
For, 'twixt the sea that riz, an' rain that fell,
    I pooty nigh was drowned!

" An' thar I stood till mornin' cum,
    Right on yon little knoll of sand,
Fre*quent*ly wishin' I had staid to hum,
    Fur from this 'tarnal land!

" When mornin' cum, I took a good
    Long look, an'—well, sir, sure's I'm *me*—
That boat laid right whar that hotel had stood,
    An' it sailed out to sea!

" No, I'll not keep you; good-by, friend:
    Don't think about it much; preehaps
Your brain might git see-sawin', end for end,
    Like them asylum chaps.

" For here *I* walk for evermore,
    A-tryin' to make it gee,
How one same wind could blow my ship to shore,
    And my hotel to sea! "

1877   *1877*

To Richard Wagner

I saw a sky of stars that rolled in grime.
   All glory twinkled through some sweat of fight.
From each tall chimney of the roaring time
   That shot his fire far up the sooty night
Mixt fuels—Labor's Right and Labor's Crime—
   Sent upward throb on throb of scarlet light
Till huge hot blushes in the heavens blent
With golden hues of Trade's high firmament.

Fierce burned the furnaces; yet all seemed well.
   Hope dreamed rich music in the rattling mills.
" Ye foundries, ye shall cast my church a bell,"
   Loud cried the Future from the farthest hills:
" Ye groaning forces, crack me every shell
   Of customs, old constraints, and narrow ills:
Thou, lithe Invention, wake and pry and guess,
Till thy deft mind invents me Happiness."

And I beheld high scaffoldings of creeds
   Crumbling from round Religion's perfect Fane:
And a vast noise of rights, wrongs, powers, needs,
   —Cries of new Faiths that called " This Way is plain,"
—Grindings of upper against lower greeds—
   —Fond sighs for old things, shouts for new,—did reign
Below that stream of golden fire that broke,
Mottled with red, above the seas of smoke.

Hark! Gay fanfares from horns of old Romance
   Strike through the clouds of clamor: who be these
That, paired in rich processional, advance
   From darkness o'er the murk mad factories
Into yon flaming road, and sink, strange Ministrants!
   Sheer down to earth, with many minstrelsies
And motions fine, and mix about the scene
And fill the Time with forms of ancient mien?

Bright ladies and brave knights of Fatherland;
  Sad mariners, no harbor e'er may hold;
A swan soft floating tow'rds a tragic strand;
  Dim ghosts, of earth, air, water, fire, steel, gold,
Wind, grief, and love; a lewd and lurking band
  Of Powers—dark Conspiracy, Cunning cold,
Gray Sorcery; magic cloaks and rings and rods;
Valkyries, heroes, Rhinemaids, giants, gods!

*   *   *   *   *

O Wagner, westward bring thy heavenly art.
  No trifler thou: Siegfried and Wotan be
Names for big ballads of the modern heart.
  Thine ears hear deeper than thine eyes can see.
Voice of the monstrous mill, the shouting mart,
  Not less of airy cloud and wave and tree,
Thou, thou, if even to thyself unknown,
Hast power to say the Time in terms of tone.

1877   *1877*

Song of the Chattahoochee

  Out of the hills of Habersham,
    Down the valleys of Hall,
I hurry amain to reach the plain,
Run the rapid and leap the fall,
Split at the rock and together again,
Accept my bed, or narrow or wide,
And flee from folly on every side
With a lover's pain to attain the plain
    Far from the hills of Habersham,
    Far from the valleys of Hall.

  All down the hills of Habersham,
    All through the valleys of Hall,
The rushes cried *Abide, abide,*
The willful waterweeds held me thrall,
The laving laurel turned my tide,

The ferns and the fondling grass said *Stay*,
The dewberry dipped for to work delay,
And the little reeds sighed *Abide, abide,*
   Here in the hills of Habersham,
   Here in the valleys of Hall.

High o'er the hills of Habersham,
   Veiling the valleys of Hall,
The hickory told me manifold
Fair tales of shade, the poplar tall
Wrought me her shadowy self to hold,
The chestnut, the oak, the walnut, the pine,
Overleaning, with flickering meaning and sign,
Said, *Pass not, so cold, these manifold*
   Deep shades of the hills of Habersham,
   These glades in the valleys of Hall.

And oft in the hills of Habersham,
   And oft in the valleys of Hall,
The white quartz shone, and the smooth brook-stone
Did bar me of passage with friendly brawl,
And many a luminous jewel lone
—Crystals clear or a-cloud with mist,
Ruby, garnet and amethyst—
Made lures with the lights of streaming stone
   In the clefts of the hills of Habersham,
   In the beds of the valleys of Hall.

But oh, not the hills of Habersham,
   And oh, not the valleys of Hall
Avail: I am fain for to water the plain.
Downward the voices of Duty call—
Downward, to toil and be mixed with the main,
The dry fields burn, and the mills are to turn,
And a myriad flowers mortally yearn,
And the lordly main from beyond the plain
   Calls o'er the hills of Habersham,
   Calls through the valleys of Hall.

1877   *1877?, 1883*

The Hard Times in Elfland

A Christmas-Eve Story for Children

Strange that the termagant winds should scold
   The Christmas Eve so bitterly!
But Wife, and Harry the four-year-old,
   Big Charley, Nimblewits, and I,

Blithe as the wind was bitter, drew
   More frontward of the mighty fire,
Where wise Newfoundland Fan foreknew
   The heaven that Christian dogs desire—

Stretched o'er the rug, serene and grave,
   Huge nose on heavy paws reclined,
With never a drowning boy to save,
   And warmth of body and peace of mind.

And, as our happy circle sat,
   The fire well capp'd the company:
In grave debate or careless chat,
   A right good fellow, mingled he:

He seemed as one of us to sit,
   And talked of things above, below,
With flames more winsome than our wit,
   And coals that burned like love aglow.

While thus our rippling discourse rolled
   Smooth down the channel of the night,
We spoke of Time: thereat, one told
   A parable of the Seasons' flight.

" Time was a Shepherd with four sheep.
   In a certain Field he long abode.
He stood by the bars, and his flock bade leap
   One at a time to the Common Road.

" And first there leapt, like bird on wing,
    A lissome Lamb that played in the air.
I heard the Shepherd call him *Spring:*
    Oh, large-eyed, fresh and snowy fair

" He skipped the flowering Highway fast,
    Hurried the hedgerows green and white,
Set maids and men a-yearning, passed
    The Bend, and gamboll'd out of sight.

" And next marched forth a matron Ewe
    (While Time took down a bar for her),
Udder'd so large 'twas much ado
    E'en then to clear the barrier.

" Full softly shone her silken fleece
    What stately time she paced along:
Each heartsome hoof-stroke wrought increase
    Of sunlight, substance, seedling, song,

" In flower, in fruit, in field, in bird,
    Till the great globe, rich fleck'd and pied,
Like some large peach half pinkly furred,
    Turned to the sun a glowing side

" And hung in the heavenly orchard, bright,
    None-such, complete.
                    Then, while the Ewe
Slow passed the Bend, a blur of light,
    The Shepherd's face in sadness grew:

" ' Summer! ' he said, as one would say
    A sigh in syllables. So, in haste
(For shame of Summer's long delay,
    Yet gazing still what way she paced),

" He summoned Autumn, slanting down
    The second bar. Thereover strode
A Wether, fleeced in burning brown,
    And largely loitered down the Road.

" Far as the farmers sight his shape
　　Majestic moving o'er the way,
All cry *To harvest*, crush the grape,
　　And haul the corn and house the hay,

" Till presently, no man can say,
　　(So brown the woods that line that end)
If yet the brown-fleeced Wether may,
　　Or not, have passed beyond the Bend.

" Now turn I towards the Shepherd: lo,
　　An agèd Ram, flapp'd, gnarly-horn'd,
With bones that crackle o'er the snow,
　　Rheum'd, wind-gall'd, rag-fleec'd, burr'd and thorn'd!

" Time takes the third bar off for him.
　" He totters down the windy lane.
'Tis Winter, still: the Bend lies dim.
　　O Lamb, would thou wouldst leap again! "

Those seasons out, we talked of these:
　　And I (with inward purpose sly
To shield my purse from Christmas trees
　　And stockings and wild robbery

When Hal and Nimblewits invade
　　My cash in Santa Claus's name)
In full the hard, hard times surveyed;
　　Denounced all waste as crime and shame;

Hinted that " waste " might be a term
　　Including skates, velocipedes,
Kites, marbles, soldiers, towers infirm,
　　Bows, arrows, cannon, Indian reeds,

Cap-pistols, drums, mechanic toys,
　　And all th' infernal host of horns
Whereby to strenuous hells of noise
　　Are turned the blessèd Christmas morns;

Thus, roused—those horns!—to sacred rage,
　　I rose, forefinger high in air,
When Harry cried (*some* war to wage),
　" Papa, is hard times ev'ywhere?

" Maybe in Santa Claus's land
  It isn't hard times none at all! "
Now, blessèd Vision! to my hand
  Most pat, a marvel strange did fall.

Scarce had my Harry ceased, when " Look! "
  He cried, leapt up in wild alarm,
Ran to my Comrade, shelter took
  Beneath the startled mother's arm,

And so was still: what time we saw
  A foot hang down the fireplace! Then,
With painful scrambling scratched and raw,
  Two hands that seemed like hands of men

Eased down two legs and a body through
  The blazing fire, and forth there came
Before our wide and wondering view
  A figure shrinking half with shame

And half with weakness. " Sir," I said,
  —But with a mien of dignity
The seedy stranger raised his head:
  " My friends, I'm Santa Claus," said he.

But oh, how changed! That rotund face
  The new moon rivalled, pale and thin;
Where once was cheek, now empty space;
  Whate'er stood out, did now stand in.

His piteous legs scarce propped him up:
  His arms mere sickles seemed to be:
But most o'erflowed our sorrow's cup
  When that we saw—or did not see—

His belly: we remembered how
  It shook like a bowl of jelly fine:
An earthquake could not shake it now;
  He *had* no belly—not a sign.

" Yes, yes, old friends, you well may stare:
  I *have* seen better days," he said:
" But now, with shrinkage, loss and care,
  Your Santa Claus scarce owns his head.

" We've had such hard, hard times this year
   For goblins! Never knew the like.
All Elfland's mortgaged! And we fear
   The gnomes are just about to strike.

" I once was rich, and round, and hale.
   The whole world called me jolly brick;
But listen to a piteous tale.
   Young Harry,—Santa Claus is sick!

" 'Twas thus: a smooth-tongued railroad man
   Comes to my house and talks to me:
I've got, says he, *a little plan
   That suits this nineteenth century.*

" *Instead of driving, as you do,
   Six reindeer slow from house to house,
Let's build a Grand Trunk Railway through
   From here to earth's last terminus.*

" *We'll touch at every chimney-top
   (An Elevated Track, of course),
Then, as we whisk you by, you'll drop
   Each package down: just think, the force*

" *You'll save, the time!—Besides, we'll make
   Our millions: look you, soon we will
Compete for freights—and then we'll take
   Dame Fortune's bales of good and ill*

" *(Why, she's the biggest shipper, sir,
   That e'er did business in this world!)*:
*Then Death, that ceaseless Traveller,
   Shall on his rounds by us be whirled.*

" *When ghosts return to walk with men,
   We'll bring 'em cheap by steam, and fast:
We'll run a Branch to heaven! and then
   We'll riot, man; for then, at last*

" *We'll make with heaven a contract fair
   To call, each hour, from town to town,
And carry the dead folks' souls up there,
   And bring the unborn babies down!*

" The plan seemed fair: I gave him cash,
  Nay, every penny I could raise.
My wife e'er cried, *'Tis rash, 'tis rash:*
  How could I know the stock-thief's ways?

" But soon I learned full well, poor fool!
  My woes began, that wretched day.
The President plied me like a tool.
  In lawyer's fees, and rights of way,

" Injunctions, leases, charters, I
  Was meshed as in a mighty maze.
The stock ran low, the talk ran high:
  Then quickly flamed the final blaze.

" With never an inch of track—'tis true!
  The debts were large . . . the oft-told tale.
The President rolled in splendor new
  —He bought my silver at the sale.

" Yes, sold me out: we've moved away.
  I've had to give up everything.
My reindeer, even, whom I . . . pray,
  Excuse me " . . . here, o'er-sorrowing,

Poor Santa Claus burst into tears,
  Then calmed again: " my reindeer fleet,
I gave them up: on foot, my dears,
  I now must plod through snow and sleet.

" Retrenchment rules in Elfland, now;
  Yes, every luxury is cut off.
—Which, by the way, reminds me how
  I caught this dreadful hacking cough:

" I cut off the tail of my Ulster furred
  To make young Kris a coat of state.
That very night the storm occurred!
  Thus we become the sport of Fate.

" For I was out till after one,
  Surveying chimney-tops and roofs,
And planning how it could be done
  Without my reindeers' bouncing hoofs.

" *My dear*, says Mrs. Claus, that night
  (A most superior woman she!)
It never, never can be right
  That you, deep-sunk in poverty,

" *This year should leave your poor old bed*
  And trot about, bent down with toys,
(*There's Kris a-crying now for bread!*)
  To give to other people's boys.

" *Since you've been out, the news arrives*
  The Elfs' Insurance Company's gone.
Ah, Claus, those premiums! Now, our lives
  Depend on yours: thus griefs go on.

" *And even while you're thus harassed,*
  I do believe, if out you went,
You'd go, in spite of all that's passed,
  To the children of that President!

" Oh, Charley, Harry, Nimblewits,
  These eyes, that night, ne'er slept a wink.
My path seemed honeycombed with pits.
  Naught could I do but think and think.

" But, with the day, my courage rose.
  Ne'er shall my boys, *my* boys (I cried),
When Christmas morns their eyes unclose,
  Find empty stockings gaping wide!

" Then hewed and whacked and whittled I;
  The wife, the girls and Kris took fire;
They spun, sewed, cut,—till by and by
  We made, at home, my pack entire! "

(He handed me a bundle, here.)
  " Now, hoist me up: there, gently: quick!
Dear boys, *don't* look for much this year:
  Remember, Santa Claus is sick! "

1877   *1877*

A Weather-Vane

A weather-vane, weatherless and vaneless,
　　Without the letters pointing each his way;
No eastless east, nor westless west, nor nothing.
　　Let us make snow-balls in the new-mown hay!

1877?　　　　　　　　　　　　　　　　　　　　*1877*

The Harlequin of Dreams

Swift through some trap mine eyes have never found,
　　Dim-panelled in the painted scene of sleep,
　　Thou, giant Harlequin of Dreams, dost leap
Upon my spirit's stage. Then sight and sound,
Then space and time, then language, mete and bound,
　　And all familiar forms that firmly keep
　　Man's reason in the road, change faces, peep
Betwixt the legs, and mock the daily round.
Yet thou canst more than mock: sometimes my tears
　　At midnight break through bounden lids—a sign
　　Thou hast a heart; and oft thy little leaven
Of dream-taught wisdom works me bettered years.
　　In one night witch, saint, trickster, fool divine,
　　I think thou'rt Jester at the Court of Heaven!

1878?　　　　　　　　　　　　　　　　　　　　*1878*

The Revenge of Hamish

It was three slim does and a ten-tined buck in the bracken lay;
　　And all of a sudden the sinister smell of a man,
　　Awaft on a wind-shift, wavered and ran
Down the hill-side and sifted along through the bracken and
　　passed that way.

Then Nan got a-tremble at nostril; she was the daintiest doe;
　　In the print of her velvet flank on the velvet fern
　　She reared, and rounded her ears in turn.
Then the buck leapt up, and his head as a king's to a crown
　　did go

Full high in the breeze, and he stood as if Death had the form
    of a deer;
    And the two slim does full lazily stretching arose,
    For their day-dream slowlier came to a close,
Till they woke and were still, breath-bound with waiting and
    wonder and fear.

Then Alan the huntsman sprang over the hillock, the hounds
    shot by,
    The does and the ten-tined buck made a marvellous bound,
    The hounds swept after with never a sound,
But Alan loud winded his horn, in sign that the quarry was nigh.

For at dawn of that day proud Maclean of Lochbuy to the hunt
    had waxed wild,
    And he cursed at old Alan till Alan fared off with the hounds
    For to drive him the deer to the lower glen-grounds:
" I will kill a red deer," quoth Maclean, " in the sight of the
    wife and the child."

So gayly he paced with the wife and the child to his chosen
    stand;
    But he hurried tall Hamish the henchman ahead: " Go
    turn,"—
Cried Maclean—" if the deer seek to cross to the burn,
Do thou turn them to me: nor fail, lest thy back be red as thy
    hand."

Now hard-fortuned Hamish, half blown of his breath with the
    height of the hill,
    Was white in the face when the ten-tined buck and the does
    Drew leaping to burn-ward; huskily rose
His shouts, and his nether lip twitched, and his legs were o'er-
    weak for his will.

So the deer darted lightly by Hamish and bounded away to the
    burn.
    But Maclean never bating his watch tarried waiting below
    Still Hamish hung heavy with fear for to go
All the space of an hour; then he went, and his face was
    greenish and stern,

And his eye sat back in the socket, and shrunken the eyeballs
    shone,
    As withdrawn from a vision of deeds it were shame to see.
    " Now, now, grim henchman, what is't with thee? "
Brake Maclean, and his wrath rose red as a beacon the wind
    hath upblown.

" Three does and a ten-tined buck made out," spoke Hamish,
    full mild,
    " And I ran for to turn, but my breath it was blown, and they
    passed;
    I was weak, for ye called ere I broke me my fast."
Cried Maclean: " Now a ten-tined buck in the sight of the wife
    and the child

I had killed if the gluttonous kern had not wrought me a snail's
    own wrong! "
    Then he sounded, and down came kinsmen and clansmen all:
    " Ten blows, for ten tine, on his back let fall,
And reckon no stroke if the blood follow not at the bite of
    thong! "

So Hamish made bare, and took him his strokes; at the last he
    smiled.
    " Now I'll to the burn," quoth Maclean, " for it still may be,
    If a slimmer-paunched henchman will hurry with me,
I shall kill me the ten-tined buck for a gift to the wife and the
    child! "

Then the clansmen departed, by this path and that; and over
    the hill
    Sped Maclean with an outward wrath for an inward shame;
    And that place of the lashing full quiet became;
And the wife and the child stood sad; and bloody-backed
    Hamish sat still.

But look! red Hamish has risen; quick about and about turns he.
    " There is none betwixt me and the crag-top! " he screams
    under breath.
    Then, livid as Lazarus lately from death,
He snatches the child from the mother, and clambers the crag
    toward the sea.

Now the mother drops breath; she is dumb, and her heart goes
    dead for a space,
Till the motherhood, mistress of death, shrieks, shrieks
    through the glen,
And that place of the lashing is live with men,
And Maclean, and the gillie that told him, dash up in a des-
    perate race.

Not a breath's time for asking; an eye-glance reveals all the
    tale untold.
They follow mad Hamish afar up the crag toward the sea,
And the lady cries: " Clansmen, run for a fee! —
Yon castle and lands to the two first hands that shall hook him
    and hold

Fast Hamish back from the brink! "—and ever she flies up
    the steep,
And the clansmen pant, and they sweat, and they jostle and
    strain.
But, mother, 'tis vain; but, father, 'tis vain;
Stern Hamish stands bold on the brink, and dangles the child
    o'er the deep.

Now a faintness falls on the men that run, and they all stand
    still.
And the wife prays Hamish as if he were God, on her knees,
Crying: " Hamish! O Hamish! but please, but please
For to spare him! " and Hamish still dangles the child, with a
    wavering will.

On a sudden he turns; with a sea-hawk scream, and a gibe, and
    a song,
Cries: " So; I will spare ye the child if, in sight of ye all,
Ten blows on Maclean's bare back shall fall,
And ye reckon no stroke if the blood follow not at the bite of
    the thong! "

Then Maclean he set hardly his tooth to his lip that his tooth
    was red,
Breathed short for a space, said: " Nay, but it never shall be!
Let me hurl off the damnable hound in the sea! "
But the wife: " Can Hamish go fish us the child from the sea,
    if dead?

Say yea!—Let them lash *me*, Hamish?"—"Nay!"—"Hus-
band, the lashing will heal;
But, oh, who will heal me the bonny sweet bairn in his grave?
Could ye cure me my heart with the death of a knave?
Quick! Love! I will bare thee—so—kneel!" Then Maclean
'gan slowly to kneel

With never a word, till presently downward he jerked to the earth.
Then the henchman—he that smote Hamish—would tremble
and lag;
"Strike, hard!" quoth Hamish, full stern, from the crag;
Then he struck him, and "One!" sang Hamish, and danced
with the child in his mirth.

And no man spake beside Hamish; he counted each stroke with
a song.
When the last stroke fell, then he moved him a pace down
the height,
And he held forth the child in the heartaching sight
Of the mother, and looked all pitiful grave, as repenting a wrong.

And there as the motherly arms stretched out with the thanks-
giving prayer—
And there as the mother crept up with a fearful swift pace,
Till her finger nigh felt of the bairnie's face—
In a flash fierce Hamish turned round and lifted the child in
the air,

And sprang with the child in his arms from the horrible height
in the sea,
Shrill screeching, "Revenge!" in the wind-rush; and pallid
Maclean,
Age-feeble with anger and impotent pain,
Crawled up on the crag, and lay flat, and locked hold of dead
roots of a tree—

And gazed hungrily o'er, and the blood from his back drip-
dripped in the brine,
And a sea-hawk flung down a skeleton fish as he flew,
And the mother stared white on the waste of blue,
And the wind drove a cloud to seaward, and the sun began to
shine.

1878

To Nannette Falk-Auerbach

Oft as I hear thee, wrapt in heavenly art,
  The massive message of Beethoven tell
With thy ten fingers to the people's heart
  As if ten tongues told news of heaven and hell,—
Gazing on thee, I mark that not alone,
  Ah, not alone, thou sittest: there, by thee,
Beethoven's self, dear living lord of tone,
  Doth stand and smile upon thy mastery.
Full fain and fatherly his great eyes glow:
  He says, " From Heaven, my child, I heard thee call
(For where an artist plays, the sky is low):
  Yea, since my lonesome life did lack love's all,
    In death, God gives me thee: thus, quit of pain,
    Daughter, Nannette! in thee I live again."

1878   *1878*

To Our Mocking Bird

Died, of a Cat, May, 1878

I

Trillets of humor,—shrewdest whistle-wit,—
  Contralto cadences of grave desire
  Such as from off the passionate Indian pyre
Drift down through sandal-odored flames that split
About the slim young widow who doth sit
  And sing above,—midnights of tone entire,—
  Tissues of moonlight shot with songs of fire,—
Bright drops of tune, from oceans infinite
Of melody, sipped off the thin-edged wave
And trickling down the beak,—discourses brave
  Of serious matter that no man may guess;
  Good-fellow greetings,—cries of light distress—
    All these but now within the house we heard:
    O Death, wast thou too deaf to hear the bird?

II

Ah me, though never an ear for song, thou hast
  A tireless tooth for songsters: thus of late
  Thou camest, Death, thou Cat! and leap'st my gate,
And, long ere Love could follow, thou hadst passed
Within and snatched away, how fast, how fast,
  My bird—wit, songs, and all—thy richest freight
  Since that fell time when in some wink of fate
Thy yellow claws unsheathed and stretched, and cast
Sharp hold on Keats, and dragged him slow away,
And harried him with hope and horrid play—
  Ay, him, the world's best wood-bird, wise with song—
  Till thou hadst wrought thine own last mortal wrong.
    'Twas wrong! 'twas wrong! I care not, *wrong's* the word—
    To munch our Keats and crunch our mocking-bird.

III

Nay, Bird; my grief gainsays the Lord's best right.
  The Lord was fain, at some late festal time,
  That Keats should set all Heaven's woods in rhyme,
And thou in bird-notes. Lo, this tearful night,
Methinks I see thee, fresh from death's despite,
  Perched in a palm-grove, wild with pantomime,
  O'er blissful companies couched in shady thyme—
Methinks I hear thy silver whistlings bright
Mix with the mighty discourse of the wise,
  Till broad Beethoven, deaf no more, and Keats,
'Midst of much talk, uplift their smiling eyes,
  And mark the music of thy wood-conceits,
    And halfway pause on some large courteous word,
    And call thee " Brother," O thou heavenly Bird!

1878   *1878*

The Marshes of Glynn

Glooms of the live-oaks, beautiful-braided and woven
With intricate shades of the vines that myriad-cloven
   Clamber the forks of the multiform boughs,—
      Emerald twilights,—
      Virginal shy lights,
Wrought of the leaves to allure to the whisper of vows,
When lovers pace timidly down through the green colon-
      nades
   Of the dim sweet woods, of the dear dark woods,
    Of the heavenly woods and glades,
That run to the radiant marginal sand-beach within
   The wide sea-marshes of Glynn;—

Beautiful glooms, soft dusks in the noon-day fire,—
Wildwood privacies, closets of lone desire,
Chamber from chamber parted with wavering arras of
      leaves,—
Cells for the passionate pleasure of prayer to the soul that
      grieves,
   Pure with a sense of the passing of saints through the wood,
   Cool for the dutiful weighing of ill with good;—

O braided dusks of the oak and woven shades of the vine,
While the riotous noon-day sun of the June-day long did shine,
Ye held me fast in your heart and I held you fast in mine;
   But now when the noon is no more, and riot is rest,
   And the sun is a-wait at the ponderous gate of the West,
    And the slant yellow beam down the wood-aisle doth seem
    Like a lane into heaven that leads from a dream,—
Ay, now, when my soul all day hath drunken the soul of the oak,
And my heart is at ease from men, and the wearisome sound
      of the stroke
   Of the scythe of time and the trowel of trade is low,
   And belief overmasters doubt, and I know that I know,
   And my spirit is grown to a lordly great compass within,
   That the length and the breadth and the sweep of the
      marshes of Glynn
   Will work me no fear like the fear they have wrought me
      of yore

14 1

When length was fatigue, and when breadth was but bitter-
ness sore,
And when terror and shrinking and dreary unnamable pain
Drew over me out of the merciless miles of the plain,—
Oh, now, unafraid, I am fain to face
The vast sweet visage of space.
To the edge of the wood I am drawn, I am drawn,
Where the gray beach glimmering runs, as a belt of the dawn,
For a mete and a mark
To the forest-dark:—
So:
Affable live-oak, leaning low,—
Thus—with your favor—soft, with a reverent hand,
(Not lightly touching your person, Lord of the land!)
Bending your beauty aside, with a step I stand
On the firm-packed sand,
Free
By a world of marsh that borders a world of sea.
Sinuous southward and sinuous northward the shimmering
band
Of the sand-beach fastens the fringe of the marsh to the folds
of the land.
Inward and outward to northward and southward the beach-
lines linger and curl
As a silver-wrought garment that clings to and follows the firm
sweet limbs of a girl.
Vanishing, swerving, evermore curving again into sight,
Softly the sand-beach wavers away to a dim gray looping of
light.
And what if behind me to westward the wall of the woods
stands high?
The world lies east: how ample, the marsh and the sea and
the sky!
A league and a league of marsh-grass, waist-high, broad in
the blade,
Green, and all of a height, and unflecked with a light or a
shade,
Stretch leisurely off, in a pleasant plain,
To the terminal blue of the main.

Oh, what is abroad in the marsh and the terminal sea?
Somehow my soul seems suddenly free

From the weighing of fate and the sad discussion of sin,
By the length and the breadth and the sweep of the marshes
of Glynn.
Ye marshes, how candid and simple and nothing-withholding
and free
Ye publish yourselves to the sky and offer yourselves to the
sea!
Tolerant plains, that suffer the sea and the rains and the sun,
Ye spread and span like the catholic man who hath mightily
won
God out of knowledge and good out of infinite pain
And sight out of blindness and purity out of a stain.

As the marsh-hen secretly builds on the watery sod,
Behold I will build me a nest on the greatness of God:
I will fly in the greatness of God as the marsh-hen flies
In the freedom that fills all the space 'twixt the marsh and
the skies:
By so many roots as the marsh-grass sends in the sod
I will heartily lay me a-hold on the greatness of God:
Oh, like to the greatness of God is the greatness within
The range of the marshes, the liberal marshes of Glynn.

And the sea lends large, as the marsh: lo, out of his plenty
the sea
Pours fast: full soon the time of the flood-tide must be:
Look how the grace of the sea doth go
About and about through the intricate channels that flow
Here and there,
Everywhere,
Till his waters have flooded the uttermost creeks and the low-
lying lanes,
And the marsh is meshed with a million veins,
That like as with rosy and silvery essences flow
In the rose-and-silver evening glow.
Farewell, my lord Sun!
The creeks overflow: a thousand rivulets run
'Twixt the roots of the sod; the blades of the marsh-grass
stir;
Passeth a hurrying sound of wings that westward whirr;
Passeth, and all is still; and the currents cease to run;
And the sea and the marsh are one.

How still the plains of the waters be!
The tide is in his ecstasy.
The tide is at his highest height:
    And it is night.

And now from the Vast of the Lord will the waters of sleep
    Roll in on the souls of men,
But who will reveal to our waking ken
The forms that swim and the shapes that creep
    Under the waters of sleep?
And I would I could know what swimmeth below when the
    tide comes in
On the length and the breadth of the marvellous marshes
    of Glynn.

1878   *1878*

Street-Cries

Oft seems the Time a market-town
    Where many merchant-spirits meet
Who up and down and up and down
    Cry out along the street

Their needs, as wares; one *thus*, one *so:*
    Till all the ways are full of sound:
—But still come rain, and sun, and snow,
    And still the world goes round.

1878?   *1884*

Remonstrance

Opinion, let me alone: I am not thine.
    Prim Creed, with categoric point, forbear
To feature me my Lord by rule and line.
    Thou canst not measure Mistress Nature's hair,
        Not one sweet inch: nay, if thy sight is sharp,
        Would'st count the strings upon an angel's harp?
            Forbear, forbear.

Oh let me love my Lord more fathom deep
  Than there is line to sound with: let me love
My fellow not as men that mandates keep:
    Yea, all that's lovable, below, above,
      That let me love by heart, by heart, because
      (Free from the penal pressure of the laws)
        I find it fair.

The tears I weep by day and bitter night,
  Opinion! for thy sole salt vintage fall.
—As morn by morn I rise with fresh delight,
    Time through my casement cheerily doth call
      " Nature is new, 'tis birthday every day,
      Come feast with me, let no man say me nay,
        Whate'er befall."

So fare I forth to feast: I sit beside
  Some brother bright: but, ere good-morrow's passed,
Burly Opinion wedging in hath cried
    " Thou shalt not sit by us, to break thy fast,
      Save to our Rubric thou subscribe and swear—
      Religion hath blue eyes and yellow hair:
        She's Saxon, all."

Then, hard a-hungered for my brother's grace
  Till well-nigh fain to swear his folly's true,
In sad dissent I turn my longing face
    To him that sits on the left: " Brother,—with you? "
      —" Nay, not with me, save thou subscribe and swear
      Religion hath black eyes and raven hair:
        Nought else is true."

Debarred of banquets that my heart could make
  With every man on every day of life,
I homeward turn, my fires of pain to slake
    In deep endearments of a worshipped wife.
      " I love thee well, dear Love," quoth she, " and yet
      Would that thy creed with mine completely met,
        As one, not two."

Assassin! Thief! Opinion, 'tis thy work.
　By Church, by throne, by hearth, by every good
That's in the Town of Time, I see thee lurk,
　　And e'er some shadow stays where thou hast stood.
　　　Thou hand'st sweet Socrates his hemlock sour;
　　　Thou sav'st Barabbas in that hideous hour,
　　　　And stabb'st the good

Deliverer Christ; thou rack'st the souls of men;
　Thou tossest girls to lions and boys to flames;
Thou hew'st Crusader down by Saracen;
　　Thou buildest closets full of secret shames;
　　　Indifferent cruel, thou dost blow the blaze
　　　Round Ridley or Servetus; all thy days
　　　　Smell scorched; I would

—Thou base-born Accident of time and place—
　Bigot Pretender unto Judgment's throne—
Bastard, that claimest with a cunning face
　　Those rights the true, true Son of Man doth own
　　　By Love's authority—thou Rebel cold
　　　At head of civil wars and quarrels old—
　　　　Thou Knife on a throne—

I would thou left'st me free, to live with love,
　And faith, that through the love of love doth find
My Lord's dear presence in the stars above,
　　The clods below, the flesh without, the mind
　　　Within, the bread, the tear, the smile.
　　　Opinion, damned Intriguer, gray with guile,
　　　　Let me alone.

1878　　　　　　　　　　　　　　　　　　　　　*1883*

How Love Looked for Hell

To heal his heart of long-time pain
One day Prince Love for to travel was fain
  With Ministers Mind and Sense.
" Now what to thee most strange may be? "
Quoth Mind and Sense. " All things above,
One curious thing I first would see—
    Hell," quoth Love.

Then Mind rode in and Sense rode out:
They searched the ways of man about.
  First frightfully groaneth Sense,
" Tis here, 'tis here," and spurreth in fear
To the top of the hill that hangeth above
And plucketh the Prince: " Come, come, 'tis here "—
    " Where? " quoth Love—

" Not far, not far," said shivering Sense
As they rode on. " A short way hence,
  —But seventy paces hence:
Look, King, dost see where suddenly
This road doth dip from the height above?
Cold blew a mouldy wind by me— "
    (" Cold? " quoth Love.)

" As I rode down, and the River was black,
And yon-side, lo! an endless wrack
  And rabble of souls," sighed Sense,
" Their eyes upturned and begged and burned
In brimstone lakes, and a Hand above
Beat back the hands that upward yearned— "
    " Nay! " quoth Love—

" Yea, yea, sweet Prince; thyself shalt see,
Wilt thou but down this slope with me;
  'Tis palpable," whispered Sense.
—At the foot of the hill a living rill
Shone, and the lilies shone white above;
" But now 'twas black, 'twas a river, this rill— "
    (" Black? " quoth Love.)

" Ay, black, but lo! the lilies grow,
And yon-side where was woe, was woe,
   —Where the rabble of souls " (cried Sense)
" Did shrivel and turn and beg and burn,
Thrust back in the brimstone from above—
Is banked of violet, rose, and fern: "
     " How? " quoth Love:

" For lakes of pain, yon pleasant plain
Of woods and grass and yellow grain
   Doth ravish the soul and sense:
And never a sigh beneath the sky,
And folk that smile and gaze above— "
" But saw'st thou here, with thine own eye,
    Hell? " quoth Love—

" I saw true hell with mine own eye,
True hell, or light hath told a lie,
   True, verily," quoth stout Sense.
Then Love rode round and searched the ground,
The caves below, the hills above:
" But I cannot find where thou hast found
    Hell," quoth Love.

There, while they stood in a green wood
And marvelled still on Ill and Good,
   Came suddenly Minister Mind.
" In the heart of sin doth hell begin:
'Tis not below, 'tis not above,
It lieth within, it lieth within ":
    (" Where? " quoth Love.)

" I saw a man sit by a corse;
Hell's in the murderer's breast: remorse!
   Thus clamored his mind to his mind:
Not fleshly dole is the sinner's goal,
Hell's not below, nor yet above,
'Tis fixed in the ever-damnèd soul— "
    " Fixed? " quoth Love—

" Fixed: follow me, would'st thou but see:
He weepeth under yon willow tree,
 Fast chained to his corse," quoth Mind.
Full soon they passed, for they rode fast,
Where the piteous willow bent above.
" Now shall I see at last, at last,
  Hell," quoth Love.

There when they came Mind suffered shame:
" These be the same and not the same,"
 A-wondering whispered Mind.
Lo, face by face two spirits pace
Where the blissful willow waves above:
One saith: " Do me a friendly grace— "
  (" Grace! " quoth Love.)

" Read me two Dreams that linger long,
Dim as returns of old-time song
 That flicker about the mind.
I dreamed (how deep in mortal sleep!)
I struck thee dead, then stood above,
With tears that none but dreamers weep ";
  " Dreams," quoth Love;

" In dreams, again, I plucked a flower
That clung with pain and stung with power,
 Yea, nettled me, body and mind."
" 'Twas the nettle of sin, 'twas medicine;
No need nor seed of it here Above;
In dreams of hate true loves begin."
  " True," quoth Love.

" Now strange," quoth Sense, and " Strange," quoth Mind,
" We saw it, and yet 'tis hard to find,
 —But we saw it," quoth Sense and Mind.
Stretched on the ground, beautiful-crowned
Of the piteous willow that wreathed above,
—" But I cannot find where ye have found
  Hell," quoth Love.

1878?   *1884*

To Bayard Taylor

To range, deep-wrapt, along a heavenly height,
    O'erseeing all that man but undersees;
To loiter down lone alleys of delight,
    And hear the beating of the hearts of trees,
And think the thoughts that lilies speak in white
    By greenwood pools and pleasant passages;

With healthy dreams a-dream in flesh and soul,
    To pace, in mighty meditations drawn,
From out the forest to the open knoll
    Where much thyme is, whence blissful leagues of lawn
Betwixt the fringing woods to southward roll
    By tender inclinations; mad with dawn,

Ablaze with fires that flame in silver dew
    When each small globe doth glass the morning-star,
Long ere the sun, sweet-smitten through and through
    With dappled revelations read afar,
Suffused with saintly ecstasies of blue
    As all the holy eastern heavens are,—

To fare thus fervid to what daily toil
    Employs thy spirit in that larger Land
Where thou art gone; to strive, but not to moil
    In nothings that do mar the artist's hand,
Not drudge unriched, as grain rots back to soil,—
    No profit out of death,—going, yet still at stand,—

Giving what life is here in hand to-day
    For that that's in to-morrow's bush, perchance,—
Of this year's harvest none in the barn to lay,
    All sowed for next year's crop,—a dull advance
In curves that come but by another way
    Back to the start,—a thriftless thrift of ants

Whose winter wastes their summer; O my Friend,
    Freely to range, to muse, to toil, is thine:
Thine, now, to watch with Homer sails that bend

Unstained by Helen's beauty o'er the brine
Tow'rds some clean Troy no Hector need defend
Nor flame devour; or, in some mild moon's shine,

Where amiabler winds the whistle heed,
To sail with Shelley o'er a bluer sea,
And mark Prometheus, from his fetters freed,
Pass with Deucalion over Italy,
While bursts the flame from out his eager reed
Wild-stretching towards the West of destiny;

Or, prone with Plato, Shakspere and a throng
Of bards beneath some plane-tree's cool eclipse
To gaze on glowing meads where, lingering long,
Psyche's large Butterfly her honey sips;
Or, mingling free in choirs of German song,
To learn of Goethe's life from Goethe's lips;

These, these are thine, and we, who still are dead,
Do yearn—nay, not to kill thee back again
Into this charnel life, this lowlihead,
Not to the dark of sense, the blinking brain,
The hugged delusion drear, the hunger fed
On husks of guess, the monarchy of pain,

The cross of love, the wrench of faith, the shame
Of science that cannot prove proof is, the twist
Of blame for praise and bitter praise for blame,
The silly stake and tether round the wrist
By fashion fixed, the virtue that doth claim
The gains of vice, the lofty mark that's missed

By all the mortal space 'twixt heaven and hell,
The soul's sad growth o'er stationary friends
Who hear us from our height not well, not well,
The slant of accident, the sudden bends
Of purpose tempered strong, the gambler's spell,
The son's disgrace, the plan that e'er depends

On others' plots, the tricks that passion plays
(I loving you, you him, he none at all),
The artist's pain—to walk his blood-stained ways,

A special soul, yet judged as general—
The endless grief of art, the sneer that slays,
   The war, the wound, the groan, the funeral pall—

Not into these, bright spirit, do we yearn
   To bring thee back, but oh, to be, to be
Unbound of all these gyves, to stretch, to spurn
   The dark from off our dolorous lids, to see
Our spark, Conjecture, blaze and sunwise burn,
   And suddenly to stand again by thee!

Ah, not for us, not yet, by thee to stand:
   For us, the fret, the dark, the thorn, the chill;
For us, to call across unto thy Land,
   " Friend, get thee to the ministrels' holy hill,
And kiss those brethren for us, mouth and hand,
   And make our duty to our master Will."

1878   *1879*

Opposition

Of fret, of dark, of thorn, of chill,
   Complain no more; for these, O heart,
Direct the random of the will
   As rhymes direct the rage of art.

The lute's fixt fret, that runs athwart
   The strain and purpose of the string,
For governance and nice consort
   Doth bar his wilful wavering.

The dark hath many dear avails:
   The dark distills divinest dews;
The dark is rich with nightingales,
   With dreams, and with the heavenly Muse.

Bleeding with thorns of petty strife,
   I'll ease (as lovers do) my smart
With sonnets to my lady Life
   Writ red in issues from the heart.

What grace may lie within the chill
    Of favor frozen fast in scorn!
When Good's a freeze, we call it Ill!
    This rosy Time is glacier-born.

Of fret, of dark, of thorn, of chill,
    Complain thou not, O heart; for these
Bank-in the current of the will
    To uses, arts, and charities.

1879   *1880*

Owl Against Robin

Frowning, the owl in the oak complained him
Sore, that the song of the robin restrained him
Wrongly of slumber, rudely of rest.
" From the north, from the east, from the south and the west,
Woodland, wheat-field, corn-field, clover,
Over and over and over and over,
Five o'clock, ten o'clock, twelve, or seven,
Nothing but robin-songs heard under heaven:
    How can we sleep?

" *Peep!* you whistle, and *cheep! cheep! cheep!*
Oh, peep, if you will, and buy, if 'tis cheap,
And have done; for an owl must sleep.
Are ye singing for fame, and who shall be first?
Each day's the same, yet the last is worst,
And the summer is cursed with the silly outburst
Of idiot red-breasts peeping and cheeping
By day, when all honest birds ought to be sleeping.
Lord, what a din! And so out of all reason.
Have ye not heard that each thing hath its season?
Night is to work in, night is for play-time;
    Good heavens, not day-time!

" A vulgar flaunt is the flaring day,
The impudent, hot, unsparing day,
That leaves not a stain nor a secret untold,—
Day the reporter,—the gossip of old,—

Deformity's tease,—man's common scold—
Poh! Shut the eyes, let the sense go numb
When day down the eastern way has come.
'Tis clear as the moon (by the argument drawn
From Design) that the world should retire at dawn.
Day kills. The leaf and the laborer breathe
Death in the sun, the cities seethe,
The mortal black marshes bubble with heat
And puff up pestilence; nothing is sweet
Has to do with the sun: even virtue will taint
(Philosophers say) and manhood grow faint
In the lands where the villainous sun has sway
Through the livelong drag of the dreadful day.
What Eden but noon-light stares it tame,
Shadowless, brazen, forsaken of shame?
For the sun tells lies on the landscape,—now
Reports me the *what*, unrelieved with the *how*,—
As messengers lie, with the facts alone,
Delivering the word and withholding the tone.

" But oh, the sweetness, and oh, the light
Of the high-fastidious night!
Oh, to awake with the wise old stars—
The cultured, the careful, the Chesterfield stars,
That wink at the work-a-day fact of crime
And shine so rich through the ruins of time
That Baalbec is finer than London; oh,
To sit on the bough that zigzags low
           By the woodland pool,
And loudly laugh at man, the fool
That vows to the vulgar sun; oh, rare,
To wheel from the wood to the window where
A day-worn sleeper is dreaming of care,
And perch on the sill and straightly stare
Through his visions; rare, to sail
Aslant with the hill and a-curve with the vale,—
To flit down the shadow-shot-with-gleam,
Betwixt hanging leaves and starlit stream,
Hither, thither, to and fro,
Silent, aimless, dayless, slow

(*Aimless? Field-mice?* True, they're slain,
But the night-philosophy hoots at pain,
Grips, eats quick, and drops the bones
In the water beneath the bough, nor moans
At the death life feeds on). Robin, pray
   Come away, come away
To the cultus of night. Abandon the day.
Have more to think and have less to say.
And *cannot* you walk now? Bah! don't hop!
   Stop!
Look at the owl, scarce seen, scarce heard,
O irritant, iterant, maddening bird! "

1879   *1881*

Ode to the Johns Hopkins University

How tall among her sisters, and how fair,—
How grave beyond her youth, yet debonair
As dawn, 'mid wrinkled mothers of old lands
Our youngest *Alma Mater* modest stands!
In four brief cycles round the punctual sun
Has she, old Learning's latest daughter, won
This grace, this stature, and this fruitful fame.
   Howbeit she was born
Unnoised as any stealing summer morn.
From far the sages saw, from far they came
   And ministered to her,
Led by the soaring-genius'd Sylvester
That, earlier, loosed the knot great Newton tied,
And flung the door of Fame's locked temple wide.
As favorable fairies thronged of old and blessed
The cradled princess with their several best,
   So, gifts and dowers meet
   To lay at Wisdom's feet,
  These liberal masters largely brought—
Dear diamonds of their long-compressèd thought,
Rich stones from out the labyrinthine cave

Of research, pearls from Time's profoundest wave
And many a jewel brave, of brilliant ray,
    Dug in the far obscure Cathay
      Of meditation deep—
      With flowers, of such as keep
Their fragrant tissues and their heavenly hues
Fresh-bathed forever in eternal dews—
    The violet with her low-drooped eye,
      For learnèd modesty,—
The student snow-drop, that doth hang and pore
Upon the earth, like Science, evermore,
And underneath the clod doth grope and grope,—
    The astronomer heliotrope,
That watches heaven with a constant eye,—
The daring crocus, unafraid to try
(When Nature calls) the February snows,—
    And patience's perfect rose.
Thus sped with helps of love and toil and thought,
Thus forwarded of faith, with hope thus fraught,
In four brief cycles round the stringent sun
This youngest sister hath her stature won.

      Nay, why regard
The passing of the years? Nor made, nor marr'd,
By help or hindrance of slow Time was she:
O'er this fair growth Time had no mastery:
So quick she bloomed, she seemed to bloom at birth,
As Eve from Adam, or as he from earth.
Superb o'er slow increase of day on day,
Complete as Pallas she began her way;
Yet not from Jove's unwrinkled forehead sprung,
But long-time dreamed, and out of trouble wrung,
Fore-seen, wise-plann'd, pure child of thought and pain,
Leapt our Minerva from a mortal brain.

And here, O finer Pallas, long remain,—
Sit on these Maryland hills, and fix thy reign,
And frame a fairer Athens than of yore
    In these blest bounds of Baltimore,—
    Here, where the climates meet
That each may make the other's lack complete,—

Where Florida's soft Favonian airs beguile
The nipping North,—where nature's powers smile,—
Where Chesapeake holds frankly forth her hands
Spread wide with invitation to all lands,—
Where now the eager people yearn to find
The organizing hand that fast may bind
Loose straws of aimless aspiration fain
  In sheaves of serviceable grain,—
   Here, old and new in one,
Through nobler cycles round a richer sun
   O'er-rule our modern ways,
O blest Minerva of these larger days!
Call here thy congress of the great, the wise,
  The hearing ears, the seeing eyes,—
Enrich us out of every farthest clime,—
Yea, make all ages native to our time,
Till thou the freedom of the city grant
  To each most antique habitant
   Of Fame,—
Bring Shakspere back, a man and not a name,—
Let every player that shall mimic us
In audience see old godlike Æschylus,—
Bring Homer, Dante, Plato, Socrates,—
Bring Virgil from the visionary seas
Of old romance,—bring Milton, no more blind,—
Bring large Lucretius, with unmaniac mind,—
Bring all gold hearts and high resolvèd wills
To be with us about these happy hills,—
  Bring old Renown
To walk familiar citizen of the town,—
Bring Tolerance, that can kiss and disagree,—
Bring Virtue, Honor, Truth, and Loyalty,—
Bring Faith that sees with undissembling eyes,—
Bring all large Loves and heavenly Charities,—
Till man seem less a riddle unto man
And fair Utopia less Utopian,
And many peoples call from shore to shore,
The world has bloomed again, at Baltimore!

1880   *1880*

[Ireland]

Heartsome Ireland, winsome Ireland,
 Charmer of the sun and sea,
Bright beguiler of old anguish,
 How could Famine frown on thee?

As our Gulf-Stream, drawn to thee-ward,
 Turns him from his northward flow,
And our wintry western headlands
 Send thee summer from their snow,

Thus the main and cordial current
 Of our love sets over sea,—
Tender, comely, valiant Ireland,
Songful, soulful, sorrowful Ireland,—
 Streaming warm to comfort thee.

1880   *1880*

The Crystal

Ye companies of governor-spirits grave,
Bards, and old bringers-down of flaming news
From steep-walled heavens, holy malcontents,
Sweet seers, and stellar visionaries, all
That brood about the skies of poesy,
Full bright ye shine, insuperable stars.
Yet, if a man look hard upon you, none
With total lustre blazeth, no, not one
But hath some heinous freckle of the flesh
Upon his shining cheek, not one but winks
His ray, opaqued with intermittent mist
Of defect; yea, you masters all must ask
Some sweet forgiveness, which we leap to give,
We lovers of you, heavenly-glad to meet
Your largess so with love, and interplight
Your geniuses with our mortalities.

Thus unto thee, O sweetest Shakspere sole,
A hundred hurts a day I do forgive
('Tis little, but, enchantment! 'tis for thee):
Small curious quibble; Juliet's prurient pun
In the poor, pale face of Romeo's fancied death;
Cold rant of Richard; Henry's fustian roar
Which frights away that sleep he invocates;
Wronged Valentine's unnatural haste to yield;
Too-silly shifts of maids that mask as men
In faint disguises that could ne'er disguise—
Viola, Julia, Portia, Rosalind;
Fatigues most drear, and needless overtax
Of speech obscure that had as lief be plain;
Last I forgive (with more delight, because
'Tis more to do) the labored-lewd discourse
That e'en thy young invention's youngest heir
Besmirched the world with.

      Father Homer, thee,
Thee also I forgive thy sandy wastes
Of prose and catalogue, thy drear harangues
That tease the patience of the centuries;
Thy sleazy scrap of story—but a rogue's
Rape of a light-o'-love—too soiled a patch
To broider with the gods.

      Thee, Socrates,
Thou dear and very strong one, I forgive
Thy year-worn cloak, thine iron stringencies
That were but dandy upside-down, thy words
Of truth that mildlier spoke had mainlier wrought.

So, Buddha, beautiful! I pardon thee
That all the All thou hadst for needy man
Was Nothing, and thy Best of being was
But not to be.

    Worn Dante, I forgive
The implacable hates that in thy horrid hells
Or burn or freeze thy fellows, never loosed
By death, nor time, nor love.

And I forgive
Thee, Milton, those thy comic-dreadful wars
Where, armed with gross and inconclusive steel,
Immortals smite immortals mortalwise
And fill all heaven with folly.

Also thee,
Brave Æschylus, thee I forgive, for that
Thine eye, by bare bright justice basilisked,
Turned not, nor ever learned to look where Love
Stands shining.

So, unto thee, Lucretius mine
(For oh, what heart hath loved thee like to this
That's now complaining?), freely I forgive
Thy logic poor, thine error rich, thine earth
Whose graves eat souls and all.

Yea, all you hearts
Of beauty, and sweet righteous lovers large:
Aurelius fine, oft superfine; mild Saint
À Kempis, overmild; Epictetus,
Whiles low in thought, still with old slavery tinct;
Rapt Behmen, rapt too far; high Swedenborg,
O'ertoppling; Langley, that with but a touch
Of art hadst sung Piers Plowman to the top
Of English songs, whereof 'tis dearest now
And most adorable; Cædmon, in the morn
A-calling angels with the cow-herd's call
That late brought up the cattle; Emerson,
Most wise, that yet, in finding Wisdom, lost
Thy Self, sometimes; tense Keats, with angel's nerves,
Where men's were better; Tennyson, largest voice
Since Milton, yet some register of wit
Wanting—all, all, I pardon, ere 'tis asked,
Your more or less, your little mole that marks
You brother and your kinship seals to man.

But Thee, but Thee, O Sovereign Seer of time,
But Thee, O poets' Poet, Wisdom's Tongue,
But Thee, O man's best Man, O love's best Love,
O perfect life in perfect labor writ,

O all men's Comrade, Servant, King, or Priest—
What *if* or *yet*, what mole, what flaw, what lapse,
What least defect or shadow of defect,
What rumor tattled by an enemy,
Of inference loose, what lack of grace,
Even in torture's grasp, or sleep's, or death's—
Oh, what amiss may I forgive in Thee,
Jesus, good Paragon, thou Crystal Christ?

1880?   *1880*

The Cloud

Sail on, sail on, fair cousin Cloud;
Oh, loiter hither from the sea.
   Still-eyed and shadow-brow'd,
Steal off from yon far-drifting crowd,
And come and brood upon the marsh with me.

Yon laboring low horizon-smoke,
Yon stringent sail, toil not for thee
   Nor me: did heaven's stroke
The whole deep with drown'd commerce choke,
No pitiless tease of risk or bottomry

Would to thy rainy office close
Thy will, or lock mine eyes from tears
   Part wept for traders'-woes,
Part for that ventures mean as those
In issue bind such sovereign hopes and fears.

Stern Cloud, thy downward countenance stares
Blank on the blank-faced marsh, and thou
   Mindest of dark affairs;
Thy substance seems a warp of cares;
Like late wounds run the wrinkles on thy brow.

Well may'st thou pause, and gloom, and stare,
A visible conscience; I arraign
   Thee, criminal Cloud, of rare
Contempts on Mercy, Right, and Prayer,
Of murders, arsons, thefts, of nameless stain.

Yet though life's logic grow as gray
As thou, my soul's not in eclipse.
  Cold Cloud, but yesterday
Thy lightning slew a child at play,
And then a priest with prayers upon his lips

For his enemies, and then a bright
Lady that did but ope the door
  Upon the stormy night
To let a beggar in,—strange spite,—
And then thy sulky rain refused to pour

Till thy quick torch a barn had burned
Where twelve months' store of victual lay
  A widow's sons had earned,
Which done, thy floods of rain returned,—
The river raped their little herd away.

What myriad righteous errands high
Thy flames *might* run on! In that hour
  Thou slewest the child, oh why
Not rather slay Calamity,
Breeder of Pain and Doubt, infernal Power?

Or why not plunge thy blades about
Some maggot politician throng
  Swarming to parcel out
The body of a land, and rout
The maw-conventicle, and ungorge Wrong?

> *What the cloud doeth,*
> *The Lord knoweth,*
> *The cloud knoweth not.*
> *What the artist doeth,*
> *The Lord knoweth;*
> *Knoweth the artist not?*

Well-answered! O dear artists, ye
—Whether in forms of curve or hue
  Or tone, your gospels be—
Say wrong, *This work is not of me,*
But God: it is not true, it is not true.

Awful is Art, because 'tis free.
The artist trembles o'er his plan,
　　Where men his Self must see.
Who made a song or picture, he
Did it, and not another, God nor man.

My Lord is large, my Lord is strong:
Giving, He gave: my me is mine.
　　How poor, how strange, how wrong,
To dream He wrote the little song
I made to Him with love's unforced design!

Oh, not as clouds dim laws have plann'd
To strike down Good and fight for Ill,
　　Oh, not as harps that stand
In the wind and sound the wind's command:
Each artist—gift of terror!—owns his will.

For thee, Cloud,—if thou spend thine all
Upon the South's o'er-brimming sea
　　That needs thee not; or crawl
To the dry provinces, and fall
Till every convert clod shall give to thee

Green worship; if thou grow or fade,
Bring mad delight or misery,
　　Fly east or west, be made
Snow, hail, rain, wind, grass, rose, light, shade;—
What is it all to thee? There is no thee.

Pass, kinsman Cloud, now fair and mild:
Discharge the will that's not thine own.
　　I work in freedom wild,
But work, as plays a little child,
Sure of the Father, Self, and Love, alone.

1880   *1882*

Marsh Song—At Sunset

Over the monstrous shambling sea,
    Over the Caliban sea,
Bright Ariel-cloud, thou lingerest:
Oh wait, oh wait, in the warm red West,—
    Thy Prospero I'll be.

Over the humped and fishy sea,
    Over the Caliban sea,
O cloud in the West, like a thought in the heart
Of pardon, loose thy wing and start,
    And do a grace for me.

Over the huge and huddling sea,
    Over the Caliban sea,
Bring hither my brother Antonio,—Man,—
My injurer: night breaks the ban;
    Brother, I pardon thee.

1880?   *1882*

[Between Dawn and Sunrise]

    Were silver pink, had pink a soul,
Which soul were shy, which shyness might
    Be visible, sure yon gloriole
That shyness is, but lately fleshed in light.

    Or, if a white rose dreamed of red
And half forgot that vision, she
    Would think what now hath overspread
Marsh, woods, yon sail, my soul, and all the sea.

1880   *1891*

A Sunrise Song

Young palmer sun, that to these shining sands
  Pourest thy pilgrim's tale, discoursing still
Thy silver passages of sacred lands,
  With news of Sepulchre and Dolorous Hill,

Canst thou be he that, yester-sunset warm,
  Purple with Paynim rage and wrack-desire,
Dashed ravening out of a dusty lair of storm,
  Harried the west, and set the world on fire?

Hast thou perchance repented, Saracen Sun?
  Wilt warm the world with peace and dove-desire?
Or wilt thou, ere this very day be done,
  Blaze Saladin still, with unforgiving fire?

1880   *1881*

[To the Sun]

Who made thee thy last spring doublet, Cavalier Earth,
That sat so trim to the curve of thy manful girth
        As thou wert a-riding?—'Twas he.—
Who brought thee, Ship, straight over the surly sea,
    Forging steadily, westward steadily,
    Sails hilarious, sea-current readily
        Serving?—He:
    Out of two caldrons of air and sea
He wrought me the trade-wind that faithfully blew me,
Set me the sea-tide that servant-wise drew me,
    Forging steadily, westward steadily,
        Over the surly sea.

1880   *1945*

A Ballad of Trees and the Master

Into the woods my Master went,
  Clean forspent, forspent.
Into the woods my Master came,
  Forspent with love and shame.
But the olives they were not blind to Him,
The little gray leaves were kind to Him:
The thorn-tree had a mind to Him
  When into the woods He came.

Out of the woods my Master went,
  And He was well content.
Out of the woods my Master came,
  Content with death and shame.
When Death and Shame would woo Him last,
From under the trees they drew Him last:
'Twas on a tree they slew Him—last
  When out of the woods He came.

1880   *1880*

Sunrise

In my sleep I was fain of their fellowship, fain
  Of the live-oak, the marsh, and the main.
The little green leaves would not let me alone in my sleep;
Up-breathed from the marshes, a message of range and of sweep,
Interwoven with wafture of wild sea-liberties, drifting,
  Came through the lapped leaves sifting, sifting,
  Came to the gates of sleep.
  Then my thoughts, in the dark of the dungeon-keep
Of the Castle of Captives hid in the City of Sleep,
  Upstarted, by twos and by threes assembling:
  The gates of sleep fell a-trembling
Like as the lips of a lady that forth falter *yes*,
  Shaken with happiness:
  The gates of sleep stood wide.

I have waked, I have come, my beloved! I might not abide:
I have come ere the dawn, O beloved, my live-oaks, to hide
    In your gospelling glooms,—to be
As a lover in heaven, the marsh my marsh and the sea my sea.

  Tell me, sweet burly-bark'd, man-bodied Tree
  That mine arms in the dark are embracing, dost know
  From what fount are these tears at thy feet which flow?
They rise not from reason, but deeper inconsequent deeps.
    Reason's not one that weeps.
    What logic of greeting lies
Betwixt dear over-beautiful trees and the rain of the eyes?

O cunning green leaves, little masters! like as ye gloss
All the dull-tissued dark with your luminous darks that emboss
  The vague blackness of night into pattern and plan,
        So,
(But would I could know, but would I could know,)
With your question embroid'ring the dark of the question of
    man,—
So, with your silences purfling this silence of man
While his cry to the dead for some knowledge is under the ban,
    Under the ban,—
    So, ye have wrought me
Designs on the night of our knowledge,—yea, ye have taught me,
        So,
  That haply we know somewhat more than we know.

  Ye lispers, whisperers, singers in storms,
  Ye consciences murmuring faiths under forms,
  Ye ministers meet for each passion that grieves,
  Friendly, sisterly, sweetheart leaves,
  Oh, rain me down from your darks that contain me
  Wisdoms ye winnow from winds that pain me,—
  Sift down tremors of sweet-within-sweet
  That advise me of more than they bring,—repeat
  Me the woods-smell that swiftly but now brought breath
  From the heaven-side bank of the river of death,—
  Teach me the terms of silence,—preach me
  The passion of patience,—sift me,—impeach me,—

And there, oh there
As ye hang with your myriad palms upturned in the air,
   Pray me a myriad prayer.

   My gossip, the owl,—is it thou
That out of the leaves of the low-hanging bough,
   As I pass to the beach, art stirred?
   Dumb woods, have ye uttered a bird?

*   *   *   *   *

Reverend Marsh, low-couched along the sea,
   Old chemist, rapt in alchymy,
      Distilling silence,—lo,
That which our father-age had died to know—
The menstruum that dissolves all matter—thou
Hast found it: for this silence, filling now
The globèd clarity of receiving space,
This solves us all: man, matter, doubt, disgrace,
      Death, love, sin, sanity,
Must in yon silence's clear solution lie.
Too clear! That crystal nothing who'll peruse?
The blackest night could bring us brighter news.
   Yet precious qualities of silence haunt
   Round these vast margins, ministrant.
Oh, if thy soul's at latter gasp for space,
With trying to breathe no bigger than thy race
Just to be fellow'd, when that thou hast found
No man with room, or grace, enough of bound
To entertain that New thou tell'st, thou art,—
'Tis here, 'tis here, thou canst unhand thy heart
   And breathe it free, and breathe it free,
By rangy marsh, in lone sea-liberty.

The tide's at full: the marsh with flooded streams
Glimmers, a limpid labyrinth of dreams.
Each winding creek in grave entrancement lies,
A rhapsody of morning-stars. The skies
   Shine scant with one forked galaxy,—
The marsh brags ten: looped on his breast they lie.

Oh, what if a sound should be made!
Oh, what if a bound should be laid
To this bow-and-string tension of beauty and silence a-spring,—
To the bend of beauty the bow, or the hold of silence the string!
I fear me, I fear me yon dome of diaphanous gleam
    Will break as a bubble o'er-blown in a dream,—
Yon dome of too-tenuous tissues of space and of night,
    Over-weighted with stars, over-freighted with light,
    Over-sated with beauty and silence, will seem
        But a bubble that broke in a dream,
    If a bound of degree to this grace be laid,
      Or a sound or a motion made.

But no: it is made: list! somewhere,—mystery, where?
        In the leaves? in the air?
    In my heart? is a motion made:
'Tis a motion of dawn, like a flicker of shade on shade.
In the leaves, 'tis palpable: low multitudinous stirring
Upwinds through the woods; the little ones, softly conferring,
Have settled, my lord's to be looked for; so; they are still;
    But the air and my heart and the earth are a-thrill,—
And look where the wild duck sails round the bend of the river,—
    And look where a passionate shiver
    Expectant is bending the blades
Of the marsh-grass in serial shimmers and shades,—
And invisible wings, fast fleeting, fast fleeting,
        Are beating
The dark overhead as my heart beats,—and steady and free
    Is the ebb-tide flowing from marsh to sea
      (Run home, little streams,
    With your lapfulls of stars and dreams);—
And a sailor unseen is hoisting a-peak,
For list, down the inshore curve of the creek
    How merrily flutters the sail,—
And lo, in the east! Will the East unveil?
The East is unveiled, the East hath confessed
A flush: 'tis dead; 'tis alive: 'tis dead, ere the West
Was aware of it: nay, 'tis abiding, 'tis unwithdrawn:
    Have a care, sweet Heaven! 'Tis Dawn.

         *   *   *   *   *

Now a dream of a flame through that dream of a flush is up-
rolled:
To the zenith ascending, a dome of undazzling gold
Is builded, in shape as a bee-hive, from out of the sea:
The hive is of gold undazzling, but oh, the Bee,
   The star-fed Bee, the build-fire Bee,
   —Of dazzling gold is the great Sun-Bee
   That shall flash from the hive-hole over the sea.

Yet now the dew-drop, now the morning gray,
Shall live their little lucid sober day
Ere with the sun their souls exhale away.
Now in each pettiest personal sphere of dew
The summ'd morn shines complete as in the blue
Big dew-drop of all heaven: with these lit shrines
O'er-silvered to the farthest sea-confines,
The sacramental marsh one pious plain
Of worship lies. Peace to the ante-reign
Of Mary Morning, blissful mother mild,
Minded of nought but peace, and of a Child.

Not slower than Majesty moves, for a mean and a measure
Of motion,—not faster than dateless Olympian leisure
Might pace with unblown ample garments from pleasure to
   pleasure,—
The wave-serrate sea-rim sinks, unjarring, unreeling,
   Forever revealing, revealing, revealing,
Edgewise, bladewise, halfwise, wholewise,—'tis done!
     Good-morrow, lord Sun!
   With several voice, with ascription one,
   The woods and the marsh and the sea and my soul
Unto thee, whence the glittering stream of all morrows doth roll,
Cry good and past-good and most heavenly morrow, lord Sun.

O Artisan born in the purple,—Workman Heat,—
Parter of passionate atoms that travail to meet
And be mixed in the death-cold oneness,—innermost Guest
At the marriage of elements,—fellow of publicans,—blest
King in the blouse of flame, that loiterest o'er
The idle skies yet laborest fast evermore—

      *   *   *   *   *

Thou, in the fine forge-thunder, thou, in the beat
Of the heart of a man, thou Motive,—Laborer Heat:
Yea, Artist, thou, of whose art yon sea's all news,
With his inshore greens and manifold mid-sea blues,
Pearl-glint, shell-tint, ancientest perfectest hues
 Ever shaming the maidens,—lily and rose
 Confess thee, and each mild flame that glows
In the clarified virginal bosoms of stones that shine,
  It is thine, it is thine:
Thou chemist of storms, whether driving the winds a-swirl
Or a-flicker the subtiler essences polar that whirl
In the magnet earth,—yea, thou with a storm for a heart,
Rent with debate, many-spotted with question, part
From part oft sundered, yet ever a globèd light,
Yet ever the artist, ever more large and bright
Than the eye of a man may avail of:—manifold One,
I must pass from thy face, I must pass from the face of the Sun:
Old Want is awake and agog, every wrinkle a-frown;
The worker must pass to his work in the terrible town:
But I fear not, nay, and I fear not the thing to be done;
 I am strong with the strength of my lord the Sun:
How dark, how dark soever the race that must needs be run,
  I am lit with the Sun.

 Oh, never the mast-high run of the seas
  Of traffic shall hide thee,
Never the hell-colored smoke of the factories
  Hide thee,
Never the reek of the time's fen-polities
  Hide thee,
And ever my heart through the night shall with knowledge
  abide thee,
And ever by day shall my spirit, as one that hath tried thee,
Labor, at leisure, in art,—till yonder beside thee
 My soul shall float, friend Sun,
  The day being done.

1880   *1882*

POEMS NOT PUBLISHED BY LANIER

———

Oh, Life's a Fever and Death's a *chill*!
'Tis a disease of which all men are ill;
Earth for a Hospital surely was given—
Hell's an eternal relapse: Health is Heaven!!

1863   *1906*

To ——

The Day was dying; his breath
Wavered away in a hectic gleam—
And I said, if Life's a dream, and Death
And Love and all are dreams—I'll dream.

A Mist came over the Bay
Like as a Dream would over an eye—
The Mist was white and the Dream was grey
And both contained a human cry—

The burthen whereof was " Love,"
And it filled both Mist and Dream with pain,
And the hills below and the skies above
Were touched and uttered it back again.

The Mist broke: down the rift
A kind ray shot from a holy star.
Then my Dream did waver and break and lift—
Through it, Cherie, shone thy face, afar.

So Boyhood sets: comes Youth,
A painful night of Mists and Dreams—
That broods, till Love's exquisite truth,
The star of a morn-clear Manhood, beams.

1863-1864   *1884*

To G. H.

Thou most rare Brown Bird on thine Eden-tree,
    All heaven-sweet to me
Cometh thy song of Love's high royalty
    And Love's deep loyalty,
And Love's sweet-pleading loneliness in thee.

Our one-star yonder uttereth her light,
    Her silver call to Night,
Who, wavering between the Dark and Bright,
    On-cometh with timid flight,
As one that could not choose 'twixt wrong and right!

O, never was a night so dark as I!
    But thou has sent a sigh
Of love, as a star would send a beam, to fly
    Downward from out the sky
And light a heart that's dark enough to die.

And so, O mine exquisite Silver-Beam,
    Let me forever dream
That I am Night and thou a Star, whose stream
    Of light like love shall seem,—
Whose love-light thro' my dark shall ever gleam!

1864   *1906*

Translation from the German of Heine

In the far North stands a Pine-tree, lone
    Upon a wintry height—
It sleeps: around it snows have thrown
    A covering of white.

It dreams forever of a Palm
    That, far i' the Morning-land,
Stands silent in a most sad calm
    Midst of the burning sand.

1864   *1884*

Ten thousand stars were in the sky,
    Ten thousand on the sea;
For every wave with dimpled face
    That leaped into the air,
Had caught a star in its embrace
    And held it trembling there.

1865?   *1945*

Wedding-Hymn, To ——

Thou God, whose high, eternal Love
    Is the only blue sky of our life,
Clear all the Heaven that bends above
    The life-road of this man and wife.

May these two lives be but one note
    In the world's strange-sounding harmony,
Whose sacred music e'er shall float
    Through every discord up to Thee.

As when from separate stars two beams
    Unite to form one tender ray:
As when two sweet but shadowy dreams
    Explain each other in the day:

So may these two dear hearts one light
    Emit, and each interpret each.
Let an angel come and dwell all night
    In this dear double-heart, and teach!

1865   *1884*

A Morning-Talk

Overheard and Transcribed by an Eavesdropper

Night loq:
    O Morn-Star stay thy flying feet:
        Send a swift beam through the maiden dream
        Of her I love, and say what seem
    The Hoverers o'er her sleep so sweet!

The Star loq:
    Ere thou hadst spoke, mine Ariel-ray
        Lit up the dream-cloud over her eyes.
        I saw one Form in the light arise.
    'Twas thine: She crowned it, crying " Stay! "

All the Stars loq:
    Come Friends, let's sleep: we've kept our sight
        Twelve hours on yonder maid, the Dawn,
        Who comes from her sleep in the East, love-drawn
    Towards the swarthy, kingly Night.

1865   1945

The Dying Words of Jackson

" Order A. P. Hill to prepare for battle."
" Tell Major Hawks to advance the Commissary train."
" Let us cross the river and rest in the shade."

The stars of Night contain the glittering Day,
And rain his glory down with sweeter grace
Upon the dark World's grand, enchanted face
        All loth to turn away.

And so the Day, about to yield his breath,
Utters the Stars unto the listening Night
To stand for burning fare-thee-wells of light
        Said on the verge of death.

O hero-life that lit us like the Sun!
O hero-words that glittered like the Stars
And stood and shone above the gloomy wars
    When the hero-life was done!

The Phantoms of a battle came to dwell
I' the fitful vision of his dying eyes—
Yet even in battle-dreams, he sends supplies
    To those he loved so well.

His army stands in battle-line arrayed:
His couriers fly: all's done—now God decide!
And not till then saw he the Other Side
    Or would accept the Shade.

Thou Land whose Sun is gone, thy Stars remain!
Still shine the words that miniature his deeds—
O Thrice-Beloved, where'er thy great heart bleeds,
    Solace hast thou for pain!

1865   *1884*

A Love-Song, To ———

A gem set in a ring of gold
Art thou, set in my happy soul—
All gem-lights, love-lights, flash and roll
About me, like a gloriole.

O never stir, O ever rest,
Thou dainty Flower on my breast—
Each odor-word thou utterest
Breathes of the gardens of the Blest.

One Star at night is strange to see,
A sweet, soft-glittering mystery—
My Star, thy ray caresses me:
I thrill, I kneel, I worship thee!

O White-Souled, break the cloudy Spell,
And fall upon my heart, and dwell,
And melt, as if a snow-flake fell
Into a glowing flower-bell!

1865   *1945*

The Wedding

O marriage-bells, your clamor tells
　　Two weddings in one breath.
She marries whom her love compels:
　　—And I wed Goodman Death!
My brain is blank, my tears are red;
Listen, O God:—" I will," he said:—
　　And I would that I were dead.

Come Groomsman Grief and Bridesmaid Pain:
Come and stand with a ghastly twain.
My Bridegroom Death is come o'er the meres
To wed a Bride with bloody tears.
　　Ring, ring, O Bells, full merrily:
　　Life-bells to *her*, death-bells to me:
　　O Death, I am true wife to thee!

1865   1884

To Willie Clopton

A white face, drooping, on a bending neck:
　　A Tube-rose that with heavy petal curves
　　Her stem: a foam-bell on a wave that swerves
Back from the undulating vessel's deck!

From out the whitest cloud of Summer steals
　　The wildest lightning: from this face of thine,
　　Thy soul, a Fire-of-Heaven, warm and fine,
In marvellous flashes its fair self reveals.

As when one gazes from the summer sea
　　On some far gossamer cloud, with straining eye,
　　Fearing to see it vanish in the sky,
So, floating, wandering Cloud-Soul, I watch thee.

1866   1884

To Carrie Ligon

That Star there, glittering above the morn,
With quiet grace hath made the Night love-lorn.
He lived upon her silvery piquancy,—
He dies beneath her twinkling coquetry.

And she's so serious!—Save that a ray
Sometimes breaks off, as if she turned away
Her dainty little head to hide a smile
That *Knights* should be so foolish all the while!

But Evening-Stars will come, to Nights and men:—
For Morn-Stars fall in love at last, and then
With a most rare and golden light thou'lt shine,
O dainty, star-eyed, serious Cousin-mine!

1866   *1945*

Will " All Be Right in a Hundred Years "?

Let life rage on: compose thyself.
Fight not with Ghibelline or Guelph.
Why shake thy heart with hopes or fears?
Why break thy heart with swelling tears?
'Twill all be right in a hundred years.
Ah, no: when grim Rebuffs affront thee
And thine own sins hound and hunt thee,
Thou dost hide thine head i' the sand,
Thou dost but wield a broken brand,
To say, " Go by, O sins, O cares,
'Twill all be right in a hundred years."

Man's soul, three score and ten years long,
Sails on towards a glittering Wrong
Which is the star by which it steers.
Rash sailor upon unknown Meres,

Wilt thou reach Home in a hundred years?
Thy voyage for ages may be painful,
For the winds are sore disdainful
And do flout a boaster's pride.
So:—choose the Right, defend thy side,
Hope manly hopes, shed loving tears,
Then, all comes right in seventy years.

1866   *1945*

Night and Day

The innocent, sweet Day is dead.
Dark Night hath slain her in her bed.
O, Moors are as fierce to kill as to wed!
    —Put out the light, said he.

A sweeter Light than ever rayed
From star of Heaven or eye of maid
Has vanished in the Unknown Shade.
    —She's dead, she's dead, said he.

Now, in a wild, sad after-mood
The tawny Night sits still, to brood
Upon the dawn-time when he woo'd.
    —I would she lived, said he.

Star-memories of happier times,
Of loving deeds and lovers'-rhymes,
Throng forth, in silvery pantomimes.
    —Come back, O Day! said he.

1866   *1884*

Night

Fair is the wedded reign of Night and Day.
Each rules a half of earth, with different sway,
Exchanging kingdoms, East and West, alway.

Like the round pearl that Egypt drank, in wine,
The sun half sinks i' the brimming, rosy brine;
The wild Night drinks all up: how her eyes shine!

Now the swift sail of our life is furled,
And through the stillness of my soul is whirled
The throbbing of the hearts of half the world.

I hear the cries that follow Birth and Death.
I hear huge Pestilence draw his vaporous breath;
" Beware; prepare, or else ye die," he saith.

I hear a haggard student turn and sigh:
I hear men begging Heaven to let them die;
And, drowning all, a wild-eyed woman's cry.

So Night takes toll of both, Wisdom and Sin.
The student's and the drunkard's cheek is thin:
But flesh is not the prize we strive to win.

Now airy swarms of fluttering Dreams descend
On souls, like birds on trees, and have no end.
O God, from vulture-dreams, my soul defend.

Let fall on Her a rose-leaf rain of dreams
All passionate-sweet, as are the loving beams
Of starlight on yon glimmering woods and streams.

1866

1884

In Cubiculo

The sun, like Cleo's pearl she dropped in wine,
Has sunk into the rosy-brimming brine,
And bacchant Night drinks up the draught divine.

Now let the straining sail of life be furled.
Here, through the stillness of my soul, is whirled
The throbbing of the hearts of half the world.

I hear the cries that follow birth and death.
I hear huge Pestilence draw laboring breath:
Beware, prepare, or else ye die,—he saith.

I hear a haggard Student turn and sigh.
I hear men begging Heaven to let them die
And women shrieking that their life's a lie.

Strict Night will have his toll of work and sin.
The Student's and the drunkard's cheek is thin.
—But flesh is not the prize all strive to win.

Now airy swarms of fluttering Dreams descend
And settle on the souls of foe and friend.
—O God, from vulture-dreams my Love defend!

Let fall on her a rose-leaf rain of dreams
Cool-pure and passionate as are the beams
Of starlight on yon glimmering woods and streams.

1866?   1945

When bees, in honey-frenzies, rage and rage,
And their hot dainty wars with flowers wage,
Foraying in the woods for sweet rapine
And spreading odorous havoc o'er the green.

1866?   1908

Lines Tangled about the Round Table

No furniture was ever found
 In history or fable
That stood so square through all its round
 As this week's strong Round Table!
On legs it never has been set,
 But stands upon its head-part;
—Which makes its whole face read,—and yet
 Its face has not a red part!

Though knights have daily round it poured
 It never was benighted!
—More strange, 'tis oft a-groaning, bored
 With people not invited!
And though a groaning board should be
 A fine sight for a stranger,
This dessert hospitality
 Gives only a blanc manger!

Good Heart!—'Twill not " expose a goose "
 (Except to her own slander!)
Yet it delights to pluck aloose
 The Herald's propa-ganda!
It does not load itself and lurch
 With bogus " News by Cable."
'Tis not the organ of a Church
 Nor is it laymen-table!

Although this Table moves, and speaks
 A rare bold revelation,
There is no spirit in its freaks
 But spirit of the nation:
And while no medium lifts its leg
 By wires hid in the ceiling,
Its feat is often raised a peg
 By ironical dealing.

Full heavily it mashes down
    On culprits white and sable,
Yet in upholding true renown
    It is inimi-table.
It is a circle, and can't end!
    In spite of plot and cabal
Let three, aye, nine full chairs commend
    This able, stable Table!!!

1866?   1945

To M. D.

I seek you. You alone I seek:
    All other women, fair,
Or wise, or good, may go their way,
    Without my thought or care.

But you I follow *day* by day
    And night by night I keep
My heart's chaste mansion lighted, where
    Your image lies asleep.

Asleep! If e'er to wake, He knows
    Who Eve to Adam brought,
As you to me: the embodiment
    Of boyhood's dear sweet thought,

And youth's fond dream, and manhood's hope,
    That still half hopeless shone;
Till every rootless vain ideal
    Commingled into one,—

You; who are so diverse from me,
    And yet as much my own
As this my soul, which, formed apart,
    Dwells in its bodily throne;—

Or rather, for *that* perishes,
    As these our two lives are
So strangely, marvellously drawn
    Together from afar;

Till week by week and month by month
  We closer seem to grow,
As two hill streams, flushed with rich rain,
  Each into the other flow.

I swear no oaths, I tell no lies,
  Nor boast I never knew
A love dream we all dream in youth—
  But waking, I found *you*,

The real woman, whose first touch
  Aroused to highest life
My real manhood. Crown it then,
  Good angel, friend, love, wife!

Imperfect as I am, and you,
  Perchance, not all you seem,
We two together shall bind up
  Our past's bright broken dream.

We two together shall dare look
  Upon the years to come,
As travellers, met in far countrie,
  Together look towards home.

Come home! The old tales were not false,
  Yet the new faith is true;
Those saintly souls who made men knights
  Were women such as you.

For the great love that teaches love
  Deceived not, ne'er deceives:
And she who most believes in man
  Makes him what she believes.

Come! If you come not, I can wait;
  My faith, like life, is long;
My will—not *little*; my hope much:
  The patient are the strong.

Yet come, ah come! The years run fast,
  And hearths grow swiftly cold—
Hearts too: but while blood beats in mine
  It holds you and will hold.

And so before you it lies bare,—
   Take it or let it lie,
It is an honest heart; and yours
   To all eternity.

1867   *1945*

To Our Hills

   Dear Mother-Earth
   Of giant-birth,
Yon hills are thy large breasts, and often I
Have climbed to their top nipples, fain to lie
And drink my mother's-milk so near the sky.

   But, Mother Earth
   Of giant-birth,
Thy mother milk comes curdled thick with woe.
Friends, blood is in the milk whereby we grow,
And life is heavy and death is marvellous slow.

   Mark yon hill-stains,
   Red, for all rains!
The blood that made them was all shed for us:
The hearts that paid them are all dead for us:
The trees that shade them groan with lead, for us.

   O ye hill-sides,
   Like giants' brides
Ye sleep in ravine-rumpled draperies,
And weep your springs in tearful memories
Of green bride-robes, now turned to bloody frieze.

   Sad furrowed hills
   By full-wept rills,
The stainers have decreed the stains shall stay.
What clement hands might wash the stains away
Are chained, to make us rue a mournful day.

O coward hand
Of the Northland,
That after honorable war couldst smite
Cheeks grimed in adverse battle, to wreak spite
For dainty Senators that lagged the fight.

O monstrous crime
Of a sick Time:
—Forever waging war that peace may be
And serving God by cheating on bent knee
And freeing slaves by chaining down the free.

Thou sorrow height
We climb by night,
Hast thou no hiding for a Southern face?
Forever will the Heavens brook disgrace?
Shall Hope sit always cooing to the base?

1867   *1916*

Strange Jokes

Well: —Death is a huge omnivorous Toad
Grim squatting on a twilight road.
He catcheth all that Circumstance
        Hath tossed to him.
He curseth all who upward glance,
        As lost to him!

Once in a whimsy mood he sat
And talked of Life, in proverbs pat,
To Eve in Eden,—" Death, on Life "
        —As if he knew!
And so he toadied Adam's wife
        There, in the dew.

O dainty Dew, O Morning-Dew
That gleamed in the world's first Dawn, did *You*
And the sweet grass and manful oaks
        Give lair and rest
To him who Toadwise sits and croaks
        His death-behest?

Who fears the Hungry Toad? Not I!
He but unfetters me to fly.
—The Germans still when one is dead
    Cry out " Der Tod! "
But, pilgrims! Christ will walk ahead
    And clear the road!

1867   *1883*

Fame

Spinning a web to hang i' the sun
    And catch that Butterfly,—Fame;
But when he's fastened, and all's done,
    What have I then for game?

A fly with two black spots on his wings,
    And a slim, slim body between,
Whose legs are the slenderest, weakest things!
    And I've even rubbed off the sheen.

1867   *1914*

———

Like a grand water-wheel his life revolved
And turned a hundred looms of useful work,
Nor broke its faith with use to serve sweet art,
In that from off the straining rim upshot
A thousand glittering drops of poetry
Each day.
        " Niagara, then, to be full grand,
Should turn a factory wheel? "
                A pause:— " Well,—yes:
Only the rich can now behold its grandeur,
—Then might it bring some help to a thousand poor:-
Indeed, its rainbow would not promise less,
Its roar would rise to a large eloquence,
And all the thunderous sparkle and wet pomp
Instead of being a world's-excuse for sloth
Would be a world's-*laudamus* to fair Work."

1867?   *1945*

Steel in Soft Hands

Poor Bayonets seized by Tyranny,
  With battle-blood still red-frothing,
Ye crushed our Lee,—but souls are free
  And ye cannot kill our loathing.

When soldiers bore you over the plain,
  E'en your foes, then, your gleaming respected.
Now, Senators thrust you at foes that lie slain
  And wound the bare breasts you protected.

Your glory is gone out in deeds malign.
  Dead hands that in battle have borne you
Reach up from their graves and wave us a sign,
  For we, your enemies, mourn you.

We mourn your fall into daintier hands
  Of Senators, rosy fingered,
That wrote, while *you* fought, complacent commands
  And afar from the battles lingered.

Most foul, most execrable steel,
  And oh, most ignobly wielded,
—Helping a Senate grind its heel
  On the men that to *you* have yielded!

1868   *1945*

Burn the Stubble!

" Wind and Fire, Wind and Fire,
  —O War, kindle and rage again.
The stubble is rank, and we desire
  To burn Life off, for the coming grain.

" Who lies a-ground, that's born to fly?
  Who loves a grief that stings his wife?
Who laughs when his hungry children die?
  Who works in vain, and likes his life?

" Let these arise and run to the sea
   And sail over Exile's mournful main.
Here's work: the stubble is rank, and we
   Must burn some room for the coming grain."
—O gasping Heart, with long desire,
   Endure, endure, till the round earth turn.
O God, come Thou, and set the fire.
   O Heart, be calm, till God shall burn.

1868   *1945*

Souls and Raindrops

Light raindrops fall and wrinkle the sea,
Then vanish, and die utterly.
One would not know that raindrops fell
If the round sea-wrinkles did not tell.

So souls come down, and wrinkle life,
And vanish in the flesh-sea strife.
One might not know that souls had place,
Were't not for the wrinkles in life's face.

1868?   *1883*

Pride

The green leaf said to the sere leaf:
   " Poor dying friend, today
Some hoof that minds not a mere leaf
   Will tread thee into the clay."

The sere leaf said to the green leaf:
   " Poor living friend, today
Some worm that likes a clean leaf
   Will eat thy green away."

The green leaf said: " Churlish sere leaf,
   Thou'lt need my pity, somewhile."
The sere leaf said: " Never fear, leaf,
   Thy pity is Pride a-smile!"

1868?   *1945*

The Jacquerie

Chapter I

Once on a time, a Dawn, all red and bright,
Leapt on the conquered ramparts of the Night,
And flamed, one brilliant instant, on the world,
—Then back in the historic moat was hurled
And Night was King again, for many years.
—Once on a time the Rose of Spring blushed out
But Winter angrily withdrew it back
Into his rough new-bursten husk, and shut
The stern husk-leaves, and hid it many years.
—Once, Famine tricked himself with ears of corn,
And Hate strung flowers on his spikèd belt,
And glum Revenge in silver lilies pranked him,
And Lust put violets on his shameless front,
And all minced forth o' the street like holiday folk
That sally off a-field on Summer morns.
—Once certain hounds that knew of many a chase,
And bare great wounds of antler and of tusk
That they had ta'en to give a lord some sport,
—Good hounds, that would have died to give lords sport—
Were so bewrayed and kicked by these same lords
That all the pack turned tooth o' the knights and bit
As knights had been no better things than boars,
And took revenge as bloody as a man's,
Unhoundlike, sudden, hot i' the chops, and sweet.
—Once sat a falcon on a lady's wrist,
Seeming to doze, with wrinkled eye-lid drawn,
But dreaming hard of hoods and slaveries
And of dim hungers in his heart and wings.
Then, while the mistress gazed above for game,
Sudden he flew into her painted face
And hooked his horn-claws in her lily throat
And drove his beak into her lips and eyes
In a most fierce and hawkish kissing that did scar
And mar the lady's beauty evermore.

—And once while Chivalry stood tall and lithe
And flashed his sword above the stricken eyes
Of all the simple peasant-folk of France;
While Thought was keen and hot and quick,
And did not play, as in these later days,
Like summer-lightning flickering in the west
—As little dreadful as if glow-worms lay
In the cool and watery clouds and glimmered weak,—
But gleamed and struck at once or oak or man,
And left not space for Time to wave his wing
Betwixt the instantaneous flash and stroke:
While yet the needs of life were brave and fierce
And did not hide their deeds behind their words,
And logic came not 'twixt desire and act,
And Want-and-Take was the whole Form of life:
While Love had fires a-burning in his veins,
And hidden Hate could flash into revenge:
Ere yet young Trade was 'ware of his big thews
Or dreamed that in the bolder afterdays
He would hew down and bind old Chivalry
And drag him to the highest height of fame
And plunge him thence in the sea of still Romance,
To lie for aye in never-rusted mail
Gleaming through quiet ripples of soft songs
And sheens of old traditionary tales.
On such a time, a certain May arose
From out that blue sea that between five lands
Lies like a violet midst of five large leaves,
Arose from out this violet and flew on
And stirred the spirits of the woods of France
And smoothed the brows of moody Auvergne hills
And wrought warm sea-tints into maidens' eyes
And calmed the wordy air of market-towns
With faint suggestions blown from distant buds,
Until the land seemed a mere dream of land
And in this dream-field Life sat like a dove
And cooed across unto her dove-mate Death,
Brooding, pathetic, by a river, lone.
O sharper tangs pierced through this perfumed May,

Strange aches sailed by with odors on the wind,
As when we kneel in flowers that grow on graves
Of friends who died unworthy of our love.
King John of France was proving such an ache,
In English prisons wide and fair and grand,
Whose long expanses of green park and chace
Did ape large liberty with such success
As smiles of irony ape smiles of love.
Down from the oaks of Hertford Castle park,
Double with warm rose-breaths of southern Spring
Came rumors, as if odors too had thorns,
Sharp rumors, how the three Estates of France,
Like old Three-headed Cerberus of Hell
Had set upon the Duke of Normandy,
Their rightful Regent, snarled in his great face,
Snapped jagged teeth in inch-breadth of his throat,
And blown such hot and savage breath upon him
That he had tossed great sops of royalty
Unto the clamorous three-mawed baying beast,
And was not further on his way withal,
And had but changed a snarl into a growl:
How Arnold de Cervolles had ta'en the track
That war had burned along the unhappy land,
Shouting, *Since France is then too poor to pay*
The soldiers that have bloody devoir done
And since needs must, pardie! a man must eat,
Arm, gentlemen! swords slice as well as knives!
And so had tempted stout men from the ranks,
And now was adding robbers' waste to war's,
Stealing the leavings of remorseless battle
And making gaunter the gaunt bones of want:
How this Cervolles (called " Arch-priest " by the mass)
Through warm Provence had marched and menace made
Against Pope Innocent at Avignon,
And how the Pope nor ate nor drank nor slept
Through godly fear concerning his red wines,
—For if these knaves should sack his holy house,
And all the blessed casks be knocked o' the head,
Horrendum! all his Holiness' drink to be

Profanely guzzled down the reeking throats
Of scoundrels and inflame them on to seize
The massy coffers of the Church's gold,
And steal, mayhap, the carven silver shrine
And all the golden crucifixes? No!—
And so the holy father Pope made stir
And had sent forth a legate to Cervolles,
And treated with him, and made compromise,
And, last, had bidden all the Arch-priest's troop
To come and banquet with him in his house,
Where they did wassail high by night and day
And Father Pope sat at the board and carved
Midst greasy jokes that flowed full greasily,
And Priest and Soldier trolled good songs for mass,
And all the prayers the Priests made were, *Pray, drink*
And all the oaths the Soldiers swore were, *Drink!*
Till Mirth sat like a jaunty postillon
Upon the back of Time and urged him on
With piquant spur, past chapel and past cross:
How Charles, King of Navarre, in long duress
By mandate of King John within the walls
Of Crevacœur and then of strong Allères,
In faithful ward of Sir Tristan du Bois,
Was now escaped, had supped with Guy Kyrec,
Had won a pardon from the Regent Duke
By half-compulsion of a Paris mob,
Had turned the people's love upon himself
By smooth harangues, and now was bold to claim
That France was not the Kingdom of King John,
But, By Our Lady, his, by right and worth,
And so was plotting treason in the State,
And laughing at weak Charles of Normandy.
Nay, these had been like good news to the King,
Were any man but bold enough to tell
The King what bitter sayings men had made
And hawked augmenting up and down the land
Against the barons and great lords of France
That fled from English arrows at Poictiers.
Poictiers, Poictiers: this grain i' the eye of France

Had swelled it to a big and bloodshot ball.
That looked with rage upon a world askew.
Poictiers' disgrace was now but two years old,
Yet so outrageous rank and full was grown
That France was wholly overspread with shade,
And bitter fruits lay on the untilled ground
That stank and bred so foul contagious smells,
That not a nose in France but stood awry,
Nor boor that cried not *faugh!* upon the air.

Chapter II

Franciscan friar John de Rochetaillade
With gentle gesture lifted up his hand
And poised it high above the steady eyes
Of a great crowd that thronged the market-place
In fair Clermont to hear him prophesy.
Midst of the crowd old Gris Grillon, the maimed,
—A wretched wreck that fate had floated out
From the drear storm of battle at Poictiers,
A living man whose larger moiety
Was dead and buried on the battle-field—
A grisly trunk, without or arms or legs,
And scarred with hoof-cuts over cheek and brow—
Lay in his wicker-cradle, smiling.
                              " Jacques,"
Quoth he, " My son, I would behold this priest
That is not fat, and loves not wine, and fasts,
And stills the folk with waving of his hand,
And threats the knights and thunders at the Pope.
Make way for Gris, ye who are whole of limb!
Set me on yonder ledge, that I may see."
Forthwith a dozen horny hands reached out
And lifted Gris Grillon upon the ledge,
Whereon he lay and overlooked the crowd,
And from gray-grown hedges of his brows
Shot forth a glance against the friar's eye
That struck him like an arrow.
                              Then the friar,

With voice as low as if a maiden hummed
Love-songs of Provence in a mild day-dream:
" And when he broke the second seal, I heard
The second beast say, Come and see.
                                    And then
Went out another horse, and he was red.
And unto him that sat thereon was given
To take the peace of earth away, and set
Men killing one another: and they gave
To him a mighty sword."
                            The friar paused
And pointed round the circle of sad eyes.
" There is no face of man or woman here
But showeth print of the hard hoof of war.
Ah, yonder leaneth limbless Gris Grillon.
Friends, Gris Grillon is France.
                            Poor France, My France,
Wilt never walk on glory's hills again,
Wilt never work among thy vines again,
Art footless and art handless evermore?
—Thou felon, War, I do arraign thee now
Of mayhem of the four main limbs of France!
Thou old red criminal, stand forth, I charge
—But O, I am too utter sorrowful
To urge large accusation, now.
                                Nathless,
My work, to-day, is still more grievous. Hear!
The stains that war hath wrought upon the land
Show but as faint white flecks, if seen o' the side
Of those blood-covered images that stalk
Through yon cold chambers of the future, as
The prophet-mood, now stealing on my soul,
Reveals them, marching, marching, marching—See!
There go the kings of France, in piteous file.
The deadly diamonds shining in their crowns
Do wound the foreheads of their Majesties
And glitter through a setting of blood-gouts
As if they smiled to think how men are slain

By the sharp facets of the gem of power,
And how the kings of men are slaves of stones.
But look! The long procession of the kings
Wavers and stops, the world is full of noise,
The ragged peoples storm the palaces,
They rave, they laugh, they thirst, they lap the stream
That trickles from the regal vestments down,
And, lapping, smack their heated chops for more,
And ply their daggers for it, till the kings
All die and lie in a crooked sprawl of death,
Ungainly, foul, and stiff as any heap
Of villeins rotting on a battle field,
—'Tis true, that when these things have come to pass
Then never a king shall rule again in France,
For every villein shall be king in France:
And who hath lordship in him, whether born
In hedge or silken bed, shall be a lord:
And queens shall be as thick i' the land as wives,
And all the maids shall maids of honor be:
And high and low shall commune solemnly:
And stars and stones shall have free interview.
But woe is me, 'tis also piteous true
That ere this gracious time shall visit France,
Your graves, Beloved, shall be some centuries old,
And so your children's, and their children's graves,
And many generations'.

Ye, O ye

Shall grieve, and ye shall grieve, and ye shall grieve.
Your Life shall bend and o'er his shuttle toil,
A weaver weaving at the loom of grief.
Your Life shall sweat 'twixt anvil and hot forge,
An armorer working at the sword of grief.
Your Life shall moil i' the ground and plant his seed,
A farmer foisoning a huge crop of grief.
Your Life shall chaffer in the market-place,
A merchant trading in the goods of grief.
Your Life shall go to battle with his bow,
A soldier fighting in defence of grief.

By every rudder that divides the seas,
Tall Grief shall stand, the helmsman of the ship.
By every wain that jolts along the roads,
Stout Grief shall walk, the driver of the team.
Midst every herd of cattle on the hills,
Dull Grief shall lie, the herdsman of the drove.
O, Grief shall grind your bread and play your lutes,
And marry you and bury you.
                              —How else?
Who's here in France, can win her people's faith,
And stand in front and lead the people on?
Where is the Church?
                         The Church is far too fat.
Not, mark, by robust swelling of the thews,
But puffed, and flabby large with gross increase
Of wine-fat, plague-fat, dropsy-fat.
                              O shame,
Thou Pope that cheatest God at Avignon,
Thou that shouldst be the Father of the world,
And Regent of it whilst our God is gone;
Thou that shouldst blaze with conferred majesty
And smite old Lust-o'-the-Flesh so as by flame;
Thou that canst turn thy key and lock Grief up
Or turn thy key and unlock Heaven's Gate,
Thou that shouldst be the veritable hand
That Christ down-stretcheth out of heaven yet
To draw up him that fainteth to His heart,
Thou that shouldst bear thy fruit, yet virgin live
As she that bore a man yet sinnèd not,
Thou that shouldst challenge the most special eyes
Of Heaven and Earth and Hell to mark thee, since
Thou shouldst be Heaven's best captain, Earth's best friend
And Hell's best enemy,—false Pope, false Pope,
The world, thy child, is sick and like to die
But thou art dinner-drowsy and cannot come;
And Life is sore beset and crieth *help!*
But thou brook'st not disturbance at thy wine:
And France is wild for one to lead her souls,

But thou art huge and fat and laggest back
Among the smoking remnants of forsaken camps.
Thou'rt not God's Pope. Thou art the Devil's Pope.
Thou art first Squire to that most puissant knight,
Lord Satan, who thy faithful squireship long
Hath watched and well shall guerdon.

       —Ye sad souls,
So faint with work ye love not, so thin-worn
With miseries ye wrought not, so outraged
By strokes of ill that pass th' ill-doers' heads
And cleave the innocent, so desperate tired
Of barbarous insult that doth day by day abase
The humblest dignity of humblest men,
Ye cannot call toward the Church for help.
The Church already is o'erworked with care
Of its dyspeptic stomach.

      Ha, the Church
Forgets about eternity.

    I had
A vision of forgetfulness. O Dream
Born of a dream, as yonder cloud is born
Of water which is born of cloud!

       I thought
I saw the moonlight lying large and calm
Upon the unthrobbing bosom of the earth
As a great diamond glittering on a shroud.
A sense of breathlessness stilled all the world.
Motion stood dreaming he was changed to Rest,
And Life asleep did fancy he was Death.
A quick small shadow spotted the white world:
Then instantly 'twas huge, and huger grew
By instants till it did o'ergloom all space.
I lifted up mine eyes—O thou just God!
I saw a spectre with a million heads
Come frantic downward through the universe,
And all the mouths of it were uttering cries,
Wherein was a sharp agony. And yet
The cries were much like laughs: as if Pain laughed.
Its myriad lips were blue, and sometimes they

Closed fast and only moaned dim sounds that shaped
Themselves to one word *Homeless,* and the stars
Did utter back the moan and the great hills
Did bellow it and then the stars and hills
Bandied the grief o' the ghost 'twixt heaven and earth.
The spectre sank, and lay upon the air,
And brooded, level, close upon the earth
With all the myriad heads just over me.
I glanced in all the eyes and marked that some
Did glitter with a flame of lunacy,
And some were soft and false as feigning love,
And some were blinking with hypocrisy,
And some were overfilmed by sense, and some
Blazed with ambition's wild unsteady fire,
And some were burnt i' the sockets black, and some
Were dead as embers when the fire is out.
A curious zone circled the spectre's waist,
Which seemed, with strange device, to symbol Time.
It was a silver-gleaming thread of day
Spiral about a jet-black band of night.
This zone seemed ever to contract and all
The frame with momentary spasms heaved
I' the strangling traction which did never cease.
I cried unto the spectre, *Time hath bound
Thy body with the fibre of his hours.*
Then rose a multitude of mocking sounds,
And some mouths spat at me and cried *Thou fool,*
And some, *Thou liest,* and some, *He dreams:* and then
Some hands uplifted certain bowls they bore
To lips that writhed but drank with eagerness.
And some played curious viols, shaped like hearts
And stringed with loves, to light and ribald tunes,
And other hands slit throats with knives,
And others patted all the painted cheeks
In reach, and others stole what others had
Unseen, or boldly snatched at alien rights,
And some o' the heads did vie in a foolish game
Of *which could hold itself the highest,* and
Of *which one's neck was stiff the longest time.*

And then the sea in silence wove a veil
Of mist, and breathed it upward and about,
And waved and wound it softly round the world,
And meshed my dream i' the vague and endless folds,
And a light wind arose and blew these off,
And I awoke.
             The many heads are priests
That have forgot eternity: and Time
Hath caught and bound them with a withe
Into a fagot huge, to burn in hell.
—Now if the priesthood put such shame upon
Your cry for leadership, can better help
Come out of knighthood?
               Lo! you smile, you boors?
You villeins smile at knighthood?
               Now, thou France
That wert the mother of fair chivalry,
Unclose thine eyes, unclose thine eyes, here, see,
Here stand a herd of knaves that laugh to scorn
Your gentlemen!
          O contumely hard,
O bitternes of last disgrace, O sting
That stings the coward knights of lost Poictiers!
I would—" but now a murmur rose i' the crowd
Of angry voices, and the friar leapt
From where he stood to preach and pressed a path
Betwixt the mass that way the voices came.

Chapter III

Lord Raoul was riding castleward from field.
At left hand rode his lady and at right
His fool whom he loved better; and his bird,
His fine ger-falcon best beloved of all,
Sat hooded on his wrist and gently swayed
To the undulating amble of the horse.
Guest-knights and huntsmen and a noisy train
Of loyal-stomach'd flatterers and their squires
Clattered in retinue, and aped his pace,

And timed their talk by his, and worked their eyes
By intimation of his glance, with great
And drilled precision.
                        Then said the fool:
" 'Twas a brave flight, my lord, that last one! brave.
Didst note the heron once did turn about,
And show a certain anger with his wing,
And make as if he almost dared, not quite,
To strike the falcon, ere the falcon him?
A foolish damnable advisèd bird,
Yon heron! What? Shall herons grapple hawks?
God made the herons for the hawks to strike,
And hawk and heron made he for lords' sport."
" What then, my honey-tonguèd Fool, that knowest
God's purposes, what made he fools for? "
                                            " For
To counsel lords, my lord. Wilt hear me prove
Fool's counsel better than wise men's advice? "
" Aye, prove it. If thy logic fail, wise fool,
I'll cause two wise men whip thee soundly."
                                            " So:
Wise men are prudent: prudent men have care
For their own proper interest; therefore they
Advise their own advantage, not another's.
But fools are careless: careless men care not
For their own proper interest; therefore they
Advise their friend's advantage, not their own.
Now hear the commentary, Cousin Raoul.
This fool, unselfish, counsels thee, his lord,
Go not through yonder square, where, as thou see'st
Yon herd of villeins, crick-neck'd all with strain
Of gazing upward, stand, and gaze, and take
With open mouth and eye and ear, the quips
And heresies of John de Rochetaillade."
Lord Raoul half turned him in his saddle round,
And looked upon his fool and vouchsafed him
What moiety of fastidious wonderment
A generous nobleness could deign to give
To such humility, with eye superb
Where languor and surprise both showed themselves,
Each deprecating t'other.

                   " Now, dear knave,
Be kind and tell me—tell me quickly, too,—
Some proper reasonable ground or cause,
Nay, tell me but some shadow of some cause,
Nay, hint me but a thin ghost's dream of cause,
(So will I thee absolve from being whipped)
Why I, Lord Raoul, should turn my horse aside
From riding by yon pitiful villein gang,
Or ay, by God, from riding o'er their heads
If so my humor serve, or through their bodies,
Or miring fetlocks in their nasty brains,
Or doing aught else I will in my Clermont?
Do me this grace, mine Idiot."
                       " Please thy Wisdom,
An thou dost ride through this same gang of boors,
'Tis my fool's-prophecy, some ill shall fall.
Lord Raoul, yon mass of various flesh is fused
And melted quite in one by white-hot words
The friar speaks. Sir, sawest thou ne'er, sometimes,
Thine armorer spit on iron when 'twas hot,
And how the iron flung the insult back,
Hissing? So this contempt now in thine eye,
If it shall fall on yonder heated surface
May bounce back upward. Well: and then? What then?
Why, if thou cause thy folk to crop some villein's ears,
So, evil falls, and a fool foretells the truth.
Or if some erring crossbow-bolt should break
Thine unarmed head, shot from behind a house,
So, evil falls, and a fool foretells the truth."
" Well," quoth Lord Raoul, with languid utterance,
" 'Tis very well,—and thou 'rt a foolish fool,
Nay, thou art folly's perfect witless man,
Stupidity doth madly dote on thee,
And Idiocy doth fight her for thy love,
Yet Silliness doth love thee best of all,
And while they quarrel, snatcheth thee to her
And saith *Ah! 'tis my sweetest No-brains: mine!*
—And 'tis my mood to-day some ill shall fall."
And there right suddenly Lord Raoul gave rein
And galloped straightway to the crowded square,

—What time a strange light flickered in the eyes
Of the calm fool, that was not folly's gleam.
But more like wisdom's smile at plan well laid
And end well compassed. In the noise of hoofs
Secure, the fool low muttered: " *Folly's love!*
So: *Silliness' sweetheart: no-brains:* quoth my Lord.
Why, how intolerable an ass is he
Whom Silliness' sweetheart drives so, by the ear!
Thou languid, lordly, most heart-breaking Nought!
Thou bastard Zero, that hath come to power,
Nothing's right issue failing! Thou mere ' pooh '
That Life hath uttered in some moment's pet,
And then forgot she uttered thee! Thou gap
In time, thou little notch in circumstance! "

Chapter IV

Lord Raoul drew rein with all his company,
And urged his horse i' the crowd, to gain fair view
Of him that spoke, and stopped at last, and sat
Still, underneath where Gris Grillon was laid,
And heard, somewhile, with languid scornful gaze,
The friar putting blame on priest and knight.
But presently, as 'twere in weariness,
He gazed about, and then above, and so
Made mark of Gris Grillon.
                                        " So, there, old man,
Thou hast more brows than legs! "
                                        " I would," quoth Gris
" That thou, upon a certain time I wot,
Hadst had less legs and bigger brows, my Lord! "
Then all the flatterers and their squires cried out
Solicitous, with various voice, " Go to,
Old Rogue," or " Shall I brain him, my good Lord? "
Or, " So, let me but chuck him from his perch,"
Or, " Slice his tongue to piece his leg withal,"
Or, " Send his eyes to look for his missing arms."
But my Lord Raoul was in the mood, to-day,
Which craves suggestions simply with a view

To flout them in the face, and so waved hand
Backward, and stayed the on-pressing sycophants
Eager to buy rich praise with bravery cheap.
" I would know why,"—he said—" thou wishedst me
Less legs and bigger brows; and when? "
        " Wouldst know?
Learn then," cried Gris Grillon and stirred himself,
In a great spasm of passion mixed with pain;
" An thou hadst had more courage and less speed,
Then, ah my God! then could not I have been
That piteous gibe of a man thou see'st I am.
Sir, having no disease, nor any taint
Nor old hereditament of sin or shame,
—But, feeling the brave bound and energy
Of daring health that leaps along the veins—
As a hart upon his river banks at morn,
—Sir, wild with the urgings and hot strenuous beats
Of manhood's heart in this full-sinew'd breast
Which thou may'st even now discern is mine,
—Sir, full aware, each instant in each day,
Of motions of great muscles, once were mine,
And thrill of tense thew-knots, and stinging sense
Of nerves, nice, capable and delicate:
—Sir, visited each hour by passions great
That lack all instrument of utterance,
Passion of love—that hath no arm to curve;
Passion of speed—that hath no limb to stretch;
Yea, even that poor feeling of desire
Simply to turn me from this side to that,
(Which brooded on, into wild passion grows
By reason of the impotence that broods)
Balked of its end and unachievable
Without assistance of some foreign arm
—Sir, moved and thrilled like any perfect man,
O, trebly moved and thrilled, since poor desires
That are of small import to happy men
Who easily can compass them, to me
Become mere hopeless Heavens or actual Hells,
—Sir, strengthened so with manhood's seasoned soul,

—I lie in this damned cradle day and night,
Still, still, so still, my Lord: less than a babe
In powers but more than any man in needs;
Dreaming, with open eye, of days when men
Have fallen cloven through steel and bone and flesh
At single strokes of this—of that big arm
Once wielded aught a mortal arm might wield,
Waking a prey to any foolish gnat
That wills to conquer my defenceless brow
And sit thereon in triumph; hounded ever
By small necessities of barest use
Which, since I cannot compass them alone,
Do snarl my helplessness into mine ear,
Howling behind me that I have no hands
And yelping round me that I have no feet:
So that my heart is stretched by tiny ills
That are so much the larger that I knew
In bygone times how trifling small they were:
—Dungeoned in wicker, strong as 'twere in stone;
—Fast chained with nothing, firmer than with steel;
—Captive in limb, yet free in eye and ear,
Sole tenant of this puny Hell in Heaven:
—And this—all this—because I was a man!
For in the battle—ha, thou know'st, pale-face!
When that the four great English horsemen bore
So bloodily on thee, I leapt to front,
To front of thee—of thee—and fought four blades,
Thinking to win thee time to snatch thy breath,
And, by a rearing fore-hoof stricken down,
Mine eyes, through blood, my brain, through pain,
—Midst of a dim hot uproar fainting down—
Were 'ware of thee, far rearward, fleeing!—Hound! "

Chapter V

Then, as the passion of old Gris Grillon
A wave swift swelling, grew to highest height
And snapped a foaming consummation forth
With salty hissing, came the friar through

The mass. A stillness of white faces wrought
A transient death on all the hands and breasts
Of all the crowd, and men and women stood,
One instant, fixed, as they had died upright.
Then suddenly Lord Raoul rose up in selle
And thrust his dagger straight upon the breast
Of Gris Grillon, to pin him to the wall;
But ere steel-point met flesh, tall Jacques Grillon
Had leapt straight upward from the earth, and in
The self-same act had whirled his bow by end
With mighty whirr about his head, and struck
The dagger with so featly stroke and full
That blade flew up and hilt flew down, and left
Lord Raoul unfriended of his weapon.
                                         Then
The fool cried shrilly, " Shall a knight of France
Go stabbing his own cattle? " And Lord Raoul,
Calm with a changing mood, sat still and called:
" Here, huntsmen; 'tis my will ye seize the hind
That broke my dagger, bind him to this tree
And slice both ears to hair-breadth of his head,
To be his bloody token of regret
That he hath put them to so foul employ
As catching villainous breath of strolling priests
That mouth at knighthood and defile the Church."
The knife ×   ×   ×   ×   ×   ×
To place the edge   ×   ×   ×   ×
Mary! the blood! it oozes sluggishly,
Scorning to come at call of blade so base.
Sathanas! He that cuts the ear has left
The blade sticking at midway, for to turn
And ask the Duke " if 'tis not done
Thus far with nice precision," and the Duke
Leans down to see, and cries, " 'tis marvellous nice,
Shaved as thou wert ear-barber by profession! "
Whereat one witling cries, " 'tis monstrous fit,
In sooth, a shaven-pated priest should have
A shaven-earèd audience; " and another,
" Give thanks, thou Jacques! to this most gracious Duke

That rids thee of the life-long dread of loss
Of thy two ears by cropping them at once;
And now henceforth full safely thou mayst dare
The powerfullest Lord in France to touch
An ear of thine; " and now the knave o' the knife
Seizes the handle to commence again, and saws
And . . ha! Lift up thine head, O Henry! Friend!
'Tis Marie, walking midway of the street,
As she had just stepped forth from out the gate
Of the very, very Heaven where God is,
Still glittering with the God-shine on her! Look!
And there right suddenly the fool looked up
And saw the crowd divided in two ranks.
And Raoul pale-stricken as a man that waits
God's first remark when he hath died into
God's sudden presence, saw the cropping knave
A-pause with knife in hand, the wondering folk
All straining forward with round-ringèd eyes,
And Gris Grillon calm smiling while he prayed
The Holy Virgin's blessing.
                        Down the lane
Betwixt the hedging bodies of the crowd,
x   x   x   x   x   x   majesty
x   x   x   x   x a spirit pacing on the top
Of springy clouds, and bore straight on toward
The Duke. On him her eyes burned steadily
With such gray fires of heaven-hot command
As Dawn burns Night away with, and she held
Her white forefinger quivering aloft
At greatest arm's-length of her dainty arm,
In menace sweeter than a kiss could be
And terribler than sudden whispers are
That come from lips unseen, in sunlit room.
So with the spell of all the Powers of Sense
That e'er have swayed the savagery of hot blood
Raying from her whole body beautiful,
She held the eyes and wills of all the crowd.
Then from the numbèd hand of him that cut,
The knife dropped down, and the quick fool stole in

And snatched and deftly severed all the wythes
Unseen, and Jacques burst forth into the crowd,
And then the mass completed the long breath
They had forgot to draw, and surged upon
The centre where the maiden stood with sound
Of multitudes of blessings, and Lord Raoul
Rode homeward, silent and most pale and strange,
Deep-wrapt in moody fits of hot and cold.

x   x   x   x   x   x   x

1868-1874?   *1884*

[Songs for " The Jacquerie "]

The hound was cuffed, the hound was kicked,
O' the ears was cropped, o' the tail was nicked.
(*All*)   *Oo-hoo-o,* howled the hound.
The hound into his kennel crept,
He rarely wept, he never slept,
His mouth he always open kept,
      Licking his bitter wound.
        The hound,
(*All*)   *U-lu-lo,* howled the hound.

A star upon his kennel shone,
It showed the hound a meat-bare bone.
(*All*)   O hungry was the hound!
The hound had but a churlish wit.
He seized the bone, he crunched, he bit.
" An thou wert Master, I had slit
      Thy throat with a huge wound,"
       Quo' hound.
(*All*)   O, angry was the hound.

The star in castle-window shone.
The Master lay abed, alone.
(*All*)   " Oh ho, why not? " quo' hound.
He leapt, he seized the throat, he tore
The Master's head from neck to floor
And rolled the head i' the kennel door
       And fled and salved his wound,
             Good hound!
(*All*)   U-*lu-lo*, howled the hound.

1868-1871?   *1884*

       May, the maiden,
       Violet-laden
Out of the violet sea,
       Comes and hovers
       Over lovers,
Over thee, Marie, and me,
       Over me and thee.

       Day, the stately,
       Sunken lately
Into the violet sea,
       Backward hovers
       Over lovers,
Over thee, Marie, and me,
       Over me and thee.

       Night, the holy,
       Sailing slowly
Over the violet sea,
       Stars uncovers
       Over lovers,
Stars for thee, Marie, and me,
       Stars for me and thee!

       1868-1871?   *1884*

Baby Charley

He's fast asleep. See how, O Wife,
Night's finger on the lip of life
Bids whist the tongue, so prattle-rife,
    Of busy Baby Charley.

One arm stretched backward round his head,
Five little toes from out the bed
Just showing, like five rosebuds red,
    —So slumbers Baby Charley.

Heaven-lights, I know, are beaming through
Those lucent eyelids, veined with blue,
That shut away from mortal view
    Large eyes of Baby Charley.

O sweet Sleep-Angel, thronèd now
On the round glory of his brow,
Wave thy wing and waft my vow
    Breathed over Baby Charley.

I vow that my heart, when death is nigh,
Shall never shiver with a sigh
For act of hand or tongue or eye
    That wronged my Baby Charley!

1869   *1883*

Them Ku Klux

Hit's nigh upon twenty year or more
    (Which my old 'oman, Nancy,
She says hit's bar'ly nineteen, *shore*
    But *I* knows women's fancy!)
That my habit's been, if it's warm and clear,
To set in my old split-bottom cheer
Out thar on the front pyāzer, near
    Them large plumgranite bushes.

I sets thar tow'rds the cool o' the day,
 To read my weekly paper,
And hears the hen a-cluckin' away
 And the pigs agin' the scraper,
And I sees the sun go down the sky
And I hopes, bein' old, that I may die
As bold as the sun, surrounded by
 Them bright and heavenly blushes.

I sot thar, some few days ago,
 A-readin' and a-noddin',
And here cum neighbor Jeems Munro
 Across the field a-ploddin',
And "Well!" says he, "Did y'ever see
Sich doins, Gracious Goodness me!
As them Ku Klux is said to be
 Eternally a-doin'?

"Why here" (says he) "'s a paper, sent
 To me from Pennsylvany;
Jest look! Hit says— *The Ku Klux went*
 That night that was so rainy,
And they tuck up a poor old colored man,
And carved him, and jinted him: made him stan'
On his head and eat up hisself: then ran
 A-howlin' and hullybalooin'!"

Now Jeems Munro h'aint lived here long,
 Fur he's a thrivin' Yankee,
That bought some land from me for a song
 When things was crinky-cranky,
Jest after the war, and then piled in
And the way he worked, hit was a Sin!
And spite of his Yankeeness, he has bin
 A fust-rate honest neighbor.

Yes sir, a fust-rate man is Jeems,
 Whatever way you strike him,
And I wish these Georgy hills and streams
 Had a million more jest like him.

But Jeems has his faults, as most men ther'n,
And one of 'em is, that he *kin not* learn
That all o' them Ku Klux lies he's hearn
    Is fools' and rascals' labor.

And so I says, " Now Jeems Munro,
    You air a man of gumption,
You know that two and two makes fo',
    And you aint much on presumption;
And now that you've lived in Bibb fo' year,
Did you ever see, or feel, or hear,
Or taste, or smell, or think you was near,
    A Ku Kluxin' assassin? "

" Caint say I hev " says Jeems. " Well now,"
    Says I, "Old Sumner's thundered,
And shuck the land, a-sayin' how
    Your folks and Grant has blundered.
I've jest been a-readin' the old man's speech,
Whar he says that far on the sandy beach
Of Santo Domingo wuss Ku Kluxes screech,
    Grate big ones, fur, fur surpassin',

" The Suthern make: but that aint shucks:
    He says that Grant's ther leader—
That Grant hisself 's a old he-Ku Klux
    —A regular Ku Klux breeder!
I'll read you," says I, " but whur air my spex?
I thought that I laid 'em right thar, jest nex
To that newspaper: Nancy, wher *air* my spex? "
    And I fumbled and grumbled horrid.

But presently I looked at Jeems:
    His jaws was fa'rly breakin',
And Nancy nigh had bust her seams
    So hard her sides was shakin',
And they both sot thar and they laughed at me,
—'Twell wife put her arms full tenderly
Round my neck, and says, " There, old man, they be
    Atop o' your own dear forrid! "

But Jeems laughed on, a good long while,
   'Twell finally he spluttered:
"Well, well, I swan, I've hed a smile!"
   And then again he stuttered:
But at last he says, "I've seed a sight
Which it makes me b'leeve that Sumner's right
And Grant's like you, so full o' spite
   A-fumblin' and a-gruntin'

"To find out whar the Ku Klux was
   (As you for your old spectikles)
And gittin' hisself in sich a buzz
   And sich a muddle o' pickles
That he clean forgot (what Nancy see)
To feel of *hisself* right keerfullee;
Then p'raps he'd 'a' found that hisself might be
   Th' identickle thing he was huntin'!"

1870-1871?   *1945*

9 from 8

I was drivin' my two-mule waggin,
   With a lot o' truck for sale,
Towards Macon, to git some baggin',
   (—Which my cotton was ready to bale, —)
And I come to a place on the side o' the pike
   Whar a piert leetle winter-branch jist had throw'd
The sand in a kind of a sand-bar like,
   And I seed, a leetle ways up the road,
   A man squattin' down, like a big bull-toad,
On the ground, a-figgerin' thar in the sand
With his finger, and motionin' with his hand,
   And he looked like Ellick Garry.
And as I driv up, I heerd him bleat
To hisself, like a lamb: "*Hauh?* Nine from Eight
   Leaves nuthin',—and none to carry?"

And Ellick's bull-cart was standin'
    A cross-wise of the way,
And the little bull was a expandin'
    Hisself on a wisp of hay.
But Ellick he sat with his head bent down,
    A studyin' and musin' powerfully,
And his forrud was creased with a turrible frown,
    And he was a werkin' appearently
    A 'rethmetic sum that wouldn't gee,
Fur he kep' on figgerin' away in the sand
With his finger, and motionin' with his hand,
    And I seed it *was* Ellick Garry.
And agin I heerd him softly bleat
To hisself, like a lamb: " Hauh? Nine from Eight
    Leaves nuthin',—and none to carry! "

I woa'd my mules mighty easy
    (Ellick's back was to'rds the road
And the wind hit was sorter breezy)
    And I got down off'n my load,
And I crep' up close to Ellick's back,
    And I heerd him a talkin' softly, thus:
" Them figgers is got me under the hack.
    I caint see how to git out'n the muss,
    Except to jest nat'ally fail and bus'!
My crap-leen calls for nine hundred and more.
My counts of sales is eight hundred and four,
    Of cotton for Ellick Garry.
Thar's eight, ought, four, jest like on a slate:
Here's nine and two oughts—Haugh? Nine from Eight
    Leaves nuthin',—and none to carry.

" Them crap-leens, O, them crap-leens!
    I giv one to Pardman & Sharks.
Hit gobbled me up like snap-beans
    In a patch full o' old fiel'-larks.
But I thought I could fool the crap-leen nice,
    And I hauled my cotton to Jammel and Cones.
But shuh! 'fore I even had settled my price
    They tuck affidavy without no bones

And levelled upon me fur all ther loans
To the 'mount of sum nine hundred dollars or more,
And sold me out clean fur eight hundred and four,
    As sure as I'm Ellick Garry!
And thar it is, down all squar and straight,
But I caint make it gee, fur Nine's from Eight
    Leaves nuthin',—and none to carry! "

Then I says " Hello, here, Garry!
    However you star' and frown,
Thar's somethin' fur *you* to carry
    Fur you've worked it upside down! "
Then he riz and walked to his little bull-cart,
    And made like he neither had seen nor heerd
Nor knowed that I knowed of his raskilly part,
    And he tried to look as if *he* wa'nt feard,
    And gethered his lines like he never keered,
And he driv down the road 'bout a quarter or so,
And then looked around, and I hollered " Hello,
    Look here, Mister Ellick Garry!
You may git up soon and lie down late,
But you'll always find that nine from eight
    Leaves nuthin' and none to carry."

1870-1871?   *1884*

Nilsson

A perfect rose, shot through and through
With silver sheens of globèd dew
Under the morning-lighted blue,

Whose rose-flame were too rich and red
Were 't not through dainty dew-drops shed
And clarified and chastenèd.

—So, Nilsson, all a-fire at heart
Thou shinest, still, serene, apart;
Through dew-pure spheres of perfect art.

Thy song hath compassed life and earth,
Wild pain of death, wild pain of birth,
The whole great chord from sin to mirth.

Thy passion throbbeth in the sphere
That Art hath wrought thee, diamond-clear,
As if a heart beat in a tear.

The listening soul is full of dreams
That shape thy wondrous-varying themes
As cries of men, or plash of streams,

Or noise of summer raindrops round
That patter daintily a-ground
With hints of heaven in the sound,

Or noble wind-tones chanting free
Through morning-skies across the sea
Wild hymns to some strange majesty.

O, if one trope, clear-cut and keen,
May type the art of Art's best queen
White-hot of soul, white-chaste of mien,

—Thou dost on Music's red heart dwell
As if a Swedish snow-flake fell
Into a glowing flower-bell

And lay, a crystal pure and bright,
Distilling sweets by day and night
That turned to music in their flight!

1871   *1883*

The Carrier's Appeal

(Written for the Carrier of " Our Saturday Night ")

Wind and rain through street and lane
Rattle your roof and shake your pane;
You turn in bed and sleep again,
    But round and round the carrier flies
        'Neath angry skies.

Snow and sleet in battle meet,
And rage in lane and whirl in street
And only make your dreams more sweet,
    But round his round the carrier goes
      Heedless of snows.

The suns arise, and through the skies
Spread news of space that distant lies,
So comes the light to reason's eyes
    When round his round the carrier runs
      Before the suns.

For morning-light has not more might
To scatter mists and banish night
Than has the Press that spreads the Right
    As round his round the carrier comes
      To all your homes.

Come words of men that wave the pen
As Richard waved his good Sword when
He drove the paynim Saracen,
    When round his round the carrier flies
      'Neath angry skies.

Here strong and weak together speak.
Rights on Wrongs great vengeance wreak,
And Wit plays many an antic freak
    When round and round the carrier goes,
      Heedless of snows.

Comes news, patch-pieced, of man and beast,
News from West and news from East,
News from greatest, news from least,
    When round his round the carrier runs
      Before the suns.

Then top my fee, my modest fee!
If you " no quarter! " cry to me
May Fate no quarter give your plea
    When round his round *No* carrier comes
      To all your homes.

1871   *1945*

Those Bonds

Georgia was held and firmly bound
    With multitudes of bonds,
And yet her very head is found
    So loose that it absconds.

Strange, with so many ligatures,
    That Bullock's still a rover,
That no attachment him secures
    Nor is he yet bound over.

And stranger still—yea, folk refuse
    To think it can be true—
We have more Clews than we can use
    Yet cannot find a clue.

1871   *1945*

———————

Have you forgot how through the April weather
    We fared into the chill and rainy west,
And how the nights wherein we played together
    Though dark were brighter than the days unblest?

Full well I mind your pretty smiles and blushings
    Whene'er I led you forth from out the wing,
Full well I mind the pleased expectant hushings
    Wherein, I thought, my feeble flute would ring!

I took the stillness for my gracious token:
    Well pleased, I trilled, and thrilled and mainly blew:
Alas, full soon my foolish trance was broken,
    —The people's senses were all eyes—for *you!*

If ears they had, I'm sure they never used them:
    All my spring-breaths of melody brought no fruit:
In truth, such right was theirs, my heart excused them
    —Your face made fairer music than my flute.

1874?   *1945*

———————

Whate'er has been, is, shall be—rind, pulp, core,
　　O' the big and pied Eve's-apple of our life—
Thou gav'st: I ate, learned good and evil lore,
　　And then was as a God, O Eve, O wife.
For who knows good, knows how the gods do grow,
　　And feeds on fruits that godlike tissues build:
And who knows ill, in truth but good doth know,
　　Ill is but good, wounding a hand unskilled.
Thus known, my Good brings double good alway,
　　As bringing roses intermixt with fruit;
And Ill—tame viper—round my neck doth play,
　　His fair white fangs not venom-bagg'd at root.
　　　Yea, thou, O sweeter Eve! my soul hast fed,
　　　And tamed, yet bruisèd not, the serpent's head.

1875   *1945*

At First

(To C. C.)

My crippled Sense fares bowed along
　　His uncompanion'd way,
And wrong'd by death pays life with wrong
—And I wake by night and dream by day.

And the morning seems but fatiguèd night
　　That hath wept his visage pale,
And the healthy mark 'twixt dark and light
In sickly sameness out doth fail.

And the woods stare strange, and the wind is dumb,
　　—O Wind, pray talk again—
And the Hand of the Frost spreads stark and numb
As Death's on the deadened window-pane.

Still dumb, thou Wind, old voluble friend?
—And the middle of the day is cold,
And the heart of eve beats lax i' the end
As a legend's climax poorly told.

Oh vain the up-straining of the hands
    In the chamber late at night,
Oh vain the complainings, the hot demands,
The prayers for a sound, the tears for a sight.

No word from over the starry line,
    No motion felt in the dark,
And never a day gives ever a sign
Or a dream sets seal with palpable mark.

And O my God, how slight it were,
    How nothing, thou All! to thee,
That a kiss or a whisper might fall from her
Down by the way of Time to me:

Or some least grace of the body of love,
    —Mere wafture of floating-by,
Mere sense of unseen smiling above,
Mere hint sincere of a large blue eye,

Mere dim receipt of sad delight
    From Nearness warm in the air,
What time with the passing of the night
She also passed somehow, somewhere.

1876   *1883*

[Beethoven]

Sovereign Master! stern and splendid power,
    That calmly dost both time and death defy;
Lofty and lone as mountain peaks that tower,
    Leading our thoughts up to the eternal sky;
Keeper of some divine, mysterious key,
    Raising us far above all human care,
Unlocking awful gates of harmony
    To let heaven's light in on the world's despair;

Smiter of solemn chords that still command
  Echoes in souls that suffer and aspire!
In the great moment while we hold thy hand,
    Baptized with pain and rapture, tears and fire,
      God lifts our saddened foreheads from the dust—
    The Everlasting God in whom we trust!

1876?   *1897*

[On the Receipt of a Jar of Marmalade]

How oft the answers to our passing prayers
  Drop down in forms our fancy ne'er foretold!
—Thus when, of late, consumed by wasting cares,
  " *Angels preserve us* " from my lips up-rolled,
    I'm sure I pictured not,—as thus I prayed,—
    Angels preserving me . . . with marmalade!

1877   *1891?, 1899*

———

Our turkey walks across the yard;
  But one sound did she utter:
" Bet, bet-bet, bet-bet, bet " a hard
  And harsh staccato sputter.

" Just hear, what an immoral bird! "
  I said, " My dear, I'll cage her."
—" For what? "—" Why, from the sounds we've heard
  I think she's laid—a wager."

1877   *1935*

Observed yon plumèd biped fine!
  To effect his captivation
Deposit particles saline
  Upon his termination.

1877   *1945*

While self-inspection it neglects,
  Nor its own foul condition sees,
The kettle to the pot objects
  Its sordid superficies.

1877   *1945*

The earliest winged songster soonest sees,
And first appropriates, the annelides.

1877   *1945*

To Mrs. S. C. Bird

(With an Empty Basket)

Elijah (so in Holy Writ 'tis said)
Was in the wilderness by ravens fed;
But my lone wastes a fairer wing supplies,
I'm pampered by a Bird-of-Paradise!

1878   *1935*

Water Lilies

Alive, yet all at rest,
The lily lieth on the water's breast;
  So may thy spirit stay
Upborne by His, that hallowed Christmas Day.

1878   *1890*

To My Class

On Certain Fruits and Flowers Sent Me in Sickness

If spicy-fringèd pinks that blush and pale
  With passions of perfume,—if violets blue
  That hint of heaven with odor more than hue,—
If perfect roses, each a holy Grail
Wherefrom the blood of Beauty doth exhale
  Grave raptures round,—if leaves of green as new
  As those fresh chaplets wove in dawn and dew
By Emily when down the Athenian vale
She paced, to do observance to the May,
  Nor dreamed of Arcite nor of Palamon,—
If fruits that riped in some more riotous play
  Of wind and beam than stirs our temperate sun,—
    If these the products be of love and pain,
    Oft may I suffer, and you love, again.

1879?   *1884*

On Violet's Wafers

Sent Me When I Was Ill

Fine-tissued as her finger-tips, and white
  As all her thoughts; in shape like shields of prize,
  As if before young Violet's dreaming eyes
Still blazed the two great Theban bucklers bright
That swayed the random of that furious fight
  Where Palamon and Arcite made assize
  For Emily; fresh, crisp, as her replies,
That, not with sting, but pith, do oft invite
More trial of the tongue; simple, like her,
  Well fitting lowlihood, yet fine as well,
—The queen's no finer; rich (though gossamer)
  In help for him they came to, which may tell
    How rich that him *she'll* come to;—thus men see,
    Like Violet's self e'en Violet's wafers be.

1880?   *1884*

Oh, what if Violet Browne were seen
    Slow walking down the way,
Attended by Miss Rosa Greene
    And Miss Vermilion Gray,

Together with Miss Paley Blue,
    And blond Miss Golding White,
Miss Die Scarlatti, and Miss Ru-
    by Hyacinth Chrysolite,—

And presently young Hugh Fitzhugh
    Should pass unnoticed by,
And all the people at that view
    Should raise the hue and cry,

To see these exquisite she-hues
    Thus by this he-Hugh go,
And mark the rainbow thus refuse
    To greet the reigning beau.

1880?   *1945*

The Poet ·

To the Pennsylvania Board of Pardons

—But I, sleek pardoners! will not pardon you.
Twice-criminals, stand forth: here, in the public blue,
Out in the common zenith, all-kenn'd, clear,
I set you in my stocks, where year on year
Shall pelt you like the muddy missile-rain
Of vulgar indignation. Spots, remain!
Who now shall slip you out from my decree
With farcic fine? The gods commissioned me.
No Boards reverse this verse that sets you high
In the stocks of shame, midmost the Ages' sky;
No quibbles, winks, nor hints, no briber's way,
No future Palmer, Stone, Duane and Quay.

Have you forgot, or, likest, never known,—
You sodden souls, you cunning-silly men,—
How, o'er the judge's bench, and o'er the bone
Of faction and all tricksters' knowing ken,
The implacable poet sits, with sovereign pen,
High on his bribe-abominating throne
And blazons on the heavens broad decrees
That true men's verdicts find, and Truth's armed self
Is Sheriff to? What shifts, what briberies,
Will buy my pardon? Blindworms, slippery lot,
With all your wriggling cares, this was forgot.

Worse than your pardoned, ye: not in the dark
Of possible concealment, no, nor in the flush
Of instant-tempting act, but sinful-stark
And impudent and free of qualm or blush
And taunting-insolent with faith in gold
You dragged the reverend Law about the land,
Lewd-laughing, loosed the general hold
Of justice, thrust in the communist's hand
His hottest torch, and taught the Mollie's tongue

A cry that rings from underground afar,
A song most terrible by dead men sung:
The purse, the purse, is made good plea in bar
By Pennsylvania law; th? poor man's jail
Is strong, the rich man's weak; what's Right? a name
For Money; down with park and down with pale,
And burn these folk that would not burn with shame,
—You first, that hung the Mollies, yea nor nay,
—They found no Palmer, Stone, Duane, nor Quay!

Think ye that gold is great, and cunning strong,
And each man has his price, and none is high?
Come, prove you: here is but a little song,
Yet who of you so rich, and who so sly,
Will juggle justice from a single line
Of this weak verse, that midst the common sky
Sets up your penal stocks, termless, condign,
Where morn by morn shall pale for fright of you,
And eve by eve shall blush at sight of you,
Nor night nor cloud shall hide the light of you,
Nor any bribe unlock, nor any pay
Bring *you* a Palmer, Stone, Duane or Quay.

1880?   *1945*

To Dr. Thomas Shearer

[Presenting a Portrait-Bust of the Author]

Since you, rare friend! have tied my living tongue
     With thanks more large than men have said or sung,
Then let the dumbness of this image be
     My eloquence, and still interpret me.

1880   *1884*

On a Palmetto

Through all that year-scarred agony of height,
   Unblest of bough or bloom, to where expands
   His wandy circlet with his bladed bands
Dividing every wind, or loud or light,
To termless hymns of love and old despite,
   Yon tall palmetto in the twilight stands,
   Bare Dante of these purgatorial sands
That glimmer marginal to the monstrous night.
Comes him a Southwind from the scented vine,
   It breathes of Beatrice through all his blades,
North, East or West, Guelph-wind or Ghibelline,
   'Tis shredded into music down the shades;
   All sea-breaths, land-breaths, systol, diastol,
   Sway, minstrels of that grief-melodious Soul.

1880?   *1891*

Struggle

My Soul is like the oar that momently
   Dies in a desperate stress beneath the wave,
Then glitters out again and sweeps the sea:
   Each second I'm new-born from some new grave.

1880-1881?   *1886*

Then, like the Dove from the dim-hulled Ark,
The Dawn flew out of the bulk of the Dark.

1880-1881?   *1945*

Wan Silence lying lip on ground,
An outcast Angel from the Heaven of sound,
    Prone and desolate
    By the shut Gate.

1880-1881?   *1908*

    Ten Lilies and ten Virgins,
        And, O mild marvel to mine eyes,
    Five of the Virgins were foolish,
        But all of the Lilies were wise.

1880-1881?   *1908*

Dream of a time when legislatures sit
    No more in public halls but private hearts,
And Love shall lie at ease, at ease,
    On the grass that greens the trading marts.

1880-1881?   *1945*

    I breakfasted on faith in God,
        I lunched on bread and tears,
    I dined on soup of boiled peascod,
        —And so passed on the years.

1880-1881?   *1945*

I said to myself *Which is I, which you?*
Myself made answer to myself,
Lo, you are I and I am you,
Yet are we twain, we two.

1880-1881?   *1887*

I'll sleep, I'll sleep, and dream a sweet death for trouble—
I'll sleep. I'll sleep, and dream that my heart beats double.

1880-1881?   *1887*

Thou and I

So one in heart and thought, I trow,
That thou might'st press the strings and I might draw the bow,
And both would meet in music sweet,
Thou and I, I trow.

1881?   *1887*

POEMS BY
SIDNEY AND CLIFFORD LANIER

To ——

'Twas Winter when I met you first,
　'Twas Winter when I saw you last:
But O, a Spring did bud and burst
　And bloom, ere that one Winter passed!

Green grass on tombs of long ago—
　A sweet, fresh Life in Death's own land—
Is what you were to me. You know
　How hard it was to drop your hand.

Ah, cold crypts love the baby-green
　That sleeps so bravely on their breast.
For this, they sacrifice their sheen,
　With this, they satisfy their rest.

So are you loved, from out the grave
　Of duty, walling me around.
Yet I am all content,—all brave:
　I wait, I wait. Sound, Trumpet, Sound!

1866   *1945*

A Song

Day is a silver veil
　God draws across the stars;
Night is a mourning-veil
　The heavens wear for wars;
Life is a bridal veil,
　Cross-wrought with gems and scars.

Day dazzles, and destroys
　The mellow lights of truth;
Night blinds us to our joys
　With tears for the day's ruth;
Life's cross-work vague decoys
　The strong right arm of youth.

Ere long, through noon-day fire
Truth's stars burn all the time;
Ere long, the heavens tire
Of Night's sad pantomime;
Ere long, Life's veiled desire
In God finds rest sublime.

1866   *1866?, 1871*

A Sea-Shore Grave

To M. J. L.

O wish that's vainer than the plash
Of these wave-whimsies on the shore:
" Give us a pearl to fill the gash—
God, let our dead friend live once more! "

O wish that's stronger than the stroke
Of yelling wave and snapping levin:
" God, lift us o'er the Last Day's smoke,
All white, to Thee and her in Heaven! "

O wish that's swifter than the race
Of wave and wind in sea and sky:
" Let's take the grave-cloth from her face
And fall in the grave, and kiss, and die! "

Look! High above a glittering calm
Of sea and sky and kingly sun,
She shines and smiles, and waves a palm—
And now we wish Thy will be done!

1866   *1871*

The Power of Prayer:

Or, the First Steamboat Up the Alabama

You, Dinah! Come and set me whar de ribber-roads does meet.
De Lord, *He* made dese black-jack roots to twis' into a seat.
Umph, dar! De Lord have mussy on dis blin' ole nigger's feet.

It 'pear to me dis mornin' I kin smell de fust o' June.
I 'clar', I b'lieve dat mockin'-bird could play de fiddle soon!
Dem yonder town-bells sounds like dey was ringin' in de moon.

Well, ef dis nigger *is* been blind for fo'ty year or mo',
Dese ears, *dey* sees the world, like, th'u' de cracks dat's in de do'.
For de Lord has built dis body wid de windows 'hind and 'fo'.

I know my front ones *is* stopped up, and things is sort o' dim,
But den, th'u' *dem*, temptation's rain won't leak in on ole Jim!
De back ones show me earth enough, aldo' dey's mons'ous slim.

And as for Hebben,—bless de Lord, and praise His holy name—
Dat shines in all de co'ners of dis cabin jes' de same
As ef dat cabin hadn't nar' a plank upon de frame!

Who *call* me? Listen down de ribber, Dinah! Don't you hyar
Somebody holl'in' " *Hoo, Jim, hoo* "? My Sarah died las' y'ar;
Is dat black angel done come back to call ole Jim f'om hyar?

My stars, dat cain't be Sarah, shuh! Jes' listen, Dinah, *now!*
What *kin* be comin' up dat bend, a-makin' sich a row?
Fus' bellerin' like a pawin' bull, den squealin' like a sow?

De Lord 'a' mussy sakes alive, jes' hear,—ker-woof, ker-woof—
De Debble's comin' round dat bend, he's comin', shuh enuff,
A-splashin' up de water wid his tail and wid his hoof!

I'se pow'ful skeered; but neversomeless I ain't gwine run away;
I'm gwine to stand stiff-leggèd for de Lord dis blessèd day.
You screech, and swish de water, Satan! I'se a gwine to pray.

O hebbenly Marster, what thou willest, dat mus' be jes' so,
And ef Thou hast bespoke de word, some nigger's bound to go.
Den, Lord, please take ole Jim, and lef young Dinah hyar below!

'Scuse Dinah, 'scuse her, Marster; for she's sich a little chile,
She hardly jes' begin to scramble up de homeyard stile,
But dis ole traveler's feet been tired dis many a many a mile.

I'se wufless as de rotten pole of las' year's fodder-stack.
De rheumatiz done bit my bones; you hear 'em crack and crack?
I cain't sit down 'dout gruntin' like 'twas breakin' o' my back.

What use de wheel, when hub and spokes is warped and split,
    and rotten?
What use dis dried-up cotton-stalk, when Life done picked de
    cotton?
I'se like a word somebody said, and den done been forgotten.

•But, Dinah! Shuh dat gal jes' like dis little hick'ry-tree,
De sap 's jes' risin in her; she do grow owdaciouslee—
Lord, ef you's clarin' de underbrush, don't cut her down, cut me!

I would not proud persume—but yet I'll bodly make reques';
Sence Jacob had dat wrastlin'-match, I, too, gwine do my bes';
When Jacob got all underholt, de Lord He answered Yes!

And what for waste de vittles, now, and th'ow away de bread,
Jes' for to strength dese idle hands to scratch dis ole bald head?
T'ink of de 'conomy, Marster, ef dis ole Jim was dead!

Stop;—ef I don't believe de Debble's gone on up de stream!
Jes' now he squealed down dar;—hush; dat's a mighty weakly
    scream!
Yas, sir, he's gone, he's gone;—he snort way off, like in a dream!

O glory hallelujah to de Lord dat reigns on high!
De Debble's fai'ly skeered to def, he done gone flyin' by;
I know'd he couldn' stand dat pra'r, I felt my Marster nigh!

You, Dinah; ain't you 'shamed, now, dat you didn' trust to
    grace?
I heerd you thrashin' th'u' de bushes when he showed his face!
You fool, you think de Debble couldn't beat *you* in a race?

I tell you, Dinah, jes' as shuh as you is standin' dar,
When folks starts prayin', answer-angels drops down th'u de a'r.
Yas, Dinah, whar 'ould you be now, jes' 'ceptin' fur dat pra'r?

1874-1875.   *1875*

Uncle Jim's Baptist Revival-Hymn

Solo.—Sin's rooster's crowed, Ole Mahster's riz,
　　De sleepin'-time is pas';
　　Wake up dem lazy Baptissis,
Chorus.—*Dey's mightily in de grass, grass,*
　　Dey's mightily in de grass.

　　Ole Mahster's blowed de mornin' horn,
　　　He's blowed a powerful blas':
　　O Baptis' come, come hoe de corn,
　　　You's mightily in de grass, &c.

　　De Meth'dis team's done hitched; O fool,
　　　De day's a-breakin' fas';
　　Gear up dat lean ole Baptis' mule,
　　　Dey's mightily in de grass, &c.

　　De workmen's few an' mons'rous slow,
　　　De cotton's sheddin' fas';
　　Whoop, look, jes' look at de Baptis' row,
　　　Hit's mightily in de grass, &c.

　　De jaybird squeal to de mockin'-bird: " Stop!
　　　Don' gimme none o' yo' sass;
　　Better sing one song for de Baptis' crop,
　　　Dey's mightily in de grass," &c.

　　And de ole crow croak: " Don' work, no, no ";
　　　But de fiel'-lark say, " Yaas, yaas,
　　An' I spec' you mighty glad, you debblish crow,
　　　Dat de Baptissis's in de grass," &c.

　　Lord, thunder us up to de plowin'-match,
　　　Lord, peerten de hoein' fas',
　　Yea, Lord, hab mussy on de Baptis' patch,
　　　Dey's mightily in de grass, grass,
　　　Dey's mightily in de grass.

1875-1876   *1876*

JUVENILE POEMS

NOTE

The following poems were apparently composed between the ages of sixteen and eighteen. Because of their early date and their inferior merit they are collected here as a separate group, preserved merely as documents in the history of Lanier's literary development and printed exactly as they were written, with all their irregularities of meter, spelling, punctuation, and the like. A few are obviously incomplete; three survive in variant versions, not here listed. About half of them are signed, either with his name or with the pen name—" Cacoethes Scrib "—used by him for other youthful compositions (see V, 199). All are definitely in his early handwriting. None of these verses have been previously published or even known by students of Lanier. The first one is dated June 22, 1858, with the note: " My only attempt at Poetry! . . . A fragment! Composite Metre!! "; the second, July 28, 1859. The rest are undated, but the script and general appearance of the manuscripts place them beyond any reasonable doubt within the period 1858-1860. The first ten, taken from Lanier's College Notebook, are arranged in the order in which they occur in its unnumbered pages; the others, from miscellaneous manuscripts, in the nearest possible approximation to a chronological order. All are in the Clifford A. Lanier Collection except the last four, which are in the Charles D. Lanier Collection, Johns Hopkins University. Three of these—" Morning on the Thermodoön " (probably an error for Thermodon, a river celebrated in the myth of the Amazons), " Lines of Devil-giants scowled," and an early draft of " As when care-wearied majesty "—are on stationery containing a letter by Lanier apparently written during his presidency of the Thalian Society, December 10, 1859–February 25, 1860; they also seem to fit the critical comments in R. S. Lanier's letter of February 21, 1861. Hence Mary Day Lanier's notation on the manuscript (" The earliest poetic effort extant ") is in error. The last one, " Hymn," exists in several forms; the text adopted is followed by over two hundred lines of roughly metered prose, entitled " Sermon," here excluded.

Wildly the Winter-wind moaneth,
Shrieking, the Night-Spirit groaneth,
   Around my chamber, dreary—
Faintly the dying embers glow
And eerie shadows round me throw,
   Musing, Solitary—

Bitterly my Spirit grieveth,
Sorely wounded it receiveth
   Consolation none—
Anon my soul is lost in wonder
And I contemplate, and ponder,
   If when life's race is run,

These longings for ideal bliss,
These Spirit-yearnings, this
   Insatiate desire
For some unearthly region, where
The Spirit, freed from earthly care,
   From passion's wasting fire,
Freed from despotic Ambition,
Blooms in Heavenly Fruition—

1858   *1945*

To Idol-Ellie!

As heavy lie yon gold-gloried, blush-bright clouds
Upon the blue beauty of the drunken, panting west
And dreamy as the filmy floating of those wondrous crowds
Of the dying day's glories waning into rest
   Thus heavy and thus beamy
   Thus glorious and dreamy
   Thus love-lighted and gleamy
   Thus sadly only dreamy
My Ellie, in my soul's most upper regions
Slumber my massive love's thought-legions!

The sun is sunk: and evening's faltering eyes
Dew dead earth with tears, in silence wept:
Out of the pearly East, and through the holy-tinted skies
The fresh moon hath risen and one ray hath swept
    One ray of a silvery slanting,
    The soft stars saucily taunting
    Tremulous, shimmering, panting,
    And floods of beauty flaunting,
Idol-Ellie, o'er my soul's upper regions
And all my massive love's thought-legions!

1859   *1945*

Spring

Now hath good Bess a rival found
And Nature hath played the Walter Raleigh
Flinging her green kirtle on the ground
Dampened with thawed frosts (copied folly
Of a fawning courtier) for fragile Spring
To walk on, earthward visiting—!

But to-night with generous emulation
The graceful moon hath nature's self outdone
In courtly etiquette: *she*, from her station
In heaven's star-trellised balcony hath thrown
Her silver brocade on the green-kirtled hills
And the vales and the jewel-flashing rills!

List ye! while soft zephyr-minstrelsy
Heralds the night-walk of the viewless queen!
The mock-bird wild-trilleth out his phantasy,
Like droppings of shattered rainbow-sheen!
Solo-singer in the orchestra of nature!
Primest speaker in her legislature!

Look! The Spring, round-zoned and hung
From heaven by light-wreathed cords of cloud
Floateth, impelled by zephys young
That, even now, in merry-flutt'ring crowd
Sipped nectar from the cups of heaven-flowers
Or loved, 'mid scented shades of heaven-bowers!

See! She's here! and as she presseth
The kirtled sward, a God-taught choir
Led by mock-bird, " All hail "! addresseth
To *her*, queen of bird's and poet's lyre,
In choral burst so rich and glad and free
As maketh blush man's labor-woven harmony!

This, is but the merry-making's signal!
Young leaves, with caperings of glee,
Dance to the south-wind's softened madrigal—
Their parent-boughs, more old, sway gracefully
(As at a ball some quiet married sett!)
Through stately motions of the minuet!

Trees, time-trusty burghers gray
Old-serving habitants of nature's town
Gravely their stately bodies sway,
And their green caps aloft wave round
As showing token of their homage loyal,
And salutation of the princess royal.

Ocean calming with the beauteous vision
Looseth his curling crests of wrath
And like some sky-blue field Elysian
Smiling, offereth waveless path
To Spring, and biddeth her a gay
" God-speed " upon her azure-tinted way!

Lakelets blue her fairy image steal
As she doth linger on the pebbly marge
And, as their bosoms, glowing, feel
The sweet influence, they enlarge
And heave, and swell and sparkle bright
And ripple o'er with tremors of delight—

Rivers, by freezing winter wind
Face-hardened and fissured yawning;
Like madmen under treatment kind
Dissolve, transparent as the dawning
Of a summer's morn and roll away
Peacefully meditating towards the sea—

1859-1860?   *1945*

What Is It?

A lone wolf by a castle-ruin howled
A moon between black drift-clouds scowled
     With baleful leer—

Wind through age-eaten port holes moaned
And weirdly shrieked wild wailings, toned
     Like cries of fear—

Far down below the jagged beetling-o'er
Of the precipice, did surly ocean roar
     Like a tiger-throng—

A Sea-gull dreaming on poised, lofty wing
Startled by some night-phantasm, 'gan to sing
     A screeching song—!

Fit scene and place were here for ghosts
To revel in, and all black demon-hosts
     Of sulphurous hell—

Fit scene and place were here for grief
Bosoms o'er-burdened by wild unbelief
     Madly to swell—

Men called me outcast on the fair, wide world
Yea, outcast, outcast: I had hurled
     Into eternity

A gory demon that from hell's ranks came
And took upon himself man's form and name
     To torture me—!   &c &c &c

1859-1860?   *1945*

Extravaganza—Ode to Coleridge—

Coleridge, thou lazy (I near said) *devil!*
Thou mongrel admixture of good and evil!
Ah, often, often have I cursed thee
Rather him or her that nursed thee
And trained thee up in such ungodly laziness!
About thy mind and character a haziness
Doth hang, indistinct, and doth envelope thee—
Ah, hadst thou th' industry of Penelope
To weave sweet songs as she did weave her garment,
Earth with thy loud-shouted praise were far-rent!
And thou art much in her position placed
For suitors wait on thee to taste
Thy charms poetic, whom thou dost refuse—
Why dost not up and work? Rather choose
To ply unceasing day and night thy shuttle-quill
To body beauty forth with all thy subtle skill
That all mankind may stand and breathless gaze
Upon the beauteous fabric of thy woven lays—?
Oft wandering with thee mid thy sylvan bowers
Sense-bound with the rare perfume of flowers,
Seeking in the rank-grown garden of my mind
For some sweet shrub to cull, and wreathe, and bind
About thy temples, compensation poor
For joys thou'st lent me from thy plenteous store;
Sudden the beauteous vision thou dost cease,
" *Fragment* " quotha, then to loved ease
Back dost betake thyself—*Then* would I throw
A thorn-crown on thy noble, hazy, brow—!
Aye, grudges do I owe thee numerous!
Coleridge, sometimes I presume Eros'
Sweet breathings on my heart to write:
Sometimes fair glories of the moon-lit night
I pen! or unskilled try to drape
With word-hangings some April-showered landscape.
Sometimes in meditative autumn twilight, I recall
Memories of the Spring in humble madrigal—

But then, when from my finished task I turn
To thy sweet " thoughts that breathe and words that burn "
Canst thou imagine how my blood runs pale
Finding that *my* freshest thoughts are stale?
When, hearty-muttering maledictions, I behold
That all my touching metaphors, my pretty things, are old?
That thou 'mongst many odes, hast long since shown
To men, ideas that I fondly thought mine own?

1859-1860?   *1945*

Yonder Cometh Spring—!

Let down from Heaven on light wreathing cords
Of fleecy clouds, through air she gently floateth
On her way impelled by Zephyrs, that but now
Did gambol o'er gorgeous meads in Paradise!
She's here! And as she steppeth on the earth
Songsters, innumerous, God-taught, greet her
With choral bursts, harmonious, singing grandly
Through dim, religious aisles of green-wood cathedrals—
Harmony so rich, so full, so glad, so free
That it putteth to the blush those labored things
That man hath woven and called music!
Flowers, beauteous hand-maids that the Princess brought
From heaven, scatter perfumes on the laden air:
Strip off their velvet mantles, and, with lavish hand
Spread them in the path for her to walk on!
Young leaves, with child-like glee, dance merrily
To the music that the winds make: older boughs,
Parents of a leafy offspring, with air sedate
Wave gracefully through stately minuets:
Trees, gray burghers of nature's populous city
Make low obeisance, and their green caps wave
Aloft, in honor of the maiden's coming!
Old Ocean, by the beauteous vision moved
Unbends his angry crests, and, glassy, smiling
Biddeth it to speed its azure-tinted way—

Fair lakes her image catch as near she lingereth
And hold it in their bosoms—that do blush
And ripple o'er with tremors of delight—
Rivers, ice-bound and seam-faced by winter
Dissolve, transparent, and gently roll away
In peaceful meditations towards the sea—
Brooklets, flashing in the sun, leap laughing
Then hurry on to bable forth, " She's come "
To flower o'erhanging, and mead, and moss-grown rock
Earth, air and sky all wake to nature's call
And to the yearning soul bring tribute joys—

1859-1860?   *1945*

Extravaganza

" Life! What is it? And its sequel
That cloud-country, of the which
No living man hath aught beheld
Save cold graves, its entrance gates?
Alas! Alas! The yore-time sages,
Their locks with silvery lore encrusted,
Their forms bent o'er under wisdom's weight
This same question, bootless, did propound—
Alas! Alas! Its mystic answer came
Not until Death their lips, pale-hued
Grimly, with fleshless fingers clutched
As twere to keep the secret from out-leaping
Unto breathless-listening ears of mortals— "
Thus my sad soul unto the winds complained
While in the desperation, and the blackness drear
Of my heart, and the wild unearthly longing
For unearthly knowledge, I prayed, God, impious
That I might die, and learn the mystery, dread—
My heart was one dry waste, and desolate
Whereon there stood the charred, unsteady trunk,
Lightning-scathed, of youthful aspirations,
That once were lusty trees, and rooted firm—
Their withered, leafless, frost-bared branches,

(Young hopes that greenly budded out, & blossomed,
In my life's spring-time,) did groan & creak
In grief's whistling wind so very mournfully!
Tis a sad thing, when a city, pestilence-blighted
Hath her wide halls filled with corpses rotten
Of her great men and fair daughters—
Tis a sad thing, when a vale, Wyoming-green
Blushing with Pomona's health-ruddy glow
Golden with crisp maize, and flower-spangled
Sudden is swept with hell-breathing fires,
And left charred waste, wolf-howling desolation!—
Tis a sad thing, when a harlot-beauty, courted
By a crowd, and by admirers jewel-covered,
Wakes up to find that *Wrinkle*, premature
Hath usurped Blush's throne, and Pleasure
Taken swift wing to flee, from misery's coming
Disgustful—When a vessel is engulphed
Amid red lightnings and the howling turmoil
Of lashed wave, mad-wind and wrathful cloud,
Air eddying with streams of darting thunder,
Tis sad to think of Ocean-monsters, slimed,
At drowning men, with talons hunger-sharpened
Clutching, fearful, alike contemptuous of age
And death and beauty—Tis sad when Mothers
Widowed and helpless, shake from tattered clothes
Thin-featured offspring, clinging there to beg
For life's necessity—Death, vengeance
Malice, betrayal, all these are sad—
But, oh! how sad unutterably, how
Past-conceivable is the wailing music,
When first upon the strained ear it strikes
Of grief-winds, sweeping gustfully
Athwart withered forests of young hopes
In wasted hearts—Wherefore was it
I prayed God, impious, to taste of death
And learn life's sequel—Like poor *Keats*
My dearest friend, yet unseen of my longing eyes
" Naught saw I earthly worth my compassing "—

1859-1860?   *1945*

Love Lost—!

Grieve, Heart! Grieve!
For thy love that is no more;
For thy love gone just before
    Thy marriage-eve!

Weep, Eyes! Weep!
Weep bitterly a briny tear;
For your delight, your Annie dear
    Doth silent sleep!

Moan, Soul! Moan!
Let it be low, and sad, and wild,
Like the wailing moan of a dying child—
    Thou art alone!

1859-1860?   *1945*

My sweet, bright dreams! *So* sweet! *so* bright!
Come, hither, all! And, while this Forest, brown,
In th' Autumnal, silent dusk, around me throweth
Mystic shadows, from out whose depths, my playful fancy
Doth suggest your cheerful countenances peeping:
Stand ye out there before me, in tableaux vivants,—
Arrayed in that same garb, so beautiful,
Which, on this very spot, some years agone,
My busy fancy wove and clothed you in!
Look! methought, as I did furtive glance
Adown that vista, that foliaged vista, where
The trees, as couples in a ball-room, stand
With arms about each other locked, prepared
To launch forth swiftly in the whirling waltz,—
Methought I saw a youth and maiden, walking,
And engaged in converse, which, to others idle,

Lovers *only* can appreciate—Sometimes, He,
Into her eyes, (*brown, soft*, eyes,) did gaze,
Till she their dark-fringed curtains would let fall,
And on his heaving bosom rest her glorious head—:
While he unto himself would murmur, softly,
" Oh, Annie, the portals of *thy* soul, too well are watched,
For black deceit, though all his store of cunning art he use,
And stealthiness, to creep in there, and poison thee,
Malignant, with his foul and lying tongue "—!
And so, when she, with naughty hands, endeavored,
His lips to keep away from *hers*, he bound them,
Playful, with her flowing hair; then, at his will,
Did feast upon the honied prize—So happy!
See! By the magic of the dreamland, here upriseth
The village-church, before our eyes, and there,
Before the Altar, blushing, kneel the couple
Upon whose heads, a white-haired pastor's hands are laid,
(The maiden's Father,) who, with earnest voice, from Heaven
Doth supplicate a blessing on their married future—

    1859-1860?   *1945*

A Shadow!

" What lack the valleys & mountains
        That once were green & gay?
What lack the babbling fountains?
        Their voice is sad to-day—
            Only the sound of a voice,
            Tender & sweet & low—

What lack the tender flowers?
        A shadow is on the sun!
What lack the merry hours?
        That I long that they were done?
            Only two smiling eyes
            That tell of joy & mirth!

What lacks my heart, that makes it
 So weary & full of pain?
That trembling Hope forsakes it
 Never to come again?
  Only *another* heart
  Tender, and *all mine own!*"

1859-1860? 1945

Hideous habitants of gloom!
Be ye harbingers of doom?
Embodied cankers on the bloom
 Of my lonely heart?

Are ye messengers of hell
Come to flap a boding knell
On my lone heart's silver bell
 On my chimeless heart—

Shriek me a sweet hell-song
The while some damned hell-throng
On a hot dome, for a hell-gong
 Beat frenzied time—

Ye look blackened with the smoke
As ye had just outbroke
From the horrid-seething coke
 And sulphurous grime—

Are red-hot hearts in hell?
Do myriad remorses, fell
Hell-hornets, on swoll'n souls dwell
 Instinging venom-death?

1859-1860? 1945

———————

There was one fled from the sound of bells' death toll
With " wetted cheeks " and with an inward " heart of flame "—
Shrivelling the finely-woven texture of his soul,
That nought but fire could shrivel, nought could tame—
Lightnings of red agony whirl and ever flashed
Until the high-wrought fabrics of his life in ruin crashed;
All wild pulsings of his blood discordant rang,
As though a steepled world of Brazen bells should clang

1859-1860?   *1945*

———————

As when care-wearied majesty, with yet lordly mien
Of lordly power, sleeps in far solitudes and rare:
So lay a mountain, clothed in sumptuous green
Haloed with dreamy glories of the sun-set air—
Adown silk masses of the rocks, wide-cleft,
And athwart trailing flowers of the circling plain,
With many a wanton petulancy, many a deft
Kissing of velvet flower-cheeks, purled amain
Full many a mirthful rill, brave flashing train
Of courtiers to the kingly river of the plain—
Only brook-monodies, whispered to the sod,
And the low, grand river's soliloquy, themed of God
Intensed around the ever brooding noiselessness
Here might silence her sister solitude caress,
And soft as the filmy fall of twilight in the west
Melt into blended stillness of the night: and rest—
While athwart the dim deeps of shoreless night,
Star-flocks, like fire-feathered aygrets, wing flight
Towards blue lakes in western lands of Light—

Beneath these stars, and by this mountain and this river,
Paced to and fro a man, low murmuring ever.
O life, O life and love, mysterious Two:
O world, and angel of the world, dim-mysteried Two—
Pacing before his cave, where river-sward sprung fair
And smiled amid the stillness and unchanging sadness there—
So ever in some lavish joy of our green earth strewed
Before the very door-way of wo's bleak abode—

1859-1860?   *1945*

Morning on the Thermodoön

Young odors have harnessed the South-winds afar
With film-woven collars of transparent mist—
On the faint-blushing seats of a rose-petal car
They pleasure ride wherever free fancies list—
A blue-eyed violet from her leaf window peeped
And the merry young visitors, seeing her, stopped
But turning her face, as the wind-coursers leaped
Past her low cottage onward, a dewy tear dropped
From her languishing eyes: For yonder harebell
Bending down to the sun-lighted dew of the dell
In its glittering freshness her velvet skin steeps
While the violet lone in its jealousy weeps.—

    *   *   *   *   *

Thermodoön! The grand-rolling! How like the flow
And the measure so stately of heroic thought
Is the march of thine unrippled majesty, slow
As the step of Despair with dead miseries fraught—
No boat keels thy breast's broad expanse have encumbered
(Like cares that plough up the weak bosom of man),
But petals of varie-hued wood-flowers unnumbered,
Make blush tinged argosies for wood-sprites and Pan!

1859-1860?   *1945*

Lines of Devil-giants scowl
Beside thy chariot of fire
Blasts of eternity howl
Athwart the world-strung lyre
With infinite, Eolian wail
Wild, wintry-melodied wail—
On waves of that universe dirge
On the woe-froth of its surge
Ride damned spirits: death
War, hypocrisy, despair,
Whose only sustenance and breath
Is the God-blaspheming prayer,
Of some lone and weary soul
Some fierce, stung, bitter soul,—
That saith, I am a lie,
A hideous lie, the world and I—
And saith unto itself, some devil,
Some malignant Potency of evil,
Some giant mocker of the world's mirth,
Some interfused hell-essence through the earth,—
This is your world—God

1859-1860?   1945

Hymn

Two white doves athwart a gray storm winging:
Two sweet children on the winter-road singing:
Two violets under the Upas-tree growing:
Two breaths of South-wind, while it is snowing:

Two bosoms bared to a guard's gun-fire:
Two dew-beads under heat of the Sun-fire:
Two petals of a rose in the Mahlstrom whirled:
Two white silken banners in a battle unfurled:
Two pilgrims journeying on through the world!

1859-1860?   1945

APPENDIX

POEM OUTLINES

NOTE

The appropriateness of the term "Poem Outlines" for many if not all of the following is evidenced by the survival of similar jottings for a dozen actually completed poems, ranging all the way from bare prose statements to partial drafts in meter and rhyme (see pp. 300, 308, 317, 321, 322, 332, 353, 354, 358-9, 360, 361, 364). Henry W. Lanier published 117 *Poem Outlines* as a slender volume in 1908 (23 of which he had first printed in *Century*, LXXVI, 847-850, Oct., 1908, and 3 more in *Current Literature*, XLV, 572-573, Nov., 1908). Three of these (from pp. 37, 85, and 100) have been treated as poems in the present volume, because they are finished quatrains; three more (from pp. 16, 39, and 47) have been omitted, because the original MSS show that they are mere extracts from Lanier's reading; the rest are reprinted in the following pages. Fourteen other outlines have been previously published, but are now first collected. To these are here added 64 new ones selected from a mass of surviving jottings as the ones most probably intended by Lanier for use in poems rather than prose, though any such selection is necessarily a matter of opinion. Only a few can be dated with certainty, but most of those in the first group were apparently written before 1877, whereas most of the others seem to have been written after that date. On May 26, 1877, Lanier first referred to the habit of noting down on odd slips of paper the ideas for poems that came to him during periods of illness or other stress that prevented composition; on Aug. 10, 1880, he announced that he had several volumes of poems "in the form of memoranda," written during the past few years. Further references in his letters (as cited in the notes) indicate the nature of three of these volumes with sufficient clarity to make possible a conjectural division of the most interesting of Lanier's poem outlines into "Songs of Aldhelm," "Credo and Other Poems," and "Hymns of the Marshes and the Mountains." The order within the several groups is simply that which seemed most appropriate to the present editor. Unless otherwise indicated in the notes, all are reproduced here from the original MSS (which are in the Charles D. Lanier Collection, Johns Hopkins University, except the items from the Ledger) with the following exceptions: Nos. 33, 42, 44, 57, 78, 94, 96, 101, 117, 125, 134, 136, 140, 149, 150, 151, 159, 172, 174, 185, 187 are from MS copies in the handwriting of Mary Day Lanier; Nos. 50, 51, 52, 53, 73, 110, 111, 121, 142, 147, 152, 155, 180, 181 are from *Poem Outlines*, pp. 95, 96, 97, 102, 94, 98, 93, 104, 99, 52, 7, 66, 119, 120, respectively. They have been numbered consecutively throughout for convenience in reference. (See pp. lxv ff., above.)

A Literary Workshop *

1

The grave is a cup
Wherewith I dip up
My draughts from the lake of life.
          (Death, loq.)

Death is the cup-bearer of Heaven, God's Ganymede, and his cup is the grave, and life is the wine that fills it.

2

Oh, man falls into this wide sea of life
Like a pebble dropped by idle hands in water—
The little circle of the stir he makes
Does lessen as it widens, until Death
Comes on, and straightway the round ripple is gone out.

3

Night's a black-haired poet, and he's in love with Day. But he never meets her, save at early morn and late eve: when they fall into each other's arms, and draw out a lingering kiss; so folded together are they at such times, that we cannot distinguish bright maid from dark lover; and so we call it Dawn and Twilight,—it being,

        Not light, but lustrous dark;
        Not dark, but secret light.

* [Lanier's Ledger, a literary journal which he apparently began in the summer of 1865 (see letter of Sept. 16 to Clifford), is preserved in the Henry W. Lanier Collection. In addition to extracts from his reading and drafts of much of his early poetry and prose, it contains numerous jottings, some of which seem definitely intended for use as poems. They are reproduced here as Nos. 1-30, in the order in which they occur in the Ledger: pp. 17 (five), 18, 20, 23 (two), 38 (two), 46 (two), 47, 61, 68, 70, 238 (two), 254, 255, 265 (two), 266, 281, 326, 329 (two), 330, 677. They may be dated roughly 1865-1875. All other surviving outlines that do not fit the categories of Lanier's three projected volumes (following) are grouped under this miscellaneous heading. Nos. 31-40, being dated (as indicated in the notes), are arranged chronologically; Nos. 41-57 keep the order in which they were printed in *Poem Outlines*; Nos. 58-67 follow in the most logical sequence.—ED.]

4

Big wars stood up in ranks, like men,
And fought with thunders and great wild fires—.

5

Pestilences whistled i' the air like bullets in a battle, and loud
world-Calamities anon exploded jarring all space.

6

The tree stood like a danseuse poised in an attitude, the vines
wreathing above its crown like the danseuse's arms above her
head—.

7

The white, austere and awful radiance of God
Too white for eyes so late unfilmed
From the earthy cataract, the flesh-disease.

8

Hunger and a whip:—with these we tame wild beasts. So, to
tame us, God continually keeps our hearts hungry for love and
continually lashes our souls with the thongs of relentless
circumstance.

9

Star-drops lingering after Sun-light's rain.

10

Those jets of warm and fragrant vapor that shoot forth from
the bursting buds of the mulberry tree in Spring, remind of the
sweet new things that are continually unfolding themselves
to the young man, who progresses from day to day in thought
and study and healthful moral tone—

11

Grave and most reverend trees, standing silently around a
Cornfield, like a Committee appointed to superintend the growing of the Corn.

12

White tents that dotted all the ground, as if
The huge war-cloud had snowed a snow of tents.

13

These green and swelling hills, crowned with white tents,
Like vast green waves, white-foaming at the top.

14

It is always Sun-rise and always Sun-set somewhere on the
earth—And so, with a silver Sun-rise before him and a golden
Sun-set behind him, the Royal Sun fares through Heaven, like
a king with a herald and a retinue.

15

Old toothless Ocean, far off, crooning by himself.

16

All men are pearl-divers, and we have but plunged down into
this strangling salt-sea of Life,—to find a pearl. This Pearl,
like all others, comes from a wound: it is the Pearl of Love
after Grief.

17

Birth is but a folding of our wings.

18

Love is a net: which an Infinite Fisher has cast with skill and
caught all men therein. Flap and struggle, with fin or claw,
like bird or beast, with never such strength, as much as we may:
we are still there, and the vast and indestructable meshes
contain us.

19

Knowledge is power in a sense: but the converse of this
proposition is not true, and power is not Knowledge. Power is
love, and Knowledge only becomes powerful when love (or
desire) has kindled it. Love is the steam, and Knowledge the
machinery, of this engine,—life.

20

John's dead, and yonder goes his Soul.
It flashes through the battle-smoke,
As if a lost sun-ray upbroke
And went back to the Sun.

21

The worlds,—
All dancing in the muddy ray of Time
Like Motes in a yellow beam from the low Sun.

22

The black nights flapped along, one after one,
Each hooting as he passed,
The ghostly days sailed by, in grinning files,
And gibbered what the nights had left unspoken.

23

The slow malignities of patient Hate,
The icy blades of persevering Scorn.

24

The earth, a grain of pollen dropped in the vast calyx of
Heaven.

25

Up from the calmèd sea of modern thought
I saw a mist arise in spiral rings.
These quickly grew into more human shapes,
That gleamed like gods and angels when the Sun
Burned upward through the far rim of the sea,
And flamed with altar-fires.

26

Man, on the one side God, on the other side hog; Tree, on
the one side a thing which we cut down at pleasure, and burn
for our mere comfort, on the other side a thing whose beauty
moves our soul and whose growths, formative processes,
balsams, therapeutic effects, are utterly beyond our ken: a stone,

which we kick from here yonder, in idlest caprice, yet which is far more venerable, for age, than Grandfather Adam, and far more inscrutable, for mystery, than the Problem of Zeno;—O how shallow is the culture of that man who will presume to argue of the World, and who will prate of understanding things! *

27

When God put Adam on the earth, did He set him up in business by fixing him a shop and stocking it with goods, and hanging it round with mottoes in large letters, such as Business Is Business, A Penny Saved Is A Penny Gained, and the like?— No, he put him in the garden (if the Bible is true) to keep it and to dress it.

28

The world has forgotten that labor is *not* a curse. Before ever Man fell, at his very creation, in the first moment when man became a living soul,—God put him in the Garden of Eden to keep it and to dress it: and this keeping and dressing are the synonym of labor. Man was to employ himself, even in Eden: and the toil of Paradise was Agriculture.

29

Jabul was the father of the tent-dwellers and them that tend sheep: Jubal his brother was the father of all such as handle the harp and organ: Tubal-Cain his brother was the father of them that work in brass and iron. It appears then that the first business men of life were the farmer, the shepherd, the musician, and the blacksmith. Go to, tradesman: I, the flute-player, I am older than thou: thou art a *parvenu.* My ancestry goes back to Adam's (if thou wdst have it accurately) great-great-great-great grandson.

30

The windy curves of yon great sail o' the sky
Tense-stretched with wafting such a hulky world
Around the sun.

* [See facsimile, vol. IX, facing p. 72, of the present edition.—ED.]

31

When June looks languidly at the cool dead May,
And dies a febrile death, under the hot breath
of summer— *

32

The beating of the hearts of half the world,
And ticking of the clocks of [half the world],
Dreams fluttering about a tossing soul like birds
about a ship in a storm &c.

33

All roads from childhood lead to hell,
Hell is but the smoke about the monstrous fires
Kindled from $\Big\}$ frictions of youth's self with self,
Rising from
Passion rubbed hard 'gainst Purpose, Heart 'gainst Brain.

34

My soul said to my sense,
Give me thy hand, dear Love.
But my Sense was angry.
Give me thy hand, O Sense, my Soul exclaimed,
I think thou art my brother.

35

So large, so blue is Harry's eye,
I think to that blue Heaven the souls do go
Of honest violets when they die.

* [No. 31 is written on the back flyleaf of Denison Olmsted's *An Introduction to Astronomy* (New York, 1859) in Lanier's handwriting of *c.* 1859-1861.
No. 32 is on the same MS with a draft of " Night and Day," a poem written
in April, 1866; No. 33 is dated " 1874-5 " in *Poem Outlines*, p. 20; No. 34 is
verso an envelope postmarked Oct. 23, 1875; No. 35 is verso a draft of a stanza
of " Psalm of the West," written in the spring of 1876; No. 36 is on the same
MS with a draft of " To ——, with a Rose," dated June 5, 1876; No. 37 is
verso a draft of " The Stirrup-Cup," dated January, 1877; No. 38 is dated by
Mary Day Lanier " Tampa, 1877."—ED.]

36

It is the easiest thing in the world to make one. falsehood out
of two truths.

37

Oft in the short-breath'd sallies of our youth,
Ere swell our Spirits' sinews manful rough
With knots from long unknotting tangled truth,
We wail anew the weakling's old rebuff
How questions ask themselves, and tease our dream
Yet when on fire for answers, forth we run
Until then near }
The answers near } yet nearer never seem
And as each nagging day's pursuit is done
Dissolve in silly dusk.

38

A Robin got drunk in a china-tree,
So drunk in fact that he could'nt see
And all he could say was " He he he."
This maudlin Robin fell from the tree,
And the Jim-Jams came in the guise of a boy,
A laughing fiend of a pitiless boy
Who spied that robin with devilish joy—

39

To Lillian

Born at the death bed of a year
That dying left a blessing here,
    My " airy, fairy " friend,
Born when the Southern soil was red,
To her sons most drear x x x x *

* [Text from *American Literature*, V, 269 (Nov., 1933), where it is said to
have been written to a young girl named Helen Harrison (whom Lanier called
" Lillian," taking his cue from Tennyson's poem), during a summer vacation in
the Allegheny mountains in 1880—probably the summer of 1879 at Rockingham
Springs. Since only this fragment has been preserved, it is treated as a Poem
Outline.—ED.]

40

Pale, at yon perilous juncture of the ways
Where Boundary's melting snows do join their tide
With tributary slush from Charles,
Not Leander swam to love-ward, in his arms
Embracing Foam, though not his Hero × × × × *

41

And then
A gentle violin mated with the flute,
And both flew off into a wood of harmony,
Two doves of tone.

42

Every rule is a sign of weakness. A man needs no rules to
make him eat, when he is hungry: and a law is a badge of
disgrace. Yet we are able to console ourselves, from points of
view which terminate in duty, order, and the like advantages.

43

How did'st thou win her, Death?
Thou art the only rival that ever made her cold to me.
Thou hast turned her cold to me.

44

Heart was a little child, cried for the moon,
Brain was a man, said, nay.
Science is big, and Time is a-throb,
Hold thy heart, Heart.

45

Ambling, ambling round the ring,
  Round the ring of daily duty,
Leap, Circus-rider, man, through the paper hoop of death,
  —Ah, lightest thou, beyond death, on this same slow-
    ambling, padded horse of life.

* [The MS copy in the handwriting of Mary Day Lanier has a note stating
that this unfinished poem was begun by Lanier in the winter of 1880-1881 to
commemorate a visit made to him in his last illness by two ladies. Boundary
and Charles are streets in Baltimore.—ED.]

Youth, the circus-rider, fares gaily round the ring standing with one foot on the bare-backed horse,—the Ideal. Presently, at the moment of manhood, Life (exacting ring-master) causes another horse to be brought in who passes under the rider's legs, and ambles on. This is the Real. The young man takes up the reins, places a foot on each animal, and the business now becomes serious.

For it is a differing pace, of these two, the Real and the Ideal.

And yet no man can be said to make the least success in life who does not contrive to make them go well together.

46

The Age is an Adonis that pursues the boar Wealth: yet shall the rude tusk of trade wound this blue-veined thigh,—if *Love* come not to the rescue; Adon despises Love.

47

For a Flower Decoration of Soldiers' Graves

Unto your house, O sleepers,
Unto these graves that house you since ye died,
Unto these little rooms wherein ye sleep,
A serenade of Love who sings in flowers,
If sense more dim than thought
May pierce through the deep dream of death wherein ye lie.

48

To stand with quietude in the midst of the prodigious Unknown which we call the World, also to look with tranquil eyes upon the unfathomable blackness which limits our view to the little space enclosed betwixt birth and death.

49

The old Obligation of goodness has now advanced into the Delight of goodness; the old Curse of Labor into the Delight of Labor; the old Agony of blood-shedding sacrifice into the tranquil Delight of Unselfishness. The Curse of the Jew of Genesis is the Blessing of the modern Gentile. It is as if an avalanche, in the very moment of crushing the kneeling villagers, should turn to a gentle and fruitful rain, and be minister not of death but of life.

50

My Desire is round,
It is a great globe.
If my desire were no bigger than this world
It were no bigger than a pin's head.
But this world is to the world I want
As a cinder to Sirius.

51

I am startled at the gigantic suggestions in this old story of the Serpent who introduces knowledge to man in Eden. How could the Jew who wrote Genesis have known the sadness that ever comes with learning—as if wisdom were still the protégé of the Devil.

52

On the advantage of reducing facts—like fractions—to a common denominator.

We explain: but only in terms of x and y, which are themselves symbols of we know not what, graphs of mystery. We establish relations betwixt this and that mystery. We reduce x and y to a common denominator, so that we can add them together, and make a scientific generalization, or subtract them, and make a scientific analysis: but more we can not do. The mystery is still a mystery, and this is all the material out of which we must weave our life.

53

Cut the Cord, Doctor! quoth the baby, man, in the nineteenth century. *I am ready to draw my own breath.*

54

How in the Age gone by
Thou took'st the Time upon thy knee,
    As a child,
A Time that smote thee in the face
Even whilst thou did kiss it
And how it tore out thy loving eyes
Even while thou didst teach it.

55

The monstrous things the mighty world hath kept
In reverence 'gainst the law of reverence:
The lies of Judith, Brutus' treachery,
Damon's deceit, all wiles of war.

56

How Twelve Stags Plowed for Saint Leonor

Ere yet to brakeward stole the feeding fawn,
While grave and lone about the greenwood lay
All soft seclusions of the dimmest dawn,
Forth from his hut, in heavenly airs to pray,

Fared Father Leonor, rapt with morn and God.
New-perfected in look and limb with sleep,
Fain of each friendly tree whereby he trod,
At dew-drop salutations smiling deep.

He paced the hollow towards his pleasant goal,
Where burst from out a tall oak's roots a spring,
As prayer from priviest fibres of the soul
Leaps forth in loneliness. There stood a stalwart ring

Of twelve great oaks about that middle Oak,
Which uttered forth the fount, as erstwhile stood
The sweetest Twelve of time round Him who spoke
The words that watered life's long drought of good.

Straight fell the father Leonor on his knees
Down by the foot of that Christ-Oak, and cried,
My master, while they sleep, I pray for these,
My soul's dear sons, my sixty, that abide

About my cell since first my wandering feet
In these Armoric wilds were stayed: O Lord,
I love it not that life on savage meat

x   x   x   x   x   x   x   x   x *

* [The fragment ends here, but cf. Lanier's essay " The Legend of St. Leonor,"
II, 247.—Ed.]

57

What Am I Without Thee?

What am I without thee, Beloved?
A mere stem, that hath no flower;
A sea forever at storm, without its calms;
A shrine, with the Virgin stolen out;
A cloud void of lightning;
A bleak moor where yearnings moan like the winter winds;
A rock on sea-sand, whence the sea hath retired, and no longer
    claspeth and loveth it;
A hollow oak with the heart riven thereout, living by the bark
    alone;
A dark star;
A bird with both wings broken;
A Dryad in a place where no trees are;
A brook that never reacheth the sea;
A mountain without sunrise thereon and without springs therein;
A wave that runneth on forever, to no shore;
A raindrop suspended between Heaven and Earth, arrested in
    his course;
A bud, that will never open;
A hope that is always dying;
An eye with no sparkle in it;
A tear wept, dropped in the dust, cold;
A bow whereof the string is snapped;
An orchestra, wanting the violin;
A poor poem;
A bent lance;
A play without plot or dénouement;
An arrow, shot with no aim;
Chivalry without.his Ladye;
A sound unarticulated;
A water-lily left in a dry lake-bed;
Sleep without a dream and without a waking-time;
A pallid lip;
A grave whereafter cometh neither Heaven nor hell;
A broken javelin fixed in a breastplate;
A heart that livth, but throbbeth not;
An Aurora of the North, dying upon the ice, in the night;
A blurred picture; ·
A lonesome, lonesome, lonesome yearning lover!

58

More than twice one, beyond all measure more,—
Doth count this singular two of thee and me.*

59

Poem. On the women who bore out their husbands on their
shoulders, as their greatest treasures, from the captured City.

60

Two of us wander on the beach,
Me and myself.

61

Oh how my neck is galled with the ragged collar of poverty!

62

Control
O Hunger, Hunger, I will harness thee
And make thee harrow all my spirit's glebe.
Of old the blind bard Herve sang so sweet
He made a wolf to plough his land.**

63

On a Certain Recent Concert
O, for thee 'tis well, 'tis well,
That music hath unmade old hell,
Else wert thou burning long
Ere now for this drear bawdy song
Of smiles, &c ———

* [Published in *Century*, XXXIV, 417 (July, 1887).—ED.]
** [Published in *Century*, XXXII, 62 (May, 1886); reprinted in *Poems*
(1891), p. 155, but here treated as a Poem Outline because obviously incomplete.—ED.]

64

Two Poems: a Contrast

The Italian Opera Singer as he is: the Singer as he should be,
preaching Love, Repentance, Faith and Hope.

> The legs that upheld him, not flesh, but dust;
> The gospel he preached, not Love, but Lust.

> The Me that is within us all,
> Music speaks by tones divine,
> The other Me—they hear and fall
> Upon their knees before this shrine
> Where Love—the Me of Me—doth shine.

65

> Time takes his worn out cast off days
> And cuts 'em up fine into little stars,
>   And gives 'em to indigent nights.
> Say, Pa, now what you 'spose
>   Time does with his worn out clothes?
> He takes all the cast off days, my dear,
>   And cuts 'em up fine in x x x x

66

I went down into the city,
I saw this one and that one, John and James
And presently ere I was aware John was telling me
How James had schemed and maneuvered and lied
And presently ere I was aware I was telling William
How John had told me how James had schemed and
      maneuvered and lied
Then presently ere I was aware, - - - -

67

A Vision of Socrates

And ever is Launcelot stained with the rose-red stain
      of Guenever,
Stained with the beautiful blemish of Guenever.
And Socrates with his uncouth rudeness [?], and
      Bacon, and Galileo, &c,
And ever the son, saint Galahad
Better his father Launcelot.

Songs of Aldhelm *

68

Come over the bridge, my merchants,
Come over the bridge, my Souls:
For ye all are mine by the gift of God,
Ye belong to me by the right of my love,
    I love
With a love that is father and mother to men,
Ye are all my children, merchants.

69

Merchant: We have no time, we have no time to listen to
    idle dreams.
Aldhelm: But I, poor Aldhelm, say you nay;
Till ye hear me, ye have no time
Neither for trade nor travelling;
Till ye hear me ye have no time to fight nor marry nor mourn;
There is not time, O World,
Till you hear me, the Poet Aldhelm,
To eat nor to drink nor to draw breath.
For until the Song of the Poet is heard
Ye do not live, ye can not live.
O noonday ghosts that gabble of losing and gaining,
Pitiful paupers that starve in the plenteous midmost
Of bounty unbounded.

* [On Oct. 20, 1878, Lanier wrote to Bayard Taylor of his "Songs of Aldhelm" as "a volume . . . which is now in a pigeon-hole of my desk half jotted down" (see also letter of June 8, 1879, and note to "Credo," below). From other references to Aldhelm (notably in the fragmentary lecture, III, 310-311), he seems to have symbolized to Lanier the ideal poet, singing his songs to a world engrossed in trade. Under this heading are here grouped all the outlines in Lanier's late handwriting dealing with the theory and function of the artist (including some that may have been intended for a preface). Nos. 68-69 are printed as one in *Poem Outlines*, p. 50; but the MS shows they are two separate items, the first entitled "The Song of Aldhelm," the second "Silken Sonnets / Songs of Aldhelm." No. 70 likewise bears the title "Songs of Aldhelm," as does a fragment with the words: "Ballads of the Bridge / Dandelion flying down, / Flying hither, flying yonder."—Ed.]

70

Songs from the Sun, Songs from the ground,
Songs from the . . . stars,
Songs, { fine souls of the body of sound,
       { joined souls and bodies of sound,
. . . ghosts of songs that died,
Songs of Birth and of Death, of . . .
Beat million-rhythmed in the heart of my hearing,
The world is all sound and still signs of sound.

71

On the difference between carrying things on as *trades*, and
as *arts*.

The trade of sculpture, the trade of painting. How can the
grocery-trade become an art.

72

You can hear Art clatter like a Cotton-Mill,—so many book-
makers, picturemakers, figuremakers, house-makers,—and no
singers, no painters, no sculptors, no temple-builders.

73

I, the artist, fought with a Knight that was cased in a mail
of gold; and my weapon, with all my art, would not penetrate
his armor. Gold is a soft metal, but makes the hardest hauberk
of all. What shall I do to pierce this covering? For I am hungry
for this man, this business man of stocks and dry-goods, and
now it seems as if there were no pleasure nor hope nor life for
me until I win him to my side.

74

The greatest trouble with the greatest artists of today is their
bitterness towards the vast world which moving in other planes
does not understand them. It is not with bitterness, it is with
Love and Compassion that the Artist must regard his fellow
men, the first artist is Christ; all men are artists.

75

I made me a Song of Serenade,
And I stole in the Night, in the Night,
To the window of the world where man slept light,
And I sang:
O my Love, my Love, my Fellow Man, My Love.*

76

Like to the grasshopper in the tall grass,
That sings to the mate he cannot see yet while,
I sing to thee, dear World;
For thou art my Mate, and peradventure thou wilt
come; I wish to see thee.

Like to the lover under the window of his Love,
I serenade thee, dear World;
For thou art asleep and thou art my Love,
And perhaps thou wilt awake and show me thine eye,
And the beauty of thy face, out of the window of thy
house of Time.

77

God let me [be] like the earth:
The farmer layeth thereupon offal and defilement,
Then the good earth giveth him grain.
So, if the world cover me with heap of insult,
Warrant me ne'er to be dead to the world,
Offer I foison of bread to the world,
Yea, let me yearn to the world
And richly return to the world
(For my wrongs)
Food for the whole of the world,
Good for the soul of the world,
In my songs.

* [Published in *Independent*, LX, 110 (Jan. 11, 1906).—ED.]

78

To many inarticulate
Like the great vague wind
Against the wire, one word larger
Than some languages, nowhere flippant,
My song is of all men and times and thoughts,
Therefore many, caring not
For aught save one man, this time, and finance,
Many, many listen not
Because I sing for all.
Sang I of that little king
That owns this special little time,
The world were mine; but oh, but oh,
I sing all Time that hath no king.
And if I sang this man or that,
Haply the singer's fee I win;
But part's too little: I sing all:
I know not parties, cliques, nor times.

79

I am but a small-winged bird:
But I will conquer the big world
    As the bee-martin beats the crow,
By attacking it always from Above.

80

If that the mountain measured earth
Had thousand-fold his mighty girth,
One violet would avail the dust
For righteous pride and just.
Then why do ye prattle of promise,
And why do ye cry *this poet's young,*
And will give us more anon?

For he that hath written a song
Hath made life's clod a flower,
What question of short or long?
As the big earth is summed in a violet,
All Beauty may lie in a two-lined stave.

Let the clever ones write commentaries in verse.
As for us, we give you texts,
O World, we poets.
If you do not understand them now,
Behold hereafter an army of commentators will come:
They will imitate, and explain it to you.

81

To him that humbly here will look,
I'll ope the heavens wide,
But ne'er a blessing brings a book
To him that reads in pride.
Whoe'er shall search me but to see
Some fact he hath foretold,
Making my gospel but his prophecy
My New, his little Old.
To him that opens his hands upwards to me like a thirsty plant,
I am Rain,
But to him that merely as a patron stands by to see me perform,
I am Zero and a Drought.

82

Thought, too, is carnivorous. It lives on meat. We never have an idea whose existence has not been purchased by the death of some atom of our fleshy tissue.

O little poem, thou goest from this brain chargeable with the death of tissue that perished in order that thou mightst live: nourish some soul, thou that hast been nourished on a human body.

83

In Malory it is told how a Damosell bled for the custom of the castle. It is so that the poet, the good man, *must* suffer at the world's hands: he must bleed for the custom of the world. Keats so bled and Wordsworth and before all Christ, and next Socrates.

84

A Business Transaction

The poet stepped into a grimy den,
  Where the sign above the door,
Said: " Money to lend, in sums to suit,
  On Real Estate, &c."

I want, said the Poet,
  (So many thousand dollars).
So said Cent per Cent, rubbing his hands,
  Where is the property?

I offer, said the Poet,
  My Castle in Spain,
'Tis a lovely house,
  So many rooms, acres, &c.

85

The Artist: he
Who lonesome walks amid a thousand friends.

86

I will be the Terpander of sadness;
I will string the shell of slow time for a lyre,
  The shell of Tortoise-creeping time,
  Till grief grow music.

87

I wish, said the poet, that you should do thus and so:
Laugh you thus, what matters a poet's wish
The poet's wish is Nature's law.
It is for the satisfaction thereof that things are,
And that Time moves.
Observe Science in modern times proving the old
  poet's dreams.
Nature with all her train of powers,
And Time with his ordered hours,
And Space, and said,
What dost thou wish, my lord!

88

When the poet says, *I wish,*
Nature appears, as Ariel to Prospero,
And says, *What, my Lord?*
It shall be done.*

89

A poet is a perpetual Adam: events pass before him, like
the animals in the creation, and he names them.

90

Facts are the products of God's imagination: fiction, of
man's.**

91

Rhythms of waving grass: Marked off in bendings and
straightenings. Last spring. From my house I looked off on a
field of buttercups; the wind blowing steadily made rhythmic
waves of green with yellow crests: steady force of wind, steady
resistance of buttercup-stem.

92

How Rhythm is mixed in with daily life: beat of pulse, rise
and fall of chest, unconscious rhythms of breath, rhythm of
walk, (even metre of walk), day and night, flood tide and ebb
tide, sleep and wake,

> The mighty breathing of the sea,
> The sea that draws two breaths a day.***

---

* [Written on the flyleaves of a copy of Sir Michael Foster's *A Textbook of Physiology* (London, 1877?—a volume now missing from Lanier's library), according to a memorandum in the Clifford Lanier Collection, Johns Hopkins University.—ED.]

** [Written verso a letter from J. R. Osgood & Co., July 21, 1876, along with a prose draft of the idea of "Clover" and several other jottings that are illegible.—ED.]

*** [Written on the back flyleaves of Lanier's copy of the Aldine *Chaucer,* vol. I.—ED.]

93

Moses' triumphal Ode on the defeat of the Egyptians was sung, danced, and timbrelled. The Israelites danced and sung at the Golden Calf; probably imitating the Egyptians. David danced before the Ark: there was an annual dance in Shiloh on the sacred festival: Greeks, Romans, and lately in Limoges the choir danced in honor of the Saint. Our own negroes.

94

Beethoven

The argument of music,
I heard thy plea, O friend;
Who might debate with thee?

95

Chopin

Betwixt the upper Mill-stone *Yes*
And the nether Mill-stone *No*,
Whence cometh *burr* and *burr* and *burr*
And much noise of quarrel,
The Miller poured the hopper full
Of corn from the bag,
And in the corn lay one violet,
(Maybe the farmer's little girl dropped it in, when
the boy went to the bin to fill the bag).
And *burr* quoth the upper Mill-stone,
And *burr you back again* the nether,
And the violet was ground with the corn,
But passed not into the bag with the meal,
Thank God!
The odor of crushed violet flew forth
And passed about the ages;
And men here and there had a sense
Of somewhat rich and high-intense,
Dewy, fiery, dear, forlorn,
Delicate, grave, new out of the morn,
But saturate yet
With the night despair that every flower will wet.*

* [Cf. Lanier's essay, "Retrospects and Prospects," V, 295: " the intense heart of Chopin, which in breaking exhaled music as a crushed flower exhales perfume."—Ed.]

96
Ornament Before Dress
Who doubts but Eve had a rose in her hair
Ere fig leaves fettered her limbs?
So Life wore poetry's perfect rose
Before 'twas clothed with economic prose.
Homer before Pherecydes,
Caedmon before Alfred.

97
Dove-flights of Sonnets out of Italy.

98
The fifteenth century is the Great Desert of English Literature, with Lydgate, Occleve, Hawes, and Skelton, for mirages,
and Dunbar and Gawain Douglass for oases.

99
This multitudinous flight of words which flutter down upon
our age out of that of Elizabeth, and like a beautiful army of
bees and butterflies fertilizes the flower of our Time with pollen
of the ideas of that.

100
O World, I wish there was room for a poet. In the time of
David and Isaiah, in the time of John and of Homer, there was
room for a poet. In the time of Hyvernion and of Herve and
of Omar Khayyam: in the time of Shakspere, there was room
in the world for a poet.
In the time of Keats there was not room:
Perhaps now there is not room.*

101
The United States in two hundred years has made Emerson
out of a witch-burner.

* [Dated " 1881 " in *Poem Outlines.*—ED.]

102

On certain Poets. (By a Japanese?)

Swinburne

He invited me to eat, the service was silver and gold, but no food therein save pepper and salt.

Emerson

He asked me to stroll with him to Nowhere: and said many wise and beautiful things on the way.

William Morris

He caught a crystal cup-full of the yellow light of sunset, and, persuading himself to dream it wine, drank it with a sort of smile.*

103

Swinburne

It is always the Fourth of July with Mr. Swinburne. It is impossible, in reading this strained laborious matter, not to remember that this case of poetry is precisely that where he who conquers conquers without strain. There was a certain damsel who once came to King Arthur's Court, " Girt " (as sweet Sir Thomas Malory, hath it) " with a sword, for to find a man of such virtue to draw it out of the scabbard."—King Arthur, to set example to his Knights, first assayed, and pulled at it eagerly, but the sword would not out. " ' Sir,' said the damsel, ' ye need not to pull half so hard, for he that shall pull it out, shall do it with little might.' "

104

Whitman is poetry's butcher. Huge raw collops slashed from the rump of poetry, and never mind gristle, is what Whitman feeds our souls with.**

---

* [The items on Swinburne and Morris were published in *Poems* (1884), p. xxxviii.—ED.]

** [This and No. 105 were published in *Poems* (1884), p. xxxviii. See also the critique of Poe, pp. xxxv-xxxvi; and of Shelley, IV, 90, of the present edition.—ED.]

105

As near as I can make it out, Whitman's argument seems to be that because a prairie is wide, therefore debauchery is admirable, and because the Mississippi River is long, therefore every American is God.

106

One of your cold jelly-fish poets that find themselves cast up by some wave upon a sandy subject and so wrinkle themselves about a pebble of a theme and let us see it through their substance—as if that were a great feat.

107

I have great trouble in behavior. I know what to do, I know what I at heart desire to do; but the *doing* of it, that is work, that labor is. I construct in my lonesome meditations the fairest scheme of my relations to my fellow-men, and to fellow-events; but when I go to set the words of solitary thought to the music of much-crowded action, I find ten thousand difficulties never suspected: difficulties of race, temperament, mood, tradition, custom, passion, unreason and other difficulties which I do not understand, as, for instance the failure of contemporary men to recognize genius and great art.

108

Do you think the 19th century is past? It is but two years since Boston burnt me for witchcraft. I wrote a poem which was not orthodox: that is, not like Mr. Longfellow's.

CREDO, AND OTHER POEMS *

109

Credo, thou'rt a domestic dog,
Stay at home and tend the women and children.
Here, Fido! dog: we'll fare into the fields.

110

I had a dog.
And his name was not *Fido*, but *Credo*.
(In America they shorten his name to " *Creed.*")
    My child fell into the water:
Then in plunged Credo, and brought me out my child,
        My beloved One,
    Brought him out, truly,
But lo, in my Child's throat and in his limbs,
In the throat and the limbs of the child of man,
    Credo's teeth had bitten deep.
(A good dog but a stern one was *Credo*)
    And my child, though sound,
    Was scarred in his beautiful face
    And was maimed in his manful limbs
        For life, alas, for life.
Thus *Credo* saved and scarred and maimed
    The Son of Man, my Child.

* [In Lanier's copy of Skeat's edition of Langland, *The Vision of William Concerning Piers the Plowman* (a volume purchased in Boston, June 3, 1879, see p. 81), p. 73, the phrase "and marchandise, leue it" is underscored, and at the top of the page is written: "Motto for Credo & other Poems: And merchandise, leave it!" Thus at about this date "Songs of Aldhelm" was merged in the newly conceived "Credo and Other Poems." (Nos. 83, 87, 95, 103, 105 in the preceding section are actually so titled on the MSS.) To preserve the original distinction between the two projected volumes, "Credo" is here restricted to those outlines in Lanier's late handwriting concerned with his beliefs about religion, science, and society. His letter of Feb. 12, 1881, refers to "My Credo and Other Poems, a thick volume, all in memoranda." Nos. 119, 120, 126, 128, 129, 133, 141, 145, 148, 153, 183, 190 are so titled on the MSS. No. 109 is written on a front flyleaf of Lanier's copy of *The Discourses of Epictetus*, purchased by him in 1879 according to a statement from Turnbull Bros., Charles D. Lanier Collection.—ED.]

111

Our beliefs needed pruning, that they might bring forth more
fruit: and so Science came.

112

    O Science, wilt thou take my Christ,
        Oh, wilt thou crucify him o'er
    Betwixt false thieves with thieves' own pain,
        Never to rise again?

    Leave me this love, O cool-eyed One,
    Leave me this Saviour.

    (Science) Down at the base of a statue,
        A flower of strange hue,
    I dug, that I might see and know the root thereof,
        And lo, the statue is prone, fallen.
    They did but crucify the godhood of Christ,
    (*My God, my God,* He said, *why hast thou forsaken me?*)

The manhood rose and lives forever, the Leader, the Friend,
the Beloved of all men and women, the Strongest, the Wisest,
the Dearest, the Sweetest.*

113

It is now time that one should arise in the world and cry out
that Art is made for man and not man for art, that government
is made for man and not man for government, that religion is
made for man and not man for religion, that trade is made for
man and not man for trade.

This is essentially the utterance of Christ in declaring that the
Sabbath was made for man and not man for the Sabbath.
Whether or not one believes in Christ [*canceled*] Whether one
is an optimist or unorthodox religionist or what not, it would
seem that faith must center upon Christ. For if Christ was God
and redeemed us, He must be the Christian's hope: but if he
was only man, x x x x **

---

* Nos. 112 and 116 are written on the same MS with a draft of " To ――,
with a Rose," dated June 5, 1876.—ED.]

** [In *Poem Outlines*, pp. 103, 106, this is printed as two separate items
(with the concluding fragmentary sentence omitted) ; but the MS, though torn
in two at " Whether," shows clearly that the second part is a continuation of the
first.—ED.]

114

In attempting to solve the problem whether one is entitled to declare one's heterodoxy, the parlous question comes up, *can you* declare yourself, is it possible, is not the mind of society in such a state that it cannot hear the words (just them and nothing else) wh. you speak, if for example you declare you believe in one God—and that Christ is not God but the sweetest man who ever lived, there are many honest people who in hearing you say this will actually *not* hear you say it but hear you say that you are an infidel and a man dangerous to trust a daughter with, and altogether a perilous person.

115

This youth, O Science, he knoweth more than thee
He knoweth that life is sweet.
But thou, thou knowest not ever a Sweet:
Tear me, I pray thee, this Flower of Sweetness-of-Life petal from petal, number me the pistils, and above all, above all, dear Science, find me the ovary thereof, and the seeds in the ovary, and save me these.
Thou canst not.

116

Come with me, Science; let us go into the Church here (say in Georgia); let alone the youth here they have roses in their cheeks, they know that life is delicious, what need have they of thee? But fix thy keen eye on these grave-faced and mostly sallow married women who make at least half this congregation—these women who are the people that carry around the subscription cards, and feed the preacher and keep him in heart always. See, there is Mrs. S., her husband and son were killed in the war; Mrs. B.—her husband has been a thriftless fellow, and she has finally found out the damnable fact that she is both stronger and purer than he is, which she is however yet sweetly endeavoring to hide from herself and all people; Mrs. C. D. and the rest of the alphabet in the same condition:—Science, I grasp thee by the throat and ask thee with vehement passion, wilt thou take away the Christ (who is to each Deficiency in this house the Completion and Hoped Perfectness) from these women?

117

The church having become fashionable is now grown crowded, and the Age will have to get up from its pew and go outside soon, if only for a little fresh air.

118

I went into the Church to find my Lord.
They said He is here, He lives here.
But I could not see Him,
For the creed-tablets and bonnet-flowers.

I went into the Church to look for a poor man.

For the Lord has said that the Poor are his children, and I thought His children would live in His house.

But in the pews sat only Kings and Lords: at least all that sat there were dressed like Kings and Lords; and I could not find the man I looked for, who was in rags;—presently I saw the sexton refuse admission to a man; lo, it was my poor man, he had on rags, and the sexton said, "No ragged allowed." *

119

Thou that in thy beautiful Church this morning art reading thy beautiful service with a breaking heart,—for that thou knowest thou art reading folly to fools, and for that thou lovest these same folk and canst not abide to think of losing thy friends and knowest not how to tell them the truth and findest them with no appetite to it nor strength for it—thou fine young clergyman, on this spring morning, there, in the pulpit, front of the dainty ladies with their breathing clouds of dresses and the fans gently waving in the still air—and thou, there, betwixt the pauses while the choir and the heavenly organ tear thy soul with music, peering down with thine eyes a-dream upon the men in the pews, the importers, the jobbers, the stockbrokers, the great drygoods house, some at a nod, some calculating with pencils on the fly-leaf of the Prayer-book, some wondering how it will be with 4's and sixes to-morrow, some vacant, three with Christ thoughts, one out of two hundred earnest—thou that

* [A shorter version of the same is written on the back of some class notes marked "Hopkins, 1880-81."—Ed.]

turnest despairing away from the men back to the women whereof several regard thee with soft and rich eyes, with yearning after the unknown whatever-there-may-be-of-better-than-this, I have a word for thee.

Thou seest and wilt not cover thine eyes; thou dost stand at the casement on a dewy morning, and sentimentalize over the birds that flit by: for thou knowest a worm died in pain at each bird song, and death sitteth in the dew; thou lookest through the rich lawn dresses of the witch women, thou lookest through the ledger-reveries of the merchant, thou seest quasi-religion which is hell-in-trifles before thee, thou seest superstition black about thee,—I have a word for thee.

Come out and declare.

120

So far from founding a church, Christ's whole labor seems to me to have been to render all future *organizations of church-followers* unnecessary. He made an altar in each man's heart, he gave means for instant approach to God by prayer at any time and in any place, he showed that every man's bosom was a possible church where every function, the mass, confession, absolution, worship, prayer, and all, could be carried on without those terrible outgrowths and ingrowths of corruption which we see successively attaching to and destroying organizations which depend upon human administration. He knew all these hot-house evils: look into the purest church in Xtendom and tell me if you do not know them. Accordingly, he proposed no creed and no form of worship; he appointed no Sabbath, and left but a single institution, which was purely memorial of his personal (not churchly) relation.*

121

The Church is too hot, and Nothing is too cold. I find my proper Temperature in Art. Art offers to me a method of adoring the sweet master Jesus Christ, the beautiful souled One, without the straitness of a Creed which confines my genuflexions, a Church which confines my limbs, and without the vacuity of the doubt which numbs them. An unspeakable gain has come to me in simply turning a certain phrase the other way: the

* [Nos. 120, 128, and 153 are written in the indelible pencil which, according to Mary Day Lanier, was used during the last illness, summer of 1881.—Ed.]

beauty of holiness becomes a new and wonderful saying to me when I figure it to myself in reverse as the holiness of beauty. This is like opening a window of dark stained glass, and letting in a flood of white light. I thus keep upon the walls of my soul a church-wall rubric which has been somewhat clouded by the expiring breaths of creeds dying their natural death. For in art there is no doubt. My heart beat all last night without my supervision: for I was asleep; my heart did not doubt a throb; I left it beating when I slept, I found it beating when I woke; it is thus with art: it beats in my sleep. A holy tune was in my soul when I fell asleep: it was going when I awoke. This melody is always moving along in the background of my spirit. If I wish to compose, I abstract my attention from the thoughts which occupy the front of the stage, the *dramatis personæ* of the moment, and fix myself upon the deeper scene in the rear.

122

The sleep of each night is a confession of God. By whose will is it that my heart beat, my lung rose and fell, my blood went with freight and returned empty, these eight hours?

Not mine, not mine.

123

It may be that the world can get along without God: but *I* can not. The universe-finity is to me like the chord of the dominant seventh, always leading towards, always inviting onwards, a Chord of Progress; God is the tonic Triad, a chord of Repose.

124

We know more than we know.
That the Lord is all I know:
That I am part I know.
But how shall we settle our provinces and diplomacies
    and boundaries, the Lord and I?
Let us talk of this matter, dear Lord, I talking in silence.

125

I fled in tears from the men's ungodly quarrel about God:
I fled in tears to the woods, and laid me down on the earth;
then somewhat like the beating of many hearts came up to me
out of the ground, and I looked and my cheek lay close by a
violet; then my heart took courage and I said:

" I know that thou art the word of my God, dear Violet:
And Oh the ladder is not long that to my heaven leads.
Measure what space a violet stands above the ground,
'Tis no farther climbing that my soul and angels have to do
    than that." *

126

You wish me to argue whether Paul had a revelation: I do
not care greatly; I have had none, but roses, trees, music, and a
running stream, and Sirius.

127

In the lily, the sunset, the mountains, the rosy hues of all life,
it is easy to trace God. But it is in the dust that goes up from
the unending Battle of Things that we lose Him. Forever
through the ferocities of storms, the malice of the never-glutted
oceans, the savagery of human wars, the inexorable barbarities
of Accident, of Earthquake and of mysterious Disease, one
hears the voice of man crying, *where art thou, my dear Lord
and Master?*

128

To believe in God would be much less hard if it were not
for the wind. Pray hold one little minute, I cry: O spare this
once to bite yonder poor old shivering soul in the bare house,
let the rags have but a little chance to warm yon woman round
the city corner, stop, stop, wind: but I might as well talk to the
wind, and lo the proverb paralyzes prayer, and I am ready to
say: Good God, is it possible thou canst stop this wind which
at this moment is mocking ten thousand babies and thin-clad
mothers with the unimaginable anguish of cold—is it possible
thou canst stop this, and wilt not? Do you know what cold is?
Story of the Prisoner, &c., &c., and the stone.

* [First published in *Poems* (1884), p. xxxix. A note in *Poem Outlines*,
p. 13, reads: " Written on the flyleaf of Emerson's *Representative Men*, between
1874 and 1879." The volume has not come down.—ED.]

129

Sometimes Providence seems to have a bee in his bonnet. Else why should hell, the greatest risk, be the most unprovable fact, and himself, the only light, be the most completely undiscoverable? If the angels are good company, why shut us out from them? I look for good boys for my children. Hide not your light under a bushel, is His own command: and yet He is completely obscured under the inexorable *quid pro quo* of Nature and the hateful measure of Evil.

130

So pray we to the God we dimly hope,
Against calamities we clearly know.

131

Pray against ills that I do know I know
Unto a God whom I but dream I dream.

132

But the corruption, the rascality, the &c., &c.,
I am not afraid.
But the stock broker, the whiskey ring,
I am not afraid.
Nay, but the war in the East,
I am not afraid.
I see God about his godly affairs,
The cat-bird sits in the tree and sings
While the boy kills the &c. beneath.

The mocking-bird hanging over the street sings, though robbery, murder, fire, &c., go on.

133

On the 1st & 4th Verses of Matthew VI.*

Didst thou say this, my Dear,
" *Otherwise, . . . no reward* "?

* [" Take heed that ye do not your alms before men, to be seen of them: otherwise ye have no reward of your Father which is in heaven. . . .
" That thine alms may be in secret: and thy Father which seeth in secret himself shall reward thee openly."—ED.]

That is, give alms in secret here,
To sell sure Futures to the Lord?
Why this is Stocks and the Bowery,
   This is bargain, high and low,
   And now my soul saith fie, and fie
     Old Clo, Old Clo,
Thou never saidst it; No, no, no!
   I will clear my Lord of slander,
   I will clear my Lord of Shame,
   O, Trade, old cunning pander
Twixt High and Low, would'st forge His name?

134

I did not think so poorly of thee, dear Lord,
As that thou wouldst wait until thou wert asked
   (As many think),
And that thou wouldst be ugly, like a society person,
Because thou wert not invited.*

135

O Lord if thou wert needy as I
If thou shouldst come to my door, as I to thine,
If thou wert an hungered as much as I
   For that which belongs to the Spirit,
   For that which is fine and good,
   Ah, Friend, for that which is fine and good,—
I would give it to thee,—if I had power.
For that which I want is first, Bread,
—Thy decree, not my choice, that Bread must be first,
Then, Music, then sometime out of the struggle for bread
   to write my poems,
Then to put out of care Henry and Robert whom I love,
O, my God, how little would put them out of care! **

* [Dated in *Poem Outlines*, p. 15, " 1881."—Ed.]
** [Published with slight differences in *Southern Bivouac*, V, 664 (Apr., 1887); reprinted in W. M. Baskervill, *Southern Writers* (Nashville, Tenn., 1896), p. 190.—Ed.]

136

How could I injure thee,
Thou art All and I am nought,
What harm, what harm could e'er be wrought
On thee by me?

137

Didst thou make me?
Some say yea.
Did I make thee?
Some say yea.
Oh, am I then thy son, O God,
Or art thou mine?
Thou art more beautiful than me,
And I will worship thee.
Lo, out of me is gone more great than me:
As Him that Mother Mary bore,
Greater far than Mary was;
As one mere woman brought the Lord,
Was mother of the Lord,
Might not my love and longing be
Father of thee?

138

Art thou creature of my brain,
Or I product of thy pain,
Am I thy son or art thou mine?
What matter? One of us must be divine!
If I'm thy father,—then my son's a God,
If thou art mine, thy son is.

139

It was not that God should descend to be man,
But that man should ascend to be God:
Not so much need we the manhood of God
As we need the Godhood of man:

140

Ah how I desire this matter!
I am sure God would give it to me if He could.
I am sure that I would give it to Him if I could.
(But perhaps He knows it is not good for you.)
I know that He could make it good for me.

141

Of one thing I am sure, that about this Matter it was not
intended we should be sure, else Christ would rise with the sun
every day, and with the stars every night, and shine into the
soul as these luminaries do, whereof no man doubts. If he
desired men to be sure, nothing would be easier.

—And doth He not rise with the sun, Yea, dear, art thou
not it? In the sun thou art sitting, and it does not hurt my
eyes to look on thee, bright, sweet, soft, One.

142

There was a flower called Faith:
Man plucked it, and kept it in a vase of water.
This was long ago, mark you.
And the flower is now faint,
For the water with time and dust is foul.
Come let us pour out the old water,
And put in new,
That the flower of faith be red again.

143

For Pray'r the Ocean is, where diversely
Men steer their course, each to a sev'ral coast;
Where all our interests so discordant be
Half begging God for winds that
Would send the other half to hell.

144

Tolerance like a Harbor lay
Smooth and shining and secure,
Where ships carrying every flag of faith were
anchored in peace.

145

How dusty it is!
In trades and creeds and politics, much wind is
 about and the earth is dry;
I must lay this dust, that men may see and breathe;
There is need of rain, and I am it.

146

To the Politicians

You are servants. Your thoughts are the thoughts of cooks
curious to skim perquisites from every pan, your quarrels are the
quarrels of scullions who fight for the privilege of cleaning the
pot with most leavings in it, your committees sit upon the land-
ings of back-stairs, and your quarrels are the quarrels of
kitchens.*

147

There will one day be medicine to cure crime.

148

The Dyspeptic

Frown, quoth my lord Stomach:
And I lowered.
Quarrel, quoth my lord Liver,
And I lashed my wife and children,
Till at the breakfast-table
Hell sat laughing on the egg-cup.
Lie awake all night, quoth my two Masters,
And I tossed, and swore, and beat the pillow,
And kicked with disgust,
And slammed every door tight that sleeps [leads?]
 to sleep and heaven.

149

A man does not reach any stature of manhood until like
Moses he kills an Egyptian (*i. e.,* murders some oppressive
prejudice of the all-crushing Tyrant Society or Custom or

---

* [Dated in *Poem Outlines,* p. 22, " 1878-9."—ED.]

Orthodoxy) and flies into the desert of his own soul, where among the rocks and sands, over which at any rate the run rises clear each day, he slowly and with great agony settles his relation with men and manners and powers outside, and begins to look with his own eyes, and first knows the unspeakable joy of the outcast's kiss upon the hand of sweet, naked Truth.

But let not the young man go to killing his Egyptian too soon: wait till you know all the Egyptians can teach you: wait till you are master of the technics of the time; then grave, and resolute, and aware of consequences, shape your course.

150

Lookest thou and longest thou for Moses to lead thee out of the captivity of that Pharaoh Sorrow? Lo, he is there within thee. I declare that in these days every man must be his own Moses. Kill thine Egyptian, flee into the wilderness of thine own heart, think upon all things, make thy mind whole and clear about the world, settle thyself as king of thyself and leader of thyself, then go back among men. Lo, he that hath helped me to do right (save by mere information upon which I act or not, as I please) he hath not done me a favor, he hath covertly hurt me: he hath insidiously deflowered the virginity of my will; I am thenceforth not a pure Me: I am partly another.

Each union of self and self is, once for all, incest and adultery and every other crime. Let me alone. God made me so, a man, individual, unit, whole, fully-appointed in myself. Again I cry to thee, O friend, let me alone.*

151

—Great shame came upon me.
I wended my way to my own house
And I was sorrowful all that night,
For the touch of man had bruised my manhood,
And in playing to be wise and a judge before men,
I found me foolish and a criminal before myself.**

* [In *Poem Outlines*, p. 41, the first four sentences were omitted. A MS copy by Mary Day Lanier has the note: " Probably in Brunswick, Apr., 1877." —ED.]

** [The MS copy in the handwriting of Mary Day Lanier has a note saying that the original was penciled on the back of a verse from " Under the Cedar-croft Chestnut," a poem written in the winter of 1877.—ED.]

152

Foul, Past, as my Master I scorn thee,
As my servant I love thee, dear Past.

153

It appears that if I were perfect, I could not be perfect.
For with whoever is perfect, there is nothing more to be done.
But if there were nothing more to do, I would be very sorry:
that is, I would not be perfect.
Therefore it appears that I would not be perfect if I were
perfect.

154

The courses of the wind, and the shifts thereof, as also what way the clouds go; and that which is happening a long way off; and the full face of the sun; and the bow of the Milky Way from end to end; as also the small, the life of the fiddler-crab, and the household of the marsh-hen; yea, and more, the translation of black ooze into green blade of marsh-grass, which is as if filth bred heaven:
This a man seeth upon the marsh.

155

As many blades of grass as be
In all thy horizontal round
So many dreams brood over thee.

156

The running [?] creek
Vein of silver, to feed the gloss of the marsh grass.

157

Silver—too black, and sea-foam gross [?]
Keep pearl for shade: **

---

* [During the last year of Lanier's life he planned a volume of poems to be called " Hymns of the Marshes " (see especially letters of Dec. 6, 1880, and Feb. 12, 1881). In addition to " The Marshes of Glynn," " The Cloud," " Sunrise," and the five songs on pp. 142-144, he probably intended to complete some of the outlines in the following group for this volume (No. 154 is so titled on the MS). And during the final summer at Lynn, N. C., he planned another volume to be called " Hymns of the Mountains " (Nos. 177, 179, 181 are so titled), to which are added the half-dozen poems concerning death written at about the same time. On the flyleaf of his copy of *Epictetus* (bought in 1879, Turnbull Bros. list, *CL*) Lanier wrote: " Hymns of the Marshes / Hymns of the Fields / Hymns of the Mountains." (The fact that two of those marked " Hymns of the Mountains " bear the alternate title " Credo " indicates that the delimitations of these various projected volumes were not clearly marked in Lanier's mind.)—ED.]

** [Written on a flyleaf of Lanier's copy of *Piers the Plowman*, ed. Skeat.—ED.]

158

Water at Dawn

Gray iris of the eyeball earth,
　　Limpid Intelligence.

159

Cousin cloud
the wind of music
blow me into wreath
and curve of grace
as it bloweth thee.*

160

The feverish heaven, with a stitch in the side,
　　Of lightning.

161

The fingers of the livid clouds
　　The scornings of the victim clouds,
Pointing at the flying Sun.

162

The horizontal bands of clouds broken about the Sun,
Like as the red ragged ends of Space,
To be fused and welded.

163

The awful ruby of the Sun
Set in the ring of the horizon.

164

　　But oh, how can ye trifle away your time at trades, and waste
yourself in men's commerce, when ye might be here in the
woods at commerce with great angels, all heaven at purchase
for a song.

* [The line arrangement follows that in *Poem Outlines*, p. 9, and a MS copy
by Mary Day Lanier (which states that the original was given to John B. Tabb
in 1895).—ED.]

165

Mediate betwixt me and men
O ye trees, O ye media.
(Thomas a K[empis].)

When I go among men I become less a man
When I go among trees I become more a man.

166

To a Certain Three Oaks in Druid Hill Park

Let me lean against you, my Loves,
Give me a place, my darlings,
I am so happy, so fain, so full, in your large company.

I knew a saint that said he never went among men without
returning home less a man than he was before he went forth.
But it is not so with you: I am always more a man when I
converse with you. Who is so manly and so manifold sweet as
a tree? There is none that can talk like a tree: for a tree says
always to me exactly that which I wish him to say. A man is
apt to say what I did not desire to hear, or what I had no need
to know at that time. A tree knows always my necessity.

167

Like the forest whose edges near man's dwellings are
embroidered with birds, while its inner recesses are the unbroken
solid color of solitude.

168

In a silence embroidered with whispers of lovers,
As the darkness is purfled with fire-flies.

169

To-day the Stars tease me, as it were gadflies:
And I cannot bear the impudent reds and yellows of the flowers.

170

The black-birds giving a shimmer of sound,
As midday hills give forth $\begin{Bmatrix} \text{transparent} \\ \text{luminous} \end{Bmatrix}$ tremors of heat and haze.

171

Wren terrors and tomtit tragedies.

172

" The Earth? " quoth a Dandelion to my Oak, " what earth?
where is any? I float, and find none! "
At that moment the wind blew.
" Nevertheless, it is here," quoth my oak, with pleasure in
all his roots, what time the dandelion was blown out of hearing.

173

While I lie here under the tree,
Comes a strange insect and poises an instant at my cheek,
And lays his antennae there upon my skin,
Then perceiving that I have nothing of nutriment for him,
He leaves me with a quiet indifference which, do all I can,
Crushes me more than the whole world's sarcasm,
And now he is gone to the Jamestown weed, there,
And is rioting in sweetness.*

174

A Garden Party

Invitation brought by the wind, and sent by the rose and the
oak. I sat on the steps—warm summer noon—in a garden, and
half cloudy with low clouds, sun hot, rich mocking bird singing,
bee brushing down a big rain-drop from a flower, where it hung
tremulous. The bird's music is echoed from the breasts of roses,
and reflex sound comes doubly back with grace of odor.—First
came the lizard, dandiest of reptiles; then the bee, then small
strange insects that wear flap-wings and spider-web legs, and
crawl up the slim green stalks of grass; the catbirds, the flowers,
with each a soul—this is the company I like; the talk, the gossip
anent the last news of the spirit, the marriage of man and
nature, the betrothal of Science and Art, the failure of the great
house of Buy and Sell (see following note [1]), a rumor out of
the sun, and many messages concerning the stars.

* [Written verso a letter from Paul Hayne, July 5, 1877.—ED.]
[1] Buy and Sell failed because Love was a partner. " This Love, now, who is

175

Then three tall lilies floated white along.
Said these words: we come from Nature,
Ambassadors, for thou gavest us consideration,
For thou said'st, Consider the lilies,
And who considers them will soon consider
And how that they did exceed the glory of Solomon

176

O Earth, O mother, thou my Beautiful,
Why frowns this shallow feud 'twixt me and thee?
Were I a bad son, deaf, undutiful,
Nor loved thy mother-talk, thy gramarye
Of groves, thy hale discourse of fact in terms
That mince not, yea, thy sharp cold winter saws
Like as the love lore thine expressive germs
Of spring do plainly petal forth,—'twere cause
Conceivable of quarrel.

177

Are ye so sharp set for the centre of the earth, are ye so
hungry for the centre of things—
O rains and springs and rivers of the mountains?
Towards the centre of the earth, towards the very Middle of
things, ye will fall, ye will run, the Centre will draw ye, Gravity
will drive you and draw you in one:
But the Centre ye will not reach, ye will come as near as the
plains,—watering them in coming so near—and ye will come
as near as the bottom of the Ocean,—seeing and working many
marvels as ye come so near:
But the Centre of Things ye will not reach,
O my rivers and rains and springs of the mountains.
Provision is made that ye shall not: ye would be merged, ye
could not return.
Nor shall my Soul be merged in God, though tending, though
tending.

he?" said a comfortable burgher oak. " I hear much of him these later days."
Why, Love, he owneth all things: trees and land and water power. [Lanier's
note.—ED.]

178

I will sail about in thy favor
As an eagle riots in the space of heaven.
I will make me a nest on the peak of thy mountain;
Blue shall be above it, blue about it and below it.
I take hold upon thee by as many fingers of desire
As the roots whereby green grass layeth hold upon
    the whole earth.
I will be a leaf and thou the wind,
I will eat thee and drink thee
And make my substance out of thine.*

179

My birds, my pretty pious.buccaneers
That haunt the shores of daybreak and of dusk,
Truly my birds did find to-day
A-strand out yonder on the Balsam hills
A bright bulk, where the night wave left it,
High upon the Balsam peaks.
Then my birds, my sweet, my heavenly day prickers,
Did open up the day
Like as some castaway bale of flotsam sunlight-stuff
And jetsam of woven Easternry: one loud exclaimed
    Upon brocaded silver with more silver voice:
And one, when gold embroideries flamed in golden
    songs of better broidered tones,
Translated them. And one from out some rare tone-
    tissue in his soul
Shook fringes of sweet indecisive sound,
And purfled all that ravishment of light with ravish-
    ment of music that not left
Heat, or dry longing, or any indictment of God,
Or question.

* [Text from the Philadelphia *Sunday School Times*, XXXV, 50 (Jan. 28, 1893), where it was published under the title "The Lord's Romance of Time," probably supplied by the editor.—ED.]

180

When into reasonable discourse plain
Or russet terms of dealing and old use
I would recast the joy, the tender pain
Of the silver birch, the rhododendron, the brook,
Or, all blest particulars of beauty sum
In one most continent word that means something
To all men, to some men everything,
To one all, but one will cover with satisfaction,
That is love.
Yet I well know this tree is a selfish saver-up of drink
Might else have nourished these laurels:
Yea, and they did not hand round the cup
To the grass ere they drank,
Nor the grass inquire if room is here for her and the phlox.
Yet my spirit will have it that Love is the lost meaning of
this Hate, and Peace the end of this Battle. Why? This is
revelation. Here I find God: what power less than His could
fancy such wild inconsequence and unreason as flies out of this
anguish, and Love out of this Murder.

181

I awoke, and there my Gossip, Midnight, stood
Fast by my head, and there the Balsams sat
Round about, and we talked together.

And "Here is some news," quoth Midnight. "What is this
word 'news' whereof we hear?" begged the Balsams: "What
mean you by news? what thing is there which is not very old?
Two neighbors in a cabin talking yesterday I heard giving and
taking news; and one, for news, saith William is dead; and
'tother for news gave that a child is born at Anne's house. But
what manner of people be these that call birth and death new?
Birth and death were before aught else that we know was." *

* [The MS copy in the handwriting of Mary Day Lanier has the following
note: "One of the last three poems outlined in the violet indelible pencil.
'Lynn' is written at head of the sheet." In *Poem Outlines*, pp. 118-120, this
and the two preceding poems are dated "Lynn, N. C., August, 1881." The
MS of No. 179, written on both sides of the sheet, is almost illegible because
the indelible penciling shows through; the MSS for Nos. 180 and 181 have not
been found. Nos. 164 and 190 are also written in indelible pencil and probably
date from August, 1881.—ED.]

182

The cricket scraping, scraping, like the creaking of the wheels
of Time.

183

When I awake in the middle of the night,
    And lie and listen,
I hear something hidden in the mass of time
    Nicking, nicking,
As the cut-worm nicks in the log.*

184

I was the earliest bird awake,
It was a while before dawn, I believe,
But somehow I saw round the world,
And the eastern mountain top did not hinder me.
And I knew of the dawn by my heart, not by mine eyes.**

185

Death lieth still in the way of life
Like as a stone in the way of a brook;
I will sing against thee, Death, as the brook does,
I will make thee into music which does not die.***

186

As the woodpecker taps in a spiral quest
    From the root to the top of the tree,
        Then flies to another tree,
So have I bored into life to find what lay therein
    And now it is time to die
        And I will fly to another tree.

---

* [Written verso letter from Percy Mason, Dec. 20, 1878.—ED.]
** [Text from W. M. Baskervill, *Southern Writers* (Nashville, Tenn., 1896), p. 226, from a MS furnished by Mary Day Lanier and dated " Camp Robin, 1881 "; a different version was published in the Atlanta *Constitution*, Oct. 19, 1890, p. 11.—ED.]
*** [This and the three outlines following (and a shorter version of No. 45) were published in a group under the title " Songs Against Death " in *Century*, XXXII, 377 (July, 1886). A MS copy of all five in the handwriting of Mary Day Lanier (New York Public Library) is marked " 1881."—ED.]

187

Look out, Death: I am coming.
Art thou not glad? what talks we'll have.
What memories of old battles.
Come, bring the bowl, Death; I am thirsty.

188

He passed behind the disc of death,
But yet no occultation knew.
Nay, all more bright therethrough
As through a jet-black foil and frame
Out-shone his silver fame.

189

For I deemed it was safer not to depart from hence before
I had acquitted my conscience with the composition of some
poems in obedience to the dream.

TEXTUAL VARIANTS AND NOTES

ABBREVIATIONS AND SYMBOLS

HA	Huntington Library and Art Gallery, San Marino, Calif.
HC	Harvard College, Cambridge, Mass.
UC	University of California, Los Angeles
HF	Hankins Family Collection, Johns Hopkins University.
FH	Family of Mrs. C. N. Hawkins, Brooklyn, N. Y.
CL	Charles D. Lanier Collection, Johns Hopkins University.
HL	Henry W. Lanier Collection, Johns Hopkins University.
RL	Robert S. Lanier Collection, Johns Hopkins University.
SL	Mrs. Sidney Lanier, Jr., Collection, Johns Hopkins University.
EM	Edwin Mims Collection, Johns Hopkins University.
JM	John S. Mayfield, Washington, D. C.
WM	Washington Memorial Library, Macon, Ga.
ET	Miss Eleanor Turnbull, Baltimore, Md.
JT	Clifford Lanier Collection, owned by Mrs. John Tilley, Montgomery, Ala.
DU	Duke University, Durham, N. C.
JU	Johns Hopkins University, Baltimore, Md.

Clover	Printer's Copy of "Clover and Other Poems," 1879, 84 pp., Henry W. Lanier Collection.
Ledger, L	Lanier's literary journal, *c.* 1865-1875, 692 pp., Henry W. Lanier Collection.
Lipp	*Lippincott's Magazine.*
MDL	Mary Day Lanier, as editor of Lanier's poems.
RT	*Round Table*, literary weekly, N. Y.

1884	*Poems of Sidney Lanier*, ed. by his wife, New York: Charles Scribner's Sons.
1891	Same as above, with seven additional poems.
1916	Same, with two additional poems. (Reprints, 1885-1929, same except pagination.)
1877	*Poems by Sidney Lanier*, Philadelphia: J. B. Lippincott & Co.
1895	*Select Poems of Sidney Lanier,* ed. Morgan Callaway, New York: Charles Scribner's Sons.

final form	Text adopted in the present edition, presumably Lanier's latest revision.
canceled	Follows matter struck out by Lanier for which nothing was substituted.
†	After a line number, signifies that the matter following was rejected in the final form.
]	Separates the final form from an earlier variant.
>	Separates an original MS reading from the form to which it was altered (understood as the final form unless combined with above).

N. B. In a few cases an abbreviation that applies to only one poem is given in the textual note to that poem.

TEXTUAL VARIANTS

(No variants have been found for 63 of Lanier's poems, and the variants for 29 of his lesser poems seemed too insignificant to be recorded. For 30 more, in which the variants were few in number or could be adequately represented by samples, the treatment is confined to a line or so in the notes. For 42 of his more important poems, however, the variants were so numerous and so interesting as to call for full treatment. In the following pages all known variants for these poems are given in formal combined collations, except in a few cases where the stages of development could be shown more clearly by separate printings of the several versions in sequence. The aim has been to employ a consistent technique as follows: (1) when the whole line or more than half of it is variant, it is given entire; (2) when only a few words are variant, they are given first in the final form, then in the earlier form, separated by]; (3) when the variant version is a MS with alterations, the earlier reading is given first, then the corrected reading, separated by 〉. If the corrected reading does not agree with the final form, that is given first, as in (2): e. g., *whistle*] *chatter* 〉 *gossip* means that the final form was *whistle*, the MS originally read *chatter*, which was altered to *gossip*, and left in that state. Variants in mechanical matters, such as punctuation, capitalization, and spelling have not been noted except when especially significant. The particular treatment accorded each poem and full bibliographical data will be found in the notes. A key to the abbreviations and symbols used in the following collations is given on the opposite page.)

A SONG OF ETERNITY IN TIME (12)

Two MSS survive: *HA*, signed " Sidney Lanier," is undated but is the revised version used in *Independent* (Mar. 3, 1881), the text adopted; *Ledger* 251, entitled " Eternity in Time:/A Song not to be sung," signed " Sidney Lanier," and dated " Macon, Georgia / July 20th 1867," is an early version with variants as follows:

      1 the manor} a lonesome
      2 long silent} in silence
      3 Amazed that any] And wondered how the
      5 aimless] idle
      6 Reached forth and] With white hand
     10 that] the
     11 his] its
     12 Within] In; her lash] my Love's eyelash
     13 " Ah, Time," I said, " is a large Tear
     14 Some one hath] That hath been
     15 Yet in his] And in its
     16 That fair One-Star, Eternity, lies beaming

This is the text used in *XIX Century* (Feb., 1870), with the variants in ll. 10, 11, and 15 altered to the final form.

THE RAVEN DAYS (15)

Two MSS survive. *Ledger* 280-281, entitled " Raven's Food " and signed " L.,"
is an undated expansion of this poem with alterations, variants, and seven
rejected stanzas:

  5 dark] slow
  11 Dumb › Prone › Pale
  12† Ah › Old burly Battle here has clanged and blundered,
      An awkward knight, with bloody eyes and (› half) blind.
      The red mail on his heel our love has sundered (› o'er us has thundered),
      And › Now, here is naught but night and a dismal wind.
      Our Night was born (› child) of Hate, and Hate has ravished
      His daughter, and a young and stronger Hate
      Has risen in the land, and reigned, and lavished
      The horrid favors of his kingly state.
      For, once when faces of our dead came smiling,
      This king arose and stamped his foot and swore
      To love the dead was plainly Hate-beguiling,
      And ordered, we should love our dead no more.
      And once when Labor brought us (› his) consolation
      And we had grasped what balm-of-work he bore,
      This king cried out that Grief was our vocation
      And work killed grief and we should work no more.
      Ah, cold sick Time; when neither Love nor Labor
      Has leave to warm or light the dreary land:
      When Hate is duty: and each silent neighbor
      Sits leaning weary on his idle hand.
  13 dark] slow
  16† " Weak Friend, below, be Sorrow's foe no longer.
      Hast thou forgot the Prophet's lot of old?
      We Ravens fed him, and his soul grew stronger:
      Out of the lone (*canceled*) woods he passed, a Poet bold.
      From flinty grief Love strikes a spark of Heaven,
      And that, from here to death will light the way.
      Aye, Love grows strong on food by Ravens given,
      And Grief's desired Tomorrow is Love's Today! "

It was probably written subsequent to the shorter version (which Lanier himself
selected for publication), but rejected because of its bitterness. An early draft of
the shorter version survives, *Ledger* 278, signed " S. L." and dated " Prattville,
Ala. / Feb. 25th 1868," with the following variants: *Dumb* for *Pale* (l. 11),
sunlight › *warm light* (l. 14), and *athwart* for *across* (l. 16); this was the
text used in *1884*, with one misreading of the MS: *ghastly* for *ghostly* (l. 3).

THE SHIP OF EARTH (15)

Ledger 411, entitled " Fear at Morning " and signed " Sidney Lanier," is an
undated early draft with alterations and variants and two rejected introductory stanzas (collated after 1-); *Round Table* (Nov. 14, 1868) contains
the rejected stanzas with slight revisions, but otherwise agrees with the final form:

  1- Enough the earth has rested in the harbor of the night *L, RT*
    With south winds blowing farewell kisses to one lingering star *L, RT*;
      lingering › gazing *L*
    She floats on tides that bear her to yon black-shored sea of light *L*; She
    drifts on tides that bear her to yon black-shored light *RT*

Whose silver breakers flash and foam upon the eastern bar *L, RT*

To sway all day upon the playing buoyance of the sea *L*; To sway all day upon the buoyant playing of the sea *RT*

To lie at high noon, a becalmed, slow-undulating barque *L*; Or lie, when noon is high, a calmly undulating barque *RT*

To sail before the gale of eve that sends her fast and free *L*; Or sail before the gale of eve, that blows her fast and free *RT*

Past the bright sunset-harbor lights into the peaceful dark *L, RT*

2 Desires] Desire *L*
4 deck] red decks; wild mutineers are] mutineers grow *L*
5 may fall from off] is fallen from *L*
6 all the] the great *L*
8 lie there among] are lying with ⟩ now lie among *L*

LIFE AND SONG (16)

Ledger 305, entitled "Work and Song" and signed "S. L.," is an early draft; *Round Table* (Sept. 5, 1868) agrees with all the early prints. They have the following alterations and variants:

4 And utter its love in love's own deed *L, RT*
5 Then, oh my God, this Clarionet *L*
6 Would type what I would that I might be *L, RT*
7 singers] Artists *L*; poets *RT*
9 clearly] wholly *L, RT*
11 Or made what God made when He wrought *L, RT*
12 The perfect one] One perfect self *L, RT*
14 Might] Should *L*
19 living aloud] his living aloud ⟩ life out loud *L*; a living aloud *RT*
20 His work a] And life was a ⟩ His work *L*; His work was a *RT*

BETRAYAL (19)

Two untitled and undated MSS survive: *JT*, the earliest draft, and *Ledger* 320, a revision. They have the following alterations and variants:

2 burned] turned *JT, L*
3 wouldst] hadst *L*
4 A violet? Who knows! *JT*; A fair blue violet still? Who knows! *L*
5 The violet lingers in the wood *JT, L*
6 The violet wears a dead-leaf hood *JT, L*
7 And] The *JT, L*
8 But ah, short passion of the rose *JT, L*
9 It] That *JT, L*
10 white] the *JT, L* ⟩ white *L*
14 O Sea, would'st thou not rather be *JT, L*; would'st ⟩ had'st; rather ⟩ liever *L*
15 A violet hiding from the day *JT, L* ⟩ A mere blue violet still? Yea, yea *L*
17 lord of love and light] lavish of love-light *JT, L*
18 But after sunset comes the night *JT, L*; comes the ⟩ it comes *L*
19 Oh thou dim anguish of the dark *JT, L* ⟩ O anguish of the lonesome dark *L*
20 Once a girl's body] A maid's body so *JT, L* ⟩ And a girl's body all *L*
21 Was laid] Laid *JT, L* ⟩ Was laid *L*

Lippincott's (Dec., 1875) has the same variants as *L* in l. 2 and in l. 19 (after correction); otherwise it agrees with *1877*, the text adopted.

NIRVÂNA (19-21)

Four MSS survive: *HF* (undated but signed " Sidney Lanier ") and *Ledger* 412-414 (signed " Sidney Lanier " and dated " Macon, Ga. / December 1869 ") agree with the text adopted; so does *CL*ᵃ (unsigned and undated, but with legal notes verso), except that it contains the rejected stanza following l. 56 (see below). But *CL,* undated and unsigned, is a rough draft in pencil. The stanzas are arranged in an entirely different order, as follows: 1, 2, 3, 11, 12, 8, 9, 10, 15, rejected stanza, 16, 17, 13, 18, 14, 4, 5, 6, 7. Rearranged as in the final form it shows the following alterations, variants, and rejected lines:

6 Arose with 〉 Up-blown by 〉 *final form*
7 Upbore me out of] And bore 〉 Did bear me up from
9 down 〉 on
13 rugged 〉 stony
14 And did immure me in his 〉 *final form*
17 dim 〉 strange
21 as a blade 〉 like a spear
22 Age it did whet my sword 〉 *final form*
27 I rose above and scorned their fierce debates 〉 I stood and scorned their foolish fierce debates
28 Looking to 〉 Calmy for thee, Nirvana
31 big] high
33 Then] And
38 Shame 〉 Blasphemy
39 stood in 〉 kept my
41 the] a
53 all 〉 Kings
55 eye 〉 lures
56† Lust, Trade, and Death, three thieves, I saw on Earth.
    Sly Lust by night stole Strength, and Death stole Birth,
    And Trade by day stole bargains at half-worth,
    —But not from me, Nirvana.
59 soars] soar'd
60 days and nights] Nights and Days
65 and 〉 ye
66 humble heavens] Heavens humble
67 all, I rise] 'bove ye all

THAR'S MORE IN THE MAN THAN THAR IS IN THE LAND (22-23)

MS *CL,* undated and unsigned, is an early draft in pencil with a few differences in spelling and the following alterations and variants:

2 In the poor hilly County of Jones
8 old red] red
9 yallerish] yaller red
14 to] down to
15 *canceled and then restored*
17 to quit] quit; cock-burrs] cockleburs *originally written as l. 9*
18 the] sich
20 Pertestin'] Declaring
25 he] they; house] place 〉 house
27 he] they; his] ther
29 That neither o' them could have the face 〉 *final form*

30 To ax more'n two dollars an acre for land
33 things > corn
37 moved out on] he moved out to
38 sleeves > breeches; greased > bared
39 rocks] stones
40† And he harrer'd it crossways and roun and roun'
50 For he was afoot > *final form*
51 To see if > *final form*
52 hum-] grum-
55 his] his > some
56 And when he had eat till he couldnt no more > *final form*
57 Brown looked him right squar in the eye, while poor > Brown told him >
   final form
58 Jones was > That whether > That it matters not whether the sile was poor

It is quite possible that l. 40† was omitted from the *Telegraph and Messenger* print (the text adopted) by mistake, for stanza 7 is one line shorter than the others. (MS *JT* is a copy in Clifford Lanier's handwriting. For a version without dialect, reproduced with contemporary illustrations, see p. 337, below.)

JUNE DREAMS, IN JANUARY (29-31)

Ledger 307-315, entitled "The Poet and the Ages," undated but probably written in the summer of 1868 (as indicated by its position in the *Ledger*), is the first form of this poem. Pp. 311-313 are a draft in ink of ll. 13-59, with alterations and variants; they also contain 8 introductory lines (listed below after 1-) and 24 other lines that were rejected in the final form (collated as *a*). Pp. 307-310 and 314-315 contain pencil drafts of various parts of ll. 1-47 and some of the rejected lines, with further alterations and variants; for the most part they seem to be a revision of the ink draft, but since it is impossible to tell in just what order they were written and since they overlap very little with each other, they are collected here as if they constituted a single draft (collated as *b*):

1- The nude bold noons lie on the grass and pant *a, b*
   With arid palpitations of hot hearts *a, b*
   Until the careless red Suns fall aslant *a, b*
   Into the wondrous bliss the West imparts *b*; Into that flaming (> awful)
      bliss the West imparts *a*
   Night, with one finger on the birds' shut beaks *a, b*
   And one uplifted to the just-lit Mars *a, b*
   With (> In) whispered tone some magic spell-word (> her dainty
      " presto!") speaks *b*; In whispered tone her dainty (> Calm with great
      magic her wild) "Presto!" speaks *a*
   Replacing songs of birds with lights of stars *a, b*; Replacing > Transform-
      ing *a*
4 With beams too bright, too pure, too > With ardors of the sun that > With
      ardors and soft loves > *final form b*
5 Breathe off the intense hours, let them exhale *b*
6 As] Like *b*
9 June-day hath] June-lights have *b*
10 Dark Pain of Passion's utter (> too bright) sweetness born *b*
11 Thou broken love-sigh (> dim love-longing) of the jealous East *b*
13 O thrilling leaves beneath the silver sky *a*; Broad leaves aflame (> afire)

beneath her thrilling eye > O leaves beneath the thrilling silver sky >
Ye leaves broad-palmed towards (> up towards) the silver sky *b*

14 O sweet mad lovers of the virgin light *a*; Catching the holy rain of dropt
star-light *b*

15 O faint pale petals, sweethearts fain to die *a*; O faint pale sweethearts >
O pallid petals, fain, so fain to die > *final form b*

16 by] with > by; keen] sweet > much *a, b* > *final form b*

17 O short-breath'd winds under the gracious moon *a*; O little (> short-
breathed) winds, beneath the mournful (> dove-like > gracious) moon >
final form b

19 Or carrying] O maiden > Or wafting *a, b* > *final form b*

20 Wafted > What way the langorous odor-current sets *a, b* > *final form b*

21 O stars, ringed flowerlike in whorls and bells *a*; O Stars arranged in
heaven like flowers in dells > O stars, ringed bright (> glittering) in
whorls and bells *b*

22 Bent over other stars (> down along the sky) in curving sprays *a*; Bent
over other stars in drooping sprays > *final form b*

23 Looped star-vines with star-blooms in panicles *a*; Or whorled, or loose
in gemmy panicles > Or vine-wound with bright blooms in panicles *b*

24 Or tracing fiery campanulas *a*; Or hung in tremulous campanulas > *final
form b*

29 Or clustering thinly round the larger stars *a* > Or clustering timid round
large mother-stars *a, b*

30 Or peeping shyly through cloud-lattices *a, b* > *final form a*

31 Or pale and bruised in the red light of Mars *a, b* > *final form a*

33 O long night-sounds that hide among the leaves *a, b*; long > strange >
final form b

34 And steady whispered chat of gloss and green *a, b* > And whispers of the
gloss unto the green *a* > *final form b*

35 in > of; the > old *a, b*

36† O all sweet sounds and lights and odors of the summer night *b*; Ye
sounds and sights and odors of the (> mild *a*) night *a, b*
That fill my heart and flow into my brain *a, b*
Dew-freshening the faded sense of Right *a, b*
And drowning in sweet dew the lust of Gain *a, b*
Dear Hearts, from what dim valley ye may come *a, b*
Ye are > Welcome right welcome in my desert place *a*; To get a > Receive
your welcome in this (> a > my) desert place *b*
Out, Trade! Out, Grief! Out lustful city-hum *a, b*
Friends, I salute you all: Health, Peace, and Grace! *a, b, all 8 lines
canceled in a*

37 "Soh!" said John Wallen (> the Poet) and laid down his pen *a*;
Wallen] Maynard > Wallen *b*

38 Old customary scorn > Old persevering scorn *b* > *final form a, b*

39 land] North *a, b*

40 the] this *a, b*

41 That bloomed erewhile *a* > That he had called to blossom in his soul *a, b*

41† For while he wrote a smile arose and dwelt *a, b*
Within his eyes, full, tender, rich and deep *a, b*
As light that lies upon (> on) open seas at morn *a*; As lights that lie
upon the seat at morn *b*
Which now went out as if a silver dawn *a, b*
Should shiver back into a rainy (> be withdrawn again into the) night *a*,
Should shiver back into a lonesome night *b*

42 " Soh! Let us date the writing. ' Given these *a, b*
42† And to men *b* > Under my hand and lawful seal affixed *a, b*
44 coldest > meanest *b*; town > world *a, b*
45 richest > greatest *b*
46 folk] fools *b*
47 By me, the poorest beggar in the world (> man beneath the sky) *b*; By me the poorest wretch beneath the sky *a, ll. 46-47 reversed in both a and b*
47† Bitter > Tis bitter! truly bitter, bitterly true *a*
48 Writ] Then *a*
49 And > While his last ember perished with the cold *a*
50† And > While fiendish winds jeered (> jibed) at the rattling pane *a*
50-51 *omitted a*
52 And while] And the > While the *a*
53 Led her sleek train of wretched revellers > *final form a*
54 Waiting in angles of church walls > Hid in church-wall angles till all passed > In church-wall angles hid till all should pass *a*
55 And he can (> let him) hobble to his rendevous *a*
55† While black mud oozed between the paving stones
    As corrupt blood from the city sinful heart
    Out-trampled by the wounding sound that roared
    Like a mad Genie up and down the streets:
    While stronger winds arose and whirled the snows
    About the faces of sleek revellers,
    Hurt Heaven uttering so its icy scorn:
    While Trade was grinding men in fearful (> spirit) mills *a*
56 While Luxury dreamed that she > And Luxury was trying to shout for pleasure *a*
57 *omitted a*

1884 agrees with MS *CL,* the text adopted, except for two emendations that follow the suggestions in pencil made by Paul Hayne on the margin of the MS: *the fervent* for *th' intense* (1. 5); *day-flower's crushing* for *crushed day-flower* (1. 10); and the omission of ll. 51-55, dealing with prostitution. *Independent* (Sept. 4, 1884) omits the same lines and has the emendation in 1. 5. Ll. 9-36 were incorporated in a revised form in " Psalm of the West " (pp. 67-68).

CORN (34-39)

MS *CL,* entitled " Corn: An Ode " and signed " Sidney Lanier," has a note at the top in pencil " 195 Dean St., / Brooklyn, N. Y.," where Lanier stayed from Aug. 25 to Nov. 16, 1874. But an exact copy of this MS in *MDL's* hand (*CL*) states that this is the original draft, written in July, that is, in Georgia. The extracts included in a letter to his father, Sept. 8, agree with this version, which is probably the one he submitted to *Scribner's* and the *Atlantic* and tried to publish in book form. It omits the first 9 and other lines, contains a dozen rejected lines, and differs widely from the final form. (On the top of p. 1 and verso p. 3 there are pencil versions of ll. 1-32, partly illegible, collated here as *CLᵃ*.) The text printed in *Lippincott's* (Feb., 1875) is a drastic revision, partly based on the criticisms of Paul Hayne and L. E. Bleckley. A further revision was made in *1877,* which itself differs in four lines from the final form. A full collation of variants follows:

1-4 *combined as* Today the woods are human; leaves caress *CLᵃ*
5 Like ladies' hands, and brother boughs express *CLᵃ*

7 And little noises out of copses start *CL^a*

8 Not louder than the ⟩ That sound anon like *CL^a*

9 talk 'twixt lips] speech from mouths *and 4 lines illegible CL^a*

10-11 *combined as* Through beechen breaths: through expirations strong *CL*

11 Through whose vague sweet float expirations strong *CL^a, Lipp*

12 Throb from] Of lithe *CL*; From lithe *CL^a, Lipp*

13 With stress of swelling limb and rounding ring *CL*; With stress and urgency of inward spring *CL^a*

15 Through thousand-plaited interweavings rare *CL*; Now since] And now *CL^a*

16 Of pungent balm with scarcely-fragrant air *CL*; Leave daintier odors (⟩ fragrancy) slow passing by (⟩ in company) *CL^a*; Come daintier smells, linked in soft company *Lipp*

17 Wafted from censer-waving pines *CL*; Like velvet-slippered ladies pacing by *CL^a, Lipp*

18 Long] Or *CL*; The *CL^a*

19 *omitted, combined with l. 17 CL*; Rich-wreathe the spacious] Like Jove's locks curled round *Lipp*

20 That breathe ambrosial passion out of Mænad-flowing hair *CL*; And breathe] Breathe out *CL^a, Lipp*

21 I pray with mosses] Or mosses, grasses *CL*; Calm mosses, grasses *CL^a*

22 Kneel down as ⟩ Kneel, lowly nuns i' the high-roofed nunnery *CL^a*

23 perfumes] odors *CL, CL^a*

24 Through fainting bridal sighs of blissful green *CL*; brown and green] blissful green *CL^a, Lipp*

25 Brief, heavenly-keen *CL*; Die into kindred silences serene *CL^a*; Dying to kindred silences serene *Lipp*

26 *omitted CL*; As far lights fringe] Like lights that melt *CL^a*; As far lights melt *Lipp*

27 I start at] And *CL*; I smile at *CL^a*

28 From mystic talk of leafy loves unknown *CL, CL^a*; souls] loves *Lipp*

29 *omitted CL*; Vague purports sweet] A perfect clear (?) *CL^a*

30 Through these, along the curving path between *CL*; Companioned thus, along the path between *CL^a*

32 radiant] glossy *CL*

33 ranging looks] ravished eyes *CL*

35 Into yon cool and radiant spaces *CL*

36 Where sky with boscage interlaces *CL*

37 So close] And ⟩ So close *CL*

39 zigzag-cornered] zigzag wandering *CL*

40 Where lissome sassafras and brambles dense *CL*

41 Contests] Contest *CL*

43 As] Like *CL, Lipp*

44 *omitted CL*; my fieldward-faring] before mine *Lipp*

45 *omitted CL*; Take harvests where the stately] Out of the silent *Lipp*

46 What silent dignities *CL*

47 What large benignities *CL*

48 What insights wise, what inward majesties *CL*

49 Thus without theft] Thus without tilth *Lipp*

50 And graces deep, by magic tilth are born *CL*; Thus without tilth] Thus without theft *Lipp*

51 A double harvest—from my field of corn! *CL*; And store quintuple harvests in my heart concealed *Lipp*; And heap] Heaping *1877*

52 Mark, now, yon eminent stem that stands *CL*; See out of line a single
corn-stem stands *Lipp*
56 ne'er mayst walk nor talk] canst not walk / And wilt not talk *CL*; canst
nor walk nor talk *Lipp*
57-69 *13 lines written as 10 in CL, as follows*:
    A braver singer hath not dreamed or sung
    (Spite of thy whole default of pen or tongue)
    Nor poet of tones, or words, or actions, fought
    More fruitful fight for any dream he sought
    In love of men, than thou.
    Thy shining brow
    Fronts heaven like a friend and intimate,
    Upreaching straight
    Full four feet nearer to the sky
    Than I *CL*
57 shalt] dost *Lipp*
68 Toward the empyrean *Lipp*
69 Thou reachest higher up than mortal man *Lipp*
70 While downward thou descendest in the mould *CL*
71 keepest] takest *CL*
73 thee] us *CL*
74 future] very *CL, Lipp, 1877*
76 unremitting] thy continuous *CL*
79 Thyself] Thy living self *CL, Lipp*
81 hardihood] lustihood *CL*
82 From wondrous-varying food *CL*; With wondrous-varying food *Lipp,
1877*
84 honest] solid *CL, Lipp*; richest *1877*; vagabond] vagrant *Lipp*
85 darkness] terrors *CL, Lipp*
88† And modern culture that with startling plow
Throws the rich Future round the roots of Now *CL*
89 wounds and] bruises and from *CL*
91 and dry] leaves and *CL*
92 Yea, from stones *CL*
93 Into thy vigorous substance] Into thy substance *CL*; Into] So to *Lipp,
1877*
94 Vigors the whole earth hath brought *CL*
95 And yet thy lucent green is one *CL*
96 White] With *CL*
106 Thou wilt— as all the poets must *CL*
107 With equal sacrifice and advocacy just *CL*
107† Expend thyself in service general *CL*
108 In equal care to] Careless if thou shalt *CL*
110 Thou took'st] Taking; mightst] mayst *CL*
111 O] Thou *CL*
112 still] yet *CL*
114 Pour thy reproachful scorn upon the land *CL*
115 Whose flimsy dwellings, built upon the sand *CL*
117 disappearance > alternation *CL*
122-124 *combined as* Send thy rebuke, sting-penetrant though still *CL*
125 Yon] Across yon *CL*
125 Bares to the sun] That bares to heaven *CL*
130† O rankest ill of wrong-eyed Discontent
    That westward blears across the Continent,

Most brightly pictures what's most dimly seen,
Clothes e'en the drear gray sage in living green,
And in each distant May-be sees a Must-have-been *CL*

131 There, on the generous swelling side *CL*; Upon that generous-swelling side *Lipp*
132 Of yonder hill, now scarified *CL*; Now scarified *Lipp*
133 By keen neglect and all unfurrowed save *CL, Lipp*
133† By blood-red gullies where the winter drave *CL*; By gullies red as lash-marks on a slave *Lipp*
134 of old who] who gravely *CL*
135 And dreamed himself a tiller of the soil *CL, Lipp*
136-147 *omitted CL*
137 heart] soul *Lipp*
146 games] a game *Lipp*
148 Aye] Prompt *CL*
150 anxious] frowning *CL*
152 Palaver'd, parley'd, plead for longer grace *CL*
153-155 *omitted CL*
155 Such troops of ills his labors could harass *Lipp*
156 Parried or swallowed] Replied with quivering lip to *CL*; Politely swallowed *Lipp*
157 And bent and fawned to melt his Dives' mood *CL*; soften] melt his *Lipp*
158 At last, his notes and pledges safe renewed *CL*
158† (The unpaid interest turned to principal,
So swelling doubly till the fatal fall) *CL*
159 fatal] deadly *CL*
161 his small borrowings] the erst plethoric purse *CL*
162 Aye] Prompt *CL*
163 I marked his bitter heart, his brooding mind *CL*
164 Ever, he groaned and whined *CL*
165 In dust, in rain] Through dust, through rain *CL*
167 Fretted and fumed now up, now down the lane *CL*
168 Snatched at] Hung on *CL*
169 with] to; wail] tale *CL*
170 In hope or] With hope and *CL*
176 Himself a life-long prey *CL*; And all] Beheld *Lipp*
177 Of quacks and scamps and all the vile array *CL, Lipp*
178 That line the way *CL, Lipp*
179 rascal] thieving *CL, Lipp*
180 Himself, at best] Yea, saw himself *CL, Lipp*
183 oblivious] desperate *CL*
188 King, but too poor for any man to own *CL, Lipp*
190 For all thy low estate *CL*
191 Thou still art rich and great *CL*
192 Beyond all cotton-blinded estimate *CL*
193 And long I marvel through the August morn *CL*; Lo] So *Lipp*
194 What largesse rich of wine and oil and corn *CL;* A vision of great treasuries of corn. *Lipp*
195 Thou bearest in thy vasty sides forlorn *CL, Lipp*
196 To render to some future bolder heart *CL*; For largesse to some future bolder heart *Lipp*

In *CL* l. 200 is transposed to l. 198; Lanier's letter to his brother, Feb. 8, 1875, says that this is the order that should have been followed in *Lippincott's,* but it was not so rearranged in *1877* or in the final revision.

IN ABSENCE (42-43)

Three MSS survive. *CL,* entitled " Laus Mariæ " and signed " Sidney Lanier," returned to Lanier in a letter from Paul Hayne, Oct. 10, 1874 (with Hayne's marginal notes in pencil), is an early draft (probably the first) of sonnets I-II, differing radically from the final form. *CLᵃ,* entitled " From ' The Wife ' " and signed " Sidney Lanier," is a revised version of II. *Ledger* 324-325, 327, entitled " Laus Uxoris (> Mariæ) In Absence," is a still further revision and contains all four sonnets. *Lippincott's* (Sept., 1875) agrees very nearly with *Ledger* after correction and shows a few variants from the final form. A full collation follows:

I

1 O were we in yon Land where dove to dove *CL*; one] fair *L, Lipp*
2 Need never call save with ecstatic tone *CL*
3 Where Love at heart's-ease walks in dreams of love *CL*; O Love!
    O Love!] O Love! O Wife! *L, Lipp*
4 Nor ever meets the cold ghost, *All-alone   CL*
5 Where every sigh is king of time and space *CL*
6 Yea, in one waving of desire's great wing *CL*
7 The wistful soul can tremble face to face *CL*
8 With his dear soul across the stellar ring *CL*
9 Where Heart his absent Heart can ne'er bewail *CL*
13 E'en there, dear Love, I still would ache for thee *CL*; lonesome] hungry *L*
14 What time the drear] Too long the drear *CL*; What time the lone (> drear)
    L; What time the lone *Lipp*

II

1 So] Oft *CLᵃ*; mottled] snaky *CL*
2 snakewise through our] through the poet's *CL, CLᵃ*; snakewise through
    my *L, Lipp*
3 in reeds and] and creep i' the *CL*; and creep in *CLᵃ*; and creep > in the
    reeds and *L*
4 our singing] the cleanest > the singing *CL*; the singing *CLᵃ*; my singing *L*
5 No *intervals* shall be in Yonderland *CL*; God's] yon *CLᵃ*
6 Their intervals are not] Of kisses or of aught *CL*
8 loving] mutual *CL, CLᵃ*; lawful > loving *L*
9 No gaps of space or time 'twixt kiss and kiss *CL*; Ah, there shall never]
    Ah never, There, shall *CLᵃ*
10 Can be where time is Now and space is Here *CL*
11 O, naught but variance sweet from bliss to bliss *CL*; There melt in one
    fine chord of ecstasy *CLᵃ*
12 And consonance of selves unlike but dear *CL*; Souls whom unlikeness
    parts yet binds more dear *CLᵃ*
13 Shall there our earthly voids represent *CL*; Yea, There, all distance, into
    music blent *CLᵃ*; wrought] rhythmed *L, Lipp*
14 To part the heights of heavenly ravishment *CL*; Divides, yet links, the
    heights of ravishment *CLᵃ*

III

2 valleys] cañons *L, Lipp*
4 unto love's delight] unto wife-delight ⟩ to true love's delight *L*; unto
    wife-delight *Lipp*
5 a mount ⟩ an Alp *L*
6 glacier-clear ⟩ icy-clear *L*
7 One] White ⟩ A *L*

IV

7 In love's great] In love's great ⟩ And in its *L*
9 skyward pointing] his up-pointing ⟩ his ascending *L*
14 But speeds] But speeds ⟩ Doth speed *L*

The alterations in ll. 7 and 14 of sonnet IV seem to indicate revision beyond the
text adopted, but they are not certainly in Lanier's hand. Lanier's letter of
Aug. 19, 1875, says that the printer for *Lippincott's* did not heed his corrections
in sonnet III.

SPECIAL PLEADING (45)

Two MSS survive, *JU* and *JM*, both undated and signed " Sidney Lanier,"
with the following variants:

1 Time bring back my lord to me *JU* ; Time bring back my love to me *JM*
4 Now and Then] this and thee *JU, JM*
10 sounds so much more] soundeth far more *JU, JM*
26 Well] Hey, well *JU, JM*
27 small] small, small *JU, JM*

Lippincott's (Jan., 1876) agrees with *JU* except in l. 26, where it agrees with
1877, the text adopted.

THE SYMPHONY (46-56)

Lippincott's (June, 1875) is the earliest version and *1877* a revision, both
with numerous variants and several rejected lines; Printer's Copy *CL* (the text
adopted) has three variants before correction:

2 Time] age *Lipp, 1877*
5 bill] coin *Lipp, 1877*
13-14 *3 lines for 2*
    Then all the mightier strings, assembling,
    Fell a-trembling, with a trembling
    Bridegroom's heart-beats quick resembling *Lipp*
13 with] like *1877*
16 Like a bridegroom by his bride *Lipp*
25 a] with a *Lipp*
26 leagues] heaven *Lipp*
34† Such manner of ills as brute-flesh thrills *Lipp, 1877*
35 and eat and die] eat, sleep, die *Lipp, 1877*
36 and the] and our *Lipp* ; our *1877*
37 Hush] And *Lipp, 1877*
38 no] never a *Lipp, 1877*
39 The rich man says, and passes by *Lipp* ; Say many men, and pass us by
    1877 ; Say many men and pass (⟩ hasten) by *CL*

40 And clamps his nostril and shuts his eye *Lipp*; With nostril· clamped
   and blinking eye *1877*
41 Did God say once in God's sweet tone *Lipp*; Did God say once in
   marvelous tone *1877*
43 But] But by *Lipp*; the] His white *Lipp*; his *1877*
44 Hath] Yea *Lipp, 1877*
45 Trade saith] the mills say *Lipp*
46 curt-tongued mills say Go] strong bank-tills say No *Lipp*; curt-tongued
   mills say No *1877*; No ⟩ Go *CL*
47 we know] Go to *Lipp, 1877, CL* ⟩ we know *CL*
50 Business is business; a trade is a trade *Lipp, 1877*
50† Over and over the mills have said *Lipp, 1877*
51 And then these passionate hot protestings *Lipp*; And then these passionate protestings *1877*
52 Changed to less vehement moods until *Lipp*; Merged in grieving moods
   until *1877*
53 They sank to sad suggestings *Lipp*; They sank to sad requestings *1877*
54 suggesting] requestings *Lipp;* suggestings *1877*
55 men] the world *Lipp*
56 'Tis not a law of necessity *Lipp*
57 That a trade just naught but a trade must be *Lipp*; That trades just
   naught but trades must be *1877*
59 Then 'business is business' phrases a lie *Lipp*
61 business] Traffic *Lipp, 1877*
63 widows] we victims *Lipp*; victims *1877*
64 Alas] But oh *Lipp, 1877*
65 In the sweeter half of life called Art *Lipp*
66 Is not a problem of head, but of heart *Lipp*
67 brain] head *Lipp*
69 And then, as when our words seem all too rude *Lipp*
70 We cease from speech, to take our thought and brood *Lipp*; We pass
   to pain that dimly sits abrood *1877*
72 gentle] heartwise *Lipp*
95 warm concave] velvet convex *Lipp*
97 As if God turned a rose into a throat *Lipp*
114 Behold I grow more bold *Lipp*
169-170 *3 lines for 2*
   Nature through me doth take their human side.
   That soul is like a groom without a bride
   That ne'er by Nature in great love hath sighed. *Lipp*
183 circled all] measure as *Lipp*
188 Yea man] His heart *Lipp, 1877*
194 their] with a *Lipp*
195 hills] heaven *Lipp*
243 greet] meet *Lipp*
244 meet] greet *Lipp*
259 For God shall] Soon shall God *Lipp, 1877*
260 And man shall] Soon shall man *Lipp, 1877*
295 may] can *Lipp, 1877*
324 Made end] Said *Lipp*
327 any] a little *Lipp*
339 high] wild *Lipp, 1877*
350 harsh] wild *Lipp*

353 chords most] tunes full *Lipp*
364 But] And *Lipp*

A copy of *Lippincott's* in *JT* has two further changes: *Bee-thighs* > *Bee-thefts* (l. 149) and *coin-spotted* > *coin-flecked* (l. 229), but the corrections seem to be in the handwriting of Clifford rather than Sidney Lanier.

A SONG OF LOVE (58)

Four MSS survive that differ so radically from each other and from the final form as to make a combined collation virtually impossible. As a clearer method of showing the stages of this poem's evolution, each version is given below entire; though none are dated, internal evidence suggests the following chronological order. MS *CL* is a copy in *MDL's* handwriting, without title or signature:

> Sweet eyes that smiled
> Now wet and wild
> An eye and tear are
> Mother and child
>
> Well Love and Pain
> Be kinsfolk twain,
> Yet if I could
> I'd love again.

MS *CL*ᵃ is an untitled draft in pencil signed " S. L.":

> Heigh, sweet eyes, Mary-mild;
> Hey, wet eyes, late beguiled:
> Oh, eye and tear's but mother and child.
>
> Hey, sweet love, twin with pain:
> Love and pain, kinsmen twain
> Yet would that I might but love again.

Ledger 675, without signature or title, is introduced by the words " The Fool Sings " and is probably the version intended for inclusion in " The Jacquerie " (see note). At the bottom of the same page is a jotting in the form of a Poem Outline: " A song irregular-sweet and dainty-rough / As any moss-rose red betwixt its prickles." This version, with alterations, follows:

> Love and a thorn > Rose is born
> Twin with a thorn
> Heigh rose and thorn, Heigh Life (> Rose) forlorn.
>
> Love is born
> Twin with scorn,
> Heigh rose and thorn, heigh love forlorn.
>
> O sweet eyes,
> O wet eyes!
> Heigh, eyes and tears, heigh, life forlorn.

MS *HA*, signed " Sidney Lanier " and entitled " Red / IV," is apparently the version sent to Dudley Buck, June, 1876 (see note); it approaches most nearly to Lanier's final revision in *Clover* (the text adopted):

> Good Rose, art born
> Twin to a thorn?
> Oh, come ye so, keen Love and Scorn?
>
> Yea, eyes that smiled
> Grow wet and wild;
> And Eye and Tear are mother and child.

> Well: Love and Pain
> Be kinsfolk twain,
> Yet who, that can, but loves again?

ROSE-MORALS (59-60)

Three MSS of "Red" survive: *DU* and *HC* are both undated but signed "Sidney Lanier" (probably copies sent to Bayard Taylor and Gibson Peacock, autumn, 1875); they are earlier drafts than *CL*, unsigned and undated, but entitled "Red" and apparently the copy sent to Dudley Buck in June, 1876. They have the following variants:

2 As sighs of roses breathed at night *HC*; As] Like *DU*
3 my] a *HC*
5 could'st] canst; breast] heart *HC*
6 yon red rose] yonder roses *HC;* yonder rose-heart *DU, CL*
7 So clean, so large with love, so calm thou art *HC*; So clean, so large, so calm with velvet rest *DU, CL*
9 Ah, good my Rose-leaves, die *HC*
10 so] drift *DU*
11 That my songs from my heart, like leaves from a stem, shall fly *HC*; That my songs from my soul as leaves from a stem may fly *DU*

The version in MS *DU* has previously been printed by J. B. Hubbell, "A Lanier Manuscript," Duke University *Library Notes,* II, 2-3 (Nov., 1937).

MS *CL* of "White," unsigned and undated (the text used in *Lippincott's,* May, 1876), has four variant lines; *CL^a* (inclosed in letter to Taylor, Mar. 20, 1876) and *1877* (the text used in *1884*) correct the first of these but show further revision of one line:

5 yet] but *CL*
10 Grow, Soul! unto such white estate *CL, CL^a, 1877*
11 Strong art and virginal prayer shall be thy breath *CL*; Strong] That *CL^a*; That virginal-prayerful art shall be thy breath *1877*
12 Thy work, thy fate *CL, CL^a, 1877*

THE CENTENNIAL MEDITATION OF COLUMBIA (60-62)

Six MSS survive. By far the most interesting is *JU,* entitled "Cantata. / Columbia's Centennial Song" and signed "Sidney Lanier." A note accompanying the MS says this was the copy originally sent to Bayard Taylor, that is, on Jan. 9, 1876; but the fact that it contains a marginal analysis of the movements indicates that it was the corrected copy sent to Taylor on Jan. 12 (see letters; but Taylor's letter of Jan. 12, commenting in detail on the version sent to him on Jan. 9, points to no differences in this lost first version, though there were undoubtedly a few). It has numerous variants and seven rejected lines and in turn omits fourteen that were added later. The analysis of movements, which differs from that printed in the present edition, is as follows: *"First Movement. Full Chorus.* Measured and sober, yet majestic:— the colossal figure of a Woman upon a height looking into the Past and meditating upon it. / *Second Movement. Full Chorus. Agitato:* the sighs of men, mingled with the raging of winds and waves. / *Third Movement. Trio: Or Quartette:* Cold, meagre, threatening: a mournful minor. / *Fourth Movement. Full Chorus.* The motive of the Second Movement might here be hinted at again, but worked up with greater fury and confusion to the climax in the last line, culminating there as a tremendous shout of voices and instruments. / [The Huguenot stanza was omitted.] *Fifth Movement. Full Chorus.* The first four lines present a sudden change from the confusion of the last movement, into a clear and animated thanksgiving: but with the fifth line enters a voice of doubt, which sinking *poco a poco decres.*, finally brings the whole chorus down to a whisper: after which should come a General Pause, for chorus and orchestra, of at least two bars. Then the next movement: Basso Solo. / *Sixth Movement. Basso Solo.* Firm, sustained, majestic: a Voice teaching and prophesying. / *Final Movement. Full Chorus.* Joyful and gracious Welcome."

MS *CL,* entitled "Cantata. / Centennial Song of Columbia" and signed "Sidney Lanier" is apparently the revised copy sent to Taylor on Jan. 15, 1876 (many of the changes being influenced by the criticisms in Taylor's letter of Jan. 12). It has the marginal analysis of movements as given in the present edition, but has a number of variants in the text. (MS *HC* is the copy sent in a letter of Jan. 18 to Gibson Peacock. MS *DU,* a transcript from the original made by Edwin Mims, is the copy sent in a letter of Jan. 15 to Dudley Buck, though it is erroneously marked as the version inclosed in the letter of Feb. 1, the final revision which has not survived in MS. Both of these agree with MS *CL.*) The variants in this version were corrected to the final form in Lanier's letters to Buck, Jan. 19, 22, and Feb. 1. Lanier's letter of Jan. 19 to Buck contains a partial revision showing two variant lines and four added lines (42-43†) that were withdrawn in his letter of Jan. 22 (here collated as *DB*). MS *HL* is a fragment, probably the first draft, of lines 13-18. The full collation follows:

2 more large with nobler] grows large with larger *JU*
3 Ranges] Ranging; yon towering] the stairéd *JU*
7 From yon misty regions where *JU*; Yonder where a weltering flow *CL*
8 Bygone battles rage in air *JU*; Ridged with acts of long ago *CL*
9-10 *omitted JU*
11 slowly hither] trembling *JU*
12 Trembling westward] Blindly *JU*
13 When this raining of day and night *HL*; *Farewell dear England*] thee homeward *JU*
14 Shall freeze and cut like hail *HL*; *But dear in vain* replying] thee home-denying *JU*
15 Wave to welkin shouted crying *HL, JU*
18 Thee, Plymouth, thee, Albany *JU*
19 Hunger cries, "Ye shall not stay" *JU*
20 *omitted JU*
21 Winter cries, "Ye shall not stay" *JU*
22 Vengeance cries, "Ye shall not stay" *JU*; *shall*] can *CL*
22† From the land as from the sea,
    "No! It shall not be!" *JU*
23-28 Then the smiting-tonguéd swords,
    War and his lieutenant lords
    —Armored Shapes, disbodied Hordes,
    Clothes as men and Oaths as Words—
    Old prescribéd Rights in throngs
    Leading new conscribéd Wrongs *JU*
30 windy night] roaring wind *JU*
31 from land and sea] they cried to me *JU*
32 *No*] "No, no, no! *JU*
33-43 *omitted JU*
33 Hark] Hark, hark *CL*

42-43 Toil e'en when brother-wars new-dark the Light
    Toil, and forgive, and forget, and unite *CL*
42-43 Toil e'en when brother-wars new-dark the Light
    Toil when wild brother-wars grasping at Right
    Sunder his head from his heart in despite,
        Toil through the after-wars,
        Scorn-wars and laughter-wars,
    Toil, and forgive, and new kiss, and o'er-plight. *DB*
44 oft-granted] good *JU, CL*
45 undaunted] firm *JU, CL*
49 Now still thee, by-past underworld *JU*
49† Lo, from beyond the thunder-world *JU*
58-61 Then break, O break, sweet Storm of harmony:
    In Music's tongue, all tongues of earth are free.
    Friends! As friends' banners be my words unfurled:
    The world's best lover doth salute the world. *JU*

    Then, Music, from this height be thou my voice:
    In thy large tongue all tongues of earth rejoice:
    Roll forth, broad tones as friendly flags unfurled,
    The world's best Wisher's welcome to the world. *CL*

PSALM OF THE WEST (62-82)

MS *SL*, entitled " To the United States of America " and signed " Sidney Lanier," is undated but an early draft consisting of 41 pp. Pp. 4-12 were originally numbered 1-9, suggesting that the first 38 lines were added later; pp. 14-20 were originally numbered 21-28, indicating that the Columbus sonnets were first planned to come later in the poem; verso p. 8 is a canceled pencil draft of ll. 141-152, 165-170 (with two lines written as one throughout), which is worked into the collation as if it were a part of the ink version. The MS has a large number of rejected lines, omissions, alterations, and variants as follows:

  6 He fashioned thine intimate Sweet and thine Eve and thy Bride
  8 For ⟩ Lo
11 Land] my land
31 shall lovingly turn] shall turn, shall turn
32 shall consciously burn] shall burn, shall burn
37 old regretting and scorn] that the night was forlorn ⟩ old regret and
    old scorn
38 Yea, the World in (⟩ stream of) the Light never dream that the Night
    hath been ever (⟩ ever hath been) forlorn
39-40 *written as one line*
43 Down the world ⟩ Forever
44 was] was nought but
45 time ⟩ day
48 the terminal ⟩ terminal
49 Till] But
51 its] a
54 lower] lowermost
56 *originally written as l. 55*
57 One wing] And one
62 O my] my
64 Till the Spark of the Dawn, as a saint in a saintly ring

65 Saying] Whispered
66 Then that Poet began in a lowly curve to pass
71 a wild] was a
73 then] next
76-77 *reversed*
79 hearing and seeing wrought] each Sense of a man caught
81 silver of sunshine and silver of > silvery sunshine and silvery
82 spirals of] curves of his
83 cinctures] cincture
84 tapering] sky-seeking
86 But] And
90 artist] Poet
93 Far spread] Far spread > Vague, far
94 The sea that names yet ne'er shall further show > The sea that fastly
    hath locks within (> in) his amplier (> looser) flow
95 Sad > The old > Sad > All secrets of Atlantis' drownéd woe
102 But ever the vacant waste seemed darker still > But ever the bleary idiot
    blur of idiot sea blurs darkened still > But ever the idiot sea-mouths
    fill and spill > *final form*
103 did > doth; or]nor
104 was > is; wrought > hath
106 dusk > sunset
108 So empty cropp'd the day behind the day > So leanly sailed > So sailed
    each day behind his day
109 Sailed to > To where; amidst > o'er glooms
110 its] his; sinks] sank > sinks > folds
122 O'er-dreaming some old tale
130 Round] Quick
135 Yet as] But as > A ghost
139 So] So > And the
141 hurled > whirled
143 First skips > Doth skip
145 Blond beards of Georgia Oaks > Blond beards with gray beards > Where
    Georgia's graybeard Oaks moss-curled (> Oaks gray-mossy curled >
    Oaks with moss-wreaths curled) > Where Georgia's oaks and wild-
    grapes curled
146 Inset with blond beards at the strand > Sway o'er (> O'er lord) the glit-
    tering strand > Green wall the shining strand
147 Wave in cross-breaths from Florida's Flower > Sway in cross-breaths >
    Sway in cross-sighs > And audit > With marrying > Where many sighs
    from > And sway in sighs from Florida's Spring > And Florida murmurs
    from her Spring
148 To > And > Or Carolina's Palm
149 Or wave > Or thrill when > What time the mocking (> Artist) bird doth
    bring > Land where the poet-bird doth bring
150 All mute his artist's balm > All mutes a poet's balm
151 Doth sing his > With singing the > Sings out his > *final form*
165-198 *omitted in ink but first six lines in pencil:*
165 Land of the pleasant-loitering feet > Or while the June with lingering
    (> loitering) feet > Fair Norseman drawn with loitering feet
166 Along the pleasant ways > By pleasant Southern ways
167 Lift up the unheard hymn of heat > Hear'st thou that Hymn to Gracious
    Heat
168 With careless minstrel's praise > The fervent hours upraise

169 bland] large
170 Through rhythmwise nights and days
219 soul > man
222 Ill doth] ills do
229 Then > And > Now; glimmered so > glimmers low
234 was > is
235 sea lay black and still > airs with darkness fill
263 is > doth
237 was > is; wrought > works
238 empty-cropp'd > leanly sails
239 Sailed to > To where; amidst > o'er glooms
240 its] his; sank > sinks
241 As when] Like as; level] slowly
242 sunset to] dusk to seek
249 be > move
253 And yearns about the sea as gods in love do yearn > *final form*
254 His heart speaks with his heart, as friend with friend less brave > *final form*
255 Firing the faiths that cool, cooling the doubts that burn
256 ff *marked in the margin " Columbus' Song "*
259 Wait, Heart! Time moves] Patience
268 No damage taking] Nor took no damage
284 sphere] globe
285 contrary > contrarious
300 How > Ho
301 by far too few > far overfew
302 multitudes of rebel] rebel murmuring and
313 Ere we had cleared Gomera > Ere we Gomera cleared
321 then > so
322 Steersman] Pilot
323 the meteor] a meteor
327 Next drive] Then drave
331 No! Freedom lies to westward, where we flee
332 Yet] But
341 So when > And then > *final form*
342 all > we
347 Yet > And
355 ranging] sweeping
356 its] his
359 Wouldst leap ashore, Heart] Heart, I will hold thee > Will jump ashore >
      Wouldst jump ashore, Heart
360 Pedro] So: Pedro
368 God's dawn i' the East, My dawn i' the West! Oh . . . Land! > God's,
      East— mine, West: my friends, behold the (> my) Land!
392 God beholds thee from the skies > *final form*
396 shall > will
409 sail no more] ply the oar
414 Cushman, Carver, Winthrop, wade
416 steered the keel] held the wheel
417 sweet > soft
422 Puritan's] Puritan's > Pilgrims
434 patriot] Warren
437 shall say > shall tell > hath told
438 And thou shalt shine as long as they > *final form*

458 'Tis not a Cock, the Future crows ⟩ A Morning shall come ere morning
    goes ⟩ *final form*
490† Even as lined for fight ye stood
491 brotherhood's stroke] brotherhood
492 *omitted*
503 Or ⟩ And
506 O patriot's God ⟩ My God, my God
516 reached ⟩ crawled to
531† Season and man at one, this blazing morn,
    To full white heat are come, old wrong and scorn
    And tyrannous stroke of toilsome years forlorn
    Have beat such tragic temper in the land
    That yeoman ask, *Why with petition bland*
    Shall we more supplicate what men demand?
    A wave, from where those French and forward Souls
    Plunge in old kinghood, rounding Westward rolls,
    And floods all marshy nooks (⟩ th' uncertain marsh) and weedy shoals
532 Jersey ⟩ Hampshire; the] the ⟩ a
549† But Doubt, small cunning rogue that e'er steals by (⟩ doth e'er steal),
    Faith-filching, when the crowd with straining eye
    Wait till some Wonder through the heavens fly.
    Wee Doubt was in the Council, *Nay, my friends, canceled*
    Quoth Dickinson, *Why declare our freedom? Can*
    Your dozen protestations add one man
    Upon your armies? And why pluck our plan
    Unripe, and break it green? Why, overbold
    Cast loose from England ere we grapple hold
    On France, or some main power? If, haply, cold
    Looks France on our ambassadors that wait
    To know her counsel in our dark debate,
    With how keen insult will we flout her State,
    Ending the thing we asked advice to end
    Before the advice can come! Shall we not send
    —France even gained— to win some further friend
    Lest our small flag no sooner be unfurled
    Than to the instant dust 'tis lightly hurled
    By the loud-laughing monarchs of this world?
550 All question] Cold question
554 its] his
561 the kindred ⟩ kindred
564 Downward athwart each] Down by the Chairman's
569 smiling ⟩ softly
601 Fain to cheat the onward ache ⟩ *final form, originally as l. 602*
603 Now] Then
618 shining ⟩ glittering
625 But Brain was bare i' the Casque,— not he
628 find] catch
645 ye] they
648 the Prime] my Prime
659 Songs ⟩ Strains
661 yet ⟩ still; godly ⟩ heavenly
663 All ⟩ Each old ⟩ Olden
669 Prophet's ⟩ Artist's
672 Thou shalt find ⟩ Son, study

674 And] And > Now
677 the] that; land] earth's land
679 The dust] That dust
693 O > Then
702 much] with
712 Oppression] Oppression > Theft
719 a righteous > Freedom's
720 For a right the Future is all free > Thy Future's voice sounds yet more
free > *final form*
727 And know and choose > And try and know time's worst and best

Lippincott's (July, 1876) has the same variant as the MS in l. 6; *1877* has
two variants, probably misprints: *give* for *shall give* (l. 38), and *once* for *that*
(l. 45). Ll. 171-189 were used in an earlier form as part of " June Dreams,
In January "; ll. 611-634 as " The Tournament. Joust First."

THE WAVING OF THE CORN (83-84)

Two MSS survive: *CL,* undated and unsigned, is a rough pencil draft of
stanzas 1 and 2, with numerous alterations and variants, some of which are
illegible; *Ledger* 471-472, signed " Sidney Lanier " and dated " West Chester.
Aug. 15th 1876 " (in the handwriting of *MDL*, but with corrections by Lanier—
she often served as his amanuensis), has alterations and variants and a rejected
stanza at the end:

1 gnarly hand yet kindly] haply undainty hand hath *CL, L*; hath > first *CL*
2 Thy prosy plough to spare this maple tree *CL, L*; maple > reverend *L*
3 His clover-carpet in the corn a-field > A clover-circle from th' exacting
field *CL*; His clover-circle midst the grain afield *L*
4 In] Whose *CL, L*
5 grain > corn *CL*
7 Who here have (> in) daily congress sweet (> meet) while (> lo) I *CL*;
Who (> That) here have daily congress sweet— lo, I *L*
9 Do stir with] Stir with fresh *CL, L*; *CL has several illegible drafts of*
ll. 7-10, followed immediately by drafts of ll. 21-23:
21 Twixt me and town spread grassy billows vast > Betwixt this heaven and
the city's hell *CL*; Betwixt this quiet heaven and Trade's loud hell >
'Twixt here, and where the louder passions dwell *L*
22 Of fair green separation > Billows of separation (> fair green separation)
roll *CL*
23 *illegible CL*; Man's (?) janglings faint where clover ridges swell *L*
24 ne'er claim] claim not *L*
29 And softly take Time's strokes as th' air of morn *L*
30† O good ten thousand corn-blades poised aloft
  Would all men's swords might blandly curve as these
  Would keen-edg'd Faiths, that even now do oft
  Behead th' unorthodox on wrong-placed knees,
  Might rise so suave and fall so heavenly-soft;
  Would many-rubbing Rights, that scrape and tease,
  Might shape (with aims but crossed for mutual good)
  Wise > Smooth polities of gentle neighborhood
  Not harshlier than doth rustle through the morn
  The waving of the corn. *L*

Several of the changes were made and the final stanza omitted at the suggestion
of Bayard Taylor (see Lanier's letter of Oct. 6, 1876, and note 140).

CLOVER (84-87)

Four MSS survive, containing separate parts of the poem and differing so much from each other and from the final form as to make a combined collation virtually impossible. Given below, in the order of composition, they indicate that the parts of the poem were conceived in reverse order from that finally adopted. *HL*, pencil notes verso letter to Lanier from J. R. Osgood, July 21, 1876, is a rough draft of ll. 95-112 in prose, as follows: "Dear billows large and quiet / Of green separation 'twixt me and [the] town. / How much dost thou charge for blooming, Clover? / And what is the price of green, / O Grass? / And as I lay in the clover I though I saw Christ like a tall clover bloom! and he was beautiful, and he saw the sun with quiet majesty; and the world came in the guise of an ass [*2 lines illegible*] and reached out its rough tongue sideways and crinkled him into its mouth and ate him. Then I saw other clover blooms: Keats, and Wordsworth, and the ass ate them also." (This MS also contains several other jottings, see Poem Outline No. 90, p. 257, and note.)

MS *CL*, verso letter to Lanier from Bayard Taylor, Aug. 16, 1876, is an untitled draft of ll. 64-86 (and two illegible pencil drafts of ll. 42-51, here omitted), with alterations, as follows:

Now through low (> my) vistas of the clover-stems
The gentle hills > Now framed in the arch (> arching) of two clover stems
Wherethrough I gaze from off (> upon) my hillside low
The hills (> fields) that wave afar (> undulate) > The fields from here to
    heaven take on
Tremors of change and large (> new) significance
To th' eye as to the ear a simple tale
Begins to hint a parable's sense beneath.
The undulating prospect breaks the bounds
Of horizontal limitings and spreads (> grows)
All-ways into the up-and-down of time *canceled*
Into a mighty- (> *illegible* > curious-) hill'd and mighty- (> curious-) valley'd
    breadth (> space)
That seems the Up-and Down of Time   *canceled*
Having no end whatever-wise I look   *canceled*
Which seems the unreasonable   *canceled*
Endless before, behind, a-side, which seems
The unreasonable Up-and-Down of Time
The clover-stems still cover it > Spread out before mine eyes: the clover-stems
Still cover all the space, but look, they bear
(For clover-blooms) men's heads, of godlike poise
one line illegible
And poets'-faces, heartsome, dear and pale,
And myriad visages of every fervent (?) soul
Whose worth or service was of artist's kind
That hath been worthy of   *canceled*
Yea every artist whether (> or) of pen or lute,
Or brush or chisel > Brush, voice, hand, chisel, act or sacrifice
Or other matter whatsoever > Or other thing (> tool) how be its substance
    bright *canceled*
Wherewith (> That men) sweet thoughts do body them withal > That e'er
    sweet inward art hath served withal
The world, in pious loving, freely. Lo (> Oh)
Here about > In arm's reach, here be Shelley, Keats, Chopin,

Beethoven, Chaucer, Schubert, Shakespeare, Bach,
And farther off and (*illegible*) bright throngs unnamable *canceled*
Of worshipful sweet faces *canceled*
And Buddha (sweetest Masters, let me round
My arms this once, this humble once about

Ledger 472-473, entitled " Clover," undated (but following " The Waving
of the Corn," dated Aug. 15, 1876), is an early draft of ll. 12-63:

The streaming day, that purled full pleasantly
O'er fretted clouds half-way from dawn to noon,
Now locked in lucent meditation spreads
Into a solemn pool of silver morn.
Eight lingering strokes of some far village-bell
Do clock the hour so inward-voiced, meseems
Life's conscience hath but whispered him eight hints
Of revolution. 'Tis that daily pause,
When nimble noises that with sunrise run
About the farms have sunk again to sleep,
When Tom across the horse-lot calls no more
To sleepy Dick, nor Dick, snore-husked in voice
Upbraids with sulphurous oath and slap on flank
Old Bob, the roan, for stamping on his foot,
What time the cart-chain clinks against the shaft
And, round the house, the rattling bucket plumps
In the well, where gathering ducks exchange loud quacks
And Susan Cook is singing. Up the sky
The hesitating moon slow trembles on,
Faint as a new washed Soul this moment up
From sin and a sad fresh grave. Far round,
A hundred hills a hundred ways do bend
Large curves of ravishment, so marvellous mild
Maybe but now the soft persuasive plain
Rose to a rain of clover-blooms, as lakes
Pout gentle mounds of plashment up to meet
The great first drops of shower. A light-heart wind
Comes zig-zag like a bee to where I lie
Mixt soul and body with the clover-tufts,
Lights on my spirit, gives from wing and thigh
Rich pollens and divine sweet irritants
To every nerve, and freshly makes from off
Hill-cheeks and hearts of flowers and souls of leaves
Report of all their secret matters fine
Unto some lordly soul-of-sense within
My frame which owns each feoffment several
And special cognizance of th' outlying five,
Yea, sees, hears, tastes, smells, touches, all in one.
And now, dear Clover, (since my soul is thine,
And I am fain give study all the day
To make thy ways my ways, thy service mine,
To find me out thy God my God to be
And utterly die to man to live with thee)
Now, Cousin Clover, tell me in mine ear:
How much a bloom dost ask for blooming, pray?
Three-Leaves, quote me the price of green this day!

In just what form the poem was submitted to *Scribner's* (and rejected in a letter of Oct. 10, 1876) cannot be stated with certainty. It may have been the *Ledger* version, a completed draft of MS *CL*, or a combination of the two.

MS *HA*, entitled " Clover " and signed " Sidney Lanier / 33 Denmead St. / Baltimore, Md.,"—Lanier's residence from Dec., 1877, to Oct., 1878—combines the above in a revised form, with the addition of the opening and closing lines; it is the text printed in *Independent* (Mar. 7, 1878) and has the following variants from the final form:

35 Faint as a death-washed soul but newly up
36 From out a fresh-sod grave. Far, round below
42 ·Descending drops of showers. Small winds as bees
43 Bow down the blooms; then wander where I lie
52 Tell me] And now
89 throngs] things
124 To quality precise for plans of His
125 The general brawn is built. Kinsman, learn this

TO BEETHOVEN (88-90)

MS *CL*, untitled, undated, unsigned, is written in pencil on the front and back fly-leaves of Lanier's copy of Pietro Blaserna, *The Theory of Sound in its Relation to Music* (New York, 1876); it consists of a rough draft of seven stanzas only, in the following order: 6, 12, 11, 15, 16, 17, and 9, with alterations and variants, and was probably written in Dec., 1876 (see note). *Galaxy* (Mar., 1877) omits three stanzas and has numerous variants and four rejected stanzas (here collated as *G*). *Clover,* the text adopted, has three variants before correction. The collation follows:

1 Clasped in a too strict calyxing *G*
2 too long] o'er long *G*
3 the] her *G*
4 bloomed] blushed *G*
5-12 *omitted and the following lines substituted G*
4† O loving Soul, thy song hath taught
   All full-grown passion fast to flee
   Where science drives all full-grown thought—
   To unity, to unity.
   For he whose ear with grave delight
   Brings brave revealings from thine art
   Oft hears thee calling through the night:
   In Love's large tune all tones have part.
   Thy music hushes motherwise,
   And motherwise to stillness sings
   The slanders told by sickly eyes
   On nature's healthy course of things.
14 thoughts] frets *G*
21 serve great] profit ⟩ serve bad *CL*
22 Christ] Christs *CL, G*
24 take no] gain their ⟩ feed on *CL*; live on *G*
28 strangely] blindly *G*
30 And spare his mate] Along with him *G*
31 Whose wives and babes may starve or freeze *G*
32† If winds of question blow from out
   The large sea-caverns of thy notes,

They do but clear each cloud of doubt
That round a high-path'd purpose floats. *G*
33 As: why one blind by nature's act *G*
34 Yet makes] Still feels *G*
35 No pitfall from our] Her precipice from his *CL*; No pitfall from his *G*
36 No] Her *CL*
37-40 *omitted G*
41 Whether the truth is best for them *CL*; Or, Can the truth be best for
   them *G*
42 eyes to bear] stomachs for *CL, G*; stomachs for〉eyes to bear *Clover*
43 Whether the sap in Culture's stem *CL*; Or, Will the sap in Culture's
   stem *G*
44 Can reach life's farthest fibre-length *CL*; E'er reach life's furthest fibre-
   length *G*
45 To know, yet hate (〉scorn) all knowingness *CL*; How to know all save
   knowingness *G*
47 To lose (〉sink) no manhood in success *CL*; To sink no manhood in
   success *G*
49 Though] How *G*; Much〉Though *Clover*
51 And midst of] How through all *G*
53 How, justly, yet with loving eyes *G*
54 Pure art from Celverness to part *G*
55 To see〉To know *Clover*
57 poor〉weak *CL*
58 O Troubadour] Time's troubadour *CL*
59 Co-Litanist] Strange Litanist *CL*
63 each〉my *CL*
65 Yea, it] Music *CL*
66 Says in my soul (〉heart), Go forth (〉Depart), O crime *CL*
67 And tunes each work (〉task) my hand begins〉And tunes what task
   each day begins *CL*
68 trumpet-note] trumpet-tone *CL*

THE STIRRUP-CUP (90)

In addition to *Clover,* the text adopted, three other MSS survive, early drafts
in pencil without title or date, showing numerous alterations and variants and
one rejected stanza. All are in *CL* and are collated below as *a, b,* and *c* in
the order of revision as indicated by internal evidence. Both *b* and *c* are signed
" S. L."; *b* is written verso *a* which is clearly the first draft; *c* is written verso
an early draft of " Tampa Robins " and is marked at the bottom in *MDL's*
handwriting " Tampa, Fla. / Jan. 1877."

   1 Death thou art but a cordial rare *a*; Death, thou art (〉thou'rt) a cordial
      rare *b*; For death is but a cordial rare *preceded by ll. 9-12 c*
   2 For look what thy compounds are〉*final form a*
   3 Time hath〉Time's wrinkles came with savoring thee (〉by culling for
      thee) *a*
   4 The best herbs〉With nectars of antiquity *a*
   5 Dear *(canceled)* David to thy brewage (〉distillage) went *a*; thy] this *c*
   6 Buddha〉*final form a*
   8 king-delight] last delight *a*
   8† These for to sweeten thee with song *a, b*; These were to sweeten it
      with song *c*

26 1

All > But > And heroes blood hath made thee strong *a*; The blood of heroes made thee strong *b*; The blood of heroes made it strong *c*

No man can call thee > Tongues cannot tell them: Man > I tell > I know them not: ah me, for shame *a* > What heroes? Ah, for shame, for shame *a, b, c*

Thy best ones > The grandest died without a name *a*; The grandest > The worthiest died without a name *b*; The worthiest died without a name *c*

11 Death if such savors be in thee > O death if these have savored thee *a* > If death such dear distilment be *a, b, c*

12 I'll drink thee very smilingly > *final form a*

Scribner's (May, 1877) has the variant in l. 11 and the rejected stanza as in *b*.

THE BEE (91-92)

MS *CL*, signed "Sidney Lanier / Tampa, / Fla.," is an early draft in ink with corrections in pencil (some of which are illegible), showing the following alterations and variants:

1 paced > ranged > paced
2 *alterations illegible*
3 Meseemed *canceled*
4 Report of chase and distant > *final form*
5 green hollow > hollow
6 *added in pencil, originated written as l. 10*
8 wavered oft] came so (> wavered) faint
9 So fickleways about, now here, now there > *final form*
11 But lo > But on a sudden, lo
12 A dainty (> little) furious shaking > I marked a blossom shiver
13 Of blossoms drew mine eye > As with a dainty inward storm
16 his > its
18 nectar > sweetest > blissful
19 Some > A
21 golden > amber; yellow > golden
22 Where low o'erhead a happy jessamine vine > *final form*
23 With > In; twine and twine > overtwine
24 Her bending live-oak, and herself did plight > *final form*
25 Unto her very > Herself unto her
27 long-desiring sense] long-desirous ear (> sense)
29† Methought my spirit through some forest grace
   Approached within a mere handshaking space
   Of brother blooms and bees
   And dear tree-families *all 4 lines canceled*
30 Till by such neighborhood the bee's faint tone > *final form*
31 Through sequence sweet (> half caught sense > sequence rich) of meaning half-unknown (> lost in air) > *final form 3 lines below*
32 Passed into words, while I, still gazing up > *final form*
33 Perceived him (> her) poising o'er a (*illegible*) fresh new cup
34 O blissful world bloom hanging full and fine
35 Upon the Universe's profuse vine
36 O World has aught > Hast nought for me
37 To thee, to thee
38-39 *reversed*
40 *e'er a poet brings*] *if a poet sings*

41 He hath a sense of pollen on > The poet hath a > He bringeth foreign dust about his wings
42 Shall fructify thy possibles > Of pollen for to make thee fruitful, nay > Shall > *final form*
43 If thou shalt (> dost) narrow up thy tubéd way > *final form*
46 And hold up stamen-prickles high > *final form*
47 To wound me hip and thigh > To break my wing and blind mine eye > *illegible* > *final form*
48 Still will I thrust me to thy central heart > Nathéless I'll force me to thy farthest heart > *final form*
49 And all more richly shall the pollen part > And (> Yea) richlier for the pain > *illegible* > *final form*
50 From off my wings; for pollens often be > From me to thee: Ah would that pollen be > *final form*
51 Dust of the battles poets fight for thee > Dust from the battles poets wage for thee > *final form*
52 But O World-bloom that hangest full and fine > *final form*
53 On the endless universal jessamine > Upon the Universe's profuse vine > Upon the Universe's planet-vine > *final form*
54-55 *reversed*
56 Hast not some little > Yield, yield the blissful (> heartsome) honey love for (> to) me
57 In thy huge > Hid in thy
58 dimmer] solemn > dearer > softer > secret > suaver
59 These words the > The pleading bee-song's burthen
60 Hast not > Wilt spare > Yield yield a little > *final form*

Lippincott's (Oct., 1877) has the variants in ll. 58-59 after correction.

TAMPA ROBINS (92-93)

Lippincott's (Mar., 1877), entitled "Redbreast in Tampa," has the following variants (with which agrees MS *CL*, a pencil draft of the first stanza only, verso MS *CL°* of "The Stirrup-Cup"):

4 us] me
5 Old Time! thy scythe reaps bliss for me
6 So blithe, so blithe, a bird can be
7-12 *omitted*
15 sky but gray wind] gray sky bending
17 No, no: I sing; and singers be
18 Too hot for Time's cold tyranny
19 Nay, windy North, I catch my clime
21 Whose constant torch my heart doth hold
22 And I'll call down] So laugh I
23 take] with
24 So passing blithe we robins be

Clover, the text adopted, has two variants before correction: *doth* > *shall* (l. 21); *laugh* > *call* (l. 22).

FROM THE FLATS (97-98)

MS *CL*, entitled "From a Flat Land" and signed "S. L.," undated, is in the handwriting of *MDL* but with corerctions in Lanier's hand (she often served as his amanuensis during periods of illness). It has several alterations and one variant (last line):

1 for ⟩ ne'er
3 sandy ⟩ drear-sand
5 And then with stupid tongues to dull the pain ⟩ *final form*
6 They ⟩ Do
10 takes the ⟩ 'gainst mine
11 thicket, leafy glen ⟩ brake or lurking dell
13 green ⟩ rich
14 Round bends of roads, or over ⟩ *final form*
15 The soul of things is tired, vigor is tame ⟩ *final form*
16 Always ⟩ Ever
20 strives straight up ⟩ heavenward strives
21 profoundest ⟩ far-falling
22 gentle ⟩ bottom
24 Bright leaps a living brook] Lapses a little brook ⟩ *Lull* sings a soothing brook

MDL followed this MS in *1884* except that she combined the two versions of l. 24 to read: *Lull sings a little brook!* (See letter to her from J. B. Tabb, Sept. 5, 1882, who suggested one other change that she did not follow.) This was restored in the *1910* edition to the final form as Lanier had printed it in *Lippincott's* (July, 1877) and in Sargent's *Cyclopaedia* (1881), the text adopted.

THE MOCKING BIRD (98)

MS *CL* (signed "Sidney Lanier," undated), *Galaxy* (August, 1877), and *1884* have the following variants:

1 a pluméd] th' extremist *CL*
2 That, still a-bud, o'er hills of leafage grew *CL*
3 in song; or typic drew] with song. With act as true *CL*; in] with *Galaxy*
4 He typed the swoop of hawks, the languorous way *CL*; watch] swoop *Galaxy*
5 Of lonesome wood-doves when their lovers stray *CL*
7 morn] dawn *CL*
8 birds did or] a bird had; could] did *CL*
11 primped] prinked *1884*
12 Sweet Science, this large] But now, Sweet Science this *CL*
13 may] could; that dull insect] dull grasshoppers *CL*

THE DOVE (99)

Three MSS survive, all omitting the fourth stanza, and showing three overlapping stages of the poem's development. *CL*, untitled, undated and unsigned, is a rough draft in pencil showing numerous alterations; *HC*, a fair copy inclosed in a letter to Gibson Peacock, Aug. 7, 1877, entitled "The Dove: A Song" and signed "Sidney Lanier," represents an intermediate stage; *CL*[a], entitled "The Dove: A Song" and signed "Sidney Lanier. / Chadd's Ford. / Pa.," shows further alterations but still differs from the final form. *HC* was printed in the *Atlantic Monthly*, LXXIV, 186 (Aug., 1894); since it agrees with *CL* after correction and with *CL*[a] before correction, it is not included in the following collation:

1 To thee, to thee *CL* ⟩ If thou, if thou, O blue and silver Morn *CL*, *CL*[a]
2 That callest o'er the curving of the (⟩ pale pursuing) sphere ⟩ *final form CL*

3 Remain, remain, O Night 〉 Sweet Night, art gone? stay (〉 Remain) CL 〉
  Sweet Night, my Love! Nay, leave me not forlorn CL, CL^a
4 'Twixt the heavenly hope and fear 〉 *final form* CL
5 If thou, bud-bosomed Spring, from yonder slope 〉 Shouldst thou maid
  (〉 past) Spring, a-cower in coverts green (〉 dark) CL; Should'st
  thou, past Spring 〉 O Spring should'st thou a-cower in coverts dark CL^a
6 Wouldst plead 〉 Shouldst set us forth thy youth and (*illegible*) in plea 〉
  In death and swift supplanting summer 〉 'Gainst great (〉 proud)
  supplanting Summer madst (〉 sing) thy plea CL
7 move] movedst CL
8 With (〉 Till) tender heartbreak throbbed (〉 burned) in every tree CL;
  mortal] tender CL^a
9 Ah, little If, how weighs thy 〉 Ah, grievous If, wilt thou be yea full
  soon CL; Ah, grievous *If,* wilt turn to *Yea* full soon 〉 And (ah,
  sad If, that turn'st to Yea full soon!) CL^a
10 Sweet] Love CL *originally written as l. 1,* CL^a
11 Should'st beat and burn in mellow measured (〉 shocks of) tune CL;
  Should'st beat and burn in (〉 my breast with 〉 Death's door with)
  mellow shocks of tune CL^a
12 Such 〉 Your moans would mock yon deep-sequestered dove CL; Each
  might but mock yon deep sequestered dove 〉 Thou needs must mock
  yon dim melodious dove CL^a

A PUZZLED GHOST IN FLORIDA (99-101)

The version in *1884,* 163-166, for which no authority has been found, is
entitled "A Florida Ghost"; it has more than fifty differences in punctuation
and spelling and the following variants:

  1 saintly] mildest
  2 slender cape and broadening] cape and fair Floridian
  6 And] Or
  19 Beneath] Under
  47 them there tall Palmettos] them Palmettos
  51 Hot Gulf] Gulf breeze

TO RICHARD WAGNER (102-103)

Clover (text adopted) has subtitle, "A Dream of the Age," canceled, and
one variant before correction, *great 〉 high* (l. 17). *1884* agrees with *Clover*
except for two careless errors: *halls* for *horns* (l. 25), *magic* for *tragic* (l. 35).
(MS *CL* is a copy in another hand and without authority.) *Galaxy* (Nov.,
1877—on the accuracy of its text see letter of Nov. 3, 1877) has the subtitle
and the following variants and rejected stanzas:

  8 high] big
  8† The workmen drove by night and snored by day:
    Young Force was fain to mould all nature new;
    Art, raging to reverse each fair old way,
    Poor Epileptic! her sad circle drew
    All zigzag— puled and laughed when she should pray
    When tongues accented life's large Word untrue—
    Shouted the trifling prefix, Time, full high,
    But slurred th' Eternal Syllable, in a sigh.

9 the furnaces] that flame of Trade; seemed] was
12 farthest] furthest
16 mind] hand; me] us
20 This] The
22 did] had
26 Strike through] Open
32 ancient] foreign
35 magic] tragic
37 grief, and love] care, love, lust
40† Now marvels fall: each shape of yon wild Past
   Dissolves, as cloud will melt away with cloud,
   In later kindred type; the modern Last
   Explains the antique First; a mighty crowd
   Of gods and powers and ancient secrets vast
   New-live in steam and crank and lever loud:
   The large Norse forces smile to man, as mild
   As tender giants to a little child.
   Then, in my dream, those accidents of sight
   Passed into heaving: life was turned to sound:
   I heard the voice of ancient day and night
   With later voices swell, so linked and bound
   That never any ear could part aright
   Those threads of tune that each through other wound:
   And yet, O mystery of mysteries!
   All seemed to sing one Fugue in many keys.
   Grim songs of sinews, metals and blown fires
   Roared as from hot clay furnace-throats expressed;
   Deep hymns, of knights' and ladies' dear desires,
   Dull hearts of smiths and clerks made manifest;
   The lissome strings of Greek and Hebrew lyres
   Twang'd out the modern Theme; East uttered West;
   Pale girls by spinning spools in factories
   Sang Elsa's woes and Brünhild's passionate pleas.
46 wave] ware *misprint*

SONG OF THE CHATTAHOOCHEE (103-104)

The reputed early printing in *Scott's Magazine* (1877), as preserved by
Painter (see note), has the following variants:
3 I hurry amain] The hurrying rain
4 Run] Has run; leap] leapt
6 Accept my] Accepted his
7 flee] fled
15 laving laurel] laurel, slow-laving
17 work] win
21 o'er] over
34 Did bar] Barred
35 And many a metal lay sad, alone
36 And the crystal that prisons a purple mist
37 And the diamond, the garnet, the amethyst *36-37 reversed*
38 Showed lights like my own from each cordial stone
43 Shall hinder the rain from attaining the plain
44 Downward] For downward

47 myriad flowers] thousand meadows
48 lordly] final
50 Calls] And

Independent (Dec. 20, 1883) has two variants that were probably misprints: *loving* for *laving* (l. 15) ; *or* for *and* (l. 37) ; both were corrected in *1884.*

TO OUR MOCKING BIRD (117-118)

A rough draft of part of the first sonnet is written on the back fly-leaves of a copy of Lucy Aiken's *Memoirs of the Court of Queen Elizabeth* (Philadelphia, 1823), inscribed " Sidney Lanier / New York, May, 1878," surviving in Lanier's library (*JU*), and probably written by him during his return trip from New York to Baltimore, end of May, 1878. Three of the lines are illegible; the other three show the following variants: *whistled wit* for *shrewdest whistle-wit* (l. 1) ; *deep* for *grave* (l. 2) ; and *tones* for *songs* (l. 7). MS *CL,* " To Bob Mockingbird / (Died May 9th 1878) / Sidney Lanier / 33 Denmead St. / Baltimore / Md.," is an early draft with the following alterations and variants:

4 Drift] Faint
6 And sing] Obscure
18 Where very love was vigilant, and passed
19 Within, and bore away full fast, full fast
21 some] a
22 stretched] reached
28 our] my *twice*
29 Not so, found Grief: thou wrongest God's own right ⟩ Nay, Bird; fond
    grief doth wrong ⟩ *final form*
30 Surely the Lord at some late ⟩ *final form*
31 Would fain have Heaven's woods all set ⟩ *final form*
33 Bird of my delight ⟩ fresh from death's despite
38 Till Shakspere, Dante, undeaf Beethoven ⟩ *final form*
39 (Who talk together) lift ⟩ 'Midst of much talk uplift
41 And pause upon some large sweet ⟩ *final form*
42 my ⟩ thou

THE MARSHES OF GLYNN (119-122)

The version printed in *A Masque of Poets* (1878) and *Poems of Places* (1879) has the following variants:

22 is a-wait] doth wait
34 miles] width
42 leaning] bending
45 Bending] Swinging
72-77 greatness] favor *4 times*
77 is the greatness] for the largeness
78 The] Is the
92 westward] nestward

OPPOSITION (130-131)

A draft of the theme lines survives on the same MS (*CLᵃ*) with Poem Outline No. 38: " Frets of my soul as frets upon a lute / That true the string unto his nicest note." Two MSS survive: *CL*, untitled, undated, and unsigned, is an early draft with numerous alterations and variants and the first and last stanzas missing (but with their refrain written down the margin: " The fret, the dark, the thorn, the chill "); *ET*, signed " Sidney Lanier / 180 St. Paul St. / Baltimore, / Md.," is a revision with further alterations and variants:

3 Direct] But shape *ET*
5 The fret of brass that runs across > The stern (> lute's) fixt fret, that runs athwart *CL*
6 The aim and striving of the strings > *final form   CL*
7 For] To *CL*
8 Doth > Gives > Restricts his passive (> wilful) wavering *CL*
10 divinest] the saintly > hallowed > helpful > divinest *CL*
12 heavenly] mighty *CL*
13 With blood that's shed > That thorns do shed in strife *CL* > When sharp doth stab the thorn of strife *CL, ET*
14 I'll] I'll > Then; my] my > thy *ET*
15 In > With *CL*
16 issues] tricklings *CL*; the] my > the *ET*
17 Take profit, Soul, from every chill *CL*; I'll > Yea thaw out grace from every chill *ET*
18 Of dank defeat and sleety scorn *CL*; Of cold neglect and stupid scorn *ET*
19 The good that lies congealed in ill > Tis Good that lies a-cold in Ill *CL*; What Good lies frozen fast in Ill *ET*
20 This earth was late from glaciers born > This rosy Age *CL* > This Age of flowers is glacier-born *CL, ET*
23 Pattern the boundary-hating will *ET*

OWL AGAINST ROBIN (131-133)

Two undated MSS survive: *CL*, a rough draft in pencil, untitled and unsigned, but in Lanier's handwriting; and *JU*, a revision in ink, signed " Sidney Lanier / Rockingham Springs, Near McGaheysville, Virginia." They have the following alterations and variants:

3 Wrongly] Rudely; rudely of] and daytime *CL*
7 or] or > and *CL*
10 chatter > whistle *CL*
11 Who is it peeps and what is > O, why peep if you will, and buy, if 'tis cheap *CL*
12 for an owl must sleep] for the love of the lord > and be still > let other folk sleep *CL*
13 and who shall be first] Fame fell the first *CL*
14 For the day (*illegible*) and the summer is curst > Each day's the same yet the last was (> is) the worst *CL*; yet the last is] but the last was *JU*
15 lunatic burst > silly outburst *CL*
16 Of idiot red-breasts] Of the idiot red-breasted *CL*
17 birds] owls *CL*
19 Fools *canceled*; heard] learned *CL*
20 Night is for song-time and work-time and play-time > Night's for activity— work-time or play-time *followed by one line illegible and canceled*, *CL*; Night's for activity, work-time or play-time *JU*
22 The vulgar day (> flaunt), the staring (> flaring) day *CL*
23 hideous > impudent *CL*
24 blot > stain; blot > secret *CL*
25 Publishing crime and gossiping bold > Of the Publisher-day > Day the reporter,—the gossip of old *CL*

27 Ho! let ⟩ Poh, shut *CL*

28 day] the day *CL*; has] doth *CL, JU*

31 Day's deadly: emit with (⟩ Look how) the stroke of the sun ⟩ Day kills. The leaf and the laborer breathe *CL*; Day kills] Day's deadly *JU*

32 cities] marshes *followed by one line illegible and canceled, CL*

35 faint ⟩ taint *CL*

36 That the ⟩ But the ⟩ That the sun can whisper ⟩ That lies in the sun, even Grace will taint ⟩ And religion will fail and virtue faint ⟩ (Philosophers say) and Religion grow faint *CL*

37 has] hath *CL, JU*

39 The loveliest land seems tame at noon (⟩ at noon looks tame) ⟩ For the mischievous sun, like a tongue ⟩ The loveliest land at noon, how tame *CL* ⟩ At noon the loveliest land shows tame *CL, JU*

40 Unshadowed, unmodest, tedious ⟩ Shadowless, brazen, the same and the same *CL*

41 For] For ⟩ Thus; there ⟩ now *CL*

42 Like the black mischievous tongue ⟩ As a tongue that tells us what ⟩ Reporting the *what,* withholding the *how* ⟩ *final form CL*

43 As a mischievous messenger ⟩ As the true-false messenger oft makes moan ⟩ As the true-false messenger mischief has sown ⟩ *final form CL*

44 but never ⟩ withholding *CL*

46 Of the tense (⟩ still), divine (⟩ the rare ⟩ the fine) Patrician (⟩ fastidious) night *CL*

47 But, Ah, to awake in the evening glow ⟩ And Oh to awake (⟩ How fine to wake) with the age (⟩ wise) old stars *CL*

48 The careful cultured (⟩ and polished) concealing stars *CL*; The cultured, concealing, and careful stars *JU*

49 *omitted CL*; work-a-day] teasing *JU*

50 That shine with a shadow ⟩ And shine so fair through the ruins of time *followed by two lines illegible and canceled, CL*

51 Baalbec is finer] Baalbec's better *CL*

52 How fine ⟩ What fun to sit where the ⟩ Where bark is rotten and moss is gray ⟩ How rare to sit on the splinters ⟩ *final form CL*

53 By the woodland pool, and mope and mow *last 4 words canceled, CL*

54 And hoot at the fools that bow ⟩ *final form CL*

55 Down to the silly sun, and then ⟩ *final form CL*

56 To flit from the woods to the dreams of men ⟩ *final form CL*

57 A (*illegible*) dreamer lies ⟩ A day-worn sleeper dreams of care *CL*

58 And stand on the sill, and stare and (⟩ straightly) stare *CL*; And perch] And stand *JU*

59 Into hidden (⟩ Into his) visions, thence (⟩ rare) to sail *CL*; Through] Into *JU*

60 Down (⟩ Aslant with) the hill and over (⟩ a-curve with) the dale *CL*

61 To] And; down] in; gleam] beam *CL*

62 Betwixt] 'Twixt *JU*

63 Hither, thither] Hither and thither *CL*

64 aimless, dayless] dayless, aimless *CL*

65 Why should I sepak of the eating (⟩ meals) of field-mice slain ⟩ *Aimless? Field-mice?* Well (⟩ True), they're slain *CL*

66 We night philosophers have *CL* ⟩ But the night-philosophy winks at pain *CL, JU*

67 Eats quick as it can and casts (⟩ drops) the bones *CL*

69 The death that all life hungrily feeds on ⟩ *final form CL*

69† O (> You) hush strenuous iterant
   Irrepressible garrulous maddening *both lines canceled, CL*
72† Leave off peeping and endless cheeping *CL, JU*
   At times when the fowls of culture are sleeping *CL*; At times when all
     fowls of high feather are sleeping *JU*
73 And *cannot* you walk now] And cultivate walking *CL, JU*

The variants in *JU* have been previously printed by the former owner of the
MS, Kenneth Rede, in the *American Collector*, III, 27-30 (Oct., 1926), with
the conclusion that the editor of *Scribner's* had taken considerable liberties with
Lanier's poem. The more tenable inference is that Lanier himself made the
final revisions in a third MS, now lost, or in proof sheets.

ODE TO THE JOHNS HOPKINS UNIVERSITY (133-135)

MS *JU*, signed " Sidney Lanier," undated but quite likely the version of the
poem read on Commemoration Day, Feb. 23, 1880, has numerous alterations
and variants (first page reproduced in Starke, facing 364). Two sets of galley
proofs survive (*JU*ᵃ and *JU*ᵇ) with corrections in ink by Lanier, clearly for
printing in the *Circular* (Apr., 1880): the former bears the date, in pencil,
"March 9," and is apparently the first proof, agreeing before correction with
the MS except in a few words (first page reprdouced in Starke, facing 366);
the latter is a revise, agreeing after correction with the *Circular*. (J. C. French,
"First Drafts of Lanier's Poems," *Modern Language Notes*, XLVIII, 27-31
(Jan., 1933), mentions all three versions and prints a few of the revisions.)
1884, which follows *Circular*, has one variant from the final form. A full collation follows:

3 mothers] *Matres, JU, JU*ᵃ, *JU*ᵇ, *1884*
6 has] hath *JU*
7 This] Such *3 times JU, JU*ᵃ, *JU*ᵇ > This *JU*ᵇ; faithful> fruitful *misprint?*
  *JU*ᵃ
8 Though born > Howbeit she was born *JU*
9 In quiet like the > Unnoised as any stealing summer morn *JU*
10 *written as l. 8 in JU, JU*ᵃ > *final order in JU*ᵃ
11 They came and ministered to her *JU, JU*ᵃ > *final form JU*ᵃ
12 Led by the] Led on by *JU, JU*ᵃ, *JU*ᵇ > Led by the *JU*ᵇ
13 That earlier] By him that *JU, JU*ᵃ > E'en him that *JU*ᵃ, *JU*ᵇ > That
  earlier *JU*ᵇ
14 strong > locked *JU*
17 So] Lo *JU*
26 With flowers of such as keep] They brought her flowers, of such as
  keep *JU, JU*ᵃ > With flowers of such as keep *JU*ᵃ
39 helps] gifts *JU, JU*ᵃ > helps *JU*ᵃ
40 And hope and faith, by guardian spirits brought *JU, JU*ᵃ > *final form JU*ᵃ
45 slow] old *JU, JU*ᵃ, *JU*ᵇ > slow *JU*ᵇ
46 did Time have > Time had no *JU*
47 bloom > spring > bloom *JU*
50 she began] to begin *JU, JU*ᵃ > she began *JU*ᵃ
55 finer] later *JU, JU*ᵃ > finer *JU*ᵃ
70 nobler] larger *JU, JU*ᵃ > nobler *JU*ᵃ
72 larger] milder *JU, JU*ᵃ > larger *JU*ᵃ
77 Till thou the freedom] The freedom *JU, JU*ᵃ > *final form JU*ᵃ
81 shall] doth *JU, JU*ᵃ > shall *JU*ᵃ
82 In] I' the *JU, JU*ᵃ > In *JU*ᵃ

86 unmaniac] restoréd *JU, JUᵃ* ⟩ unmaniac *JUᵃ*
93 undissembling] sure and level *JU, JUᵃ* ⟩ undissembling *JUᵃ*
98 See how this Pallas blessed her Baltimore *JU, JUᵃ* ⟩ *final form JUᵃ*

THE CRYSTAL (136-139)

The germ of this poem has survived in the form of a Poem Outline (MS *CL*):

I forgive thee the rape and blood, David,
I forgive thee thy lusts and [*illegible*], Solomon,
I forgive thee rout and riot, Shakspere,
    thee fable and ass's stupidity, Homer,
    thee absurdity and grim lack of deep smiles, Milton,

But oh, my sweet One, O my dear One,
My fair lord whom Pilate loved not
    But John loved.
What freckle spots thy lily Soul,
What flaw is in thy framed whole,
That asks my pardon? None, none.
Naught's to forgive in thee, my Love, my Only One.

Two other MSS survive: *HA,* undated but signed " Sidney Lanier / 435 N. Calvert St. / Baltimore, / Md.," agrees with the text adopted (*Independent,* July 15, 1880) ; *CL,* unsigned and undated, is an earlier draft. All contained 12 introductory lines, rejected from the present edition by Lanier's authority, but reproduced below (unnumbered) from the text of *1884,* with alterations and variants from *CL*:

At midnight, death's and truth's unlocking time *1884*
When far within the spirit's hearing rolls *1884*; far] deep; the spirit's] the sense of ⟩ our inmost *CL*
The great soft rumble of the course of things *1884*; great soft] soft great *CL*
A bulk of silence in a mask of sound *1884*; bulk of] mighty ⟩ bulk of *CL*
When darkness clears our vision that by day *1884*; When] And *CL*
Is sun-blind, and the soul's a ravening owl *1884*
For truth and flitteth here about *1884*
Low-lying woody tracts of time and oft *1884*; Low-lying woody] The trees of time ⟩ Low-lying woody *CL*
Is minded for to sit upon a bough *1884*
Dry-dead and sharp of some long-stricken tree *1884*
And muse in that gaunt place,—'twas then my heart *1884*; 'twas then my heart] 'twas there I cried ⟩ at such a time ⟩ 'twas then my soul *CL*
Deep in the meditative dark, cried out *1884*; cried out] my soul ⟩ exclaimed ⟩ cried out *CL*

MS *CL* then shows the following alterations and variants from the text of the poem as adopted:

4 O seers and sweetest ⟩ Sweet seers and stellar
6 How bright ye burn, how heavenly bright, my stars ⟩ *final form*
9 heinous] palpable
10 not one but] or else doth
11 opaqued with] athwart some
19† And would 'twere more, that more my love might work
20 Small curious] O'er-curious
23 Which] That
38 Thy sleazy] And slazy

42 Thee, also dear and ⟩ Thou dear and very
43 Thine unclean cloak, and bearish carriage rude ⟩ *final form*
44 was ⟩ were; and ⟩ thy
46 Thee ⟩ So; will forgive ⟩ pardon thee
47 to offer ⟩ for needy
52 boil ⟩ burn
64 So, unto] Likewise
66 freely] thee will
69 hearts] souls
73 Whiles] Oft
75 touch] jot
79 And singing sterterous, as cowherds may that sleep ⟩ *final form*
80 In straw among the cattle ⟩ *final form*
82 sometimes] at times
90 But thee, O manful Man, O tender Heart ⟩ *final form*
91 breathed ⟩ writ
92 Friend ⟩ King
93 more or less ⟩ if or yet

THE CLOUD (139-141)

Three MSS survive. *JT* is a copy, probably by *MDL,* with the title " The Cloud " canceled and " Individuality " substituted, but otherwise agreeing with the text adopted. *JU* is an untitled rough draft of stanzas 1, 2, 10, the interlude, 13, and 17 (with stanza 2 of " Marsh Song— At Sunset " included), written on the fly-leaves of Lanier's copy of the Bohn Library edition of the *Discourses of Epictetus* (London, 1877), i-ii, 440-441, purchased on Apr. 11, 1879 (Turnbull & Bros. statement, *CL*), with numerous alterations and variants. *CL,* the text adopted, shows variants before correction. *1884,* for which no authority has been found, is entitled " Individuality," and has variants in five lines. (*Century,* Dec., 1882, agrees with *1884* except for omission of ll. 13-15 and 67-71, and is not included.) A full collation follows:

1-5 Come on,
    Sail on, sail on, fair Cousin Cloud,
    Come on and ⟩ Come brood upon the marsh with me.
    Still ⟩ Dream ⟩ Gray-eyed and shadow brow'd,
    Mist
    Film *JU*
  5† Over ⟩ Above the humped and fishy sea
    Slow think thyself along,
    Above the growling Caliban sea,
    White Ariel, dream thyself along.
    And ⟩ Above the ⟩ Quite unafraid above the fearsome sea
    all circled for omission and later used in " Marsh Song " JU
6-10 And heartseas'd still for straining mast ⟩ Heartseas'd for all yon straining
    sail
    And laboring smoke that not for thee
    Bear ventures, o'er the treacherous vast (⟩ while thy soul is pale)
    Of risk and tease and bottomry ⟩ With teasing risk and bottomry *JU*
12 self ⟩ lock *CL*
13 Wept for my fellows woes ⟩ *final form* CL
14 Though most ⟩ Part for *CL*
15 Strait-lace so many ⟩ In issue bind such *CL*

16 Dark 〉 Stern *CL*; Stern] Lo *1884*
21-25 *stanza 5 originally written between stanzas 8 and 9 CL*
26 Though this 〉 Yet though *CL*
33 stormy] storming *1884*
39 of rain] with winds *1884*
47 Yon 〉 Some *CL*
67-71 The maker's greater than his song 〉 The maker's 〉 The Lord of all's
       too rich to covet one 〉 The maker's Lord's too great and strong
       To covet goods of one that He Himself
       Hath made his neighbor.
       For if, O Lord, they rob me of my songs 〉 What can I give thee? Piteous
           (*illegible*) farce
       To think Thee giving to Thyself through me! *JU*
83 thou 〉 mad *CL*; mad] on *1884*
86 is it all] matters it *1884*
88 Discharge] Go work 〉 Fulfill *JU*; Fulfill 〉 Discharge *CL*
91 Sure of my Father and myself (〉 my Lord, my Self, our Love, 〉 the Lord,
       of Self, and Love 〉 the Lord, of Me, of Love) alone *JU*; Sure of the
       Lord, of Self, of Love 〉 *final form CL*

[BETWEEN DAWN AND SUNRISE] (142)

The version printed in *Independent* (Apr. 30, 1891) and reprinted in *1891*
differs widely, except in l. 2, from the text adopted, but no authority has been
found for it. From the incomplete rhyme in the second stanza it seems to be
an earlier draft; it is given entire following:

       Were silver pink, and had a soul,
           Which soul were shy, which shyness might
       A visible influence be, and roll
           Through heaven and earth— 'twere thou, O light!

       O rhapsody of the wraith of red,
           O blush but yet in prophecy,
       O sun-hint that hath overspread
           Sky, marsh, my soul, and yonder sail.

SUNRISE (144-149)

The first draft, on "pale blue leaves faintly penciled" (see note), has not
come down. Three MSS survive: *RL,* the final version (and the text adopted),
has one variant before correction: *sunshine 〉 great Sun* (l. 129); *CL,* a copy
in the handwriting of J. B. Tabb, agrees with this; *JT,* entitled "Hymns of
the Marshes. / II. / Sunrise," undated and with the signature cut away, is the
intermediate version, with the following rejected lines, alterations, and variants
(see facsimile facing p. 275, vol. X):,

1 that 〉 their
4 A (〉 Much) glory of breadth from the marshes, exhaled with a land-
       ward sweep 〉 Soft message of breadth from the marshes, sweep and
       (〉 on) sweep
5 And (〉 All) inwove with wild sea-liberties, inland drifting 〉 Soft lisp
       (〉 wafture) of wild sea-liberties, landward drifting
9 glooming 〉 hid in
14 Then the 〉 The

15 my beloved! I might not abide] ere the dawn has, Beloved! to hide〉
   my Beloved! my Live-Oaks!〉 *final form*
16 O] my
17 In your gospelling darks (〉 shadows 〉 glooms), my live-oaks (〉 to
   tremble and hide)
17† Oh, and to be
   By your beauty 〉 O marsh and sea
18 As a lover alone with you, my marsh, my sea 〉 *final form*
20 dost know] tell me, dost know
27 velvety 〉 dull-tissued
28 vague blackness] vast vagueness
31 dark] blank
36 Designs in the under-dark knowledge hath brought me
37 So ye have taught me
41 Ye] Blest
43 your] the
48 river] valley
54 This owlet that 〉 An owlet out of the low-hanging bough
55 But now
56 As I brushed it hath whirred 〉 As I brushed it, stirred
57† *"A Ballad of Trees and the Master," untitled, follows*
66 darkness, light, the heart, the eye 〉 sanity
69 could] would
70 haunt] be
71 About these margins of the marsh and sea
71† Deafened with *mine and thine,* with *out and in,*
   With noises Christians make, to drown their sin
   Of war, of party, and of winking wealth,—
   Here, steeped in rest, thine ear may have his health.
   Yea, richer ministries (〉 essences) of freedom sweep (〉 haunt)
   About these margins of the marsh, the deep 〉 About these margins
   ministrant
74 when] for
75 No man with room enough, and girth (〉 or grace) of bound
76 and art 〉 thou art
98 marvellous 〉 mystery
100 of dawn 〉 made
101 Is a rumor about, of dawn 〉 *final form*
105 heart] soul are quick; are] is
122 palpable-bright 〉 unwithdrawn
123 Sweet Baptist, prepar'st thou the way of the light? 〉 O Heaven, be
   careful! (〉 have care!) How delicate-fair this Dawn *and one line below*
   take heed! it is done, it is Dawn.
123† *"Between Dawn and Sunrise," untitled, follows*
124 Now] But
127 the Bee] of dazzling gold is the Bee
128 build-fire] builder
129 *omitted*
130 flash] flash full soon
131 Yet] But
132 live] have
133 Or ever they pass away
145 unjarring, unreeling] not whelmed, not reeling

150 my] the
158† *"To the Sun,"* *untitled, follows*
159 Thou] O *twice*
160 Laborer] artisan
161 sea's] sea is
163 perfectest hues] simile-hues
168 Thou] O
172 globe of ⟩ globèd
173 bright] more bright
175 I must pass from the face of my lord, from the face of the sun
176 Wants are griding, hunger and cold are at frown
179 I am strong, I am strong with the strength of my lord the sun
182 run] running
191 lord ⟩ friend

1884 has five words variant, probably misreadings of MS *RL* which it otherwise follows: *waftures* for *wafture* (l. 5); *charity* for *clarity* (l. 64, corrected in *1885*); *moon* for *morn* (l. 135, corrected in *1885*); *the* for *thy* (l. 175, corrected in *1885*); and *politics* for *polities* (l. 186).

TO OUR HILLS (166-167)

In addition to the text adopted (*Ledger* 256, 259), four other MSS survive: *CL*, entitled " Our Hills " and signed " Sidney Lanier," is undated but apparently the earliest draft; *SL* and *Ledger* 246, 249 (here collated as *L*), both signed " Sidney Lanier / Macon, July 14, 1867," are also early drafts—all three lacking two stanzas and following a different order for the other six: 1, 3, 4, 5, 2, 9. *Ledger* 439, without title, date, or signature, is a draft of the last three stanzas only (here collated as *L*ª). They have the following alterations and variants:

2 giant] Titan *CL*
3 thy] your *CL, SL, L*
4 to lie] and dry *CL, SL, L* ⟩ to lie *L*
5 And] To *CL, SL, L* ⟩ And *L*
6 But] O *CL*; Good *SL, L*
7 giant] Titan *CL*
8 Thy mother's-milk is curdled with aloe *CL, SL, L* ⟩ thick with woe *L*
9 Like hills, Men, lift calm heads through any woe *CL, SL, L* ⟩ Aye ⟩ final form *L*
10 And weep, but bow not an inch for any foe *CL, SL, L* ⟩ final form *L*
11 Mark yon] O ye *CL, SL*; Ye red ⟩ Mark the *L*
13 them was all shed] you has all bled *CL*; you was all bled *SL*; you ⟩ them was all shed *L*
14 them] you *CL, SL, L* ⟩ them *L*
15 them] you *CL, SL, L* ⟩ them *L*
16 O ye] And O *CL*
20 Of days that stained your robes with stains like these *CL, SL, L* ⟩ Of bridal green ⟩ final form *L*
21 Sleep on, ye hills *CL*; Sleep on, O hills *SL*; Sleep on, O (⟩ sad ⟩ my) ⟩ final form *L*
22 Weep on, ye rills *CL*; Weep on, O rills *SL*; Weep on, O (⟩ sad) ⟩ final form *L*
24 What clement] They chain the *CL, SL, L* ⟩ final form *L*; stains] stains ⟩ blood *L*

25 They wait with cold hearts will we " rue the day " *CL, SL, L* 〉 **Are** chained to make us " rue the day " *L*

26-35 *omitted CL, SL, L*

26 O] O 〉 Thou *L*[a]

28 How dared you after adverse battle smite 〉 That, after honorable war, didst (〉 couldst) smite *L*[a]

29 Cheeks grimed with honorable battle (〉 war) poor (〉 girl-) spite 〉 *final form L*[a]

30 For dainty Senators] Of dainty senators (〉 congressmen) 〉 For dainty Congressmen *L*[a]

31 O monstrous crime] O monstrous joke 〉 Thou monstrous crime *L*[a]

·32 Of a sick Time] Of a crazy folk 〉 Of the mad (〉 sick) Time *L*[a]

35 all 〉 down *L*[a]

38 Thou hast no hell-deep chasm save disgrace *CL, SL, L*

39 To stoop will fling us down its fouléd space *CL, SL, L*; And will the sweet Right never 〉 And will the Right forever wear disgrace 〉 And 〉 *final form L*[a]

40 Stand proud! The Dawn will meet us face to face *CL, SL, L*; Will 〉 Shall Hope stay *always* only with the base *L*[a]

40† For ever the top-rocks, yonder 〉 For down the steepest hills 〉 For down steep hills the dawn loves best to race *CL*

1916, the first printing, follows *CL* after correction.

NILSSON (196-197)

Ledger 416, an early draft (see notes), differs so radically from the final form it is given here entire:

> A rose of perfect red, embossed
> With silver sheens of crystal frost,
> Yet warm, nor life nor fragrance lost;
>
> High passion-breathing in a sphere
> That Art hath wrought of diamond clear:
> A great heart beating in a tear:
>
> Star-sparkles caught in rain-drops round
> And pattered daintily a-ground
> With hints of heaven in the sound:
>
> Large noble wind-tones chanting free
> Through morning-skies across the sea
> Wild hymns to some strange majesty:
>
> (Or, if one trope, clear-cut and keen,
> May type the art of Art's best queen,
> So chaste in skill, so warm in mien)
>
> On Music's heart doth Nilsson dwell
> As if a Swedish snow-flake fell
> Into a glowing flower-bell!

A SONG (213)

MS *JT,* entitled "The White Veil," undated and unsigned but in Lanier's handwriting of 1866 or earlier, is a first draft of the opening stanza. In a different stanza form, with the metaphor put to a personal rather than an abstract application, this is apparently Sidney Lanier's original contribution (undoubtedly addressed to Mary Day):

> The Stars grow pale, behind the silver veil
> Of day, that God draws o'er them.
> O Sweet my Star, *thine* eyes seem brighter far
> For this white veil before them.

Ledger 30, dated " March 1866 " and signed " Clifford and Sidney Lanier," is the first form of the collaboration (MS *CL,* inclosed in Lanier's letter of Mar. 26, 1866, and an unidentified print in *JT,* agree with this). Though in Sidney's handwriting, it may be conjectured from the form of the signature that Clifford's share was a large one. Since it differs from the final form in 12 out of 18 lines, it is given here entire:

> Day is a silver veil
> God draws across the Stars.
> Night is the old Earth's wail
> From out her prison-bars.
> Life is an obscure tale
> Of wild but needless wars.
>
> The dazzling day destroys
> The mellow lights of truth.
> Night shouts, with a loud noise
> The cry of sinful ruth.
> Life's vague reward decoys
> The strong right arm of Youth.
>
> Ere long, through noon-day fire
> Truth's Stars shine all the time.
> Night's grief and groan and ire
> Change to an Angel's chime.
> Life's aimless, strong desire,
> In God, finds rest sublime.

Ledger 279, signed " Sidney and Clifford Lanier," undated, is a revised version made in Prattville, 1868 (the nearest dated entry, p. 278, is Feb. 25, 1868). It is in Sidney's handwriting, and from the form of the signature and the fact that they were living apart at the time, it may be conjectured that the revisions are his. It agrees with the final form (*Southern Magazine,* July, 1871) except for the following alterations and variants:

> 5 chequered 〉 bridal
> 14 burn] shine
> 17 Life's wild 〉 Youth's veiled
> 18 God finds rest 〉 death finds God

THE POWER OF PRAYER (215-216)

An early MS draft has recently been published in W. R. Benjamin's *Collector* (June-July, 1945) with ll. 34-51 omitted and showing numerous variants (here collated as *WB,* with Mrs. Benjamin's permission) and several differences in spelling such as *hear* for *hyar. Scribner's* (June, 1875), besides several differences in spelling such as *Mah'sr* for *Marster* (unwarranted editorial changes according to Lanier's letter of May 27, 1875), has a few variants, three of which were retained probably by oversight in *1884.* A full collation follows:

> 2 De Lord, *He* made dese] My Jesus made dem *WB*
> 6 yonder] far off *WB*

 8 Dese] My; cracks] chinks *WB*
 9 Yea, God has built my cabin wid some windows 'hind and fore *WB*
10 my] de *WB*
12 show] shows; dey's] dey *WB*
14 dis] my *WB*
17 holl'in'] callin' *WB*
25 I'se pow'ful skeered] Good Lord, Good Lord *WB*
27 *You* screech, and howl, and swish de water, Satan! Let us pray *WB,*
       Scribner's
28 hebbenly] Jesus *WB*
31 Marster; for] O good Lord *WB*
32 to scramble up de homeyard] to start to climb upon de *WB*
33 traveller's] nigger's *WB*
34-51 *omitted in WB*
38 de] my *Scribner's, 1884*
39 I'se like a word dat somebody done said, and den forgotten *Scribner's;*
       somebody] dat somebody *1884*
43 but yet] but *misprint? 1884*
52 O glory hallelujah] Nor glory, glory, glory *WB*
53 he done gone flyin'] I hear him passin' *WB*
54 dat] de; felt my Marster] know'd my Lord was *WB*
55 didn'] could'n' *WB*
59 When folks *is* prayin', Jesus sets a-listenin' in de a'r *WB*
60 Yas] Yea; jes' 'ceptin'] exceptin' *WB, Scribner's*

All of these changes and the addition of the omitted lines in the final form
were presumably made by Sidney Lanier; there is no other evidence of the
respective shares of the two brothers in this collaboration.

NOTES

(For a key to the abbreviations used in the notes see p. 286, above. No annotations are given for persons, places, or events that are generally known or readily available in standard reference works, unless identification seemed necessary to an immediate understanding of the poem.)

ON READING OF ONE WHO DROWNED HERSELF (5)

Written at Oglethorpe University, Midway, Ga., Feb. 5, 1861. Apparently not published, but submitted by Lanier to an unidentified "Monthly" (see letter of Feb. 5, 1861).

Text: *Ledger* 10, signed "S. C. L.," undated, but probably 1865 since the Ledger was not begun until after the war (with period for dash, end of poem). MS *CL*, attached to letter of Feb. 5, 1861, the first draft, has one variant line.

This is the first poem of Lanier's known to have been intended for publication, but the early printing, if there was one, has not been found; it is quite possible, of course, that the letter inclosing it was never sent.

SPRING GREETING (5)

Written in prison at Point Lookout, Md., Dec., 1864.

Published anonymously in *Round Table*, III, 443 (July 14, 1866); reprinted with changes and addition of subtitle, "From the German of Herder," in *1884*, 225.

Text: *Round Table*. *Ledger* 9 (the text followed in *1884*), entitled "Translation of Herder's 'Spring-Greeting,'" signed "S. C. L.," and dated as above, has three minor variants. (An inaccurate copy survives in *MDL's* handwriting in her Notebook, p. 93, dated "Summer of /65," *CL*.) MS *CL*, an early literal translation, was included in Lanier's letter of July 1, 1864, and is printed in the present edition (VII, 155-156), along with translation of a quatrain from Tanner.

The first poem of Lanier's known to have been published, this is actually a free rendering of Heine's (not Herder's) "Neuer Frühling," VI, in *Neue Gedichte* (Hamburg, 1844), 9. (See Clifford Lanier's *Thorn-Fruit*, New York, 1867, 40, and note 29, Letters of 1864.) This and "Translation from the German of Heine" (154), both of which are in the nature of original compositions merely based on the German originals, are the only two of Lanier's translations that are treated as poems in the present volume. He made a number of other more or less literal renderings, in prose and verse, with no intention of original poetic creation but for the specific purpose of presenting texts to the modern reader that would not otherwise be available to him, especially from Old and Middle English poems to illustrate various matters in his Peabody and Hopkins lectures and in *The Science of English Verse*. (See vols. II and III of the present edition; see also IV, 290, and the uncollected modernization of John Barbour's "Bruce" in *Music and Poetry*, New York, 1898, 212-248; see also the conclusion of the note to "To Richard Wagner," p. 354, below.)

THE TOURNAMENT: JOUST FIRST (6)

Probably written at Scott's Mills, near Macon, Ga., Aug., 1865.

Published in *Round Table*, V, 365 (June 8, 1867); reprinted without change, except for omission of subtitle, in *1884*, 226-227. (Salem Dutcher's letters of

July 12 and 30, and Lanier's letters of Sept. 11, 12, and 20, 1867, indicate that it was widely reprinted in contemporary newspapers.)

Text: *Round Table*. Four MSS survive: *JT*[a] and *CL*, both undated; *Ledger* 11, signed " S. C. L." and dated " Summer 1865 " in *MDL's* handwriting; and *JT*[b], inclosed in letter of Sept. 1, 1865, entitled " Love and Duty." (MS *HF* is a copy in the handwriting of Clifford Lanier.) They show several minor variants, but agree with each other. A revised version was used over ten years later in " Psalm of the West " (see p. 79, above).

Lanier gave a copy of this poem to Mary Day on Aug. 13, 1865 (see her letter of Aug. 7 and his letters of Sept. 1, 1865, and Oct. 27, 1866). It was apparently just written and was, at least in part, a symbol of their misunderstanding and parting; on Oct. 31, 1866, he wrote to her: " Dost thou remember that a little more than one year ago . . . my brain took steely fingers and clasped them about my heart and strangled it to death, at *thy* bidding! " (See also notes 38 and 52, Letters of 1866, 1867, and Mary Day's verse reply, " The Bequest," sent to him at the time of their reconciliation, and printed in VII, 293-294.) No authority has been found for the date in *1884*, " Camp French, Wilmington, N. C. / May, 1862," nor for the notation on MS *CL* in the handwriting of *MDL*, " sent from the battle-ground, in 1863 "; but it is possible that a lost early draft was written during the war, for the poem is used as an allegory of the conflict between North and South in " Psalm of the West." Clifford Lanier wrote to his mother, Jan. 7, 1864, of attending a " grand tournament and coronation ball " at Kinston, N. C., at which his brother was probably present also. Certainly Lanier was familiar with this traditional southern game long before the occasion many years later when he is said to have made the address to the knights (see note 52, Letters of 1879).

THE TOURNAMENT: JOUST SECOND (6-8)

Written in Macon, June, 1867 (see letter of June 15).

Published in *Round Table*, VI, 13 (July 6, 1867); reprinted, with one change and with subtitle omitted, in *1884*, 227-229.

Text: *Round Table*. No authority has been found for the variant in *1884*, *Cried Love, unarmed, yet dauntless there* (l. 22). No other variants known.

TO J. L. (8)

Written at Scott's Mills, near Macon, Ga., Oct., 1865.

Published anonymously in *Round Table*, III, 443 (July 14, 1866); reprinted with a few changes in *Independent*, XLVI, 849 (July 5, 1894), entitled erroneously " In 1865 / To J. L. / An Unpublished Poem." Previously uncollected.

Text: *Round Table*. Three MSS survive: *Ledger* 21, " To Janie Lamar from S. C. L.," dated " Scott's Mills, Oct. 1865 "; *JT*[a], " To ———," and *JT*[b], " To Janie Lamar " (both unsigned and undated, but latter inclosed in Gertrude Lanier's letter to Clifford, Oct. 15, 1865). They agree in showing three minor variants, the text followed in *Independent* (with one further change for which no authority has been found: *this our* for *our*, l. 6).

Addressed to Jane Taliaferro Lamar of Orange Court House, Va., the widow of Lanier's friend John Hill Lamar, who had been killed in battle in 1864. (She later married Lanier's brother-in-law, Harry Day.)

LITTLE ELLA (9)

Written in Montgomery, May 10, 1866.
Published as sheet music by R. W. Offutt & Co., Montgomery, Ala., title-page: " Little Ella. A Beautiful Ballad / Dedicated to / Ella S. Montgomery / by her friend / S. C. Lanier / May 10, 1866." The date is apparently that of composition; it was published in the spring of 1868 (see review in New Orleans *Picayune*, Mar. 19, 1868). Printed as a poem without music as " To ———," in *Mid Continent*, VI, 86 (May, 1895). Previously uncollected.
Text: sheet music (set in stanzas). *Ledger* 57, " To Ella Montgomery. / With Music. By Sidney Lanier," and *Mid Continent* have a few minor variants.
Lanier set several of his own poems to music, but this is the only one for which both words and music have been found. The dedicatee (see illustration, VII, facing 379) was the small daughter of his friend Mrs. Mattie Montgomery.

A BIRTHDAY SONG. TO S. G. (9-10)

Written in Montgomery, Oct. 4, 1866; revised in Macon, July 15, 1867.
Published in *Round Table*, VI, 61 (July 27, 1867), dated " Macon, Ga., July 15, 1867 "; reprinted without change in *1884*, 219-220.
Text: *Round Table*. Three MSS survive: *JT*, entitled " To S. E. G.," with stanzes 9 and 11 missing, clearly the earliest version; *Ledger* 64-65, " To S. E. G. on her Birthday:— From S. C. L. / Montgomery, Ala. / Oct. 4th 1866 "; and *CL*, " To S. E. G. On Her Birthday: / From Her Friend, / Sidney Lanier," inclosed in a letter of Oct. 6 (?) 1866. They show a dozen or more variants, the most interesting of which is the following: in *CL* the last line reads, *Whereat two Pearl-Gates opened, fold on fold*; in *Ledger*, the same reading ⟩ *And whispered, ' Love, forever fair, is never old!'*
Addressed to Sallie Given, daughter of the lessee of the Exchange Hotel, Montgomery, where Lanier was a clerk. (MS *CL* contains a second poem, " To S. E. G. / with a copy of Tennyson," written by Clifford Lanier. The influence of Tennyson is apparent in both poems.)

TO CAPTAIN JAMES DEWITT HANKINS (10-11)

Written in Montgomery, Nov., 1866 (see both letters of Nov. 5).
Published posthumously in *Century*, XXXII, 378 (July, 1886), as " To J. D. H.," with the first and last stanzas omitted (on the advice of R. W. Gilder, the editor of *Century*, according to letter from Clifford Lanier to Virginia Hankins, Feb. 28, 1885); reprinted without change in *1891*, 156.
Text: MS *HF*, entitled " To Captain James DeWitt Hankins / Bacon's Castle, Virginia / Killed October 19th 1866— Aged 25 years " and signed " From His Friends / S. & C. L. / of Montgomery, Alabama." (There is no evidence that Clifford Lanier collaborated in writing the poem.) This MS is in the handwriting of Virginia Hankins, but is adopted as the basic text since it was written for her and since it is identical with the next two MSS, both dated " Nov. 1866 " and signed " Sidney Lanier," which seem like finished copies: MS *JTa*, entitled " To J. H."; and *Ledger* 66, entitled " To James Hankins," showing a few variants before correction, the most interesting of which is: *The generous stars fling me no gold* (l. 10). MS *JTb*, " To James Hankins," unsigned and undated, is an earlier draft with a few minor variants. The four stanzas in *1891* show only one variant, *wrinkled, old* for *wrinkle-old* (l. 10).

Lanier intended it for publication in the Richmond and Petersburg newspapers, as indicated in his letter to Virginia Hankins, Nov. 5, 1866, but no such printing has been found. (The following files have been searched: Richmond *Dispatch*, *Enquirer, Examiner, Times, Whig*, and others; Petersburg *Index*.) James Hankins, a friend of Lanier's when he was stationed at Ft. Boykin, 1863-1864, had been killed in a duel at Surry Court House, Va. The episode was romanticized many years later in a novel (C. E. Williams, *The Penalty of Recklessness; or, Virginia Society Twenty Years Ago*, Boston, 1884).

BARNACLES (11)

Written in Macon, July 16, 1867 (so dated in *Ledger* 245; the early prints are dated July 30, 1867).

Published in *Round Table*, VI, 312 (Nov. 9, 1867); reprinted without change in Montgomery *Weekly Mail*, Dec. 4, 1867; in J. W. Davidson, *Living Writers of the South* (New York, 1869), 322; and in *1884*, 235 (with misprint, *waters* for *water*, l. 10).

Text: *Round Table*. No variants known.

Ledger bears the early title: "Forgetting what is behind, press forward." Written at a time when the Old South had been destroyed by war and reconstruction, "Barnacles" is Lanier's challenge to the past. He wrote to his brother, Nov. 19, 1867, that the poem had been "highly applauded."

Just what Lanier had in mind by "sea-mells" (l. 4) cannot be determined for no record of such a word has been discovered (letter to the editor from M. M. Mathews, editor of the *Dictionary of American English*, Nov. 20, 1945).

A SONG OF ETERNITY IN TIME (12)

Written in Macon, July 20, 1867 (see *Ledger* 251); revised in Baltimore, probably Nov.-Dec., 1880 (apparently one of the "two little Songs just sent," mentioned in letter of Dec. 6 to W. H. Ward, editor of *Independent*).

Published in *XIX Century*, II, 708 (Feb., 1870), as "Eternity in Time"; revised version with present title published in *Independent*, XXXIII, 1 (Mar. 3, 1881); and reprinted without change in *1884*, 46.

Text: *Independent*. Two MSS survive; for a full collation of variants, including the early version, see p. 287, above.

The germ of the second stanza is contained in an essay on "Desire and Thought," *Ledger* 87, c. 1867-1868: "A colossal star may reproduce itself in the tear that one weeps under the skies at night: and so Man, who is mainly a tear, may hold the image of god shining, brokenly, within his bosom." Also (according to a memorandum in the handwriting of Clifford Lanier, *JT*), it was written on a flyleaf of Lanier's copy of Sir Michael Foster's *A Textbook of Physiology* (a volume now missing from his library) in the following form:

> I hold in my soul the whole thought of God
> As a drop of liquid no larger than a tear
> May hold in its bosom the image of a star, which is a world.

The poem may refer to Virginia Hankins (note 61, Letters of 1867).

IN THE FOAM (12-13)

Written in Prattville, Ala., Dec. 9, 1867.

Published in *Round Table*, VII, 60 (Jan. 25, 1868); reprinted with changes in *1884*, 234.

Text: *Round Table*, the version chosen by Lanier for publication, and apparently the latest revision. Two MSS survive, with a half-dozen minor variants:

Ledger 260, signed " S. L. / Prattville Ala. Dec. '67 " (the text used in *1884*);
CL, entitled " To M.," inclosed in Lanier's letter to Mary Day, Dec. 9, 1867
(the first draft).

The existence of a copy of this poem in *HF* suggests that it may have been
Lanier's farewell to Virginia Hankins on the eve of his marriage to Mary Day
(Dec. 19, 1867); for though in one draft (*CL*) it is entitled " To M.," it deals
in both mood and subject matter with a parting.

TYRANNY (13-14)

Written in Prattville, Ala., Jan. 23, 1868 (see letter of Jan. 24); revised
in 1879.

Published in *Round Table*, VII, 124 (Feb. 22, 1868), as " Spring and
Tyranny "; reprinted, with title and one word changed, in *1884*, 93-94.

Text: *Clover* 65, early print corrected, as IV of " Street-Cries " (see p. 359,
below). *1884* is apparently based on this text, but *MDL* failed to substitute
barren for *sickly* (l. 16) and *in your natal* for *with your dainty* (l. 18). Three
MSS survive: *JT*, *CL*, and *Ledger* 262-263, all signed " S. L." and bearing the
early title; the last two are dated " Jan. 23, 1868." They show three minor
variants in addition to those given above.

This is one of a group of poems dealing with the evils of Reconstruction (see
Introduction). The attitude towards commerce and industrialism—Prattville had
been a prosperous manufacturing town—is markedly different from Lanier's later
tirades against Trade (see especially " The Symphony ").

LAUGHTER IN THE SENATE (14)

Written in Prattville, Ala., Jan. 26, 1868.

Published in *Round Table*, VII, 236 (Apr. 11, 1868); reprinted without
change in Baltimore *Leader*, I, 1 (May 2, 1868); and in *1916*, 223.

Text: *Round Table*. *Ledger* 261, signed " S. L. Prattville Ala. / Jan'y 26th
1868," has five minor variants.

One of a group of poems dealing with the evils of Reconstruction (see Introduction). The denunciation in the concluding stanza is echoed in a public address
the following year, when Lanier referred to " the national Senate . . . mumming
and capering in clownish follies, utterly unrebuked " (V, 253, of the present
edition).

THE RAVEN DAYS (15)

Written in Prattville, Ala., Feb. 25, 1868 (as dated on a surviving MS).

Published in *Scott's Monthly*, VI, 873 (Dec., 1868); reprinted without change
in *Banner of the South*, I, 2 (Jan. 30, 1869), and *New Eclectic*, IV, 248 (Feb.,
1869); and with three changes in *1884*, 213.

Text: *Scott's Monthly*. Two MSS survive, one of which contains 28 rejected
lines; for a full collation see p. 288, above.

This is one of a group of poems dealing with the evils of Reconstruction (see
Introduction).

THE SHIP OF EARTH (15)

Probably written in Prattville, Ala., spring of 1868 (dated " Prattville, 1868 "
in *1884*; but in *Ledger* it follows " Resurrection," which was written in the
summer or early autumn after leaving there).

Published in *Round Table*, VIII, 328 (Nov. 14, 1868); reprinted with omission of first two stanzas in *1884*, 89.

Text: *Clover* 56, *Round Table* uncorrected, but with first two stanzas rejected, as II of " Street-Cries " (the text followed in *1884*). One MS survives entitled " Fear at Morning "; for a full collation of variants see p. 288, above.

This is one of a group of poems dealing with problems in the South during Reconstruction (see Introduction; see also letter of Jan. 30, 1867, for evidence of an autobiographical element).

LIFE AND SONG (16)

Probably written at Scott's Mills, near Macon, Ga., summer of 1868 (from evidence of publication date and the relationship of the poem to the facts of Lanier's life at this period): revised in 1879.

Published in *Round Table*, VIII, 157 (Sept. 5, 1868); reprinted without change in *Scott's Monthly*, VI, 718 (Oct., 1868); and in *New Eclectic*, III, 250 (Oct., 1868); revised version in *1884*, 94-95.

Text: *Clover* 66, *Round Table* print revised and numbered V of " Street-Cries " (the text followed in *1884*). " Life " and " Song " have been capitalized, l. 11. One MS survives; for a full collation of variants see p. 289, above.

Written at a time when untoward circumstances were turning Lanier aside from an incipient career as author, this poem may have found its germ in Milton's " he who would not be frustate of his hope to write well hereafter in laudable things, ought himself to be a true poem " (" Apology for Smectymnuus," *Works*, III, 303, Columbia Edition). Ironically, it was his first success, a favorite with anthologists, and widely copied at the time of its publication; in addition to the reprintings given above, may be cited the Atlanta *Constitution* and an unidentified Montgomery newspaper (clipping dated Sept. 13, 1868, *JT*, with an editorial note replying to an inquiry in the former as to the identity of the author).

RESURRECTION (16-17)

Probably written at Scott's Mills or Vineville, near Macon, Ga., late summer or early autumn, 1868 (from evidence of publication date and the reference to " early fall," l. 2).

Published in *Round Table*, VIII, 281 (Oct. 24, 1868); reprinted with changes in *1884*, 221.

Text: *Round Table* (with periods changed to commas, ll. 5, 7). *Ledger* 410, entitled " New Life," signed " S. L.," undated but in Lanier's handwriting of *c.* 1868, has ten minor variants (the text followed, with two changes, in *1884*).

The obscurity is due to the imperfect rendering of Lanier's depression, resulting from his illness and economic troubles (see note to " Life and Song," above). The variant title and l. 7 may owe something to the birth of Lanier's first son, Charles, on Sept. 12, 1868.

THE GOLDEN WEDDING OF STERLING AND SARAH LANIER (17-18)

Written in Macon, Sept., 1868 (see letter of Oct. 1).

Published in a pamphlet of four pages, bearing on the cover: " For / The Golden Wedding, *etc.* / September 27, 1868. / By the Eldest Grandson "; reprinted in *1884*, 207-208. (See also letter of Nov. 4, 1868, and note 55.)

Text: pamphlet (with misprint corrected, l. 35, by authority of a copy revised in Lanier's handwriting, *CL*). No other version known.

Sterling Lanier (1794-1870) and Sarah Vivian Fulwood (1803-1877) had been married in 1818. (See A. H. Starke and Lena Jackson, "New Light on the Ancestry of Sidney Lanier," *Virginia Magazine of History and Biography*, XLIII, 165-166, Apr., 1935.)

BETRAYAL (19)

Apparently written in Macon, autumn of 1868 (from position in *Ledger* 320, but see note to "The hound was cuffed," p. 375, below).

Published in *Lippincott's*, XVI, 711 (Dec., 1875); reprinted with two changes in *1877*, 87-88; and without further change in *1884*, 205.

Text: *1877*. Two MSS survive; for a full collation of variants see p. 289, above.

Intended as an intercalary song for "The Jacquerie" (see note, p. 375, below). But the point in the story where it was to be inserted was not reached in the fragment of that poem that has come down, as indicated by a prose note in Lanier's handwriting on "Betrayal," MS *JT*: "Sung by a peasant maiden to whom *the Duke* has made proposals: written for her by one Master Peter of Orleans, a fair clerk and scrivener. The scene is just at sun-set." Down the left margin of the same MS is written: "You find parallels to this style in Shakespeare, and in the old Virelays and love-songs of Provençal."

NIRVÂNA (19-21)

Written in Macon, Dec., 1869 (receipt of copy acknowledged by Paul Hayne in a letter of Dec. 11).

Published in *New Eclectic*, VI, 294-296 (Mar., 1870); reprinted without change in *1884*, 210-212.

Text: *New Eclectic*. In *1884* capitals were removed from abstract nouns, though not consistently, on the theory that this early habit, resulting from Lanier's interest in German literature, was opposed to his later style (see *MDL* to Lawrence Turnbull, July 22, 1882); but the printer's copy of *Clover*, made up in 1879, indicates the contrary, and the capitals have been retained. Four MSS survive; for a full collation of variants see p. 290, above.

The *New Eclectic* print had a footnote to the title which read: "The Highest Paradise of Buddha, attainable only by long contemplation, and by perfect superiority to all passions of men and all vicissitudes of Time." That Lanier's orientalism was picked up at second hand is indicated by an early notation in the *Ledger* 17, *c.* 1865, "Hindo, life-weariness—(Novalis)"; and evidence that he did not adopt this philosophy himself, even at this time, is found in his explanation to Virginia Hankins: "Of course it is a rapt Hindu who speaks" (letter of Jan. 7, 1870, inclosing a copy of the poem). Indeed it is directly opposed to the direction of Lanier's development. In his copy of the *Discourses of Epictetus*, purchased in 1879 (see Turnbull Bros. statement, *CL*), opposite a passage on p. 305 advocating that man should not desire anything that he does not possess, he wrote disapprovingly: "But this is Buddha: freedom to lose desire; then we lose all, we are nought. It shows the lack of personality." Though phrased in the vocabulary of Buddhism, "Nirvâna" seems merely to symbolize Lanier's quest for spiritual peace at a crucial period of his life when, suffering from ill health and torn between his desire for authorship and the hard necessity of earning a living under the blight of Reconstruction, he was trying to force himself into the groove of legal practice (for a similar mood see his letter to Hayne, Mar. 15, 1869, where the final appeal is to Christ instead of Buddha). In its attitude towards problems of his own and of the South and the nation, it is a recapitulation of much that he had said before in prose and verse. (See Arthur Christy, "The Orientalism of Sidney Lanier," *Aryan Path*, V, 638-641, Oct., 1934.)

THAR'S MORE IN THE MAN THAN THAR IS IN THE LAND (22-23)

Written in Macon, 1869-1871 (from the evidence of publication and the date in *1884*, "Macon, Georgia, 1869").

Published in the Macon *Telegraph and Messenger*, Feb. 7, 1871 (clipping in *CL*), with headnote indicating original publication; reprinted without change in *Southern Farm and Home*, II, 253 (May, 1871), and in *1884*, 172-174. (Apparently copied in newspapers throughout the South; reprinted in a version without the dialect in the Toledo, Ohio, *Blade*, May 18, 1871, and elsewhere, and in one unidentified newspaper with illustrations, entitled "Jones"—see facsimile.)

Text: *Telegraph and Messenger* (with correction of misprints in punctuation, ll. 42-43, and *waggin* for *wagin,* following *1884* and the magazine printing of "Jones's Private Argument"). One MS survives; for a full collation of variants see p. 290, above.

In spite of the statement in *1884*, vii, that it was published in a "Georgia Daily, 1869," no evidence has been found of publication earlier than 1871, and the earliest reference to it is in a letter of Mar. 11 (?) 1871—both being suggestive of recent composition. (It is dated "1871" in *MDL's* handwriting in a MS list of poems, *CL*.) This letter and note 17, Letters of 1871, tell of reprintings in Georgia and Virginia newspapers; and an unidentified clipping from a Galveston, Texas, newspaper (*CL*) reprints the poem with the following editorial note: "This is the sort of doggerel with which the Georgia newspapers persuade their people to cease emigrating and stay at home. There is not a word of truth in the story. Had there been time for the five years to elapse, poetic truth would have made Jones rich." Though no conclusive evidence has been discovered for Lanier's authorship of the version without dialect, it is quite likely that he published it so in the *Telegraph and Messenger* (no file for this period discovered); for the reprint in the Toledo *Blade* credits that newspaper as its source. It also seems probable that the version with illustrations, signed "O. J. Hopkins &c Toledo O.," appeared in the *Blade* (probably the weekly edition, no file of which has been discovered); for the advertisements verso, dated May 27, 1871, are from Summit City, Mich., and Ft. Wayne, Ind.—neighboring cities to Toledo—and the editor of the *Blade* at this time was "Petroleum V. Nasby" (David R. Locke), who would have sponsored both verse and drawings of this genre, nor would he have removed the dialect editorially.

In a reminiscent letter, Sept. 25, 1883, Robert S. Lanier recorded an anecdote of its composition, but unfortunately did not give the date: "While practicing law with us, a youngish fat well to do looking farmer came in the office . . . [and] told Sidney how, a year or two before, he had bought an adjoining 'worn out' farm from a neighbor who took the purchase money & himself & family to newer lands in Texas, & how that, a few days before, this neighbor came back from Texas to his house while he was at breakfast without money, in rags—: came back to see this farm renewed, & *thrift* all around, &C, &C. Shortly after . . . Sidney turned to his desk and composed the poem, . . . that was then published in The Daily T & M^r. here & republished all over the country." Jones county is east of and adjoining Bibb County, in which Macon is located. Lanier was later to see and describe the "Cracker" emigrant on his

Clipping from the

Toledo, Ohio, *Blade*(?), May, 1871.

"JONES."

A STORY FOR PEOPLE WHO WANT MORE LAND.—
ILLUSTRATED BY O. J. HOPKINS.

I KNOW a man and he lived in Jones—
Which Jones is a county of red hills and stones—
And he lived pretty much by getting of loans;
And his mules were nothing but skin and bones,
And his hogs were as flat as his cornbread pones,
    And he had bout a thousand acres of land.

This man—and his name was also Jones—
He swore that he'd leave them old red hills and
    stones,
For he couldn't make nothin' but yellowish cot-
    ton,
And little of that, for his fences were rotten,
And what little cotton he had, that was boughten,
    And he couldn't get a living from the land.

And the longer he swore the madder he got,
And he rose and he walked to the stable lot,
And he hallooed to Tom to come there and hitch,
For to emigrate somewhere where the land was
    rich,
And to quit raising cock-burs, thistles and sich,
    And wasting their time on barren land.

So him and Tom they hitched up their mules,
Protesting that folks were mighty big fools
That 'nd stay in Georgia their lifetime out,
Jest scratching a living, when all of them
    mought
Get places in Texas where cotton would sprout
    By the time you could plant it in the land.

And he drove by a house where a man named
    Brown
Was living not far from the edge of the town.

But Brown moved out on the old Jones farm,
And he rolled up his breeches and bared his arm,
And he picked all the rocks from off'n the ground,
And he rooted it up and plowed it down,
    And sowed his corn and wheat in the land.

Five years glide by, and Brown one day,
(Who got so fat that he wouldn't weigh)
Was sitting down sorter lazily,
To the pleasantest dinner you ever see,
When one of the children jumped on his knee
    And says, "Yon's Jones which you bought
    his land."

And there was Jones standing out at the fence,
And he hadn't no wagons, nor mules, nor tents,
For he had left Texas a-foot and come
To see if he couldn't get some
Employment, and he was looking as hum-
    Ble as if he had never owned any land,

But Brown he asked him in, and he sot
Him down to his victuals smoking hot,
And when he had filled himself and the floor,
Brown looked at him sharp, and rove and swore
That ' whether men's land was rich or poor,
    There was more in the man than there was in
    the land."

    —*Macon (Ga.) Telegraph.*

And he bantered Brown for to buy his place,
And said that seeing as money was skace,
And seeing as sheriffs were hard to face,
    Two dollars an acre would get the land.

They closed at a dollar and fifty cents,
And Jones he bought him a wagon and tents,
And loaded his corn, and his woman and truck,
And moved to Texas, which it took
His entire pile with the best of luck,
    To get there and get him a little land.

way to Texas (letter of Nov. 22, 1872). For a discussion of his dialect poems, both their historical importance and their relationship to current economic problems in the South (treated in serious prose and poetry as well as humorous), see Introduction.

JONES'S PRIVATE ARGUMENT (24-25)

Written in Macon, 1870-1871 (dated 1870 in *1884* and published in 1871—not mentioned in Lanier's letters).

Published in *Southern Farm and Home*, II, 338 (July, 1871), with headnote indicating original publication; reprinted with changes in *1884*, 175-176.

Text: *Southern Farm and Home* (with comma supplied, l. 3; apostrophe, l. 32; capital for *Hit's*, l. 41; and misprint in punctuation corrected, l. 17). MS *CL*, undated and unsigned, has legal notes verso, suggesting composition in the law offices of Lanier & Anderson. It agrees with above except in a few minor points and is the text followed in *1884*. Before correction it shows a dozen or more variants mostly altered for the sake of the rhyme scheme, dialectal spellings such as *Tennessy* and *tuk*, and first drafts such as the following (ll. 33-34):

> He'd tied the lines (to read, you know)
> Around his leg, and driv on slow.

Published in a local agricultural magazine, it advocates diversified crops as the salvation of the southern plantation system—a recurrent theme in Lanier's prose and poetry, both humorous and serious (see Introduction). The thriftless conservative farmer "Jones" is the same character satirized in "Thar's More in the Man" (22, and note, above). "Clisby" (l. 47) was Joseph Clisby, of the Macon *Telegraph and Messenger*, who had written editorials urging the planting of corn instead of cotton.

THE HOMESTEAD (25-28)

Apparently written in Macon, summer of 1871 (from evidence of publication date).

Published in *Southern Farm and Home,* II, 392 (Aug., 1871). Previously uncollected.

Text: *Southern Farm and Home* (with quotation marks removed, l. 2, and semi-colons supplied, ll. 92, 96). It is signed with Lanier's name, and the headnote indicates original publication. MS *CL* is a modern copy from the magazine print. No other version known.

The theme of a diversified agriculture to solve the economic plight of the South connects it with the dialect poems written during the same period and "Corn," three years later.

JUNE DREAMS, IN JANUARY (29-31)

Apparently written in its first form in Macon, summer of 1868; revised in San Antonio, Texas, winter of 1873.

Published posthumously in *Independent*, XXXVI, 1121 (Sept. 4, 1884); reprinted with one change in *1884*, 237-240.

Text: MS *CL*, signed "Sidney Lanier," undated (but the pencil annotations in the handwriting of Paul Hayne prove this to be the draft sent him on Mar. 12, 1873, see note 40, Letters of 1873). This is the text followed in *1884* with editorial emendations and deletions. An earlier MS survives (*Ledger* 307-315), entitled "The Poet and the Ages," undated, but probably written in the summer of 1868 (from its position in the *Ledger* between " Life and Song " and " The hound was cuffed," but *1884*, 240, dates it " 1869 ") ; it has numerous variants and forty-odd rejected lines, but breaks off at l. 59. For a full collation of variants see pp. 291-293, above.

Not published by Lanier but submitted through a friend to *Galaxy, Scribner's,* and *Atlantic* (see letter from Ronald MacDonald, Apr. 9, 1874, and note 112, Letters of 1874). Stanzas 3-9 were incorporated in a revised form in " Psalm of the West " (see pp. 67-68, above). The rejection by three magazines makes the autobiographical theme doubly ironical. The poem fits the circumstances of Lanier's life in June, 1868, when he was recovering from his first serious attack of tuberculosis but without employment and with his wife pregnant, and even more so those in January, 1873, when he was separated from her in Texas because of illness and desperately revolving the plan to give up law for a career in art. (Both wife and eldest son are named in the poem, ll. 67 and 78.)

ON HUNTINGDON'S " MIRANDA " (32)

Written in Baltimore, Jan. 31, 1874.

Published in New York *Evening Post*, Mar. 6, 1874, p. 1; reprinted without change in *1884*, 107.

Text: *Evening Post.* MS *HL*, entitled " Miranda," inclosed in letter of Jan. 31, 1874, and printed in the present edition (IX, 20), is the first draft with numerous variants. *Ledger* 544, signed " S. L.," undated, has a few variants, the most interesting of which is, l. 11, *'Twixt flame and shame of love's surprise* ⟩ *With mystic tears of love's surprise* (the alteration having been made as a result of the request in his wife's letter of Feb. 5, 1874). MS *CL* is a copy in the handwriting of *MDL*.

Lanier saw Daniel Huntington's " Miranda " at the home of a Baltimore friend, J. Stricker Jenkins, and described it in a letter of Jan. 4, 1874. The painting was sold at auction in 1876 and cannot be located (note 2, Letters of 1874). A fragmentary musical composition by Lanier has survived entitled " Mem. for ' Miranda,' " MS *CL*.

MY TWO SPRINGS (32-34)

Written in Baltimore, Mar., 1874 (see letters of Mar. 15 and 20).

Published posthumously in *Century*, XXIV, 838-839 (Oct., 1882), entitled " My Springs "; reprinted without change in *1884*, 71-73.

Text: MS *CL*, entitled " My Two Springs " and signed " S. L.," inclosed in letter of Mar. 15, 1874 (with correction of l. 47, *lady-loves* for *loves* (*no less*), by authority of letter of Mar. 20, and l. 50, *littles* for *Littles*). No other variants known, nor any authority for the shortened title printed by *MDL*.

Unpublished by Lanier, but intended for publication and submitted unsuccessfully to the *Atlantic* (see letter of Mar. 15, 1874, and Ronald MacDonald's letter of Apr. 9). The *Century* paid $40 for it to *MDL* (letter from R. W. Gilder, Apr. 19, 1882).

Of the many poems Lanier addressed to his wife, this is the first one he considered worthy; it seems to have been inspired by a photograph sent him on his birthday (see illustration, IX, facing 23, and the description in letter of Feb. 3, 1874). A fragmentary musical composition by Lanier has survived (*CL*) entitled " The Spring that feeds the Lake of Dreams," echoing the opening stanza of the poem. Other poems to his wife were " Acknowledgment," " Evening Song," " In Absence," " Laus Mariæ," and " Special Pleading."

CORN (34-39)

Written at Sunnyside, near Griffin, Ga., July, 1874 (receipt of a copy is acknowledged in Paul Hayne's letter of July 30); revised in Brooklyn, Oct., 1874 (see letter of Oct. 25), again slightly in *1877* and afterwards.

Published in *Lippincott's*, XV, 216-219 (Feb., 1875); reprinted in the Philadelphia *Evening Bulletin*, Jan. 20, 1875, and copied in other newspapers; reprinted with revisions in *1877*, 9-19; and with further changes in *1884*, 53-59.

Text: *CL* copy of *1877*, corrected in Lanier's handwriting (the text used in *1884*). Two MSS and a rough draft of the opening lines survive; for a full collation of variants see pp. 293-296, above.

"Corn," Lanier's best poem to date, was the first to bring him anything like a national reputation. No account of its composition is preserved in his letters, but a credible story of its origin has been recorded by a friend and neighbor at Sunnyside (see J. M. Kell, *Recollections of a Naval Life*, Washington, 1900, pp. 296-297, conveniently recounted in Starke, 182.) The region was a prosperous farming section of middle Georgia, about 60 miles above Macon, where the cultivation of corn had replaced the conventional money-crop of cotton, described by Lanier later as: "that ample stretch of generous soil, where the Appalachian ruggednesses calm themselves into pleasant hills before dying quite away into the sea-board levels, [where] a man can find such temperances of heaven and earth—enough of struggle with nature to draw out manhood, with enough of bounty to sanction the struggle—that a more exquisite co-adaptation of all blessed circumstances for man's life need not be sought" (quoted from "The New South," an essay concerned with the same economic problem, see V, 357). With this inspiration, Lanier made a serious plea for the same agricultural reform in the South that he had advocated three years before in his dialect verses (cf. especially pp. 38-39 with pp. 22-25, 194-196). Confident that he had written an important poem, he went to New York at the end of August to arrange for its publication. It was rejected by *Scribner's* and the *Atlantic*, and an ambitious scheme to publish it as an illustrated booklet fell through (letters of Sept. 4, 8, 13, 17, Oct. 3, 14). After submitting it to friends for criticism, chiefly Hayne and L. E. Bleckley, he made a complete revision and finally sold it to *Lippincott's*, who upon publication doubled the price originally offered and sent him a check for $50 (Bleckley's analysis is given in note 117, 1874; see letters of Oct. 25, Dec. 1, 1874, and Jan. 24, 1875; also J. F. Kirk's letter of Jan. 16, 1875). Upon its appearance in mid January it met with instant success, especially because of the editorials of Gibson Peacock in the Philadelphia *Evening Bulletin* (see letters of Jan. 18, 24, 26, and notes 25, 28). Through this new friend, who did much to sponsor Lanier's career from this time on, he also met Charlotte Cushman and Bayard Taylor and made his entry into the world of established artists. One ironical result was that this first successful poem brought him the commission to write a travel book, *Florida*, his first sustaining pay for literary work (Mar. 24, 1875, to his wife). "Corn" is further interesting as Lanier's initial effort to break away from conventional verse-forms, in pursuance of plans announced in a letter of the previous spring (Mar. 15, 1874).

CIVIL RIGHTS (40-42)

Written on the train between Bristol and Lynchburg, Va., Aug. 21, 1874 (see letter of Aug. 22, and note 72).

Published in Atlanta *Herald* (no file discovered, but see letter of Sept. 17,

1874) ; reprinted in Savannah *Daily Sun* (no file discovered, but undated clipping in *CL*) ; in Savannah *Morning News*, Oct. 28, 1874; and in Macon *Daily Telegraph and Messenger*, Oct. 29, 1874. Previously uncollected.

Text: *Telegraph* (with restoration of *to hold*, l. 40, and *make his 'davy 'fore the co'te* for *take his " davy " for the Cote*, l. 49, by reference to MS *CL*). MS *CL*, undated and unsigned, but in Lanier's handwriting and apparently a second draft (first draft, see letter of Aug. 22, 1874, not found), has a few variants, including dialectal spellings such as *curioosesest* and *firenilly* (*finally*), altered in the print. Two other MSS survive, but they are copies in the handwriting of *MDL*. The newspaper printings agree except in matters of typography.

These verses, Lanier's bitterest denunciation of Reconstruction politics, were provoked by Charles Sumner's " Supplementary Civil Rights Bill " (debated in Congress throughout 1874 though not passed until Mar. 1875), which was considered in the South as tantamount to conferring social equality on the negro and was the occasion of riotings. Lanier wrote, Nov. 2, 1874, apropos the printing of his poem: " The rascals have put my name to it,—when I expressly instructed the Herald *not* to do so. Not that I'm ashamed of it at all,—but May [his wife] is still in the country and I did not want the negroes to have any ground for twisting me into an enemy."

In a letter of Sept. 17, 1874 (omitted from the present edition) Lanier wrote: " I am glad to know that my ' Civil Rights ' is published. I wrote to the ' Herald ' inclosing it, and offering it for $25.00. I have not heard from them:— but of course publication is an acceptance." He was apparently never paid. The reprinting in the Savannah *Sun* was accompanied by an editorial (not found) comparing Lanier's poem to Bret Harte's "The Heathen Chinee" (letter of Nov. 3, 1874, and note 136; see also Introduction).

IN ABSENCE (42-43)

I-III written in Brooklyn, autumn of 1874; IV probably in Baltimore, the following winter, along with revisions of the others (see letters of Oct. 7, note 126, 1874, and Feb. 7, Mar. 21, 1875; also *MDL's* letter of Oct. 12, 1874).

Published in *Lippincott's*, XVI, 341-342 (Sept., 1875) ; reprinted with revisions in *1877*, 79-82; and without further change in *1884*, 74-76.

Text: *1877*. Three MSS survive; for a full collation of variants see pp. 297-298, above.

Of this sequence, addressed to his wife, Lanier wrote (letter to *MDL*, Feb. 7, 1875) that he was revising No. I, which had been criticised by Paul Hayne as " too ripe and luxuriant," a " Swinburnian misconception " that he resented; he added: " I will have to abandon the title *Laus Mariæ* for my sonnets: it wd. be misleading, as every one wd. take it to be praise of the Virgin. Perhaps I will head them *Laus Uxoris* (' Praise of a Wife '), for I wish to preserve the pious tone of the *Laus* form of expression." These early titles are used in the surviving MSS. A fifth sonnet, which retained the title of " Laus Mariæ " (44, and note, below), was originally intended as part of this sequence, and probably a sixth " Whate'er has been " (200) ; the four sonnets entitled " Acknowledgment " (56), written the following summer, were considered an extension of this series. Lanier was apparently paid $35 for " In Absence " by *Lippincott's* (letters to his wife, July 22, 23, 1875).

LAUS MARIÆ (44)

Written in Brooklyn, autumn of 1874 (letter of Nov. 2 and note 134).

Published in *Scribner's*, XI, 64 (Nov., 1875); reprinted with one change in *1884*, 80.

Text: *Scribner's*. In *1884*, l. 8 reads: *Shake the green tussocks of malign disgrace*, but no authority has been found for this. No other variants known.

A comment in Lanier's letter of Nov. 3, 1874, "Scribner's has accepted No. III of the Sonnets," indicates that this was originally a part of "In Absence" (see note, above); for "Laus Mariæ" is the only sonnet composed at about this time which was published in *Scribner's*, and it was the name originally given to the "In Absence" sequence. Like the others it was written in praise of Mary Day Lanier. (A fragmentary musical composition by Lanier has survived entitled "Laus Mariæ," *CL*.)

TO MISS CHARLOTTE CUSHMAN (44)

Written in Baltimore, Jan. 27, 1875.

Published in Emma Stebbins, *Charlotte Cushman* (Boston, 1878), 268. Previously uncollected.

Text: Stebbins, dated as above. (Several MSS survive, *HC, CL, JT,* and *JM,* but they are all copies and without authority.) No variants known.

Presented to Charlotte Cushman by Lanier on the day after his first meeting with her (see letter of Jan. 26, 1875), accompanied with a copy of *Lippincott's Magazine* containing "Corn." He addressed three other poems to her: "To Charlotte Cushman" (58), "Dedication" (83), and "At First" (200).

SPECIAL PLEADING (45)

Written in Baltimore, probably Feb., 1875 (see letter of Feb. 11).

Published in *Lippincott's*, XVII, 89 (Jan., 1876); reprinted with changes in *1877*, 89-90; and without further change in *1884*, 81-82.

Text: *1877*. Two MSS survive; for a full collation of variants see p. 298, above.

Originally written as an intercalary song for "The Jacquerie" (see note, p. 375; see also letter of Feb. 11, 1875, which suggests that it likewise refers to Lanier's enforced separation from his wife), but it is not clear from the surviving fragment of that poem just where it was to be inserted. "He" (l. 9) is probably the same character, the Duke, mentioned in the note to "Betrayal" (see note, p. 335, above). "Special Pleading" is obviously an experiment in vocabulary and in metrics, and Lanier set considerable store by it as a new departure in his literary technique (see letters of Feb. 11 and Dec. 21, 1875).

MARTHA WASHINGTON (46)

Written in Baltimore, Feb., 1875 (letter of Feb. 26 tells of correcting the proofs four days before).

Published in *Martha Washington Court Journal*, Feb. 22, 1875, p. 1, a Baltimore occasional, one issue only (copy in the Lanier Room); reprinted in the Philadelphia *Evening Bulletin* (see letter of Mar. 2, 1875) and without change in *1884*, 113.

Text: *Martha Washington Court Journal*. No other version known.

THE SYMPHONY (46-56)

Written in Baltimore, Mar. 20-28, 1875 (see letters of Mar. 24 and 28); revised in 1876 and again in 1879.

Published in *Lippincott's*, XV, 677-684 (June, 1875); reprinted without change in *Dwight's Journal of Music*, XXXV, 41-42 (June 26, 1875); reprinted with revisions in *1877*, 20-38; and with further revisions in *1884*, 60-70.

Text: Printer's Copy, 19 pp., *CL*, originally prepared for inclusion in *Clover* but omitted (see letter of May 16, 1879). This is clearly Lanier's latest revision and was used in *1884*, with a few exceptions as noted below. But a special problem is created by the fact that preparation of this "copy" was not completed by Lanier (see, for example, ll. 310-311, where words have been deleted but no substitutions made). Pp. 1-4, 6, 8, 10, 12, 14, 16, 18 consist of pasted sheets from *1877* with revisions or of new drafts in MS, indicating that he was using the *1877* text as the basis of his revised version; but the remaining pages consist of pasted clippings from a newspaper reprint of the *Lippincott* text, uncorrected. On the assumption that if Lanier had completed preparation of this Printer's Copy he would have corrected these pages in accordance with the *1877* text—or with even further revisions—I have followed *1884* in using the *1877* text for these passages (ll. 72-90, 111-131, 153-173, 194-212, 234-254, 276-295, 316-334, 354-368). I have also followed *1884* in making two mechanical changes: *violins'* for *violin's* (l. 15) and restoration of quotation marks (l. 50), but I have not followed the changes in punctuation or the correction *may* for *can* (l. 295—two other changes by *MDL* appear in the "copy," ll. 127 and 136, but were not used in *1884*); further I have restored several stanza divisions, obliterated in the process of pasting (and hence omitted in *1884*), by reference to *Lippincott's* and *1877*. Otherwise I have followed the Printer's Copy exactly. For a full collation of variants see pp. 298-300, above.

Lippincott's paid Lanier $100 for "The Symphony" (see J. F. Kirk's letter of Apr. 4, 1875). Elizabeth Stuart Phelps used l. 3 as a text for her poem, "What the Violin Said," published in the New York *Daily Graphic*, VIII, 910 (Oct. 27, 1875). The second of Lanier's long ambitious poems to be published, "The Symphony" won him the friendship of Bayard Taylor through a copy sent by Gibson Peacock (who had recently become Lanier's sponsor because of his admiration of "Corn"): and it prompted the first serious consideration of Lanier's poetry by a literary critic of national reputation, G. H. Calvert's article in the *Golden Age*, V, 4-5 (June 12, 1875). The poem epitomizes Lanier's life-long devotion to music, which he was convinced would "revolutionize the world" through harmony and love, and his continuing conviction that the blight on modern life was the tyranny of commercialism, here with the added note of social protest because of its oppression of the poor (see Introduction).

The allusion in ll. 42-43 is to *Matthew* iv:4; in l. 178, to *Matthew* xix:19; in l. 182, to *Luke* x:29 ff.; in ll. 333-334, to *Luke* xviii:17. The reference in ll. 311-312 is apparently intended to be to Sir Philip Sidney, who, because of his sister's marriage, was sometimes referred to as "Pembroke's brother"; the description fits the character and career of Sidney, a favorite of Lanier's, but does not apply to any of the Earls of Pembroke.

ACKNOWLEDGMENT (56-58)

Written in Brooklyn and New York City, late summer of 1875 (II, III, and IV were inclosed in a letter of Aug. 30; I, in a letter of Oct. 2).

Published in *Lippincott's*, XVIII, 554-555 (Nov., 1876); reprinted with one change in *1877*, 83-86; and in *1884*, 77-79.

Text: *1877*. No variants known, except *Lippincott's*, l. 38, *Those* for *These*. Written in continuation of "In Absence" (42-43) and probably prompted by the appearance of that series in the Sept., 1875, issue of *Lippincott's* and by an evening of talk with Bayard Taylor (see letters of Aug. 29 and 30). Though addressed to his wife, they deal principally with the problem of religious faith in an age of scientific doubt (see Introduction).

TO CHARLOTTE CUSHMAN (58)

Probably written in Brooklyn, late summer of 1875 (see letters of Aug. 30, Sept. 5, and Oct. 3).

Published in *Lippincott's*, XVII, 375 (Mar., 1876); reprinted, with one line revised, in *1877*, 91; and without further change in Emma Stebbins, *Charlotte Cushman* (Boston, 1878), 268-269, and in *1884*, 44.

Text: *1877*. *Lippincott's* has one variant, *round an arduous* for *o'er a strenuous* (l. 10). Two MSS survive, both in *HC*, one signed "Sidney Lanier," the other "Address: Westminster Hotel, N. Y."—where Lanier moved on Sept. 25, 1875. Of a half-dozen variants the most interesting is l. 4, which reads in the two MSS respectively: *Fulfilment leaving Heaven to match a dream* and *Fulfilment charmed from God by a yearning dream*.

Charlotte Cushman saw this sonnet in MS, but it is doubtful if she saw it in print, for she died on Feb. 18, 1876 (see Lanier's letters of Sept. 5, 1875, and Feb. 16, 1876). For other poems addressed to her see "To Miss Charlotte Cushman," note, p. 342, above.

A SONG OF LOVE (58)

Probably written in Brooklyn, late summer of 1875 (this and "To Charlotte Cushman" are probably the "little snatches" mentioned in letter of Aug. 30, 1874); revised in Baltimore, 1879.

Published posthumously in *Century*, XXVII, 559 (Feb., 1884); reprinted without change in *1884*, 97.

Text: *Clover* 70, MS, *numbered* VII of "Street-Cries" (the text used in the posthumous prints). A draft of the idea and four other MSS survive showing widely different versions; for a full collation of variants see p. 300, above.

MS *HA* is numbered "IV," indicating that this was one of the "4 songs of roses" sent to Dudley Buck in June, 1876, for a musical setting (see note to "Rose-Morals," p. 345, below). Turned down by Buck, it was later set to music by B. F. Gordon. A note in *1884*, 244, reads: "*A Song of Love*, like *Betrayal*, belongs to the early plan of *The Jacquerie*. It was written for one of the Fool's songs and, after several recastings, took its present shape in 1879." MS *Ledger* has in place of a title the caption "The Fool Sings." The surviving fragment of "The Jacquerie" (see note, pp. 373 ff., below) introduces the Fool, but the narrative does not reach the point at which this song was to be inserted. *MDL* was paid $85 for this poem, and "How Love Looked for Hell" (see letters from *Century*, Sept. 29, Oct. 1, 1883), presumptive evidence that it was not published in Lanier's lifetime; but its inclusion in his projected volume *Clover* indicates his intention to publish.

A SONG OF THE FUTURE (59)

Probably written in New York, autumn of 1875. (No other undated poem fits so well the "little song" mentioned in Lanier's letter of Oct. 3. A receipt for it has survived dated Nov. 9, 1875, signed by Lanier in acknowledgment of $10 paid by *Scribner's Monthly*, MS *JM*.)

Published in *Scribner's* XII, 543 (Aug., 1876); reprinted without change in *1884*, 50, where it. is dated in error 1878.

Text: *Scribner's*. No variants known.

ROSE-MORALS (59-60)

"Red" written in Philadelphia, Oct. 15, 1875 (see letter to Taylor and note 175); "White" written in Baltimore, Mar., 1876 (letter of Mar. 20).

Published in *Lippincott's*, XVII, 587 (May, 1876); reprinted with two changes in *1877*, 92-93; and without further change in *1884*, 52. A revised version of "White" was printed·in Epes Sargent, *Harper's Cyclopaedia of British and American Poetry* (New York, 1881), 916.

Text: "Red," *1877*; ".White," Sargent (by authority of Lanier's letters of Aug. 19 and 26, 1880). Three MSS of "Red" and two MSS of "White" survive; for a full collation of variants see p. 301, above.

MS *CL* of "Red" has a note at the top in Lanier's handwriting: "Four (—You can name them what you like—Songs of Roses, or what not)." This was obviously his instruction to Dudley Buck to whom he sent "four little poems" to be set to music (see Lanier's letter to his wife, June 28, 1876; for Buck see note to Cantata, below). Turned down by Buck, it was later set to music by B. F. Gordon. Two of these songs were thus the two parts of "Rose-Morals"; a third was "To ———, With a Rose," written on June 5 (one MS of which bears the numeral III); a fourth was "A Song of Love," written in ·Aug., 1875 (one MS of which bears the numeral IV)—these being the only "songs of roses" ever written by Lanier. All four were returned in Buck's letter of Aug. 21, 1876, with the comment that they appealed as literature but not as texts for musical settings: "I am right sorry to say that I cannot handle the four songs sent. You refer to their not being 'conventional' songs—Suppose you try your hand at one that *you would call* 'conventional.'" (See note to "Evening Song," pp. 350-351, below.) That Lanier thought of "Rose-Morals," at least part two, as embodying a new poetic technique, see his letter to Taylor, Mar. 20, 1876, inclosing a draft; but the idea of symbolic rose-morals Lanier may have learned from Thomas Carew and Robert Herrick (see *1895*, pp. 71-72).

THE CENTENNIAL MEDITATION OF COLUMBIA (60-62)

Written in Baltimore, Jan. 1876.

Published by G. Schirmer, New York, 1876, with music by Dudley Buck, probably in March (see Lanier's letter of Mar. 18); text printed in New York *Tribune*, Apr. 12, 1876, with introduction by Bayard Taylor; reprinted in Macon *Daily Telegraph and Messenger*, Apr. 18, and copied in whole or in part by newspapers and music journals all over the country; and in *1884*, 249-251—all without change.

Text: Schirmer, the official publication (with musical annotations from the MSS as a substitute for the omitted score). Six MSS survive, in addition to numerous alterations included in Lanier's letters; for a full collation of variants see pp. 301-303, above.

The full story of the composition, publication, performance, and contemporary reception of Lanier's Cantata is given in his letters of Jan.-June, 1876, and the notes thereto, so that only a summary need be given here. The official invitation was sent to Lanier on Dec. 31, 1875, by Gen. J. R. Hawley, President of the U. S. Centennial Commission, upon the suggestion of Bayard Taylor (see note 216, Letters of 1875). Dudley Buck (1839-1909), who was selected to compose the music, had been appointed assistant conductor of Theodore Thomas's orchestra in 1875. His greatest reputation came as a composer of religious music and concert cantatas—a reputation that was first established on a national basis by his music for Lanier's Cantata. A first draft of the poem was sent to Taylor for criticism on Jan. 9, 1876, and a corrected copy three days later. On Jan. 15 a revised version was sent to Taylor and to Buck (two drafts: a continuous copy and a working copy with musical annotations), and on Jan. 18 to Peacock. Partial corrections were made in Lanier's letters to Buck of Jan. 19, 22, and 25, and the final revision including these was sent in his letter of Feb. 1. Corrected proof sheets were sent to Buck in a letter of Feb. 14, Lanier's alterations being apparently confined to matters of punctuation. · (Some of the revisions were influenced by Taylor's and Buck's criticisms.)

The text and music were printed by Schirmer early in the spring, for the purposes of rehearsing the orchestra and chorus. Through some misunderstanding, and against Lanier's wishes, it was released to the press for review. It was noticed by the music critic in the New York *Tribune*, Mar. 31, with praise of the score but considerable criticism of the words, and the controversy began. Taylor tried to stem the tide by printing the entire text in the *Tribune*, Apr. 12, with an introduction explaining the musical nature of the composition and stating that it should not be judged by a mere reading. The actual performance of the Cantata by Theodore Thomas's Orchestra of 150 musicians and a chorus of 800 voices (with Myron Whitney as soloist) at the opening ceremonies of the Centennial Exposition, Philadelphia, May 10, seems to have been a success (see Starke, 243-244). But the occasion only served to renew the newspaper criticism, and Lanier finally published his own defense in a long article in the *Tribune* on May 20 (reprinted in the present edition, II, 266-273), which satisfied the judicious in both literary and musical circles. Out of this controversy came two parodies of his Cantata, testimonials of a growing reputation. One was published in the New York *World*, May 13, 1876, accompanied by a burlesque letter from "The Grand Lama of Thibet," entitled: "Fiat Justitia. Mr. Lanier's Plagiarism Exposed—The Centennial Cantata in its Original Form." The other, preserved in an unidentified newspaper clipping (*CL*) with a note in pencil "by Richard Scudder," follows:

"A CANTATA."

THE HOOSIER AUNT.

I.

From that hundred-citied west,
West that grows like weed possessed,
Ranges down on all my doors
Country cousins, countless scores:
    In posish, in posish
    To enjoy the exposish;
    Come to stay, come to stay,
    Till the show has passed away;

While loud voices rise and call—
" Put some more cots in the hall; "
Weltering, my children cry,
Sweltering, my children cry,
As they wander to-and-fro:
" Well, this is indeed a go! "
While their guests of both the sexes,
Moveless guests of both the sexes,
Move about from day to day,
Doing buildings and annexes.

II.

Hoosier aunt, hoosier aunt, hither, swiftly flying,
Gitting eastward o'er the air-line rail,
Heart within, " I kinder hate to leave you, Oshkosh," sighing,
But, " Osh, you've got no show in this Centennial year, during which you have
    no show and Philadelphia has the show," replying,
Telegrams in showers addressed to the old aunt from Philadelphia crying—
" Don't come; we're over full: particulars by mail."

III.

Oshkosh, not for thee,
Nor thee, O Kankakee,
Nor thee, dear Coney Island, sitting by the sea,
Nor thee, Skowhegan, and in very truth,
Not e'en for thee, Duluth, Duluth,
Will Winter cries, I write away,
Nym Crinkle cries, I write a play,
Jim Bennett cries, I polo play.
But the Hoosier aunt cries, " I'm bound to go to
Philadelphia, and I'm bound to stay."

IV.

Then old bunks and hooks and things,
The kind that one from garret brings,
Ghosts of goods once fresh and fair,
Grown ragged quilts in the attic air,
Lounges with their broken springs,
Settees where the sly moth clings—
   Parents, children, hired girls,
   While each aching head swift whirls,
Write to the hoosier aunt with faces very glum,
" No! thou shalt not come! "
      Hoopla!
Hoosier aunt coming east in throbbing train—
East, the remonstrances are all in vain—
East, like an arrow shot swift and well
By some such archer as old Bill Tell,
Flies for the apples and " rings the bell "
     Unfoiled and lusty,
     Albeit a trifle dusty,

Gits she by day and under the stars,
Gits in Wagner and Pullman cars,
Gits while the hoosier heart heaves and hums
With a sweet expectancy that nothing mars.

Now, Laus Deo, the journey's past,
Now praise for railways running fast
Despite of those who waved her away,
She's started, is here, and has come to stay—
How long, good gracious! how long is it
That she's going to protract her visit?
How long, how long? O give us an answer
And tell us the truth in one brief stanza.

" Long as the art hall's open found,
Long as the Corliss wheel turns round,
Long as the gatemen do not cease
To gather in the half-dollar piece;
Long as there's anything to see,
So long, in short, as the show shall be,
So long dear aunt will be on hand
As summer blithest morning bland."

O exposish, from top of George's Hill unfold
The star-strewn banner loved with love untold,
Wave us swift onward to that golden age
When right alone shall hold the world's broad stage,
When love alone shall human thought engage;
Scream, eagle, scream, from Schuylkill unto Niger,
And sound the world's best lover's welcome—
         cheers, cheers, each cheer's a " tiger."

(For a discussion of the importance of the Cantata in Lanier's career as a poet, see the Introduction and Starke, 235-248.) There are several echoes in Lanier's poem from Elizabeth Barrett Browning, notably in l. 50, which paraphrases a line from *Aurora Leigh* that he had written in his *Ledger* 94: " Who lives true life will love true love."

PSALM OF THE WEST (62-82)

Written in Baltimore, winter-spring of 1876 (see letters of Feb. 16 and Apr. 4).

Published in *Lippincott's*, XVIII, 39-53 (July, 1876); reprinted with one change and two misprints in *1877*, 39-78; and with misprints corrected in *1884*, 114-138.

Text: *CL* copy of *1877* with revisions in Lanier's hand (with end commas supplied, ll. 77, 455; all numerals for stanzas omitted; and correction of Lanier's careless error, *past* for *passed*, p. 71, l. 12, as in *1884*, which otherwise followed this text). One MS survives, entitled " To the United States of America "; for a full collation of variants see pp. 303-307, above.

On Sept. 26, 1875, he wrote to Clifford Lanier that he had been engaged by the editor of *Lippincott's* to write a centennial poem; on Feb. 16, 1876, he wrote that he had begun work on it. Illness during the first half of March interrupted him, but on Mar. 11 he sent his wife a draft of the " invocation " (probably pp. 62-65, not found but see letter of Mar. 18 and note 66). On Mar. 24 he wrote Taylor that he was only about half through; on Mar. 26, to his wife, "for several days . . . the poem has grown fast"; on Apr. 4, to both, "finished," with the implication that most of it had been written during the past three weeks. *Lippincott's* paid him $300 for it (letter to Peacock, Apr. 11). In May he corrected proofs and made "such emendations as I desire" (letters to wife, May 8 and 15). Apparently illustrations had been originally planned for it (letter of Mar. 14); though none accompanied its publication, it was made the feature of the July issue of *Lippincott's*, with the name of both author and poem in bold type across the front cover.

Lanier incorporated in the "Psalm of the West" revised versions of two poems written a number of years before: stanzas 3-9 of "June Dreams, In January" (29, cf. 67-68) and all of "The Tournament: Joust First" (6, cf. 79). In many respects a companion piece to his Cantata, the "Psalm" was, like it, conceived in relation to a musical setting; in fact, Lanier himself began such a composition entitled "Choral Symphony," but no trace of it has survived (see letter of Feb. 12, 1881). As a poem celebrating the centenary of American independence, the geographical and historical allusions (which are correct except for the spellings of a few proper names) will be sufficiently clear to the reader without specific identification.

TO ———, WITH A ROSE (82)

Written in Philadelphia, June 5, 1876.
Published in *Lippincott's*, XVIII, 371 (Sept., 1876); reprinted without change in *1877*, 94; and in *1884*, 106.
Text: *1877*. MS *CL^a*, entitled "To M. F. P." and signed "S. L. / June 5th 1876," is an early draft showing a few variants. MS *CL^b*, a revision entitled "Red. / (To M. ———, with a rose, on her birthday.) / III," has two interesting variants: *On Mariquita's natal day* (l. 3) and *What fits her grace most gracefully* (l. 6). (MS *JT* is a copy by J. A. Fisher; MS *HC*, a copy by Gibson Peacock.)
Addressed to Mariquita da G. A. de la Figanière Peacock, wife of Lanier's friend and sponsor Gibson Peacock, at whose Philadelphia home he was visiting in June, 1876. The title of MS *CL^b* indicates that this revision was sent to Dudley Buck as one of the "4 songs of roses" to be set to music (see note to "Rose-Morals," p. 345, above).

DEDICATION (83)

Probably written at West Chester, Pa., late summer or early autumn 1876. The Lippincott volume of *Poems* (1877) to which it formed the dedication was in preparation as early as Aug. 15 (see letter to A. H. Dooley) and was issued on Nov. 12, 1876.
Published in *1877*, 5; reprinted without change in Emma Stebbins, *Charlotte Cushman* (Boston, 1878), 269, and in *1884*, 43.
Text: *1877*. No variants known.
This is one of four poems addressed to the same friend (see "To Miss Charlotte Cushman," note, p. 342).

THE WAVING OF THE CORN (83-84)

Written at West Chester, Pa., Aug. 15, 1876 (so dated on one of the MSS); revised in October (see letter of Oct. 6).

Published in *Harper's*, LV, 439 (Aug., 1877); reprinted without change in *1884*, 23.

Text: *Harper's* (with hyphen supplied, l. 3). Two MSS survive; for a full collation of variants, including a rejected stanza, see p. 307, above.

Lanier was paid $15 for it by *Harper's* (see letter to Peacock, Dec. 27, 1876). Originally intended for inclusion in *Clover* 43-44, as indicated in the table of " Subjects for Illustration," but these pages of the Printer's Copy have not come down (see Introduction).

CLOVER (84-87)

Written at West Chester, Pa., Aug.-Sept., 1876 (see notes 131 and 135, Letters of 1876); revised in Baltimore, 1879.

Published in *Independent*, XXX, 1 (Mar. 7, 1878); reprinted with revisions in *1884*, 19-22.

Text: *Clover* 1-5, *Independent* print revised (with hyphen supplied, l. 27, the text used in *1884*). Two MSS and two rough drafts survive; for a full collation of variants see pp. 308-310, above.

Submitted to *Scribner's* in a letter of Sept. 25, 1876, with the following comment: " The enclosed grew out of a mood of solemn protest against the doctrine of ' Art for Art's Sake,' which has led so many of our young artists into the most unprofitable and even blasphemous activities" (see note 135, Letters of 1876; it was rejected in a letter of Oct. 10). Lanier was paid $25 for it by the *Independent* (see W. H. Ward's letter of Mar. 10, 1878), the first of his poems to be accepted by that magazine. The issue in which it was published contained an editorial note (p. 16), as follows: " We have seen poems of Sidney Lanier's which appeared to us almost incomprehensible; but such is not the case with the lines we publish this week. There is a strength about them and a flavor, withal, of Walt Whitman which will deserve attantion [*sic*]."

The poem reflects Lanier's depression in the summer of 1876, caused by ill health and disappointments and perhaps by a lingering resentment of the severe criticism of his Cantata; it was inscribed to the memory of Keats, in whose career he found a parallel to his own (cf. the echo of the " Ode on a Grecian Urn," l. 6). As a statement of his theory of the artist's function, he planned it as the title poem for his projected volume, " Clover and Other Poems" (see Introduction).

EVENING SONG (88)

Written at West Chester, Pa., early autumn of 1876.

Published in *Lippincott's*, XIX, 91 (Jan., 1877); reprinted without change in Philadelphia *Evening Bulletin* (no file discovered, but undated clipping in *CL*); in Epes Sargent, *Harper's Cyclopaedia of British and American Poetry* (New York, 1881), 916; and in *1884*, 151.

Text: Sargent. MS *HA* is a fragment of ll. 1-2, *O Love, look off across yon sallow sands / To where.* Dudley Buck's letter of Nov. 7, 1876, indicates that l. 5 originally read, *Now in the sea's red cordial melts the Sun.* No other variants known.

Written to be set to music, in response to a request from Dudley Buck, Aug. 21, 1876, for " an ' Evening Song,' a sort of ' Ueber allen Gipfeln ist Rüh ' but longer." On Nov. 7 Buck wrote, " I composed your song last night at ' one heat,' " suggesting one alteration which Lanier made (see above) and a change of title to " On the Sea Shore." (See note 117, Letters of 1876; for Buck, note to " Centennial Meditation," pp. 345-346, above.) A posthumous printing in *Independent*, XLIX, 1489 (Nov. 18, 1897), apparently from a MS in the possession of H. C. Wysham, gives the title as " On the Shore." It was published with Buck's music under the title *Sunset*, and has been set to music by several other composers, including Henry Hadley. The figure in the second stanza, an allusion to the tradition that Cleopatra dissolved a pearl in the drink with which she toasted Antony's health, had been used ten years before in " Night " (161). This lyric, addressed to Lanier's wife, is one of his best and has been a favorite with anthologists. He was paid $10 for it by *Lippincott's* (see letter to Peacock, Dec. 31, 1876).

TO BEETHOVEN (88-90)

Begun on the train between Philadelphia and Baltimore, Dec., 1876 (see letter of Mar. 15, 1877), and probably finished in Tampa, Jan. 1877 (see letter of Jan. 11) ; revised in 1879.

Published in *Galaxy*, XXIII, 394-395 (Mar., 1877) ; reprinted in a revised form, with four stanzas rejected and three new ones added, in *1884*, 98-100.

Text: *Clover* 37-41, MS (the text used in *1884*). A rough draft in MS also survives; for a full collation of variants see pp. 310-311, above.

Lanier was paid $25 for it by *Galaxy* (see letter from Bayard Taylor, Feb. 5, 1877). This poem and the sonnet " Beethoven " (201) were written for the semi-centennial celebration of the death of Beethoven. It is interesting to note that Lanier, to whom music was the religion of the new age, praises the message rather than the technique of his favorite composer (see Introduction and H. C. Thorpe, " Sidney Lanier: A Poet for Musicians," *Musical Quarterly*, XI, 373-382, July, 1925).

THE STIRRUP-CUP (90)

Written in Tampa, Jan., 1877 (so dated in *MDL's* handwriting on MS *CL*[b]).

Published in *Scribner's*, XIV, 28 (May, 1877) ; reprinted with one variant line and one stanza rejected in *1884*, 45.

Text: *Clover* 42, MS (the text used in *1884*). Three other MSS survive; for the rejected stanza and a full collation of variants see pp. 311-312, above.

Lanier was paid $20 for it (see letter from *Scribner's*, Jan. 19, 1877, which indicates that the title was originally " Life's Stirrup-Cup "). This poem, written a few weeks after he went to Florida by order of his doctor, reveals Lanier's courageous facing of the prospect of death. The names alluded to include some of those he had listed the previous summer in " Clover "; the following year he added further names in " The Crystal."

THE BEE (91-92)

Written in Tampa, Jan.-Feb., 1877 (see letter of Feb. 7).

Published in *Lippincott's*, XX, 493 (Oct., 1877) ; reprinted with two changes in *1884*, 83.

Text: *Clover* 46-48, *Lippincott* print with last 8 lines in MS (the text used in *1884*). One other MS survives with numerous variants, collated on pp. 312-313, above.

Submitted without success to the *Atlantic* and to *Harper's* (see Taylor's letter of Apr. 15 and Lanier's letters of Apr. 26, May 25, 1877, and note 40). The poem states Lanier's theory of the function of the poet; in this and in the personal experience of nature, which forms the setting, it seems to reflect his recent reading of Emerson. For Lanier's concern with the scientific accuracy of his description of the bee, see his letter to Taylor, Feb. 11, 1877, and note 17.

TAMPA ROBINS (92-93)

Written in Tampa, Jan.-Feb., 1877 (the issue of *Lippincott's* containing it was out by Feb. 18, according to a letter from Emma Stebbins).

Published in *Lippincott's*, XIX, 355 (Mar., 1877), as " Redbreast in Tampa "; reprinted with revisions and one additional stanza in *1884*, 28.

Text: *Clover* 16-17, MS, a revision with new title (the text used in *1884*). A MS rough draft of the first stanza also survives, verso a draft of " The Stirrup-Cup," dated Jan., 1877; for a full collation of variants see p. 313, above.

This poem and the complementary " Stirrup-Cup " are statements of Lanier's attitude toward life and death, the figure of Time appearing in both but with reversed applications; the MS mentioned above suggests that they were written at about the same time.

UNDER THE CEDARCROFT CHESTNUT (93-94)

Written in Tampa, Mar., 1877 (see letter of Mar. 4).

Published in *Scribner's*, XV, 380-381 (Jan., 1878); reprinted with two changes in *1884*, 149-150.

Text: *Scribner's*. No authority has been found for the two variants in *1884*, which are probably misprints: *Trim set* for *Firm-set* (1. 1); *quickly* for *prickly* (1. 16). MS *CL*, a draft of the last two stanzas only, signed " Sidney Lanier," has three minor variants before correction. (A letter from Taylor, Mar. 12, 1877, indicates that a lost first draft contained the word *colic*—probably for *worries*, l. 21—changed at Taylor's suggestion.)

The *Scribner* print was illustrated with a woodcut by Thomas Moran made from a sketch by Taylor (see note 86, Letters of 1877) and accompanied with the following note: " This chestnut tree (at Cedarcroft, the estate of Bayard Taylor, in Pennsylvania) is estimated to be more than eight hundred years old." Lanier had visited him there in the summer of 1876, while staying at nearby West Chester. (See note 25, 1877, for Taylor's response to this poem, written in appreciation of his many literary services, especially for placing Lanier's poems with the magazines during the illness in Florida.)

A FLORIDA SUNDAY (94-97)

Apparently written in Florida winter-spring, 1877 (dated by *MDL* " Tampa," where Lanier remained until Apr. 5; his letter of June 13, 1877, refers to it as printed).

Published in *Frank Leslie's Sunday Magazine*, II, 72-73 (July, 1877); reprinted without change, except for correction of misprint, in *1884*, 142-145.

Text: *Leslie's* (with correction of misprint, *joys* for *jays*, l. 64, by authority of Lanier's letter of June 13, 1877, which added: " the punctuation is also quite mutilated in some places," though only one such correction seemed necessary— the colon supplied, 5th line from the end). No variants known.

During the winter of 1877 Lanier made his first serious reading of Emerson (see letter of May 25), whose influence is apparent not only in specific lines (see the concluding couplet) but in the central idea of the poem: the spiritual unity behind nature and the essential kinship of each and all. Based upon a personal religious experience (cf. the autobiographical allusion in ll. 5-6), it foreshadows " The Marshes of Glynn " and " Sunrise." The influence of Keats may be seen in the delight in color and sound (and cf. the specific echo of the " Ode on a Grecian Urn " in ll. 16-17).

FROM THE FLATS (97-98)

Probably written in Tampa, spring of 1877 (see *1884*, 26; Lanier left Florida on Apr. 5).

Published in *Lippincott's*, XX, 115 (July, 1877); reprinted without change in Epes Sargent, *Harper's Cyclopaedia of British and American Poetry* (New York, 1881), 917; and with one line altered in *1884*, 26, but restored in *1910*.

Text: Sargent (with omission of comma after " beauty," l. 10). One MS survives, entitled " From a Flat Land "; for a full collation of variants, see pp. 313-314, above.

Lanier's letter of July 12, 1872, is a prose counterpart of this poem. See also his comment in the Peabody lecture on *Phoenix*: " A modern poet would never have described a Happy Land as an unbroken plain where no mountains stand; the picture of a landscape without broken ground is to our eyes intolerable " (III, 48, note 2).

THE MOCKING BIRD (98)

Probably written in Brunswick, Ga., Apr.-May, 1877 (see letters of Apr. 26, July 23, Aug. 1, and note 62, 1877).

Published in *Galaxy*, XXIV, 161 (Aug., 1877); reprinted with changes in *1884*, 27.

Text: *Clover* 12, MS (the text used in *1884* with *prinked* for *primped,* l. 11). An earlier version survives in MS; for a full collation of variants see p. 314, above.

A note in *1884*, 243, quotes from a lost college note-book Lanier's jotting: " A poet is the mocking-bird of the spiritual universe. In him are collected all the individual songs of all individual natures." (See also " To Our Mocking Bird " and note, p. 358, below.)

THE DOVE (99)

Written at Chadd's Ford, Pa., Aug. 7, 1877 (letter to Peacock); revised, with addition of the fourth stanza, later in the year.

Published in *Scribner's*, XVI, 140 (May, 1878); reprinted without change in Philadelphia *Evening Bulletin*, Apr. 19, 1878 (clipping in *CL*); and in *1884*, 105.

Text: *Scribner's*. Three MSS survive; for a full collation of variants see pp. 314-315, above.

For an account of its composition see letter to Peacock, Aug. 7, 1877. The figure in the first stanza drawn from *Othello* had been used in a poem written more than ten years before, " Night and Day " (160). Lanier was paid $20 for it (letter from *Scribner's Monthly*, Jan. 14, 1878).

A PUZZLED GHOST IN FLORIDA (99-101)

Written at Chadd's Ford, Pa., late summer of 1877 (letter of Nov. 25 confirms the place; Lanier was there from Aug. 1, to Sept. 12, 1877).

Published in *Appleton's Journal*, III [n. s.], 568 (Dec., 1877); reprinted with changes in *1884*, 163-166, as " A Florida Ghost."

Text: *Appleton's*. No authority has been found for the title or variants in *1884*, and since it seems in no way an improvement, the version published by Lanier has been adopted. For variants see p. 315, above.

A note in *1884*, 245, reads: " The incidents recorded of this storm are matter of history in and around Tampa." Lanier probably heard the story from the proprietor of the Orange Grove Hotel, where he stayed during the winter and spring of 1877. Unlike Lanier's other poems in Cracker dialect, it has no serious message beneath the humor and was probably written as a potboiler.

TO RICHARD WAGNER (102-103)

Probably written at Chadd's Ford, Pa., late summer or early autumn, 1877 (first mentioned in letter of Oct. 8 as in press, and Lanier had been traveling constantly for the past month).

Published in *Galaxy*, XXIV, 652-653 (Nov., 1877), with subtitle " A Dream of the Age "; reprinted with revisions and omission of four stanzas in *1884*, 95-96.

Text: *Clover* 67-69, MS, as VI of " Street-Cries " (the text used in *1884* except for two careless errors). For a full collation of variants, including the four rejected stanzas, see pp. 315-316, above. (The asterisks between the last two stanzas are Lanier's.)

The germ of the poem has survived in a fragmentary prose jotting (MS *CL*): " . . . to look upon the complex actions of gods: he [Wagner?] can make the gods misty, but the eye of the scientific age would much prefer the immeasurable profounds of music (which it knows it cannot pierce) to the quite measurable shallows of this old Scandinavian godhood (which it knows it could pierce easily if it had a mind to)." Lanier's admiration for Wagner's "music of the future" is amply testified to in the letters, in " Mazzini on Music," and in three short prose pieces (see II, 307-315, 336-339). The solution of social problems through music is similar to that in " The Symphony," for he considered Wagner the prophet of the new age of industry (see " To Beethoven," note, p. 351, above; see also the Introduction for a general treatment of this theme). Lanier began a translation of Wagner's *Das Rheingold*, but did not get beyond fifty lines (see IX, 112, and note).

SONG OF THE CHATTAHOOCHEE (103-104)

Written in Baltimore, end of Nov., 1877 (see letters of Nov. 27, 30, and note 103).

Said to have been published in *Scott's Magazine* in 1877 (see *1884*, iii, and F. V. N. Painter, *Poets of the South*, New York, 1903, p. 227); first verified publication in *Independent*, XXXV, 1601 (Dec. 20, 1883), from which it was reprinted with correction of two misprints in *1884*, 24-25.

Text: *Clover* 6-10, MS (the text used in the posthumous prints). Capitals have been supplied in ll. 13, 15, 17. The variants from the " early printing," as preserved in Painter, 184-186, are given on pp. 316-317, above.

The evidence concerning the first publication of this poem is confusing. Lanier's letters of Nov. 27, 30, 1877, state that it was " written for a little paper at West Point, Ga.," just being started by a friend of his, and sent off on the former date; but no such periodical has been found. Painter says (p. 227) that it was "first published in *Scott's Magazine*, Atlanta, Georgia, from which it is here taken. It at once became popular, and was copied in many newspapers throughout the South. It was subsequently revised, and the changes, which are pointed out below, are interesting as showing the development of the poet's artistic sense." He then reproduced this different early version; though he does not specifically date this printing, he speaks of it (p. 94) as being two or three years after 1875; and *1884*, iii, dates it specifically as "Scott's Magazine, 1877." But the only periodical bearing this title that has been discovered, *Scott's Monthly Magazine*, ceased to exist in 1869, and a search of its files fails to reveal Lanier's poem. The *Macon Daily Telegraph and Messenger* for 1877-1878 has also been searched for a possible reprinting. Here the matter rests.

The theme of the poem is suggested in a passage in "Sketches of India," written in the autumn of 1875, describing a waterfall where the river Nerbadá "leaps out eagerly toward the low lands he is to fertilize, like a young poet anxious to begin his work of grace in the world" (see VI, 277, of the present edition). The Chattahoochee River Lanier was familiar with from his summers spent at Marietta, Ga. It is described in *1895*, 78, as follows: "The Chattahoochee River rises in Habersham County, in northeast Georgia, and, intersecting Hall County, flows southwestward to West Point, then southward until it unites with the Flint River at the southwestern extremity of Ga." Lanier's most popular poem, it has frequently been praised for its technical skill. A note by W. H. Ward, accompanying its publication in the *Independent*, said that it was "written just as he was formulating to himself the principles of poetic art." One commentator has suggested that Coleridge's "Song of Glycine" was the musical source of the poem, a fact which "throws light on Lanier's method of poetic composition, suggesting that his poems had their genesis in music rather than in idea" (Philip Graham, "A Note on Lanier's Music," University of Texas *Studies in English*, XVII, 111, 1937). The most common comparison has been to Tennyson's "The Brook," a poem from which Lanier quoted in a letter of Feb. 3, 1878. (An elaborate analysis of its versification is made by C. W. Kent, "A Study of Lanier's Poems," *PMLA*, VII, 33-63, Apr., 1892; see also Introduction.)

THE HARD TIMES IN ELFLAND (105-111)

Written in Baltimore, end of Nov., 1877 (see letters of Nov. 21, 22, 27, and 30).

Published in the Baltimore *Every Saturday*, Christmas Supplement, Dec. 22, 1877, p. 1, with early subtitle "A Story of Christmas Eve" (photo in *JU*); reprinted with correction of errors in mechanics in *1884*, 152-160.

Text: *Clover*, 75-85, *Every Saturday* print, pasted, unrevised except for new subtitle. As in *1884* the following corrections have been made in mechanics: *To* for *to* (l. 63); *If* supplied (l. 67); *flapp'd* for *flap'd* (l. 70); semi-colon supplied (l. 84); *Look* for *look* (l. 101); *Claus* for *Klaus* (ll. 205, 215); and missing quotation marks supplied. No other version known.

One of Lanier's most successful ventures in light verse, this is a humorous solution of his economic distress in the autumn of 1877. He had returned to Baltimore after an absence of eighteen months, including the long illness in Florida, and was living in a cheap flat at 55 Lexington St., as yet unable to secure remunerative employment sufficient to support his family, whom he had brought with him for the first time. His wife and three sons, Charles, Henry, and Sidney ("Nimblewits"), are referred to specifically; "Newfoundland Fan" was a neighbor's dog. *MDL* testifies to the autobiographical content in a letter printed in " The Sons of Sidney Lanier and ' Hard Times in Elfland,' " *Young Southron*, I, 31, Christmas, 1896. See also the suggestion by Starke, 290, that it may be taken as an allegory, in which " Elfland is the South, and Santa Claus is the southern planter who has [been ruined by] the honeyed persuasions of the industrialist and the stock-broker." Further, it may reflect the financial depression which had lasted into 1877, with railroad riots in Pittsburgh during the summer and autumn. Lanier's letter of Nov. 14, 1877, says that he was to be paid $50-$75 for " Hard Times," but there is no further evidence on this point. He later tried to get it published with illustrations (see letters to Taylor, Jan. 6, 1878, and to Scribner, May 22, 1879; the *Every Saturday* print was accompanied by one smudgy woodcut).

A WEATHER-VANE (112)

Probably written in Baltimore, autumn of 1877 (from evidence of publication date).

Published in *Dial of the Old South Clock*, 7 (Dec. 10, 1877), an occasional issued daily (except Sunday), Dec. 5-15, 1877, at a fair for the benefit of the Old South Church, Boston; reprinted without change by J. H. Birss, " A Humorous Quatrain by Lanier," *American Literature*, V, 270 (Nov., 1933). Previously uncollected.

Text: *Dial*. No other version known.

According to Birss: " *The Dial* . . . does not seem to contain deliberate parodies of named authors [the poem was printed over Sidney Lanier's signature], and there is no reason to doubt the authenticity of Lanier's lines." A possible explanation of the meaning of the poem is that the magazine was originally intended to be called *The Weather-Vane*, and that Lanier replied to a request to contribute with a humorous comment on this title.

THE HARLEQUIN OF DREAMS (112)

Apparently written in Baltimore, winter of 1878 (from evidence of publication date; possibly one of the two poems referred to in Lanier's letter to Peacock, Jan. 6, 1878).

Published in *Lippincott's*, XXI, 439 (Apr., 1878); reprinted without change in Epes Sargent, *Harper's Cyclopaedia of British and American Poetry* (New York, 1881), 917, and in *1884*, 85.

Text: Sargent. No variants known. (Originally included in *Clover* 49, as indicated in " Subjects for Illustration," but now missing. MS *CL* is a copy, apparently in the handwriting of W. R. Thayer.)

The best of Lanier's sonnets, this is one of half-a-dozen written during the first part of 1878, probably growing out of his studies in Renaissance sonneteers for the Bird lectures (see III, viii). It was singled out for special praise by the London *Spectator* (undated clipping, *JU*).

THE REVENGE OF HAMISH (112-116)

Probably written in Baltimore, winter of 1878.

Published in *Appleton's Journal*, V [n. s.], 395-396 (Nov., 1878); reprinted with slight revision in *1884*, 33-38.

Text: *Clover* 20-27, MS and early print (the versions followed in *1884* with one careless error). *Appleton's* has four variants, two of which are significant:

and her little keen ears made turn for *and rounded her ears in turn* (l. 7) ; and
.ll unweeting, stood watching and for *never baiting his watch tarried* (l. 30).
Written as an experiment in logaœdic dactyls, growing out of Lanier's metrical
studies for the Bird lectures (see letter of Oct. 20, 1878, and III, vii-viii). It
was based on an episode in William Black's novel, *Macleod of Dare*, Chap. III,
printed serially in *Harper's*, XVI, 412-413 (Feb., 1878), which it follows
identically in plot, though the name of the henchman is borrowed from another
character (*1895*, 79, states that Lanier discussed the source of the poem with
his friend J. R. Tait). Charles Mackay's poem, " Maclaine's Child " (*Poetical
Works*, London, 1876, 99-101) is similar in plot, but was clearly not a source
for Lanier. " The Revenge of Hamish," the most ambitious narrative poem he
ever completed, has the spirit if not the form of medieval balladry, and was
included in Henry F. Randolph's *The Book of Latter-Day Ballads* (New York,
1888), 187-194, along with selections from Whittier, Lowell, Bret Harte,
Tennyson, Browning, Meredith, Morris, Rossetti, and others. For a recent criticism see Yves Bourgeois, " Sidney Lanier et le Goffic," *Revue Anglo-Americaine*,
VIII, 431-432 (June, 1931). He was paid $30 for it by *Appleton's* (letter from
O. B. Bunce, Mar. 15, 1878).

TO NANNETTE FALK-AUERBACH (117)

Written in Baltimore, Mar. 27, 1878 (so dated in the first printing).
Published in the Baltimore *Gazette*, Mar. 28, 1878; reprinted without change
in *1884*, 102.
Text: *Clover* 71, MS (same text as in the prints). No variants known.
This sonnet was first written in German, a copy of which was sent to Bayard
Taylor in a letter of Mar. 25, 1878 (for Taylor's comments see note 36, Letters
of 1878). A note in *1884*, 244, says that this version was published in " a
German Daily of Baltimore," but a search of all available files of such news-
papers fails to reveal it (see *Volksfreund und Biene* and *Der Deutsche Cor-
respondent*). A MS survives in *CL* with a few errors in the mechanics of the
German script; these were corrected, probably by *MDL*, when it was printed in
1884, 101, the text reproduced below:

An Frau Nannette Falk-Auerbach

Als du im Saal mit deiner himmlischen Kunst
  Beethoven zeigst, und seinem Willen nach
Mit den zehn Fingern führst der Leute Gunst,
  Zehn Zungen sagen was der Meister sprach.
Schauend dich an, ich seh', dass nicht allein
  Du sitzest: jetzt herab die Töne ziehn
Beethovens Geist: er steht bei dir, ganz rein:
  Für dich mit Vaters Stolz sein' Augen glühn:
Er sagt, " Ich hörte dich aus Himmelsluft,
  Die kommt ja näher, wo ein Künstler spielt:
Mein Kind (ich sagte) mich zur Erde ruft:
  Ja, weil mein Arm kein Kind im Leben hielt,
Gott hat mir dich nach meinem Tod gegeben,
  Nannette, Tochter! dich, mein zweites Leben! "

Mme. Auerbach, instructor in piano at the Peabody Conservatory and a distinguished concert-artist, was a close friend of Lanier's. He admired her extrava-

gantly, especially for her interpretation of Beethoven. In describing her rendition of his *Concerto in G* for piano at the Maryland Musical Festival in May, 1878 (two months after writing this sonnet), Lanier declared: "Her greatness and simplicity seem to be genuine emanations from Beethoven's genius" (see II, 324).

TO OUR MOCKING BIRD (117-118)

Written in Baltimore, May-June, 1878 (shortly after the bird's death, which was on May 9, according to MS *CL*).

Published in *Independent*, XXX, 1 (Aug. 29, 1878); reprinted without change in *1884*, 103-104.

Text: *Clover* 72-74, *Independent* print revised in punctuation only. Two MSS survive; for a full collation of variants see p. 317, above.

In "Bob: The Story of Our Mocking-Bird" (VI, 340-349), juvenile prose, Lanier tells of this family pet whose death was the occasion of the poem, treating him as the symbol of the poet: "in consideration that he is the Voice of his whole race, singing the passions of all his fellows better than any one could sing his own, he is clearly entitled to be named William Shakespere." (See also "The Mocking Bird" and note, p. 353, above.)

THE MARSHES OF GLYNN (119-122)

Written in Baltimore, probably summer of 1878 (see letter of July 13).

Published in *A Masque of Poets* (Boston, 1878), 88-94; reprinted without change in H. W. Longfellow's *Poems of Places. America. Southern States* (Boston, 1879), 252-257; and with revisions in *1884*, 14-18, as IV of "Hymns of the Marshes."

Text: *1884*. The authority for this version is conjectural but strong. All of the changes in the twelve lines that show variants are distinct improvements in artistic form or in meaning, and are such as Lanier himself would have made. The poem is marked on the Chronological List in *MDL's* handwriting (*CL*) as "1878-1879," indicating a revision in the latter year; and it was originally included in *Clover* 11-19, printer's copy of a projected volume made up in May, 1879 (these pages are now missing, but the contents are proved by the accompanying table of "Subjects for Illustration"). Hence it is reasonable to assume that Lanier made a revision, which was the one followed in *1884*. (The variants in the earlier prints are given on p. 317, above.)

The marshes of Glynn County are on the coast of Georgia, near Brunswick, and persistent legend has tried to connect the composition of the poem with the locale, as early as 1875 (see Starke, 279 and note 9). Lanier had known the region thoroughly for many years, his latest visit being in the spring of 1877 returning from Florida (see letter to Taylor, Apr. 26); and it is possible that he may have written the first two stanzas at this time, as the most convincing account reports (see Mattie T. Northen in the Atlanta *Journal*, May 19, 1929, supposedly quoting from a lost letter from Lanier to Mrs. Jas. H. Couper, a Brunswick friend). All that can be established with certainty on this point is that the poem grew out of Lanier's actual experience of the region. A foreshadowing of the opening lines may be found in an unpublished prose jotting (*Ledger* 602-603), made before he left Tampa:

"In among the trees in Florida. Here walking one presently finds a host of contrasts exhaling from one's contemplation of the forest, one glides out of the idea that this multiform beauty is familiar, that it is a clump of trees and vines and flowers: No, it is Silence, which, denied access to man's ear, has caught form, and set forth its fervent appeal to man's eye: it is Music, in a siesta; it is Conflict, dead, and reappearing as Beauty: it is amiable Mystery, grown communicative: it is Nature, with her finger on her lip,—gesture of double significance, conveying to one, that one may kiss her, if one will say nothing about it: it is Tranquillity, suavely waving aside men's excuses for wars, . . . it is Trade, done into a flower, and blossoming as perfect type of honest *quid pro quo*, in the lavish good measure of that interchange whereby the undersides of leaves use man's breath and return him the same in better condition, paying profitable usuries for what the lender could not help loaning: it is a Reply, in all languages, but untranslateable in any, to the multitudinous interrogations . . . of students who dimly behold the unknowable world of the something unexplainably sweet beyond the immediate field of thought, itself yet far from being crossed,—interrogations of business-men, who, with little time for thinking of the things beyond their routines, yet occasionally desire some little concise revelation of the enormous Besides and Overplus which they suspect to lie beyond all Trade,—interrogations of the pleasure-seeker who cannot but hope that there will be Something Else, when the ball is over at the hotel,— interrogations of the sick man, petulantly wondering if he shall ever find companions who will not shudder when he coughs, nor coddle him with pitying absurdities . . . ."

On Apr. 20, 1878, he was invited by G. P. Lathrop to contribute to an anthology in the "No Name" Series being published by Roberts Brothers, Boston. Lanier's reply has not been found, but it seems clear that "The Marshes of Glynn" was written specifically as his contribution to *A Masque of Poets*. Just when he began the composition of it is not known, but probably not many weeks before the known date of its completion in mid July (letter of July 13 says he has just sent it off "hot from the mint"). Part of it is said to have been written on the schoolhouse steps at Pen Lucy, the academy of R. M. Johnston, where Lanier was teaching at this time (see VII, xxxviii, and notes 95 and 96). At any rate, it was published in Nov., 1878, and attracted some little attention in spite of its anonymity. (For an account of the contents and the reception of *A Masque of Poets* see A. H. Starke, "An Omnibus of Poets," *Colophon*, IV, part 16, Mar., 1934.)

Like "The Revenge of Hamish" (112), it was another experiment in logaœdic dactyls, growing out of his metrical studies in the "Physics of Poetry," in process of composition during the summer of 1878 (see II, viii-xiii). Another influence, especially in the rhythmical freedom of the long loose lines, came from Whitman, whose poetry he had read for the first time in Jan., 1878, and a copy of whose *Leaves of Grass* he had bought on May 5 (see Lanier's letter of that date to Whitman). The treatment of nature and the touches of mysticism reflect the medieval poets he had been reading during this year (see letter to Peacock, Dec. 21, 1878; cf. the closing paragraphs of the seventh Peabody lecture and the quotation from his own poem in the twelfth Johns Hopkins lecture, III, 39-40, 334). Beyond all this, however, it is essentially original and typical of its author, "the poem of Lanier's spiritual maturity" according to Starke, and generally conceded to be one of his very best.

STREET-CRIES (122)

Probably written in Baltimore, summer of 1878.

Published posthumously in *1884*, 86, as the introductory stanzas to seven poems grouped under this general heading.

Text: *Clover* 50, MS (the text followed in *1884*). MS *CL*, untitled, undated, and unsigned, is a rough draft showing several alterations and variants.

The two poems immediately following, "Remonstrance" and "How Love Looked for Hell," were apparently written *c.* July 13, 1878 (see notes below), and it seems safe to assume that these introductory lines were written about the same time. The subject matter and general theme of all three seem to mark them as the nucleus of Lanier's projected volume, "Songs of Aldhelm," mentioned in a letter of Oct. 20, 1878, as "now in a pigeon-hole of my desk half-jotted down." When this volume was abandoned, they were transferred in May, 1879, to another projected volume, "Clover and Other Poems." Here, along with five earlier poems and with these two stanzas as a sort of proem to be set in smaller type, they were assembled under the general title of "Street-Cries," as follows: I. "Remonstrance" (122), II. "The Ship of Earth" (15), III. "How Love Looked for Hell" (125), IV. "Tyranny," (13), V. "Life and Song" (16), VI. "To Richard Wagner" (102), and VII. "A Song of Love" (58). This grouping was followed in *1884*, but was abandoned in the present edition, and the inclosing quotation marks omitted. (For a fuller account of Lanier's projected volumes, see Introduction.)

REMONSTRANCE (122-124)

Written in Baltimore, summer of 1878.

Published posthumously in *Century*, XXV, 819-820 (Apr., 1883); reprinted with correction of one misprint (*clods* for *clouds*) in *1884*, 86-88.

Text: *Clover* 50-55, MS, numbered I of "Street-Cries" (with *lovable* for *loveable*, l. 11, as in *1884*, which followed this text). This MS shows one alteration, *struggling* > *hideous* (l. 48); no other variants known.

Though not published by Lanier, this poem was submitted to *Lippincott's* but rejected because of its attack on orthodoxy (see letter of Aug. 24, 1878, and note to "How Love Looked for Hell," below); his intention to publish is further indicated by its inclusion in *Clover*. MDL was paid $75 for it by *Century* with the comment, "How did such a poem escape publication?" (letters to her from R. W. Gilder, Dec. 23, 1882, and Apr. 4, 1883).

In theme this poem fits with the Poem Outlines grouped under the heading "Credo and Other Poems" (pp. 262-275, above); indeed, the germ of it has been preserved in just such unfinished form (MS *JT*, a copy made in 1883 by J. A. Fisher), entitled "Free":

> Opinion, let me alone—
> Damned be he (cried the Saxon) that doth not believe
> That Christ had black eyes and black hair.
> Damned be he (cried the Spaniard) that doth not believe
> That Christ had black eyes and black hair.
> Who is he that will fasten creeds before mine eyes, &c.

The allusions in l. 55 are to Nicholas Ridley, an English bishop, and Michael Servetus, a Spanish scientific and theological writer, both burned at the stake during the Inquisition.

HOW LOVE LOOKED FOR HELL (125-127)

Probably written in Baltimore, summer of 1878.

Published posthumously in *Century*, XXVII, 733-734 (Mar., 1884); reprinted without change in *1884*, 89-92.

Text: *Clover* 57-64, MS, numbered III of "Street-Cries" (with punctuation supplied in ll. 10, 20, 21, 34, 35, 63, 84, 111—the text used in *1884*). MS *CL* is a rough draft of the first stanza, unrhymed, with minor variants.

Probably one of the three poems mentioned in Lanier's letter of July 13, 1878, as just sent off "hot from the mint"; one of these was "The Marshes of Glynn," another seems to have been "Remonstrance," and this the third—it being the only poem of this period (dated "1878-1879" in *1884*) not specifically accounted for. It is possibly the unnamed poem submitted to the *North American Review* and rejected in a letter of Aug. 25, 1878. At any rate, Lanier's intention to publish it is indicated by its inclusion in *Clover*. *MDL* was paid $85 by *Century* for this poem (and "A Song of Love"; see letter to her from R. W. Gilder, Oct. 1, 1883), presumptive evidence that it was not actually published in Lanier's lifetime.

The germ of the poem is contained in a prose note in the *Ledger* 330-331, undated but *c.* 1874: "In all times and peoples, the same old gigantic Tale appears, in never-exhausted forms, how that Love went down into Hell, and rose again: Ishtar, Venus, Proserpine, Eurydice, Virgil, Dante, Goethe's Faust, Bailey's Festus, Christ. This is indeed the Story of Life. Childhood, pure Love, goes down into the fires and smokes of youth,—that time when desires burn, when we plunge ourselves into great [*illegible*] darknesses of sins, when we scorch our hearts with insane rushings through the fires of life, when we are beasts and revel in the brutalities that make our faces grave forever afterward, when we scorn our mothers (and would die ten deaths, afterwards in later life, if we might blot it out) when we laugh at our fathers, when we are simply a pitchy flame of Self. In Manhood, we rise again,—those of us who do not die eternally in the youth stage. (Poem). S. L." (Cf. the implied theme of the poem, that evil is the absence of good, with Lanier's later philosophy in "Opposition.")

TO BAYARD TAYLOR (128-130)

Written in Baltimore, Dec., 1878 (accepted by Scribner, Dec. 28; see also Lanier's letter of Jan. 1, 1879).

Published in *Scribner's*, XVII, 642-643 (Mar., 1879); reprinted without change in *1884*, 39-42.

Text: *Clover* 28-31, *Scribner* print, unchanged. MSS *HA* and *UC* are both signed "Sidney Lanier" and undated. They agree with each other in showing several variants, the most interesting of which are: *And burns towards* for *Wild-stretching towards* (l. 42) and *drooping* for *dolorous* (l. 76).

Bayard Taylor, the subject of this elegy, had died in Berlin on Dec. 19, 1878. (Lanier had earlier addressed another poem to him, "Under the Cedarcroft Chestnut," 93.) Stanzas 7-8 contain allusions to Taylor's *Prince Deukalion* (1878), his translation of *Faust* (1870-1871), and his projected biography of Goethe. "Opposition" (130), written the following year, takes its refrain from l. 80. "To Bayard Taylor," the only poem published by Lanier in 1879, reflects in its "literary" qualities the studies Lanier was pursuing for his Peabody lectures during this winter.

OPPOSITION (130-131)

Written in Baltimore, probably in the spring of 1879.

Published in *Good Company*, IV, 444 (Jan., 1880); reprinted without change in *1884*, 51.

Text: *Good Company*. Two MSS and a draft of the idea, dated Tampa, 1877, survive; for a full collation of variants see pp. 317-318, above.

The conception apparently dates from 1877. The opening line echoes l. 80 of "To Bayard Taylor," written in Dec. 1878. The inclusion of this poem (under the title "The fret that's fixed across the Lute" and marked "MS") on a list drawn up by Lanier apparently in preparation for his projected volume *Clover* indicates that it was probably written by May, 1879. MS *ET* is dated "1879 / 180 St. Paul St.," Lanier's residence until Sept. 25, 1879, and hence must have been written before he went on his vacation to Rockingham Springs on July 18. The theme of the poem—that both rhythm and moral development stem from "opposition"—had been expounded in his Peabody lectures in the winter of 1879 and was further elaborated in his *Science of English Verse* written the following summer, and elsewhere. This theory, his most important contribution to literary criticism, grew out of his reading in contemporary science (treated in Introduction). "Opposition" is Lanier's most philosophical poem and one of his most significant to recent critics, being chosen by Conrad Aiken, for example, as the single poem to represent its author in his Modern Library Anthology, *American Poetry, 1671-1928* (New York, 1929).

OWL AGAINST ROBIN (131-133)

Written in Boston, June 2, 1879; revised at Rockingham Springs, Va., July-Aug. (see Lanier's letter of June 4, MS *JU*, and letter from *Scribner's* Aug. 14).

Published in *Scribner's*, XXII, 453-454 (July, 1881); reprinted without change in *1884*, 47-49.

Text: *Scribner's*. Two MSS survive; for a full collation of variants see pp. 318-320, above.

In accepting the poem *Scribner's* wrote: "We have handed it to the artist to see what he can do with the illustrations." These did not materialize, but negotiation concerning them may explain the delay of two years between acceptance and publication. This is a rare example of humor in Lanier's poems other than the dialect verse. It probably represents a good-natured reversal of his own trouble in sleeping during nights of illness.

"Baalbec" (l. 51) was an ancient city of Syria, near Damascus, the center of worship of the sun-god Baal.

ODE TO THE JOHNS HOPKINS UNIVERSITY (133-135)

Probably written in Baltimore, Feb., 1880.

Published in *Johns Hopkins University Circular*, No. 4, pp. 38-39 (Apr., 1880); reprinted with one change in *Baltimore Christmas Magazine*, pp. 59-61 (Dec., 1880); and, as originally, in *1884*, 108-111.

Text: *Christmas Magazine* (by authority of Lanier's letter to the editor, G. E. Dorsey, Nov. 29 (?) 1880, where he speaks of correcting "some important errors of punctuation in the Circular imprint"). A MS and two sets of corrected proof sheets survive (see facsimiles in Starke, facing 364, 366); for a full collation of variants see pp. 320-321, above.

Read on the fourth Commemoration Day, Feb. 23, 1880 (Feb. 22, the regular anniversary, fell on Sunday this year), during the first year of Lanier's lectureship at the Johns Hopkins University. The *Circular* print contained a footnote explaining the allusion in ll. 12-14: "An algebraic theorem announced by Newton was demonstrated and extended by Sylvester" (reprinted in *1884*, 244). An account of Lanier's relations with the university and his friendship with J. J. Sylvester and the other professors is given elsewhere in the present edition (see VII, xl-liii; see also III, 411-419, for an encyclopædia article on the early history of Johns Hopkins written by Lanier at about the same time). Though an occasional poem, it is interesting for its revelation of Lanier's devotion to science and to literature (see Introduction, and cf. the note to " The Crystal," below).

[IRELAND] (136)

Written in Baltimore, Mar., 1880 (see letter of Mar. 26).

Published in *The Art Autograph* (New York, 1880), plate 10, facsimile of MS, untitled; reprinted without change but with title added in *1884*, 148.

Text: *Art Autograph* (with punctuation supplied end l. 12). No variants known.

This was Lanier's contribution to a project organized by the New York *Herald* to raise money for the relief of the Irish famine. Most of the prominent American authors contributed to the volume, which was issued in May, 1880 (see letter of May 21).

THE CRYSTAL (136-139)

Probably written in Baltimore, spring, 1880 (from evidence of publication date).

Published in *Independent*, XXXII, 1 (July 15, 1880); reprinted without change in *1884*, 29-32.

Text: *Independent* (with 12 introductory lines rejected by authority of Lanier's letter to Sarah Bird, Feb.-Mar., 1881). For the rejected lines, a rough draft, and a full collation of variants in two surviving MSS see p. 321, above.

The circumstances of composition are not mentioned in Lanier's letters, but it must have been after Sept., 1879, when he moved to N. Calvert St., the address written on MS *HA*; and since he usually submitted his poems to the magazines shortly after composition, the date can be placed at about two months before its publication. He was paid $20 for it by W. H. Ward (letter of July 23, 1880), editor of the *Independent*, who wrote a note in the same issue in which it appeared (p. 18) calling attention to it as " a sermon in verse " and mentioning the fact that Lanier was a lecturer on literature at Johns Hopkins. The allusions in " The Crystal " to the great whom Lanier loved reflects his recent studies; he had paid similar reverence before (in " Clover," " The Stirrup-Cup," and elsewhere), but here there were new names and a more critical attitude. Treated at length in the Peabody and Hopkins lectures are Æschylus, Cædmon, Langland, and Shakespeare (the plays here referred to— *Romeo and Juliet, Richard III, Henry IV Pt. 2, Two Gentlemen of Verona, Twelfth Night, The Merchant of Venice,* and *As You Like It*—were not Lanier's favorites; see III and IV, *passim*). Copies of these and the following are preserved in Lanier's library, Johns Hopkins University, many with annotations: Dante's *Divine Comedy, The Discourses of Epictetus,* Homer's *Odyssey,* and Lucretius's *De Rerum Natura* (a copy of Socrates, bought from Turnbull & Bros., Apr. 11, 1879, has not survived—see list in *CL.*) Keats, Milton, and Tennyson had been life-long favorites; Emerson since 1877. Nothing further is known of Lanier's interest in Marcus Aurelius, Jakob Behmen, and Thomas à Kempis, whom he probably knew only at second-hand. (For his interest in Buddhist philosophy see the note to " Nirvâna," p. 335, above.) Defects in all these are " forgiven " to point up the perfection of Christ, though Lanier's concern here as always is more with ethics than with theology (see Introduction). A further kinship with " Clover " may be found in the echoed phrase " the course of things " (l. 3 of the omitted introduction), allegorized as an Ox in the earlier poem.

THE CLOUD (139-141)

Probably written in Baltimore, June, 1880 (see letter of June 15).

Published posthumously in *Century*, XXV, 222-223 (Dec., 1882), as "Individuality"; reprinted without change, except for addition of eight lines, in *1884*, 10-13, as "Hymns of the Marshes / II / Individuality."

Text: MS *CL*, entitled "Hymns of the Marshes / II / The Cloud," signed "Sidney Lanier," undated but in his late handwriting (apostrophe added l. 21; capitals ll. 50, 61). No authority has been found for the variants in the posthumous prints, and the title there used seems to have been an earlier one (see Lanier's letter of June 15, 1880, and the alteration on MS *JT*). MS *CL* is apparently the latest revision. For a full collation, including the variants in two MSS, see pp. 322-323, above.

Although not published by Lanier, it was submitted to *Lippincott's* in a letter of June 15, 1880 (containing an explanation of its genesis and meaning); it was also intended for inclusion in his projected volume, "Hymns of the Marshes." *MDL* was paid $75 for it by *Century* (letter to her of Jan. 19, 1882), presumptive evidence that it had not been previously published.

This poem reveals, more fully than any other by Lanier, his interest in the conflict between evolution and religion, between scientific determinism and the responsibility of the individual. There also survives a similar prose jotting (MS *CL*), which shows how Lanier frequently made memoranda without being certain whether he intended to use them in prose or poetry, and which points up the relationship of "The Cloud" to the theme of "Personality" developed in the lectures at Johns Hopkins, winter, 1881 (see IV, 6). It is written on a blank envelop, with a note at the top: "J. H. The Sacred Difference between me and you. The Modern Personality." Then beneath: "Marsh Hymns. It is at this difference, as I understand it, that Evolution stop[s]: See Fiske in Jany Atlantic, Darwin, Spencer &c. You cannot account for it. Here it would seem the direct hand of God is involved [?] in world's economy. The inconceivably thyself. . . . Tennyson ["De Profundis"]." On the reverse side: "The mystery in us which calls itself I. No man would voluntarily exchange personalities: nature has taken care of this sacred difference. (Shakspere's Sonnet) Vedder's picture. Whitman's mistake: he has only sung the average man: the reserve of *me* he has overridden in the most shocking manner. This force, what becomes of it on the principle of conservation? You cannot account for origin. A new function [*illegible*]. . . ." (See Introduction.)

MARSH SONG—AT SUNSET (142)

Probably written in Baltimore, late autumn of 1880 (dated "Fall of 1880" in the handwriting of *MDL* on a MS list of Lanier's poems, *CL*; see also note 124, letters of 1880).

Published posthumously in *Our Continent*, I, 4 (Feb. 15, 1882); reprinted without change in *1884*, 13, as III of "Hymns of the Marshes."

Text: *Our Continent*. No other text known except a draft of five lines included in an early version of "The Cloud" (see p. 322, above).

Not published by Lanier, but apparently intended for inclusion in his projected volume, "Hymns of the Marshes." The allusions to Shakespeare's *The Tempest*, without which the poem is unintelligible, will be readily identified by the student.

[BETWEEN DAWN AND SUNRISE] (142)

Written in Baltimore, Nov.-Dec., 1880 (see note to " Sunrise " and note 124, Letters of 1880).

Published posthumously in *Independent*, XLIII, 625 (Apr. 30, 1891) ; reprinted without change in *1891*, 157.

Text: MS *JT* of " Sunrise," following l. 123, with the marginal notation: " This song, like the other [Ballad of Trees and the Master], in smaller print " (see note to " Sunrise," p. 366, below). The title, here retained in brackets from *1891*, was probably supplied by *MDL*. No authority has been found for the radically different version in the posthumous prints, given entire on p. 323, above, but *JT* has been adopted because it is in Lanier's handwriting and is unquestionably a more perfected form—the rhyme being completed in the last line. (Of the variant version, a note in the *Independent* print, by the editor, W. H. Ward, says: " This draft for one of the *Marsh Hymns* was found among Mr. Lanier's papers." It may have been withheld from publication for ten years because of the faulty rhyme.)

Though unpublished by Lanier, it was obviously intended for inclusion in his projected volume, " Hymns of the Marshes."

A SUNRISE SONG (143)

Written in Baltimore, Nov.-Dec., 1880 (probably one of the " two little Songs just sent," mentioned in letter to W. H. Ward, Dec. 6, inclosing " A Ballad of Trees and the Master ").

Published in *Independent*, XXXIII, 1 (Apr. 28, 1881) ; reprinted without change in *1891*, 152.

Text: *Independent*. No variants known.

Apparently intended for inclusion in Lanier's projected volume, " Hymns of the Marshes."

[TO THE SUN] (143)

Written in Baltimore, probably Nov., 1880 (see letter of Dec. 6, and note 124). Previously unpublished, but clearly intended by Lanier as one of his " Hymns of the Marshes," a projected volume.

Text: MS *JT* of " Sunrise," following l. 158 (with italics removed and period supplied at the end). No other version known. Title supplied by the present editor.

Of three intercalary songs included in the first drafts but omitted from the final version of " Sunrise " (see note, p. 366), this one is now first made known to students of Lanier.

A BALLAD OF TREES AND THE MASTER (144)

Written in Baltimore on or shortly before Dec. 1, 1880 (see note 124, Letters of 1880).

Published in *Independent*, XXXII, 1 (Dec. 23, 1880) ; reprinted without change in *1884*, 141.

Text: *Independent*. No variants known.

The finest of Lanier's lyrics and probably the most perfect poem he ever wrote, it was composed at one sitting in " fifteen or twenty minutes . . . just as we have it without erasure or correction " (see Mary Day Lanier's accounts quoted in Starke, 407-408, and note 124, Letters of 1880). It is also incorporated in a surviving MS of "Sunrise" (*JT*) following line 57, with the marginal notation: "This little intercalary song to be in italics, or, perhaps better, in smaller print than the main text." (See facsimile facing p. 275, vol. X; *1884*, 245, says erroneously that it followed line 53.) One of three such songs, this is the only one that Lanier extracted for separate publication; he was paid $15.00 for it by the *Independent* (see W. H. Ward's letter of Dec. 24, 1880, and the note to "Sunrise," following). It has been set to music by various composers, notably George W. Chadwick and Francis Urban. According to *Luke* xxii:39 the olive grove in Gethsemane was the place where Christ was wont to go for prayer. For the place of this poem in Lanier's religion see the Introduction to the present volume.

SUNRISE (144-149)

Written in Baltimore, Dec., 1880; revised, Jan., 1881.

Published posthumously in *Independent*, XXXIV, 1 (Dec. 14, 1882); reprinted with a few changes in spelling and punctuation in *1884*, 3, as I of "Hymns of the Marshes."

Text: MS *RL*, entitled "Hymns of the Marshes / I / Sunrise," signed "Sidney Lanier / 435 N. Calvert St. / Baltimore, Md.," undated but clearly the final version, both from the appearance of the MS and from the fact that it does not contain "A Ballad of the Trees and Master." (A note in *1884*, 245, says that the first copy and first revision of "Sunrise" included the "Ballad," which was omitted from the final version. The present text is apparently the one followed in *1884*, but with a few changes in punctuation and five errors in reading the MS, as indicated in the collation, below. The MS is here reproduced exactly, except for a few changes in mechanics, following *1884*: capitals removed from *sleep*, ll. 11, 14; *silence's* for *silence'*, l. 67; hyphen for *build-fire*, l. 128; capital for *Sun*, ll. 175, 181.) Two other MSS survive; for a full collation of variants see pp. 323-325, above.

This poem was written when Lanier had a fever temperature of 104° (*1895*, xviii). A note by *MDL* in H. W. Lanier, *Selections from Sidney Lanier* (New York, 1916), 164, reads: "The lines of *Sunrise* were so silently traced that for successive days I removed the little bedside desk and replaced in its sliding drawer the pale-blue leaves faintly penciled, with no leisure for even mental conjecture of them. . . . That hand 'too weak to sustain the effort of carrying food to the lips,' I had propped to the level of the adjustable writing desk. After New Year the perfect manuscript was put into my hand, and I was bidden to read it." A letter from *MDL* to Charlotte Ware, Sept. 13, 1910, describing the composition of "A Ballad of Trees and the Master," written shortly before Dec. 2, 1880 (see note 124, Letters of 1880), says that the "Ballad" was incorporated "a month later" in the first draft of "Sunrise"; but a letter to Katherine Tyler, Feb. 23, 1923, states specifically that the latter was written in "December, 1880"—hence probably near the end of the month. A note in *1884*, 243, says that "Sunrise" was Lanier's "latest completed poem," and this is in a general sense true; for it was written at the beginning of the final illness that all but incapacitated him during the last eight months of his life. Some of the brief untitled verses on pp. 208-210 of the present edition may have been written thereafter, however, and a number of the Poem Outlines definitely were. A note to the "Ballad," *1884*, 245, says: "It was one of several interludes which he at first designed, but, for some reason, afterwards abandoned." Lanier himself extracted "A Ballad of Trees and the Master" (144) for separate publication;

MDL published a second posthumously, " Between Dawn and Sunrise " (142) ; a third is now first published, " To the Sun " (143). Asterisks indicate their position in the MS. Though Lanier did not live to publish " Sunrise " himself, the MSS reveal his intention of making it the initial poem in his projected volume, " Hymns of the Marshes." The general consensus of critical opinion has ranked it, along with " The Marshes of Glynn," at the head of his poetry (see Introduction).

"OH, LIFE'S A FEVER AND DEATH'S A CHILL " (153)

Written at Fort Boykin, Va., Sept., 1863 (inclosed in letter of Sept. 15).
Published posthumously in *Independent*, LXI, 1095 (Nov. 8, 1906) ; reprinted without change in G. H. Clarke, *Some Reminiscences . . . of Sidney Lanier* (Macon, Ga., 1907), 19. Previously uncollected.
Text: Clarke. No variants known.
These burlesque lines refer to a recent attack of the " James River ague " from which Lanier had suffered (see letter of Aug. 5, 1863).

TO ——— (153)

Written at Ft. Boykin, Va., Dec., 1863 (see letter of Dec. 7 and note 50). Completed in Jan., 1864 (see letter of Jan. 18).
Published posthumously in *1884*, 222.
Text: *Ledger* 5, signed " S. C. L." and dated " Boykin's Bluff. 1864 " (March or later, since Jan.-Feb., 1864, were spent on an expedition to North Carolina)—probably a revision made *c.* 1865, since the *Ledger* was not begun until after the war. *Mist* and *Dream* have been capitalized consistently. Two other MSS survive, both in *CL,* inclosed in Lanier's letters to his father, Dec. 7, 1863, and Jan. 18, 1864 (printed in VII, 128, 136), and in his letter to Mary Day, Feb. 28, 1864; they have a few minor variants, but are earlier versions. *1884* shows one variant (l. 16): *Through it, O Love shone thy face, afar,* for which no authority has been found.
This poem, apparently addressed to Virginia Hankins (see note 50, letters of 1863), is the first Lanier had written since his college days, except for the burlesque quatrain above.

TO G. H. (154)

Written at Ft. Boykin, Va., May 23, 1864.
Published posthumously in *Independent*, LXI, 1095 (Nov. 8, 1906) ; reprinted without change in G. H. Clarke, *Some Reminiscences . . . of Sidney Lanier* (Macon, Ga., 1907), 17-18. Previously uncollected.
Text: *Ledger* 7, signed " S. C. L." (with commas supplied, ll. 1 and 8). This is the best of three surviving MSS, and though dated " 1864 " (apparently in another hand) is probably a revision made *c.* 1865, since the *Ledger* was not begun until after the war. MS *HF*, " To G. H.; alias ' *My* Love Bird '—by S. C. L.—May 23/64," the copy sent to Virginia Hankins, and MS *WM*, undated and unsigned, agree with each other and with the posthumous prints in showing a half-dozen variants, one sample of which will demonstrate their metrical inferiority: *Like one who hesitateth* for *As one that could not choose* (l. 10).
On p. 6 of the *Ledger* Lanier copied an extract from an undated lost letter written to him at Ft. Boykin by Virginia (" Ginna ") Hankins: " Do you remember the ' Brown Bird ' in the Drama of Exile, whose song as he sat on his tree in Paradise, was the last sound heard by Adam as he fled with Eve,

'along the glare'? So, O Friend, do I send my cry for you across these broad stretches of moonlight that lie between us." Lanier's poem, copied on the opposite page, was his reply. Elizabeth Barrett Browning's *A Drama of Exile*, a favorite with Lanier at this time, was the literary source (see her *Poems*, p. 72, ll. 328-355, Cambridge Edition).

TRANSLATION FROM THE GERMAN OF HEINE (154)

Written in prison at Point Lookout, Md., Dec. 11, 1864.
Published posthumously in *1884*, 224, with title "The Palm and the Pine," apparently added by *MDL*.
Text: *Ledger* 8, entitled "Translation," etc., signed "S. C. L.," and dated as above. (A copy in Lanier's handwriting, without title, is in *MDL's* Notebook, 94, *CL*.) No variants known.
This may have been submitted for magazine publication by Lanier, since in the issue of the *Round Table*, III, 443 (July 14, 1866), containing "Spring Greeting" (5) and "To J. L" (8), the editor appended the following note: "The translations from the German below, selected from a number sent us, appear to be very well done. The name of the original author is not stated." ("To J. L.," however, was not a translation.) It is a somewhat free rendering of Heine's "Lyrisches Intermezzo," XXXIII, in *Buch der Lieder* (Hamburg, 1841), 131.

"TEN THOUSAND STARS WERE IN THE SKY" (155)

Probably written in Macon, summer 1865. Previously unpublished.
Text: MS *CL*, in *MDL's* Notebook, 95, untitled, undated, and unsigned, but definitely in Lanier's early handwriting. It follows immediately after a copy in the same handwriting of Lanier's "Translation from the German of Heine" (see above); and though the latter was written in Dec., 1864, both transcripts were probably made in the summer of 1865, his first reunion with Mary Day after the war. No other version known.

WEDDING-HYMN, TO ——— (155)

Written at Scott's Mills, near Macon, Ga., July, 1865.
Published posthumously in *Independent*, XXXVI, 1057 (Aug. 21, 1884), as "Wedding-Hymn"; reprinted without change in *1884*, 233.
Text: *Ledger* 3, "Wedding-Hymn, To ——— / Scott's Mills— July— 1865," signed "S. C. L." (the text used in *1884*, except l. 15, which retained the early reading *to-night* for *all night*). MS *JT* has several minor variants; though sent in Lanier's letter of Sept. 16, 1865, it is an earlier version than that in *Ledger* (the last two lines of which, before correction, agree with *JT*).
This song, written for the wedding of his friends Augusta Lamar and James Monroe Ogden, on Sept. 19, 1865, was set to music by Lanier as a duet with contralto solo (see letters to Clifford Lanier, Sept. 1 and 16), but only the words have come down.

A MORNING-TALK (156)

Written at Scott's Mills, near Macon, Ga., Sept. 10, 1865. Previously unpublished.
Text: MSS *JT* and *HL*, inclosed in letters to Clifford Lanier and Mary Day, Sept. 16, 1865. *Ledger* 18, signed "S. C. L. / September 10th 1865," and MS *CL*, entitled "The Lover," unsigned and undated, are earlier drafts with a number of minor variants.
This song, dedicated to Virginia Lamar Bacon, was set to music by Lanier for contralto and soprano voices with flute obligato (see letters of Sept. 16, 1865), but only the words have come down.

THE DYING WORDS OF JACKSON (156-157)

Written at Scott's Mills, near Macon, Ga., Sept. 24, 1865.

Published posthumously in *1884*, 230-231, with "Stonewall" added to the title.

Text: *Ledger* 19, "The Dying Words of Jackson," signed "S. C. L. / Scott's Mills, Sept. 24, 1865" (with *Day* for *day*, l. 1; *hero* for *Hero*, l. 12). MS *JT*, unsigned and undated, but in Lanier's handwriting and probably sent with his letter of Sept. 30, 1865, has a half-dozen variants; *Ledger*, which before correction is identical, is the latest revised version.

Stonewall Jackson was shot by accident after the battle of Chancellorsville, May 1-5, 1865; the Signal Corps of which Lanier was a member, covering the retreat from Suffolk, was at nearby Franklin, Va. (see Clifford Lanier's letter to his father, May 5, 1863).

A LOVE-SONG, TO ——— (157)

Probably written at Point Clear, Ala., or Montgomery, end of 1865. Previously unpublished.

Text: *Ledger* 23, signed "From S. C. L. / 1865" (the nearest dated entries are Oct., 1865, p. 21, and Mar. 2, 1866, p. 28). No other version known. Periods have been substituted for dashes, ll. 4 and 8; a comma has been removed after the first *O*, l. 5.

The dedicatee cannot be definitely identified. "White-Souled" (l. 13) is a description frequently used of Virginia Hankins in Lanier's letters; he was not in correspondence with Mary Day at this time. The last two lines, altered, were used in a poem written six years later ("Nilsson," p. 197, ll. 29-30).

THE WEDDING (158)

Probably written at Point Clear, Ala., or Montgomery, end of 1865.

Published posthumously in *Independent*, XXXVI, 1057 (Aug. 21, 1884), with title "Wedding Bells"; reprinted without change, except title "The Wedding," in *1884*, 223 (dated "Macon, Georgia, 1865").

Text: *Ledger* 45, entitled "The Wedding," signed "S. C. L.," and dated "1865" in the handwriting of *MDL* (the text used in *1884*). Before correction it shows three variants, which agree with MS *JT*, undated but clearly an earlier draft with six variants, the most interesting of which are: *she* for *he* (l. 6) and *O God, how canst thou let this be!* for *O Death, I am true wife to thee!* (l. 14).

On Nov. 1, 1865, Mary Day wrote to Lanier (then at Point Clear, Ala.) that she was definitely going to marry Fred Andrews, to whom she had been engaged for several years. "The Wedding," in spite of the mixed metaphor in the last line (which did not appear in the early draft), seems to be Lanier's response to this news, colored also by his extreme illness at the time.

TO WILLIE CLOPTON (158)

Written in Montgomery, Mar. 2, 1866.

Published posthumously in *Manhattan Magazine*, IV, 380 (Sept., 1884), entitled "To Wilhelmina"; reprinted without change in *1884*, 232. (Title in both probably supplied by *MDL*.)

Text: *Ledger* 28, entitled "To Willie Clopton / From S. C. L. / March 1866." Two other MSS survive: *JT*, "To Cousin Willie / Montgomery, Ala., Mar. 2, 1866"; and *CL*, attached to letter of Mar. 26, 1866, thus bearing the latest date but invalidated by a careless error in l. 4. Otherwise both MSS agree with *Ledger*, which is the most finished version mechanically. No other variants known.

Wilhelmina Clopton, to whom the poem was addressed, was a distant cousin; she was married to Lanier's brother Clifford in Nov., 1867. The opening figure is also applied to one of the characters in *Tiger-Lilies*, Felix Sterling (V, 71).

TO CARRIE LIGON (159)

Written in Montgomery, Mar., 1866 (see letter of Mar. 21 and notes 9 and 13). Previously unpublished.

Text: *Ledger* 29, dated "March 1866" and signed "From S. C. L." MS *CL*, attached to letter of Mar. 26, 1866, has two minor variants, and is a slightly inferior version.

Addressed to a distant cousin, whom Lanier had recently visited in Tuskeegee, Ala. (see letter of Mar. 21, 1866).

WILL "ALL BE RIGHT IN A HUNDRED YEARS"? (159-160)

Written in Montgomery, Mar. 30, 1866; revised, Nov. 6. Previously unpublished.

Text: MS *JT*, unsigned, dated "Nov. 6. / 66" (with commas supplied, end of ll. 8, 9, 12, 15). *Ledger* 33, signed "Sidney Lanier / 1866," agrees except that it is inferior in mechanics. MS *CL*, inclosed in Lanier's letter of Mar. 30, 1866, is an earlier draft with minor variants in the last three lines.

MS *JT* has a puzzling notation in Lanier's handwriting beneath the title: "Anon. / Read from / M. L. S.'s Gazette." Though the words "read from" are ambiguous, this seems to indicate that Lanier published the poem, but the periodical referred to has not been identified. Similarly the word "Anon." cannot be explained, for the evidence of the other two MSS makes Lanier's authorship certain (see letter of Mar. 30, 1866).

NIGHT AND DAY (160)

Probably written in Montgomery, spring of 1866.

Published posthumously in *Independent*, XXXVI, 833 (July 3, 1884); reprinted without change in *1884*, 218.

Text: *Ledger* 41, signed "Sidney Lanier," dated "1866" and immediately preceding "Night," p. 42, which was written on Apr. 19 (with dash removed from beginning of l. 3—the text followed in the posthumous prints.) MS *JT*, untitled, unsigned, and undated, is an earlier draft with a few minor variants.

The use of Othello's slaying of Desdemona as a metaphor for sunset will also be found in "The Dove" (99), written over ten years later.

NIGHT (161)

Written in Montgomery, Apr. 19, 1866.

Published posthumously in *Independent*, XXXVI, 545 (May 1, 1884); reprinted without change in *1884*, 236.

Text: *Ledger* 42, signed " S. C. L. / 1866." MS *CL*, signed "Sidney C. Lanier" and dated "Montgomery, / April 19ᵗʰ 1866," is an earlier draft with one variant before correction. Notes on this MS by *MDL* and John B. Tabb show that the two variants in the posthumous prints were the result of editorial emendation: *straining* for *our* (l. 7); *Wisdom as of* for *both Wisdom and* (l. 16).

The figure in the second stanza was used ten years later in a revised form in "Evening Song" (88). See note to "In Cubiculo," below.

IN CUBICULO (162)

Probably written in Montgomery, late autumn of 1866. Previously unpublished.

Text: *Ledger* 69, signed "Sidney Lanier," undated (nearest dated entry, p. 66, is Nov., 1866). It has two minor variants before correction.

"In Cubiculo" is actually a revised version of "Night," but this was discovered too late to relegate it to the notes without invalidating over a hundred cross-references (in vols. VI-X) to the remaining poems. The oversight may be partially explained by the fact that printer's copy of the manuscript poems (including "In Cubiculo") was not prepared until many months after the texts of the previously collected poems (including "Night") had been set up. And there are consolations: this error gives the reader two drafts of the same poem side by side, to facilitate a study of Lanier's craftsmanship; and it gives the general editor, emerging from his cubicle, a renewed sense of being, after all, human.

"WHEN BEES, IN HONEY-FRENZIES, RAGE AND RAGE" (162)

Probably written in Montgomery, Nov., 1866.

Published in *Poem Outlines* (New York, 1908), 85. Previously uncollected as a poem, but here treated as such because it is a finished quatrain.

Text: *Ledger* 68, untitled, signed "L.," undated (but nearest dated entry, p. 66, is Nov., 1866). (The text used in *PO*.) Before correction it has two variants.

LINES TANGLED ABOUT THE ROUND TABLE (163-164)

Probably written in Montgomery, end of 1866. Previously unpublished.

Text: *Ledger*. 72-73, signed " S. C. L.," undated (nearest dated entry, p. 66, is Nov., 1866). Before correction it shows a half-dozen unimportant variants. No other version known. (Italics labelling the puns, first two stanzas only, have been omitted.)

Lanier had made his entry into the world of literature through the *Round Table* (letter of May 12, 1866, and Starke, 76-77), the first magazine to publish his poems.

TO M. D. (164-166)

Written in Montgomery, Feb. 14, 1867. Previously unpublished.

Text: MS *CL*, dated "February 14ᵗʰ, 1867"; the signature looks like "Valetine / L." No other version known.

The poem, definitely in Lanier's handwriting, was addressed to Mary Day during the months of misunderstanding prior to their engagement.

TO OUR HILLS (166-167)

Written in Macon, July 14, 1867; revised in Prattville, Ala., Dec., 1867 (as stated on the MSS).

Published posthumously in *1916*, 222, as " Our Hills."

Text: *Ledger* 256, 259, entitled " To Our Hills " and signed " S. C. L. Prattville, Dec. 1867." This is clearly the revised version, since it contains two extra stanzas, bears the latest date, and is superior to the other surviving MSS, two of which are dated " July 14th 1867 " and the third (the text used in *1916*), though undated, agrees more nearly with the early MSS than with that here adopted. For a full collation of variants see pp. 325-326, above.

This is one of a group of poems dealing with the evils of Reconstruction (see Introduction).

STRANGE JOKES (167-168)

Written in Macon, July 21, 1867.

Published posthumously in *Independent*, XXXV, 1281 (Oct. 11, 1883), with subtitle " In a Whimsey Mood "; reprinted without change, except for omission of subtitle, in *1884*, 209.

Text: *Ledger* 244, signed " Sidney Lanier / Macon, July 21, 1867." No variants known, except the use of singular for plural in ll. 21-22, *1884*.

In the *Ledger* 16 Lanier wrote a prose version of the opening lines: " Death, an omnivorous Toad, that catches and swallows whatever you pitch him, shot, hot coals, or peas! " This note, rather than the poem itself, may have been prompted by Mark Twain's " Celebrated Jumping Frog of Calaveras County," first published in 1865 and copied in newspapers all over the country.

FAME (168)

Written in Montgomery, probably during Nov.-Dec., 1867, at the time of the publication of his first volume, *Tiger-Lilies*, as suggested by the subject matter.

Published posthumously in Mary E. Burt, *The Lanier Book* (New York, 1914), 49. Previously uncollected.

Text: *Ledger* 252, unsigned, dated " Montgomery, Ala. / 1867 " (the next dated entry, p. 256, is Dec., 1867). No other version known.

Lanier was living in Prattville, Ala., at the time, but probably wrote the poem during a visit to his brother in Montgomery.

" LIKE A GRAND WATER-WHEEL HIS LIFE REVOLVED " (168)

Written in Prattville, Ala., probably in Dec., 1867. Previously unpublished.

Text: *Ledger* 252-253, signed " L.," undated (but preceded by " Fame," p. 252, written in Nov.-Dec., 1867, and followed by " In the Foam," p. 260, written on Dec. 9). No other version known.

The earliest treatment of social-economic problems in Lanier's poetry, this anticipates " The Symphony." (See Introduction; for an account of Prattville as a manufacturing town, see note 70, Letters of 1867.) The influence of Carlyle, an early favorite, is clearly discernible both in the poem and in the prose note that follows it in the *Ledger* 253-254:

" The impossibility of doing anything for the *mass*: this is the dreariest of all those impossibilities which inevitably rise up in the path of advancing youth, when it attempts to settle the great problem of Me and Not-me. Here am I: yonder are the poor: I am one, the wretched are millions: through the ages I observe the wretched Mass drag and drag, the sand of rough life clings to them in the dragging and dirt changes to misery, this dirt becomes a grave-mound in what minute another draggee is born, the round goes on, who has stopped it, who has changed it, who *can* alter it, is it not folly to try?

" Those who, in youth, answer this self-asked question in the affirmative, become tradesmen, bankers, belly-gods, corporation-men, paying open respect to the laws which protect their property and secret disrespect to the laws which protect other men's property. They subscribe to churches because religion is conservative and because church-affinities bring custom. They build opera-houses through a certain unadmitted fondness, which somehow seems to advance along with age and baldness, for well-turned legs of coryphees."

STEEL IN SOFT HANDS (169)

Written in Prattville, Ala., Feb. 7, 1868 (see below). Previously unpublished except for the fourth stanza in *Mims*, 93, incorrectly.

Text: *Ledger* 276, signed " S. L. Prattville / Feby 7th 1868." Variant before correction, *of* for *seized by* (l. 1). No other version known.

This belongs with the group of poems dealing with the evils of Reconstruction (see Introduction), probably withheld from publication because of its bitterness.

BURN THE STUBBLE! (169-170)

Written in Prattville, Ala., Feb. 23, 1868. Previously unpublished (see note to " Steel in Soft Hands," above).

Text: MS *JT,* signed " Sidney Lanier," undated but clearly the latest revision (with quotation marks supplied, ll. 5, 9). *Ledger* 277, signed " Sidney Lanier / Prattville, Ala. Feby 23rd 1868," has several minor alterations and variants, such as *flame* for *rage* (l. 2), *salty* > *bitter* for *mournful* (l. 10).

SOULS AND RAINDROPS (170)

Probably written at Scott's Mills, near Macon, Ga., summer of 1868.

Published posthumously in *Lippincott's*, XXXII, 117 (July, 1883); reprinted without change in *1884*, 216.

Text: *Ledger* 306, signed " S. L.," undated (but follows immediately after " Life and Song," p. 305, apparently written in summer of 1868). No variants known.

PRIDE (170)

Probably written in Macon, autumn of 1868. Previously unpublished.

Text: *Ledger* 316, signed " S. L.," undated (it follows " Life and Song," p. 305, apparently summer of 1868, and precedes " The hound was cuffed," p. 317, apparently the song referred to in Lanier's letter of Nov. 4, 1868). No other version known.

THE JACQUERIE (171-189)

Written at various intervals between 1868 and 1874 (?), but left at his death in fragmentary form.

Published posthumously in *1884*, 183-203.

Text: a composite of the several surviving MSS. Chap. I, ll. 1-59, *HL*, entitled "Jacquerie," undated and unsigned, but clearly superior to and apparently in a later hand than the other two versions of this part (*Ledger* 438, 440-442 and *JTᵃ*). Chap. I, l. 60 to end, and Chaps. II-V, *Ledger* 442-460, entitled "The Jacquerie," undated and unsigned, apparently in a later hand and more complete than the other version for this part, with which it frequently agrees before correction (*JTᵃ* contains Chap. I; *JTᵇ* contains Chaps. II-IV, lacking the last 22 lines and all of V). This is apparently the text followed in *1884*, but with a dozen careless errors and editorial emendations and numerous changes in mechanics. The present text has been transcribed literally from the MSS, with the exception of the following corrections for the sake of a reasonable consistency: capitals supplied (p. 173, l. 24; p. 174, ll. 15 and 16; p. 180, ll. 27 and 28; p. 183, ll. 32 and 37; p. 188, l. 28); colon supplied (p. 172, l. 17); commas supplied (.p 173, l. 35; p. 180, l. 24; p. 183, l. 35); *prove* for *Prove* (p. 182, l. 18); quotation marks regularized (p. 187, ll. 32 ff.). (The last folio of the MS—*Ledger* 459-460—is torn at the top, leaving *lacunae* in the text on pp. 187-188. The last line of the fragment is followed by the caption "Chap. VI.") The state of some of the MSS, with many illegible lines and alterations, is such as to make a full collation virtually impossible; and careful study of the variants has convinced the present editor that such results as could be shown, after great labor, would add little if anything to the evidence of Lanier's craftsmanship given above in the textual variants of his more important poems. The MSS are available in the Lanier Room, Johns Hopkins University, where they may be examined by the curious.

Lanier is said to have planned it originally as a sort of music-drama, jotting down "hints and fragments" as early as his college days (Clifford Lanier, "Reminiscences of Sidney Lanier,," *Chautauquan*, XXI, 406, July, 1895). The first mention of the poem, however, occurs in Lanier's letter of Nov. 4, 1868, where it is referred to as a new book: "It is to be a novel in verse, with several lyric poems introduced by the action. The plot is founded on what was called 'the Jacquerie,' a very remarkable popular insurrection wh. happened in France about the year 1359, in the height of *Chivalry*. . . . But, unfortunately, I have only the very meagre account of the business given in Froissart, and am terribly crippled in my historical allusions by this fact." Paul Hayne's letter of Jan. 14, 1869, acknowledges receipt of a lost letter from Lanier containing an installment of the poem. It is quite possible that this is MS *JTᵃ*. The first page is missing, but there are two lines of prose at the top of p. 2 which seem to be the end of an explanation of its historical background: "years after the battle of Poictiers—(*three* years after, according to Froissart)." Then follows an early draft of "The Jacquerie," Chap. I, followed by a prose summary of what the rest of the poem was to contain (p. 8): "And so on, diddle-daddle &c, through a marvellous plot of Dukes' Fools, swords, *Droits de Seigneurs*, catapults, ladies besieged in Meaux by the Jacquerie, jewels, by-play, love, lyrics, rescues, and the like, all winding up with the most barbarous and altogether historic hanging of Master Jacques Bonhomme, the hero of the tale and the leader of the Jacquerie." The MS concludes with a request for criticism of "my foolish little book," and is signed "Your Friend / Sidney Lanier." Lanier's letter of Mar. 15, 1869, indicates that he had temporarily suspended work on the poem.

The next references to it come in the winter and spring of 1871, when he sent further installments, including two of the intercalary songs, to Hayne (see note 4, Letters of 1871). Over a year later he wrote to his father from Texas, Dec. 6, 1872, that he had found a French history that enabled him "to advance very largely" his conception of "The Jacquerie," and it is possible that he did further work on it at that time. How important he considered this poem is indicated by the fact that one of his reasons for moving to Baltimore was to consult some of the authorities on the subject in the Peabody Library (see letters of Nov. 21 and Dec. 23, 1873, and note 145). The result of all this and the new plan that he was evolving for his "*Magnum Opus*" is revealed in a letter to L. E. Bleckley, Nov. 15, 1874, in which he says of the uprising of the Jacquerie: "It was the first time that the big hungers of *the People* appear in our modern civilization: & it is full of significance. . . . Trade arose & overthrew Chivalry . . . it is *now* the *gentleman* who must arise and overthrow Trade." It seems likely that it was the introduction of this economic theme that finally led Lanier to abandon his medieval narrative for the more modern handling of a similar problem in "The Symphony," written the following winter (for a discussion of the historical background of "The Jacquerie" and the relationship of the two poems, see Introduction).

Though there are occasional references to "The Jacquerie" in later years (see letters of Mar. 25 and Sept. 27, 1877, and Jan. 30, Feb. 3, 1878), Lanier seems to have done little if any further work on it after 1874, and it remained at his death a fragment of five chapters which, however promising, scarcely justify the high estimate he seems to have placed upon it. The state of the surviving MSS—unfinished both in extent and in the matter of revision—indicates that he did not consider any of it in final form, except for three of the intercalary songs. Two of these he published separately, "Betrayal" (19) and 'Special Pleading" (45), and a third was included in his projected volume of "Clover and Other Poems," "A Song of Love" (58). The grouping of "Songs for 'The Jacquerie'" in *1884* includes only the first of these, along with the two that Lanier did not show any intention of publishing: "The hound was cuffed" (189) and "May, the maiden" (190). It is possible that he expected to make musical settings for these songs, all of which reveal an interest in verse technique rather than either the medieval story or its modern social application.

"THE HOUND WAS CUFFED, THE HOUND WAS KICKED" (189-190)

Apparently written in Macon, autumn of 1868 (see letter of Nov. 4; however, of the five songs written for "The Jacquerie," this seems to fit best the description in Hayne's letter of Jan. 10, 1871: "a true medieval song . . . showing your familiarity with antique balled poetry"; see also notes 89 and 4, *Letters* of 1870, 1871).

Published posthumously in *1884*, 206.

Text: *Ledger* 317, untitled, undated, and unsigned, but in Lanier's handwriting of *c.* 1868 (with italics and roman reversed). No variants known, except in *1884*, l. 11, *That* for *It,* apparently an editorial emendation.

Intended for insertion in "The Jacquerie" (171 and note, see above), probably in Chap. I, following l. 24. It has been set to music by H. R. Thatcher.

"MAY, THE MAIDEN" (190)

Apparently written in Macon, autumn of 1868 (see note to "The hound was cuffed," above).

Published posthumously in *1884*, 204.

Text: *Ledger* 321, untitled, undated, but signed "S. L." (with commas supplied, end of ll. 10 and 12). No variants known.

Intended for insertion in "The Jacquerie" (172 and note, see above), probably in Chap. I, following l. 72. It has been set to music by several composers, including Reginald DeKoven.

BABY CHARLEY (191)

Written in Macon, Dec., 1869.

Published posthumously in *Lippincott's*, XXXI, 58 (Jan., 1883); reprinted without change in *1884*, 214.

Text: *Ledger* 415, unsigned but dated " Macon, Ga. / December 1869." No variants known.

Lanier's first son, Charles Day Lanier (named for his maternal grandfather), had been born on Sept. 12, 1868. (See the letter written to him by Lanier on July 20, 1881.)

THEM KU KLUX (191-194)

Probably written in Macon, Dec.-Jan., 1870-1871. Previously unpublished.

Text: MS *CL*, entitled " Whar Air Them Ku Klux " (with first two words canceled), undated, signed " S. L." The MS shows alterations in 15 lines, ten of which were made for the sake of meter and rhyme. Those of interest to the student of dialect verse are: *several* > *some few* (l. 17); *farmin'* > *thrivin'* (l. 34); *moved in* > *piled in* (l. 37); *knave's* > *rascals* (l. 48). (One other change is discussed below.) The following corrections in mechanics have been made: apostrophees supplied for all missing letters; comma supplied, l. 5; missing quotation marks, ll. 25, 65, 89; commas for dashes, l. 69; *that* for *that that*, l. 70; *There* for *there*, l. 79. No other version known, except an inaccurate copy in the handwriting of Sidney Lanier, Jr.

The internal evidence of stanzas 5 and 7 would seem to place the poem in 1869: " Jeems " the Yankee had bought land in Georgia " jest after the war " and has now " lived in Bibb fo' year." But before alteration the MS read *six* for *fo'*, which would make the year 1871. This is borne out by the allusion in stanzas 8 and 9 to Sumner's speech about Grant and Santo Domingo, which the speaker says he has just read. The reference is to the scathing speech by Charles Sumner delivered in the U. S. Senate on Dec. 21, 1870, denouncing President U. S. Grant for his project of annexing Santo Domingo and for failing to suppress the activities of the Ku Klux Klan (entitled " Naboth's Vineyard," *Works*, Boston 1883, XIV, 89-130, 168-249). Lanier's poem was probably written shortly thereafter. Sumner had had many clashes with Grant and had previously denounced President Andrew Johnson's Reconstruction policy as too light. For an account of the Ku Klux Klan see Paul H. Buck, *The Road to Reunion, 1865-1900* (Boston, 1937), *passim*. (Lanier's dialect poems are discussed in the Introduction.)

9 FROM 8 (194-196)

Written in Macon, 1870-1871 (dated 1870 in *1884* and 1871 in *Independent*—not mentioned in Lanier's letters).

Published posthumously in *Independent*, XXXVI, 321 (Mar. 13, 1884), entitled " Nine From Eight "; reprinted with a few changes in dialectal spelling in *1884*, 169-171.

Text: MS *CL*, entitled " 9 from 8," signed " S. L.," undated (with the following corrections: apostrophes supplied for all missing letters; hyphen for *two-mule*, l. 1; commas, ll. 1, 73; *Hello* for *hello*, l. 71). Before correction it shows a dozen or more variants, the most interesting of which is, l. 10, *whar the sand was smooth and white* > *a figgerin thar in the sand*. No authority has been found for the changes in the posthumous prints in title, spelling, and mechanics.

Apparently not published by Lanier, unless in some local newspaper (no file of the Macon *Telegraph* has been discovered for Jan. 1867-July 1871, but several other Georgia and Alabama newspapers have been searched). Though the plea for diversified crops is not explicitly stated, it is implied in the theme of bankruptcy through exclusive planting of the money-crop, cotton. The provincialism in l. 37 is explained in a note to the *Independent* print: " ' Under the hack ' is a familiar Cracker expression denoting perplexity or trouble. Hack is probably a contraction of *hackle*"—an instrument used in the breaking of flax. " Crap-leen," l. 40, is dialectal for " crop-lien." The allusions in ll. 47 and 51 are to Hardeman & Sparks and Campbell & Jones, cotton factors and warehouse and commission merchants in Macon (see advertisements in the July, 1871, issue of *Southern Farm and Home*, containing " Jones's Private Argument ").

NILSSON (196-197)

Written in New York, Oct. 4, 1871.
Published posthumously in *Independent*, XXXV, 385 (Mar. 29, 1883); reprinted without change in *1884*, 217.
Text: *Ledger* 417-418, entitled " Nillson," signed " Sidney Lanier," and dated " N. Y. 1871 " (with correction of spelling in title). *Ledger* 416, entitled " Nilsson," signed " Sidney Lanier," and dated " N. Y. Oct. 4, 1871," is a shorter version and apparently an earlier draft since it precedes the above and seems less finished in structure and metaphor; it is reproduced entire on p. 326, above. The version given in *1884* is a composite of the two MSS, apparently made for *MDL* by John B. Tabb, since MS *HA* is an identical composite in his handwriting.
In a letter of Sept. 24, 1870, Lanier described enthusiastically the singing of Christina Nilsson, Swedish soprano; he may have heard her at another concert the following year. Ll. 29-30 were revised from " A Love-Song, To ———— " (157), written six years before.

THE CARRIER'S APPEAL (197-198)

Written in Macon on Dec. 23, 1871. Previously unpublished.
Text: *Ledger* 419-420, in pencil, signed " S. L. / Dec. 23rd 1871." No other version known.
Bridges Smith, the newspaper friend at whose request this New Year's " Address " for the local carrier was written, has left an account of its origin, saying in part: " It required considerable begging to get him to promise. He did not like to write poetry to order." (See Macon *Daily Telegraph*, Nov. 17, 1917; a later article, issue of Nov. 10, 1926, suggests that it may have been printed as a broadside.)

THOSE BONDS (199)

Written in Macon, Dec. 24, 1871. Previously unpublished.
Text: *Ledger* 420, signed " S. L. Dec. 24th " (following " The Carrier's Appeal," pp. 419-420, dated Dec. 23, 1871). No other version known.
R. B. Bullock (l. 6), Reconstruction Governor of Georgia, was accused of selling state bonds and appropriating the proceeds; fearing criminal indictment, he resigned and fled the state on Oct. 23, 1871 (see note 72, Letters of 1871). Henry Clews & Co. (l. 11), Wall St. bankers, had been Bullock's financial agents; during the fight over the repudiation of the bonds, they published a

card in the Atlanta *Constitution* admitting that the proceeds of the bonds had been misapplied but urging that the state of Georgia take no action that would injure her credit.

" HAVE YOU FORGOT HOW THROUGH THE APRIL WEATHER " (199)

Probably written in Baltimore, end of Apr., 1874. Previously unpublished.
Text: MS *CL*, untitled, undated, and unsigned, but definitely in Lanier's handwriting (minor variants before correction). No other version known.
A note on the MS by *MDL* reads: " Sidney Lanier / 1874—Baltimore—On a Concert Tour." Lanier went on a concert tour to West Virginia and Ohio, Apr. 15-24, 1874, as one of several instrumentalists accompanying Miss Jenny Busk, the addressee of the poem (see letters of Apr. 14, 19, 1874, and notes 54, 55).

" WHATE'ER HAS BEEN, IS, SHALL BE—RIND, PULP, CORE " (200)

Probably written in Baltimore, Dec., 1875. Previously unpublished.
Text: MS *EM*, entitled " VII," undated, signed " S. L." MS *CL*, entitled " II," written verso Lanier's letter of Dec. 7, 1875, is an earlier version, as two examples of its several variants will show: *And with all foods* for *And feeds on fruits* (l. 6); *like as rose-odors* for *As bringing roses* (l. 10).
The titles of the two MSS, omitted because meaningless without explanation, suggest that this sonnet may have been originally included in the " In Absence " sequence (see note, p. 341, above); like them, it is written in praise of Lanier's wife.

AT FIRST (200-201)

Written in Baltimore, Feb. 27, 1876 (see letter to Taylor).
Published posthumously in *Independent*, XXXV, 897 (July 19, 1883); reprinted without change in *1884*, 139-140.
Text: MS *CL,* signed " S. L." (with *Frost* capitalized, l. 11, and comma supplied, l. 25). Two other MSS survive: *HA,* a copy in the handwriting of *MDL*; and *JM*, which shows one variant, l. 15, *And the heart of the night beats lax at the end,* as in *CL* before correction. No other variants known.
Inspired by the death of Charlotte Cushman, Feb. 18, 1876; though their friendship lasted only a little over a year, it was an intimate one. (See " To Miss Charlotte Cushman," note, p. 342, above.)

[BEETHOVEN] (201-202)

Probably written in Dec., 1876, at the same time as the longer " To Beethoven " (see note, p. 351). During the winter of 1876-1877 there were nationwide celebrations of the semi-centennial of Beethoven's death.
Published posthumously, *Independent*, XLIX, 1489 (Nov. 18, 1897), in an article by Lanier's friend H. C. Wysham, without title or indication of source, and described as " hitherto unpublished." Previously uncollected.
Text: *Independent*. No other version known. Title supplied by the present editor.

[ON THE RECEIPT OF A JAR OF MARMALADE] (202)

Written in Tampa, winter of 1877 (note 9, Letters of 1877).

Published posthumously in New Castle, Va., *Record*, Apr. 11, 1891 (according to *1895*, 90—no file discovered); reprinted in W. M. Baskerville, *Southern Writers* (Nashville, Tenn., 1899), I, 147. Previously uncollected.

Text: MS *FH*, photo *JM* (with comma and dash reversed, end l. 5, and title supplied from *1895*). The Baskerville print has a variant, or careless error, in the last line.

Sent to Mrs. C. N. Hawkins, wife of the editor of the Tampa *Sunland Tribune*, in appreciation of a gift (see Starke, 266).

"OUR TURKEY WALKS ACROSS THE YARD" (202)

Written in Tampa, probably on Feb. 4, 1877 (see letter of Feb. 4 and notes 9 and 10).

Published posthumously by J. S. Mayfield with a supplied title, "An Immoral Bird," in *American Book Collector*, VI, 200-203 (May-June, 1935). Previously uncollected.

Text: MS *FH* (photo *JM*), verso letter from Lanier dated Feb. (4?) 1877, a copy by Mrs. C. N. Hawkins, who vouches for the authenticity of the poem with the following notation: "copied from a borrowed 'Atlantic Monthly'—written [by Lanier] on a fly-leaf." No variants known.

Mayfield gives a plausible conjecture of its conception: Lanier was sitting on the balcony of the Orange Grove Hotel in Tampa reading a copy of the Feb., 1877, *Atlantic*, which contained an article by his friend Bayard Taylor, "Studies in Animal Nature," with a passage on parrots and other talking birds; an actual turkey walking across the yard at the moment prompted Lanier's comic poem. The copy of the *Atlantic* containing the verse was loaned to Mrs. Hawkins, and though it has not survived, her transcription has.

[UNTITLED VERSES] (203)

Written in Tampa, Feb. 6, 1877. Previously unpublished.

Text: *Ledger* 304, dated as above, untitled, and unsigned. All three are in the handwriting of *MDL*, but are indisputably Lanier's compositions. She frequently served as his amanuensis and always signed or initialed her own contributions, chiefly prose notes, in the *Ledger*. The verses are in the same vein as "Our turkey walks" (see above), known to be by Lanier, and were probably written under similar circumstances. No other versions known.

TO MRS. S. C. BIRD (203)

Written in Baltimore, Jan. 14, 1878.

Published posthumously in Lincoln Lorenz, *The Life of Sidney Lanier* (New York, 1935), 208. Previously uncollected.

Text: MS *CL*, in the autograph of *MDL*, dated "Jany 14th 1878." No variants known.

Sarah C. Bird has recorded in her Reminiscences (MS *HL*, copy): "He dropped into an empty basket, in which I had sent some hothouse grapes, a little verse, which I found after some days." Mrs. Bird, a native of Hancock County, Ga., had moved to Baltimore in 1869. Wealthy and socially active, she was a devoted friend and valuable sponsor of Lanier: "Her home on East Mount Vernon Place was for more than a generation the seat of an elegant and cultured hospitality, and among her guests have been many distinguished in literature and music." It was here, under her auspices, that he began his career as a lecturer. (See *Baltimore: Its History and Its People*, by many contributors, New York, 1912, III, 651; for the series of lectures see III, vii-viii, of the present edition.)

WATER LILIES (204)

Written in 1878, probably in Baltimore.

Published as an illustrated Christmas card by L. Prang, Boston, in 1890, signed "Sidney Lanier" (copy in the Lanier Room, Johns Hopkins). Previously uncollected.

Text: Prang. No other version known.

A note by *MDL* (MS *CL*) reads: "Mrs. Wallen to whom the water-lily was written in 1878—and for whom I got a friend to make the design that both might be sold for Mrs. Wallen's sore need." Mary R. Wallen, a devoted Macon friend and a life-long invalid, was the subject of an extended tribute in Lanier's English Novel lectures at Johns Hopkins in 1881 (see IV, 48-49). Though he may have written several poems to her, this is the only one that has survived, and is probably the same as the two described following: "He once wrote a poem in honor of Mrs. Wallen, which he called 'The White Rose'" (letter from J. T. Boifeuillet, Mar. 23, 1925, MS *JT*); and "To 'The White Flower' of the English Novel," described in *1895*, 90, as written in 1878 and first printed on an illustrated Christmas Card by L. Prang, Boston, 1890. (The collection of Prang's cards in the Boston Public Library from 1875 to 1896 has been searched, but "Water Lilies" is the only poem by Lanier discovered.)

TO MY CLASS (204)

Probably written in Baltimore, Christmas, 1879. The date in *1884*, 146 ("Christmas 1880") is apparently in error. *MDL* said in her note (*1884*, 255) that it was addressed to a class of young girls who had been studying Chaucer''s "Knight's Tale" with Lanier; and at the bottom of the surviving MS she wrote, "At Mrs. Singleton's." Lanier did teach at Mrs. M. C. Singleton's Eutaw Place School in the winter of 1879-1880, but not the following year (see note 59, Letters of 1879, and letter of Sept. 29, 1880). Further, the imagery is drawn from the same source as in "On Violet's Wafers" (see below), definitely known to have been written in Jan., 1880. Hence this poem must have been written during the illness of Dec., 1879-Jan., 1880, probably at Christmas as *1884* states. Lanier was at this time also preparing his Class Course at Johns Hopkins based partly on Chaucer's "Knight's Tale" (III, xiii); during his illness of Dec., 1880-Jan., 1881, he was much sicker, and at that time he was studying more recent literature in preparation for his lectures on the English Novel.

Published posthumously in *Independent*, XXXVI, 1409 (Nov. 6, 1884); reprinted without change in *1884*, 146.

Text: MS *HL*. (It is included in *Clover*, probably by accident because written on the same size paper; but the paper is of an entirely different kind, the page is unnumbered, and the poem was written more than six months after that collection was made.) No variants known.

ON VIOLET'S WAFERS (205)

Written in Baltimore during the serious illness that lasted from Dec. 22, 1879, to Jan. 15, 1880. (The acknowledgment of Violet Browne, daughter of Lanier's friend W. H. Browne, is dated Jan. 10, 1880; *1884*, 147, gives the year incorrectly as " 1881.")

Published posthumously in *Independent*, XXXVI, 1409 (Nov. 6, 1884); reprinted in *1884*, 147, without change except for misprint, *for* for *to*, l. 12.

Text: MS *HL* (included in *Clover* by accident as was " To My Class," above). No variants known, except in *HL* before correction: *Fresh* > *More* (l. 9); *high* > *fine* (l. 10); *better* > *finer* (l. 11).

The imagery is drawn from Chaucer's " Knight's Tale," as in the case of " To My Class "; it was " addressed to a member of the same class, and is similarly conceived " (see *1884*, 255).

" OH, WHAT IF VIOLET BROWNE WERE SEEN " (205)

Probably written in Baltimore, winter of 1880. Previously unpublished.

Text: MS *CL*, untitled, undated, and unsigned, but in Lanier's late handwriting (with *by* for *-By*, l. 8). There are several variants before correction.

Preserved with the poem is a note of thanks from the addressee and some nonsense verses written in reply, both in the handwriting of her father, W. H. Browne, but undated. Another poem from Violet Browne to Lanier has survived (*CL*), dated Feb. 14, 1880, as well as Lanier's other poem to her, " On Violet's Wafers," written early in Jan., 1880 (see above). The present verses were probably written about the same time. (No other version known.)

THE POET TO THE PENNSYLVANIA BOARD OF PARDONS (206-207)

Apparently written in Baltimore, spring of 1880. Previously unpublished.

Text: MS *CL*, signed " Sidney Lanier." No other version known.

A note written by *MDL* on July 20, 1920 (MS *CL*), beneath a copy of the first twelve lines of this poem, says in part: " The above . . . [was] never submitted to any publisher,—written after the notorious action of the Penn^a Board of Pardons in 1880 in setting free one William Kemble, convicted of bribery, April 27th, and pardoned on May 1st of the same year. In 1898, eighteen years later, two very prominent men from the Philadelphia newspapers gave me the legal facts of the case, confirming all of Mr. Lanier's charges. . . . But a band of criminals cannot be pilloried in 1920 for their deeds of 1880." It was probably not printed by Lanier for the same reasons as the three Reconstruction poems (see Introduction), and is included here only for the sake of completeness. The following summary is taken from *Appleton's Annual Cyclopaedia* (New York, 1881), 621-622: W. H. Kemble, *et al.*, were convicted of bribing the Pennsylvania state legislature early in 1880. An appeal to the Board of Pardons, Mar. 27, resulted in a divided decision, and sentence was pronounced on Apr. 26; but a review by the Board granted the pardons and the prisoners were discharged early in May, 1880, on the grounds that they were the first offenders under a new law and the punishment inflicted by the court had been too severe. The Board, whom Lanier denounced, consisted of A. K. Dunkel (not " Duane "), Secretary of Internal Affairs; H. W. Palmer, Attorney General; M. S. Quay, Secretary of State; and C. W. Stone, Lieutenant-Governor.

TO DR. THOMAS SHEARER (207)

Written in Baltimore, Sept., 1880 (see letter of Sept. 20).

Published posthumously in *1884*, 112, with a subtitle, here retained in brackets.

Text: inscription on a plaster copy of Ephraim Keyser's bust of Lanier presented to Dr. Thomas Shearer, dated " September, 1880," now owned by Walter Buck, Baltimore. *1884* has three minor variants; MS *CL*, signed " Sidney Lanier," four.

The addressee was a Baltimore doctor, whose services and kindness Lanier was partially repaying with this gift.

ON A PALMETTO (208)

Probably written in Baltimore, 1880 (no evidence for date except in *1891*, 153, which gives the year as " 1880 ").

Published posthumously in *Independent*, XLIII, 1265 (Aug. 27, 1891), with the note: " Since the collection of Mr. Lanier's poems in a volume this penciled draft of a sonnet has been found among his papers. It is not known when it was written." Reprinted with changes in *1891*, 153.

Text: *1891* (with comma supplied, end of l. 11). *Independent* has two variants, *its* for *his* (1. 3); *praise* for *love* (1. 5); and two misprints. MS *HA* is a copy in the handwriting of *MDL*. No other variants known.

MDL's letter to W. H. Ward, Mar. 23, 1891, suggests that Lanier withheld the poem from publication because of the " defect " in l. 13, the misspelling of *diastole* to make it rhyme with *soul*. The setting and mood are similar to " From the Flats " (97), written in Florida in 1877.

STRUGGLE (208)

Probably written near the end of Lanier's life (see note to the Untitled Verses, below).

Published posthumously in *Century*, XXXI, 572 (Feb., 1886); reprinted without change in *1891*, 154.

Text: MS *CL*, pencil, undated and unsigned, but in Lanier's late handwriting. Canceled version of last line illegible. No other variants known.

[UNTITLED VERSES] (208-210)

These seven poems were apparently written at the end of Lanier's life. They are similar to the jottings during his last years collected in the present volume as " Poem Outlines." The 2nd is taken from the volume *Poem Outlines*, 3rd from MS *JT*, and the others from MSS *CL*—untitled and unsigned but all in Lanier's late handwriting. The 3rd was also published in *Poem Outlines*; 6th and 7th in *Century*, XXXIV, 417 (July, 1887), under the titles " Two in One " and " One in Two," apparently supplied by *MDL*, to whom they were addressed. No variants known. Previously unpublished or uncollected.

THOU AND I (210)

Probably written near the end of Lanier's life. The only evidence for dating is the year " 1881 " printed at the bottom of the page by *MDL*, to whom it was addressed, in *1891*, 158.

Published posthumously in *Century*, XXXIV, 417 (July, 1887); reprinted without change in *1891*, 158.

Text: *Century*. No variants known.

TO ———— (213)

Written in Montgomery, Mar. 24, 1866. Previously unpublished.

Text: MS *CL*, attached to Lanier's letter of Mar. 24, 1866, which states that it was written in collaboration with his brother Clifford. Two other MSS survive, *Ledger* 31 and *HF*, but *CL* seems superior in mechanics. No variants known except in an earlier draft written by Clifford Lanier in his Notebook, p. 18 (*JT*), entitled " To W— " and dated " Montgomery Mch. 8, 1868." The differences between this and the final form indicate that Sidney's revisions were extensive: 5 lines were entirely changed; 9 more were reworded to polish the meter; only the first two remained intact. In the same Notebook, p. 19, is a draft in Sidney's handwriting agreeing with the final form.

A SONG (213)

Written in Montgomery, Mar., 1866; revised in Prattville, 1868 (from the evidence of the MSS).

Published in *Southern Magazine*, IX, 127 (July, 1871). Previously uncollected. (An early version was published in an unidentified religious periodical, probably in 1866 since it is marked " just written," clipping in *JT*.)

Text: *Southern Magazine*. Four MSS survive. Though not an important poem, the several stages of its development are given in full, pp. 326-327, above, for the light they shed on the respective shares of Clifford and Sidney Lanier in this collaboration.

A SEA-SHORE GRAVE (214)

Written in Montgomery, Apr., 1866; revised in Prattville, 1868.

Published in *Southern Magazine*, IX, 127 (July, 1871); reprinted without change in *1884*, 215.

Text: *Southern Magazine*. *Ledger* 275, signed " Sidney and Clifford Lanier," undated but a revised version made in 1868 and submitted to the *Round Table* (the nearest dated entry, p. 276, is Feb. 7, 1868; see letter of Mar. 3, 1868), has one variant line. *Ledger* 40, signed " Sidney and Clifford Lanier " and dated " April 1866," an earlier version, varies considerably (11 out of 16 lines) but the variants are not significant. Four still earlier drafts, the last of which agrees with *Ledger* 40 except in a few words, were written by Clifford Lanier in his Notebook, pp. 19-22 (*JT*); this suggests that the poem was written in its first form by Clifford and that the revision was probably made entirely by Sidney, since it is in his handwriting and they were living apart at the time (see variants to " A Song," p. 326, above). The poem was addressed to their mother, Mary J. A. Lanier, who had died in May, 1865 (see Starke, 120).

THE POWER OF PRAYER (215-216)

Written in Brooklyn, early autumn of 1874; revised the following spring in Baltimore (see letters of May 28, Sept. 5, 28, Oct. 14, 1874; and Apr. 12, 1875).

Published in *Scribner's*, X, 239-240 (June, 1875); reprinted without change in the Macon *Daily Telegraph and Messenger*, May 26, 1875, and apparently widely copied (see letter of June 17, 1875); and with a few changes in *1884*, 177-180. (An early version with considerable differences has recently been published in Benjamin's *Collector*, LVIII, 106-107, June-July, 1945.)

Text: *Scribner's* with revisions in Lanier's handwriting, *CL* (apparently the text used in *1884* except for a few careless errors). For a full collation of variants see pp. 327-328, above.

Clifford Lanier has left a brief account of the origin of the poem (quoted in *1895*, 67). He once saw a newspaper squib of about ten lines telling how a negro was greatly frightened on first seeing a steamboat coming down the river; he then "wrote out in metrical form the plot of *The Power of Prayer*, substantially as we now have it," and sent it to his brother Sidney who "polished it up." The first reference to it in the letters is in Lanier's to his brother, May 28, 1874, "I hope soon to polish up de ole blind darkey." On Aug. 7 he wrote that he had changed the metre from dactyllic to iambic and the form from narrative to dramatic, though retaining "pretty nearly the same ideas." On Oct. 14, reporting that it had been accepted by *Scribner's*, he wrote: "I did not feel the right exactly, to a half interest in the poem: but your solicitation to me to father it was so earnest,—and our two names look so brotherly in print!—that I signed it 'Sidney and Clifford Lanier.'" On Apr. 12, 1875, he wrote: "I have written four more verses to it, in order to intensify the climax by postponing it a little." This part of the poem definitely known to have been contributed by Sidney Lanier was probably ll. 34-51, actually six stanzas rather than four (the portion omitted from the early version printed in *Collector*). Nothing further is known about the collaboration, though a similar poem by Clifford Lanier alone, "The Power of Affection," is certainly inferior.

When the editor of *Scribner's* pointed out the resemblance of the plot to a story by Mark Twain, Lanier replied that neither he nor his brother was familiar with any such story (see letters of Sept. 28, Oct. 1, 1874); but Clifford Lanier suggested, years later, that the newspaper squib which formed the germ of the poem may have been based on an episode in *The Gilded Age*, Chap. III (see *1895*, 67-69, where the episode is conveniently reprinted). The scene and situation in "The Power of Prayer" and Mark Twain's chapter entitled "Uncle Daniel's Apparition and Prayer" are almost identical, but there is no real similarity in phrasing. The most marked parallels are as follows:

Gilded Age	"Power of Prayer"
"It's de Almighty! Git down on yo' knees."	"De Debble's comin' round dat bend . . . I'se gwine to pray."
	(ll. 23, 27)
"Good Lord, . . . some po' sinner's a gwine to ketch it . . . let dese po' chil'en hab one mo' chance . . . Take de ole niggah if you's got to hav somebody."	"O hebbenly Marster . . . some nigger's bound to go. "Den, Lord, please take ole Jim, and lef young Dinah hyar below."
	(ll. 28-30)
"Dis chile would like to know whah we'd a ben now if it warn't fo' dat prah?"	"Yas, Dinah, whar 'ould you be now, jes 'ceptin' fur dat pra'r."
	(l. 60)

But the differences are considerable: in the *Gilded Age* the scene is the Mississippi River (not the Alabama), the negro is middle-aged (not old and blind), there are three white children with him (not his daughter Dinah), and the protagonist is God (not the Devil). According to *1895* Mark Twain testified that the story was written by him (rather than Warner) and that it was pure fiction. "The Power of Prayer" preceded by several years the work in negro dialect of Thomas Nelson Page and Joel Chandler Harris and was contemporary with that of Irwin Russell (see Introduction).

UNCLE JIM'S BAPTIST REVIVAL-HYMN (217)

Written in Baltimore, end of 1875.

Published in *Scribner's*, XII, 142 (May, 1876); reprinted without change, except for repetition of both lines of "chorus" after each stanza, in *1884*, 167-168.

Text: *Scribner's* (with headnote omitted, see below). No variants known.

Evidence for the respective shares of Clifford and Sidney Lanier follows. After their successful collaboration on "The Power of Prayer" (published in June, 1875), Sidney wrote to his brother, Sept. 26, 1875: "I wish you would sketch another negro poem, and let me do my half with it." On Nov. 16, his wife wrote to Clifford: "Your 'Plantation Matins' is pronounced a brilliant success. . . . Sidney says that . . . he proposes to make some of the slightest of alterations and to expunge two of the couplets which are less clear and forcible than the others." Sidney's revisions were apparently made during the last part of December (see letter of Dec. 21). On Jan. 8, 1876, he wrote to his wife, announcing that Scribner had accepted the poem: "I altered it considerably in shape, little in matter." On Jan. 22 he added that he was writing an introduction for it, at the request of R. W. Gilder "'for the illumination of the secular reader' upon some of Uncle Jim's idioms." This was printed as a headnote to the poem in *Scribner's* and reprinted in *1884*, as follows:

[Not long ago a certain Georgia cotton-planter, driven to desperation by awaking each morning to find that the grass had quite outgrown the cotton overnight, and was likely to choke it, in defiance of his lazy freedmen's hoes and ploughs, set the whole State in a laugh by exclaiming to a group of fellow-sufferers: "It's all stuff about Cincinnatus leaving the plough to go into politics *for patriotism*; he was just a-runnin' from grass!"

This state of things—when the delicate young rootlets of the cotton are struggling against the hardier multitudes of the grass-suckers—is universally described in plantation parlance by the phrase "in the grass;" and Uncle Jim appears to have found in it so much similarity to the condition of his own ("Baptis'") church, overrun, as it was, by the cares of this world, that he has embodied it in the refrain of a revival hymn such as the colored improvisator of the South not infrequently constructs from his daily surroundings. He has drawn all the ideas of his stanzas from the early morning phenomena of those critical weeks when the loud plantation-horn is blown before daylight, in order to rouse all hands for a long day's fight against the common enemy of cotton-planting mankind.

In addition to these exegetical commentaries, the Northern reader probably needs to be informed that the phrase "peerten up" means substantially *to spur up*, and is an active form of the adjective "peert" (probably a corruption of *pert*), which is so common in the South, and which has much the signification of "smart" in New England, as *e. g.*, a "pert" horse, in antithesis to a "sorry"—*i. e.*, poor, mean, lazy one.]

For further treatment of Lanier's poems written in dialect, see the Introduction.

INDEX OF TITLES AND FIRST LINES

INDEX OF TITLES AND FIRST LINES